Cities

Cities

Missions' New Frontier

Roger S. Greenway
Timothy M. Monsma

BAKER BOOK HOUSE
Grand Rapids, Michigan 49516

Copyright © 1989 by Baker Books
a division of Baker Book House Company
P.O. Box 6287, Grand Rapids, MI 49516-6287

ISBN: 0-8010-3831-6

Fourth printing, May 1994

Printed in the United States of America

Library of Congress Cataloging-in-Publication Data

Greenway, Roger S.
    Cities, missions' new frontier.

    Bibliography: p.
    Includes index.
    1. Missions.   2. Evangelistic work.   3. City churches.
4. Cities and towns—Religious aspects—Christianity.
I. Monsma, Timothy M., 1933–   .   II. Title.
BV2653.G74   1989   266'.009173'2   89–6962
ISBN 0–8010–3831–6

Teaching aids that supplement *Cities: Missions' New Frontier* are available.
More information on "The Gospel in the City," five videocassettes prepared
by John Perkins and Roger Greenway, can be obtained by writing:

> Priority One Resources
> Home Mission Board
> Southern Baptist Convention
> 1350 Spring Street NW
> Atlanta, GA 30367

A complete course including assigned readings, collateral material, a study
guide, and twenty-four lectures by Roger Greenway on audiocassette is
available from:

> The Institute of Theological Studies
> 1553 Plainfield NE
> Grand Rapids, MI 49501

The authors dedicate this book
to all whom God uses to announce
and demonstrate his love and salvation
on the urban frontier of missions

Contents

Illustrations

Tables

Preface

In view of the rapid growth of cities in Asia, Africa, and Latin America and the internationalization of cities in Europe and North America, it is no exaggeration to call cities the new frontier of Christian missions. For, like the world at large, missions tomorrow will be mostly urban. Christ calls the church to bring the gospel not only to tribes and villages, but also to modern, socially complex centers of population, culture, and political power.

The urbanization of Christian missions is an urgent and serious need. Cities determine the destiny of nations, and their influence on the everyday affairs of individuals is incalculable. As cities grow in number, size, and influence, it is incumbent on those responsible for world evangelization, which includes the tasks of teaching, planning, and recruitment of missionaries, to focus attention on cities. Likewise, in the years ahead students of missions at Christian colleges and seminaries will need to wrestle with urban issues if they are to be prepared for ministry in tomorrow's world.

The purpose of this book is to provide students and practitioners of Christian missions with a basic introductory textbook for urban ministry. Other valuable books on the subject have appeared in recent years, such as *The Urban Christian* by Raymond J. Bakke, *World-Class Cities and World Evangelization* by David B. Barrett, and *A Clarified Vision for Urban Mission* by Harvie M. Conn. We have tried not to duplicate what is already available in other volumes, but to provide a global overview of urban mission and introduce students to some exciting new dimensions of Christian ministry centered in cities.

In these pages we have not hidden our personal experience of years of urban ministry in Asia, Africa, Latin America, and North America. Frequently we use personal pronouns when describing events and ministry in which we have been intimately involved. For that reason we identify the author at the beginning of each chapter.

Discussion questions are placed at the end of each chapter to facilitate the book's use in classrooms and small groups. More research needs to be done in areas related to urban mission, and we hope that this textbook will stimulate wide investigation of the subjects we have addressed. In a real sense, there are no experts in urban mission, just learners and practitioners pursuing greater effectiveness before the Lord in the growing cities of the world.

The bibliography found at the end of the book represents a major effort to provide students and urban-mission specialists with a comprehensive source of references for further investigation. Like the book as a whole, the bibliography includes urban-mission materials not only from all the major regions of the world, but also from the viewpoint of the social sciences as well as religion and missiology. Admittedly, the bibliography is not complete; new titles appear every year. Yet it is a significant start, and students will find it useful. We are grateful to Arthur Hall, who compiled many of the entries for this bibliography, and to Edna Greenway, who put the entries in their final form.

We also gratefully acknowledge the editorial assistance of Susan Lutz of Philadelphia. A published author and professional editor, she has used her skills to blend the styles and content of two different authors into a consistent and integrated book. We express appreciation as well to Nelvina Ilbrink for her time and skill in preparing the manuscript for publication.

Beyond question, the new chapter in world and mission history is entitled "Cities," and the church of tomorrow will be largely an urban church. It follows that education in and for the church, at whatever level, must give major attention to cities. Religious education must provide the theological perspective, practical training, and strong motivation needed to make the Christian faith a saving and transforming force in cities. To advance that goal, this book is presented.

It is presented also with humble optimism that God is at work in worldwide urbanization, and through it is providing the greatest opportunity in history to reach all peoples with the gospel. Let these studies lead us, therefore, from our books and classrooms to the streets, homes, slums, and high-rise buildings of a thousand cities, offering everywhere our hands and voices for the kingdom of God.

Definitions

Cities—concentrations of people living in close proximity and interacting with one another under some form of municipal incorporation and government. *Towns* are small cities; cities are large and important towns. "Cities" frequently is used to denote urban or metropolitan areas.

    Megacity—a concentration of over one million people.

    Supercity—a concentration of over four million.

    Supergiant—a city of over ten million inhabitants.

Urban—that which pertains to or characterizes cities in distinction from rural areas. An *urban area* comprises a city and the communities that are related to and affected by it. An *urban region* may include a number of cities, towns, and related communities.

Metropolis—a large and very important city. A *metropolitan area* includes one or more cities and towns with their contiguous communities.

Inner city—the old, economically depressed central sections of North American cities, characterized by racial and cultural diversity, unemployment, crime, and social problems.

Urbanization—the process by which, in a particular country or region, the percentage of people living in cities increases relative to the rural population, with consequent effects on human life. Where there is rapid urbanization, there is a relative decline in rural population.

Industrialization—the process by which, in a particular country or region, modern industry provides employment and manufactured goods for people. Industrialization may parallel, lag behind, or move ahead of urbanization, with resulting effects on employment and social well-being. *Overurbanization* means that the urban population is growing faster than industry can provide jobs. This is a common phenomenon in developing countries.

A Biblical Framework
Roger S. Greenway

The kind of mission work that pleases God and can expect his blessing is done carefully on sound biblical foundations. Christian ministry, after all, is a projection of theological beliefs; its vigor and form reveal the base on which it rests. We cannot expect lives to be changed, city neighborhoods improved, and vital churches established if our labors spring from feeble, even distorted, theological roots. The urban missiologist, therefore, must blaze a trail that the missionary practitioner can follow. Workers in the streets will not move forward as they should unless there are urban missiologists ahead of them, behind them, and alongside them, sounding true and prophetic notes.

As evangelical churches and mission organizations awaken to the challenges of a rapidly expanding urban world, there is the danger that the urgency of the task will cause them to neglect biblical foundations. The needs in the city are so many and so pressing that we are tempted to move in multiple directions without pausing to take our theological bearings. Urban mission has suffered a great deal from such negligence in the past. As a new era of urban ministry unfolds, we must not repeat the mistake.

The apostle Paul, in 1 Corinthians 3, describes himself as an expert builder, a builder who laid an excellent foundation in Jesus Christ and the gospel. He hoped that the builders who came after him would build carefully. We who follow the apostles, whether as students or practitioners of urban mission, must continually reflect on the foundation of our work, Christ as the fullness of biblical revelation. We must build on that foundation alone and build with the best materials. Sound urban strategies and mission operations require firm theological foundations. This takes much prayer, biblical study, the constant stretching of our mental horizons, and plain hard work.

1

Warnings from Europe

There are grave consequences when Christian leaders neglect serious theological reflection on the city and its significance for the church and missions. Religious conditions in European cities serve as a warning. Christianity is in serious trouble there. Places that once were strongholds of the faith have in recent years become mission fields.

How did the churches lose the cities? Various factors entered the picture. One factor is that evangelical scholars have neglected the cities. This explanation is given by C. Henk Koetsier, a European scholar who lives and works in Amsterdam. Personally engaged in urban missions for many years, Koetsier assesses the situation in Europe:

> There has been little theological analysis and reflection on what is happening in cities. It seems as if theology has lost interest in the world of the modern city. Only recently have a few theologians left their ivory towers of theological erudition to confront the turmoil of inner city life. Hence, churches have not been able to cope with the situation in the cities. They have withdrawn from the cities sociologically by migration and theologically by a similar abandonment. Churches simply have not been willing to reflect critically and creatively on the challenges posed to them by the cities.[1]

There are signs that what has happened in Europe will be repeated in the cities of North America, and later in other parts of the world. Everywhere we see the tendency of churches to flee and scholars to ignore the awesome challenges of the cities. What little attention is given to urban ministry tends to focus on methods and strategies rather than on foundational questions that are biblical and theological in nature.

Recognizing this tendency, I choose to focus first on the scriptural picture of cities. After we have examined the biblical framework, we can discuss the practical issues involved in urban ministry. It is important that we look carefully at both, for a great deal is involved. As we think through the subject from a biblical perspective, our vision of God, creation, redemption, cities, and evangelism will inevitably be stretched.

1. C. Henk Koetsier, "The Church Situation in European Cities," *Urban Mission* 3.3 (Jan. 1986): 45.

The Biblical Picture of Cities

We turn first to the cities that might have been and then to the city that will be. When we have done that, we will see more clearly the cities that are, the cities where you and I live and minister. By means of this analysis we will, I am sure, come to understand in a deeper and more comprehensive way our mission in and to these cities.

The Cities That Might Have Been

The cities that might have been are the communities that would have arisen if the fall had not occurred. In an unfallen state, the gifts that come to expression in human culture, the arts, craftsmanship, architecture, and technology, would all have developed at a heightened rate, to a superb level, and without the corrupting influences of evil. They would have appeared in a vast assortment of ways, all of them bringing glory to God and benefiting the human family. Human gifts would have come to their highest expression in cities, in communal and institutional life, as sinless people worked together, shared their talents and labor, and produced great things with the resources of God's good and rich creation.

The world that might have been would most certainly have been an urban world. The human race was created in a garden, but their destiny as God's image-bearers and as social beings lay in the city. Moreover, the cultural mandate which God gave Adam (Gen. 1:28) implied, even required, city building. Adam was commanded to cultivate the earth's resources and build with the things placed at his disposal. He was to organize and govern, under God, the world God had made. From the nuclear family to the extended family to the whole human race the unfallen community would have expanded, and cities would naturally have resulted. These cities would have been wonderful places, a sheer joy and delight to their inhabitants. Without sin, corruption, or disharmony, all urban life would have contributed to human welfare and God's glory.

The cities of an unfallen race would have been cultural centers beyond imagination. The myriad gifts and potentials of God's image-bearers would have produced an endless variety of cultural achievements dedicated to God's glory and the holy development of the human race. It is often observed that cities today contain the highest expressions of human knowledge, skill, and cultural achievement. But the cities in an unfallen world would have surpassed today's cities in every way. Who can imagine what achievements there might have been if sin and evil had not entered the world, turning human potentials to dark and devious purposes?

These cities without sin would have been temple cities, and all the worship and praise would have been to the one true God. They would have been theocentric, covenant cities, honoring God by perfect obedience and benefiting the inhabitants in every way. Each might appropriately have been called "Holy City of God."

But such cities did not happen. They are not part of history as we know it. What they might have been we can deduce from Scripture's account of how God created things and to what end creation's resources were meant to be used. But the fall occurred, and a different world developed. We shall look at that world and its cities in a few moments. But first we must examine another part of Scripture.

The City That Will Be

The city that will be is known and entered by grace alone. The Bible describes it in Revelation 21, calling it the Holy City, the new Jerusalem. This city is not of human making but comes down out of heaven from God. It is beautiful beyond description, unblemished by sin, like a virgin bride coming to her husband.

In this city, community life is peaceful, harmonious. There are no tears, nor cause for them. Death and mourning are gone. There is no pain. The things that blighted former cities are gone forever. Best of all, God dwells with his people in perfect relationship.

This new city is a temple city. The temple is Jesus Christ, who is the presence of God with his people. Scripture describes him as the Lamb slain as a sacrifice for sinners' redemption. As the Lamb, he has earned the right to receive the glory and praise of all the inhabitants of the new city.

The world to come, Scripture teaches, will be an urban world. The redemption drama that began in a garden will end in a city, the new Jerusalem. Heaven's citizens will be urbanites. Drawn by bonds of grace from all races, nations, and language groups, new-city citizens will live together in perfect harmony as God's redeemed people, his new covenant community. This city to be will enjoy everything the cities that might have been would have possessed, and one thing more: the citizens of the new city will not only be sinless, they will be sinners washed clean. Theirs is the story of redemption. Their songs are about the Savior and his blood (Rev. 5:9).

The Cities That Are

Between the dying rays of a lost opportunity and the promise of a gracious future stand the cities that are. Postfall cities certainly are not the same as those cities that might have been. Because of sin, cities today are human-centered, often violent, and rife with friction, greed, and carnality. Sin runs freely through the streets and markets. Sin sits enthroned in high places of civic life. Cities are characterized by many broken covenants, most of all the broken covenant with God.

Yet these cities are habitable. Life goes on in them every day. Sin is evident in every area of urban life, but still things are not as bad as they might be. By God's mercy, even pagan cities still reflect some of the greatness of the God who created the inhabitants, stamped his image on them, and restrains their worst intentions. We can call them, therefore, "common grace" cities, because they survive and even prosper as a result of the mercy and goodness of God richly distributed to all humankind.

Life in these cities is adapted to the fallen condition of the inhabitants. There are police officers, courts, and prisons. There are laws to protect and punish. Every aspect of urban life now reflects the presence of sin and corruption. Urban life, in fact, can continue and keep from degenerating to utter chaos only because of the corporate defense mechanisms city dwellers develop to cope with their common fallen condition.

Meredith Kline makes a great deal of Genesis 4:1–6:8, a passage which most of us probably ignore. Kline shows how this passage illuminates the nature of cities. He points out that it was plainly by an act of grace and mercy that, after Adam and Eve had fallen into sin and broken covenant with God, God again appointed a city structure for the benefit of the human race.[2]

The world's cities are evidences of God's preserving and preventative grace. For the sake of his elect, he has appointed cities to preserve human life and restrain the course of humankind's self-destructive tendencies. It should not surprise us that the murderer Cain built a city, for urban life structures and protects human life. In a more formal way, the cities of refuge (Num. 35) offered protection and life to people who inadvertently had killed another person.

The judicial command announced in Genesis 4:15—the word of God to Cain concerning the law that would protect him—is a prelude to the account of the historical beginnings of the city (v. 17). Genesis 4:15, says Kline, is thus a virtual city charter. The city is established as a

---

2. Meredith Kline, "Kingdom Prologue II," mimeographed course material, pp. 22–23.

refuge from the wilderness, a sanctuary from one's adversaries, and a place of cultural development and creativity. The city soon becomes also, as evidenced in the Lamech story (vv. 23–24), a place of pride and violence.[3]

This postfall city was not the same city that the Lord would have established at the beginning. That is, it was not a theocratic, covenant city with an institutional integration of divine worship and human culture. Such a holy temple-city God would one day provide through the program of redemption to be accomplished by Christ. But the cities that fallen humans build are "common grace" cities, made possible only by God's mercy to all humankind. These are temporal cities, not permanent. Each one bears the seeds of its own downfall. The cities that are, the cities of history as we know it, are subject to decay and eventually to destruction. Perhaps the restlessness so common to urban life stems from the city's corporate uneasiness about its future, and an unconscious awareness of its vulnerability and eventual doom.

As a result of the fall, fundamental changes have occurred in the city. They are visible ramifications of the curse. For example, every city now has its cemeteries, reflecting the fact that all urban life eventually turns from metropolis to necropolis. Another of the changes in the city that are due to sin and evil is that urban efforts to gather resources and human strength and talent are no longer just a means for fulfilling God's mandate to subdue the world; they have become a pooling of power for war and for defense against outside attackers. Cities throughout history have assumed the character of fortresses surrounded by walls and moats to protect the inhabitants.

No longer is the city mainly a geographical center for commerce, a marketplace to expedite the flow of the earth's abundance and the products of humankind's cultural endeavors. Rather, the city has become an administrative center to provide welfare and relief to people in distress. It must supply police officers, courts, and prisons to protect its citizens and punish wrongdoers. It must cope with the general frustration of cultural efforts that results from the common curse, as well as with all the negative consequences of human selfishness, greed, and violence.[4]

We see, therefore, that while there is a kind of structural continuity between the cities that might have been and the cities that are, there is also a deep and prevailing discontinuity because of sin and its consequences, and the common curse leveled by God upon the whole human race. This discontinuity shows itself in all areas of human

3. Ibid., p. 25.
4. Ibid., p. 26.

life—in the obvious things such as the existence of crime and violence, and in the host of subtle ways by which city dwellers organize their lives to cope with the world as it now is.

A Framework for a Biblical Urban Missiology

This perspective gives us a general framework from which we can approach many of the questions that arise in urban missions. The cities we know today are not to be identified with either the kingdom of Satan or the kingdom of God. Cities are the result of God's common grace. Through them God restrains the development of evil, blesses his creatures, and works out his sovereign purpose in both judgment and grace. Awareness of this biblical perspective on the nature of cities has several ramifications:

1. Given the truth that today's cities are the result of common grace, we can see the essential nature of the religious warfare that takes place every day in cities around the world. Today's cities are by nature apostate corporations. Even their best accomplishments bear the marks of sin and active hostility to God and his Word.

Scripture depicts the religious warfare of the city as a battle between Babylon and Jerusalem. Babylon is the representative city of humankind, rebellious, greedy, violent, idolatrous, and doomed. Jerusalem, on the other hand, is the representative city of God. It is a theocracy, for there God reigns. It symbolizes God's peace, unity, and righteousness. In Jerusalem Messiah is King, while in Babylon he is despised and opposed. True citizens of Jerusalem are in covenant with God, citizens of Babylon are in league with the devil.

Herein lies the nature of the religious warfare that rages in the city. There are, as Augustine pointed out, two cities within every single city. There are Babylon with its citizens and Jerusalem with its citizens. These two are essentially at odds, for they serve different masters and live by different standards. The master of the one is Christ; of the other, Antichrist.

2. Christians living and working in cities can understand things that remain largely a mystery to persons lacking the biblical framework. Christians are very realistic about the city's essential nature and the cause of the unending frustrations that occur when citizens try to improve city life. Christians understand the root of the problem. It is the moral malignancy that lies buried deep in the city's heart. It is the legacy of Cain and the spirit of Lamech, which have never gone away.

Because Christians understand this, they should never make the

error of humanistic idealists who suppose that somehow, by enlightened planning, greater leaders, and more dedicated efforts, the city's ills
can be cured. All utopian schemes for the creation of a perfect city on
earth are immediately discarded once the postfall city is understood in
biblical perspective.

Followers of Jesus Christ, aspirants to the city that will be, have
important roles to play in the common-grace cities of this world. But
they should never be deceived into thinking that through their combined efforts and best intentions, in some fashion or to some degree,
these cities will become the kingdom of God and the city of King Jesus.
Neither gradually nor suddenly will the cities of humankind become
the city of God. These cities are temporary, under the curse, and someday will be removed to make way for the heavenly city which the
Scriptures promise. A clear understanding of this fact is extremely
important for urban workers. Naive utopianism should find no place in
urban missiology, for it is as self-defeating as it is unbiblical.

3. Because of the biblical framework by which cities are understood,
Christians can take a positive stance vis-à-vis cities. Instead of giving
up on cities, Christians can and should affirm them and accept their
share of responsibility for the cities' care. Proof is found in Jeremiah
29:7: even in wicked Babylon, captive Israel is commanded by God to
"seek the peace and prosperity of the city. . . . Pray to the LORD for it,
because if it prospers, you too will prosper."

By God's common grace, the cities that now are were built and are
maintained. The development of human culture and civilization depends on them. In cities the fiercest battles for human minds and
hearts take place. For that reason, cities are center stage for the Christian mission, the great drama of redemption. Understanding this, Christians ought not flee the urban battlefield, but rather they should pur-
posely choose to be in the city and occupy all the corners of urban life,
bearing the light, salt, and leaven of the gospel.

The work of God's people in the cities that are ought never to be
narrow or isolationist. The church in the city has a task to perform
that carries its members into all the systems and all the areas that
constitute urban life. Whether in education or politics, city hall or the
marketplace, the responsibility of Jerusalem's citizens is to proclaim
who really reigns. They must pray for the city's welfare, attack its
abuses, and promote its true good. God's people know where the crucial issues lie. They know that the city's deepest struggle is religious.
Precisely because they know this, they must not allow anything to
remain outside the scope of their work and witness. All that is in the
city must be confronted with all that is in Christ.

4. Because biblically enlightened Christians have begun to under-

stand the nature of the city and have heard the missionary injunction to go into all nations and make disciples of all peoples, they approach cities realistically and evangelistically. Christians need not be shaken or surprised by anything that happens in the city. They expect to find much that is beautiful and beneficial, because God's common grace is operative there, and the very nature of the city encourages cultural development. But the spirit of Cain is there also, with its greed, oppression, and ungodly ways. The line of Cain does not escape the Christian's attention. He knows that it runs without interruption from primitive Enoch through Lamech's violent though culturally progressive industrial center to Babel and to Sodom, and finally to "BABYLON THE GREAT THE MOTHER OF PROSTITUTES AND OF THE ABOMINATIONS OF THE EARTH" (Rev. 17:5).

Christians know what is really going on in cities. They understand that sin and evil are at work in the city, both in the lives of individuals and in the social structures people devise. They know, too, that because of God's common grace there is a form of beauty and good in the city, the spirit of Cain is restrained, and demonic potentials are kept from escalating too quickly.

Christians know also that because of God's special grace another force has intervened and is at work in the city. It engages the forces of evil and builds a community of a different kind. It is the Spirit of Christ enlisting God's people in the mission of salvation. This Spirit longs to hear the message of Jesus proclaimed in the streets.

The Call to Urban Mission

In Scripture, the call to urban mission begins with the prophet Jonah and God's commission to go to Nineveh to preach God's word (Jon. 1:2; 3:2). Paul and the other apostles of the New Testament took up this mission and applied it to the cities of their day. In chapter 2 we will examine certain aspects of the New Testament mission, but here we will reflect simply on Jonah, with whom the urban apostolate began.

In the words of Scripture, Nineveh was a "great city" (Jon. 1:2). God's common grace was richly displayed there. It was not only a large metropolis, the capital of a powerful empire, it was famous for its beauty. Many people considered it the fairest city ever built on earth. Militarily, Nineveh appeared impregnable. It was reported, at least among the ancients, to have had outer ramparts that stretched for sixty miles and inner walls a hundred feet high. Horse-drawn chariots, three abreast, could ride its battlements. To build the king's palace in Nineveh required the labor of ten thousand slaves for twelve years, and the city's parks and public buildings were praised throughout the world. Nineveh lasted for fifteen hundred years, which makes most modern cities seem like adolescent upstarts. It was indeed a "great city."

The Nineveh of Scripture was also a representative city, symbolic of cities throughout the ancient and modern worlds. It was a city of cultural achievement and also of injustice, oppression, and violence. It was the wickedness of Nineveh that God said was its fundamental problem and the reason why Jonah's mission was needed (1:2).

Despite its beauty and strength, Nineveh was a city under divine judgment. Its gods were idols, and the entire political and economic life of the city was based on the exploitation of weaker nations, military conquest, and slave labor. The prophet Nahum spared no words in describing Nineveh as the betrayer of nations and a city of harlotries (Nah. 3:4). Every form of vice and witchcraft was practiced, and even its artistic achievements were fouled by obscenities and idolatry. Rightfully Nahum called Nineveh "the city of blood" (3:1), for violence and plunder made it what it was.

God knew exactly what the city was like; its wickedness provoked his wrath. The sin of the city was individual, for it was committed personally by Nineveh's thousands of citizens. It was also collective, for the sum total of Nineveh's life, culture, and achievements had wickedness stamped across it. The spirit of Cain and of Lamech was highly evident there. It was an apostate corporation. The warp and woof of Ninevite life was totally depraved, and the city's only hope was a repentance as wide and deep as the sin that polluted it.

The significance of the Book of Jonah for urban mission can be studied from many angles.[5] The mission strategist sees in it a familiar pattern: God commissions his messenger, who goes to the city and announces God's word, and as a result city dwellers repent and turn to God. From the standpoint of mission strategy, Jonah is often looked upon as a model for all times.

The theologian is moved by the fact that the initiative in mission is taken by God. The story is about Jonah, but the principal actor is not a man, but God. God calls the prophet and hounds him until he is willing to obey. God's mercy toward the wicked city motivates the entire operation, despite Jonah's reluctance and negative mood. It is God's mission, properly speaking, and not Jonah's. God wants Nineveh saved, and by his grace he forces the prophet into action and the city into repentance.

---

5. For an extended treatment of the mission of Jonah to Nineveh, see Roger S. Greenway, *Apostles to the City: Biblical Strategies for Urban Missions* (Grand Rapids: Baker, 1978), pp. 15–28.

Most importantly, Jonah's mission is a sign of the call of God to his people to proclaim his message of repentance and salvation to the cities which are, even horribly wicked cities that are hell-bound for eventual destruction. Despite its shortcomings, Nineveh was important in the sight of God, and he wanted his message proclaimed in its streets. Jonah's task, and by extension the task of God's people as a whole, was to be God's messenger in this citadel of power and evil, and to join God in his judgment-and-grace struggle with the city.

The story of Jonah and what happened in Nineveh deserves continued analysis and reflection. Just as urban mission began in that city many centuries ago, there is a sense in which it must begin there again today. God still speaks through Jonah about the nature of urban mission, God's mercy toward city dwellers, and his desire that they hear his word. The Jonah story reminds us also of the rebellious spirit that refuses to recognize cities as strategic places of mission.

Imagine how the story might have turned out if Jonah had remained to minister in Nineveh, teaching the law, establishing justice, and serving as a light to that pagan nation, as Israel was called to do in Isaiah 42:1–9. Jonah might have sent a message to his fellow prophets in Israel, informing them that a great awakening had begun in Nineveh, and urging them to join him there to follow up on what had started. This might have led to a new day for Israel, a momentous turning point in its understanding of God and especially of his care for the world—even for cities as wicked as Nineveh. Israel might have come to perceive its own election in a new light, that is, as God's messenger-nation to the world.

But Jonah's distaste for ministry in Nineveh prevailed. The overall failure in terms of mission sprang from Jonah's and Israel's stubborn refusal to understand both God's concern for all nations and the responsibility of the citizens of Jerusalem to be lights to the Ninevehs of the world. It was in order to expose Israel's misconstrued theology that the Holy Spirit inspired the writing of this short book and included it in the Bible. The Book of Jonah served ancient Israel, as it serves the Christian church, as an instructor, a rebuke, and a reminder about mission.

As it turned out, Jonah withdrew from the city, and Nineveh's repentance was short-lived. Eventually the city was destroyed. Yet Jesus affirmed the genuineness of Nineveh's repentance: "The men of Nineveh will stand up at the judgment with this generation and condemn it; for they repented at the preaching of Jonah, and now one greater than Jonah is here" (Luke 11:32). Since the time of his coming, the issue for cities and their populations is what they do with Christ and the gospel.

Nineveh's repentance, for as long as it lasted, remains a sign of what can happen in cities and neighborhoods when God's message is proclaimed and his Spirit moves. The pity is that the Nineveh story finds its place in religious history as the record of an aborted opportunity rather than the birth of a great movement for the kingdom of God.

The issue of Nineveh still stands before God's people. In this time of worldwide urbanization, will God's people seize the opportunity to evangelize modern Ninevehs, or will they turn away like Jonah, preferring service in less threatening places? And if they do go to the cities, how extensive will their message be? Will it challenge the cities' wickedness in all places where it lurks, calling forth repentance that reaches from shops and streets to city hall?

The closing verses of Jonah are sad in terms of the prophet's failure that they unmask, but they are splendid in terms of their theology and framework for urban mission. In words of great feeling, God reveals himself to be the great demographer who counts the city's population and who cares about its children and even its animals. Idolatrous, cruel, and greedy Nineveh is not beyond the heart of God.

The whole length and breadth of urban mission is implied in this revelation. The God of the Bible is the initiator and the director of the missionary enterprise. He cultivates green plants and governs the creation order for the well-being of the human race, but his chief concern is focused particularly on people. For their salvation he sends his prophets, as he sent his Son, to the city.

Discussion Questions

1. What evidence do we have that God cares about cities and their inhabitants? How should this affect our sense of calling to urban mission?
2. Identify at least ten examples of sin and evil in urban life today. What would a real Nineveh-style repentance from such sin and evil be like?
3. Given the biblical data, what do you think should be the cutting edge of Christian mission in the city?
4. Jonah fled when God told him to go preach to Nineveh, and in modern times cities continue to intimidate missionaries. What connection might there be between the sad condition of many cities and their frequent neglect by missionaries?

2

The Urban-Mission Movement of the New Testament

Roger S. Greenway

The mission movement of the New Testament was primarily an urban movement. After Pentecost the gospel spread from city to city and from cities to the surrounding countryside. It was in the cities of the Roman Empire that Christianity enjoyed its greatest success until well after the time of Constantine in the fourth century, and the urban environment shaped the way early Christians thought, acted, and evangelized. Because the twenty-first century will be largely in an urban world and the influence of the cities will be felt everywhere, the urban character of early Christianity and particularly of the mission work of the apostles needs careful examination.

More than historical interest motivates this study. We are looking for principles and models to guide us as we seek to minister biblically and relevantly in the world's expanding cities. Most of the information about the subject comes from the Bible, the Spirit-inspired authority for Christian faith and practice; accordingly, it is not naive to expect that the Spirit has placed in Scripture important indicators to guide us in urban mission.

In one brief chapter, we can only scan the skyline and pick out the main features of the early movement of Christianity. The work of the apostle Paul will receive our major attention. I want to underscore, however, that the mission work of Paul was a team effort; the Bible itself clearly indicates this. In addition, much of what was happening

Parts of this chapter were excerpted from Roger S. Greenway, *An Urban Strategy for Latin America* (Grand Rapids: Baker, 1973).

in evangelism during the first century was never recorded. We must conclude that the missionary movement of the New Testament period was not the work of a few individuals, but of an extended group of apostolic associates, the details of whose work we know nothing about.[1]

The Holy Spirit inspired the New Testament writers to provide the church of all times with historical examples of believers fulfilling God's will for the world in obedience to Christ's commission. These people, whose labors and achievements are recorded in Scripture, serve as models for Christ's disciples everywhere. Through them the apostolate continues until the end of the age. Their ministries provide invaluable insights into the kind of mission work that pleases God.[2]

The apostle Paul was not alone among first-century Christians in his focus on the cities. Before Paul's conversion, the believers in Messiah Jesus had already carried the gospel message to Jewish communities in various Greco-Roman cities. We recall that it was the success of this early evangelism in Damascus that aroused Paul, the angry zealot, to travel to that city to arrest and imprison the converts.[3]

Of equal importance was the planting of the church in the city of Antioch. This happened while Paul was still a rabid persecutor of the Christian movement. The church in Antioch was founded by laypersons whose names were not recorded but whose labors began an important new chapter in the story of Christianity. The founders were Hellenists, natives of Cyprus and Cyrene, who had been forced to leave Jerusalem because of persecution. Arriving in Antioch they took the significant step of preaching the gospel to Gentiles, thereby beginning the mother church of the Gentile Christian movement (Acts 11:19–26).[4]

1. Wayne A. Meeks, *The First Urban Christians: The Social World of the Apostle Paul* (New Haven: Yale University Press, 1983), p. 8.

2. Paul stated explicitly that he regarded his way of life and ministry as a model for others to follow (2 Thess. 3:9). I do not agree with Meeks's position that the Pauline authorship of a number of the Epistles attributed to Paul in the canon is questionable, and that the identification of Paul as the leading actor of the New Testament accounts may have originated among later Christians who affiliated themselves with the Pauline movement (ibid., pp. 7–8). My position is that Paul was the author of the Epistles which the church traditionally attributes to him, that he was the leader and mentor of a movement involving countless associates and co-workers, and that the Holy Spirit chose the accounts of missionary activity recorded in Scripture as instruction for Christ's followers in all times.

3. Ibid.

4. For a more extensive treatment of the role of the church at Antioch, see chapter 3, "Antioch: A Biblical Model of Urban Church Development," pp. 31–42. A better model for city churches cannot be found than this church at Antioch.

Paul and the City

Wayne Meeks points out that Paul was a city person through and through; the city breathes through his language. Paul's language and metaphors are drawn primarily from the urban world; his Greek is fluent, and it evokes the classroom more than the farm. Paul is at home with the speech used in gymnasiums, stadiums, and workshops. The manual work with which he often supported himself was not that of a farmer but of an artisan, a blue-collar worker, the kind of person who belonged thoroughly to the city. "When Paul rhetorically catalogs the places where he has suffered danger," observes Meeks, "he divides the world into city, wilderness, and sea (2 Cor. 11:26). His world does not include the *chōra*, the productive countryside; outside the city there is nothing—*erēmia*." Not uncharacteristically, Paul boasted to the Roman officer arresting him that he was "a citizen of no ordinary city" (Acts 21:39).[5]

From the hour of his conversion when the Lord told him to arise and go to the city (Damascus), where he would receive further instructions (Acts 9:6), until the last we hear about Paul (his imprisonment in Rome—Acts 28:31), a consistent picture is given of a missionary focusing his main efforts on cities. It was not by meditating in the desert nor by visiting small villages in out-of-the-way corners that Paul engaged the principalities and powers in moral and spiritual battle. He went to the flourishing Hellenistic cities, and in that environment he planted the evangelistically vibrant and growing churches of the New Testament period.[6]

Making Disciples

At the heart of New Testament missionary strategy lies the presupposition that people everywhere need to be converted to faith and allegiance to Jesus Christ and enrolled in continuing active discipleship. They will then be baptized and will seek membership in Christ's visible body on earth, the church.

There is no exception to this in the New Testament. The apostles shared the presupposition that sin had alienated all people from God and none can enter the kingdom without the new birth (John 3:3, 5;

5. Meeks, *First Urban Christians*, p. 9.
6. Ibid., p. 10.

Rom. 1–3). Conversion to Christ, in the mind of the apostles, was the universal need, and in that conviction they preached and witnessed to Jews and Gentiles alike. They baptized the converts and organized churches wherever a nucleus of believers was gathered.

Because the kingdom of Jesus Christ cannot be extended without the conversion of sinners, the growth of the church, and the ever-widening application of Christ's new order by the faithful discipleship of his followers, the agenda for Christian missions is fairly clear. It is hard to understand, therefore, why in some churches evangelism has been given a different meaning, and "conversion" is almost considered an outdated word.

Not long ago, Bishop Stephen Neill reflected on the change that he had observed in many mainline churches, and how it contrasted with the Pauline emphasis on conversion.

> It is constantly said that old ideas of mission must be completely replaced by those that are new and relevant. This is a statement that needs elucidation, and much useful discussion can arise out of it. But I wonder whether the heart has not gone out of the missionary enterprise in all the mainline Churches for another and deeper reason.
>
> If we put the plain question, "Do we want people to be converted?" from many of our contemporary ecumenical theologians the answer would be a resounding "No." If we are evangelicals, must not the answer be a resounding "Yes"?
>
> For years I have been looking for a word which will take the place of the now very unpopular word "conversion," and have not found it. I am well aware of all the possible objections to the word. But I have an uneasy feeling that those who hesitate to use the word are also rejecting the thing.
>
> Those of us who have come to Christ, even from a profoundly Christian background, have known what it means to be "without hope and without God in the world" (Eph. 2:12). Are we prepared to use Paul's language, however unpopular it may be? We desire all men to say Yes to Christ. But there are countless ways of saying Yes to Christ which fall short of the surrender that leads to salvation. Do we know what we are really talking about?
>
> It seems to me that the time has come when we ought to be done with circumlocutions and not be ashamed to say exactly what we mean.[7]

Recently, I was asked to speak at the annual conference of a national council of Protestant churches in an African country. Before and after my presentations I had opportunity to hear the reports of the various

---

7. Stephen Neill, "Church of England Newspaper," 13 November 1970, cited in *Church Growth Bulletin* 8 (May 1971): 145.

committees and organizations that had been active the previous year. I was particularly interested to hear and read the report of the evangelism committee, because I considered that country to be extremely ripe for harvesting, and some churches were growing enormously.

The evangelism report, however, was very disappointing. The only action that this group of churches had apparently taken the previous year had been to hold some ecumenical services. There was not a whisper about overt united efforts to win Muslims and animists to Christ. Certain churches reported that their members received evangelism training and were involved in mission programs, but in every case these were organized and directed by outside, parachurch organizations. The entire report contained not a single word about engagement in what, by New Testament standards, we understand as evangelism. These were mainline churches, representing traditions that once were strong in missions and evangelism. But they had fallen into the very error that Stephen Neill discussed.

What must head the list of things to be done in today's cities? If the New Testament shapes our strategy, we will begin with the proclamation of the gospel of Jesus Christ as Savior and Lord. Like Paul, we will do everything in our power to win converts and will openly affirm that to be our goal (1 Cor. 9:19–23).

Religious conversion was not a popular notion in Paul's day any more than it is in ours. In his book *Evangelism in the Early Church*, Michael Green discusses at length the idea of conversion in Greco-Roman society. He finds, contrary to the conclusions of certain modern writers whom he mentions, that nothing in the religions of that period resembled Christian conversion. The Christian faith that Paul preached demanded a complete break with all other religious commitments and a radical moral change in the lives of its adherents. All this was utterly contrary to the customary attitude of Hellenistic people, who did not regard belief as necessary for worship, nor ethics as part of religion, and could not understand why a person could not adopt a new faith while still adhering to some degree to his old ones.[8]

Regardless of its foreignness to the Greco-Roman mind, Paul persisted in his conviction that repentance and conversion are absolutely necessary for entrance into the kingdom of God.[9] Christ and the apostles did not preach about a kingdom of God to which entrance can be gained, or whose program can be realized in the world, without the

---

8. Michael Green, *Evangelism in the Early Church* (Grand Rapids: Eerdmans, 1970), pp. 144–46.

9. Geerhardus Vos, *The Kingdom and the Church* (Grand Rapids: Eerdmans, 1958), pp. 91ff.

demands of repentance and conversion being met. New Testament discipleship involves a radical and continued change of faith, worship, and ethics. "All things are become new" (2 Cor. 5:17 KJV). Christian conversion, with its implications for the whole of life, was the basic step toward changing what was wrong in Roman society.

Focus on the Family

Paul's conversion approach to urban missions was family-centered. The households mentioned in the New Testament (Acts 16:15; 1 Cor. 1:16; Gal. 6:10) were not unlike the extended families and kinship ties found in Southern (frequently called "Third") World cities today, and Paul used these households to establish the faith in each area he evangelized.

> While individual contacts and personal friendships marked the beginnings of a new church, it was through the Greek "household" that the new faith spread rapidly in St. Paul's world. The Greek *oikos* or *oikia* formed the basic social unit that was best fitted for the extension of the church. There is no exact equivalent in Greek for the English word "family." The *oikos* or household was a kind of extended family, many of whom lived together. It was composed not only of members of the family (in our sense) but also of employees, slaves, tenants, and other dependents.[10]

Thousands upon thousands of extended-family households are found all across the cities of Southern World countries. They can be found as well in the ethnic neighborhoods of North American and European cities. They represent the modern equivalent of the social unit Paul used as his base of operation. What can Pauline mission strategy teach us about evangelism through extended families and households? Let's look at what Paul did and then draw some conclusions.

The Book of Acts and the Epistles often refer to the rulers of households, people through whom entire families were brought to conversion and baptism. Cornelius "and all his family were devout and God-fearing" (Acts 10:2). When the Spirit fell on them, they were all baptized in the name of Jesus Christ (Acts 10:48). To the trembling jailer at Philippi, Paul said, "Believe in the Lord Jesus, and you will be saved— you and your household" (Acts 16:31). The jailer then took Paul and Silas up into his house, the word was preached to his entire household,

10. Joseph A. Grassi, *A World to Win: The Missionary Methods of Paul the Apostle* (Maryknoll, N.Y.: Maryknoll, 1965), p. 85.

and that very same night the jailer "and all his family were baptized" (Acts 16:33).

At Philippi it was a woman who was the first contact; through her the faith entered her family, and the entire household was baptized (Acts 16:15). At Thessalonica it was Jason and his house (Act 17:5–9). At Corinth, Crispus, the president of the local synagogue, accepted the new teaching and was baptized along with his household (Acts 18:8). His home provided direct access to the Jews. Paul, however, chose as his place of residence the house of Titus Justus, a Gentile who worshiped God and lived next door to the synagogue (Acts 18:7). Being a Gentile, Titus could be the channel for other non-Jews to come to hear Paul preach. Scattered throughout the Epistles are other references to the households where Paul stayed, preached, and established his first converts (1 Cor. 1:15–16; Col. 4:15; Philem. 2).

Changed Homes and Society

Parents, children, servants, slaves, visitors, relatives, and friends all heard the gospel preached in the environment of the home, and there Paul generally made his first converts. Households were baptized together and shared the Lord's Supper together.

The first blow against pagan racial and social barriers was struck at the communion table where master and slave, women and men, Jew and Gentile sat together around a common table and celebrated the same salvation. The first and most basic lessons concerning the nature of the church as the household of God (Gal. 6:10; Eph. 2:19) were taught at the very beginning of the Pauline mission in each city as the faith was planted in the extended family of the Greek household. There, along God-appointed covenant lines, the gospel could travel its swiftest course until even distant relatives might be converted.

There was a period during which urbanologists maintained that family ties tend to disintegrate in the city and that the home plays a lesser role in shaping the lives and attitudes of city people. Based on this premise, the "industrial mission" strategy was developed. Industrial missionaries theorized that in the urban setting vocational, educational, recreational, and political relationships take on larger significance than do primary-group relationships, particularly family relationships. They reasoned that urban people are best reached in the places where they work and spend their leisure time, and not primarily in the setting of the home and family.

That theory about the urban family, and the mission strategy stemming from it, have now largely been set aside. There is an ample body of research that suggests that the family continues to play very important roles in meeting the needs of companionship, affection, and basic security. The urban person's most fundamental identity is still connected with the family.[11]

The holistic approach to missions and evangelism taken in this book neither restricts the definition of sin and evil to individual conduct nor limits urban ministry to personal and family matters. The societal dimensions of what needs to be done in the city are readily acknowledged, as is the importance of ministries for community development and the promotion of social justice. But at the same time the holistic perspective on urban mission recognizes that nothing is more crucial for social change in the city than the conversion of persons, families, and groups to evangelical Christianity. There is both theological and empirical evidence to substantiate this position.

Some valuable research was done in the 1960s by sociologist Emilio Willems. Willems was interested in the Pentecostal movement in South America and curious to know both the social conditions that fostered its spread and the effects the movement had on the people who became part of it. The data that Willems collected led to this conclusion: *conversion to the evangelical faith is the most important single factor in the reorientation of individual and family lives and in general upward mobility in the urban setting.*

Willems examined the lives of people who were part of the evangelical and Pentecostal movements in Chile and Brazil, particularly among the masses of the poor who had poured into the cities. He observed that before adopting the new faith, their lives were generally marked by drunkenness, tavern brawls, wife beatings, illegitimacy, neglect of children, untidy personal appearance, failure to improve their poor housing conditions, and similar traits. But after conversion to evangelical Christianity, these traits began to disappear. In their place appeared new attitudes and values which greatly changed the lifestyle and economic conditions of the converts' households. Willems was by no means an evangelical believer looking for evidence to substantiate his preconceived notions about the social benefits of conversion. Yet this is what he observed about the typical convert: "He refrains from alcohol, his attitudes toward his family change, and instead of violence there is now patience and the 'desire to forgive.' If he lives in concubinage he seeks to legalize his union; he begins to enjoy home life and, thanks to his newly acquired money-saving virtues, he is soon able to ameliorate

---

11. Harvie M. Conn, *A Clarified Vision for Urban Mission* (Grand Rapids: Zondervan, 1987), pp. 40–42.

somewhat the shanty he may be living in. The place is kept cleaner and so are the children."[12]

Willems tended to ascribe these changes to the poor person's "desire to become respectable, that is, to adopt middle-class behavior."[13] But desire alone is not enough to explain what happens in such people's lives. The poor may have the desire for improvement, but desire by itself does not produce the change. Even changes in outward circumstances guarantee nothing. There must be new power from within. The secret of Christian conversion and its effect on human social conditions lies in the answer to the question: What is the source of the convert's power to stop drinking, carousing, and fornicating and to begin living the kind of life that is a joy to himself and those around him?

That power, according to the Bible, comes from the Holy Spirit's indwelling the believer (Rom. 8:2–4). That is why conversion has beneficial social consequences. Through the work of the Holy Spirit, hearts of people are changed—they think new thoughts, alter their wills and desires, love what before they despised, and hate what previously they enjoyed. Sociologists like Willems can describe what occurs after people are converted, but their explanations of what makes it happen are inadequate. They supply only part of the answer, for the spiritual dynamics of conversion must be theologically explained.

Converts and Churches

New Testament mission strategy emphasizes evangelism, winning converts, and multiplying churches. Paul's approach to the cities of the first century illustrates this very well. Within a period of ten years, by means of three missionary journeys, Paul founded churches in the four Roman provinces of Galatia, Macedonia, Achaia, and Asia. His sights were set on Spain, the farthest western frontier of the empire (Rom. 15:24, 28); and he may have reached there. Everywhere Paul went he and his co-workers preached, gathered converts, and formed them into local self-governing churches.

Deep theological presuppositions lay behind Paul's emphasis on church planting. Fundamental was his conviction that God had intervened in the world to establish a new community of people centered

12. Emilio Willems, *Followers of the New Faith: Culture Change and the Rise of Protestantism in Brazil and Chile* (Nashville: Vanderbilt University Press, 1967), pp. 130–31.

13. Ibid., pp. 131, 251.

around Jesus Christ. Paul, like any Jew well-grounded in the Old Testament, knew full well that God had a goal in history—the formation of a people who would serve him and carry out his purpose. Paul believed, too, that the Messiah would establish a community of people through whom God would, in the last days, act mightily and climactically in the affairs of humankind. When, on the Damascus road, the glorified Lord announced to Paul, "I am Jesus, whom you are persecuting," Paul sensed at once what Jesus was referring to. He was referring to the church, the community of men and women whom Paul was persecuting; they were so well known to and so much loved by the risen Lord that he identified himself with them.

That settled the issue for Paul. The persecutor of the church would become a church planter. From the moment of his conversion, he regarded the church as the unique community of believers in and through whom God was carrying forward his design and purpose in the world. The church, for Paul, was the long-awaited messianic community with worldwide dimensions. It was to be the bearer of the Good News to all races and nations, and would in that way fulfil God's plan in history.

The founding of a church, for Paul, was a tremendous thing. It was an act of incorporating individuals and families into a new community of Christ, a mini-Jerusalem within the cities of the world. As an establisher of churches, Paul regarded himself as God's colaborer, building a community which would endure for eternity.[14]

Paul was realistic about the world and the evils it contained. He made no empty boasts about establishing utopia or ridding the world of injustice. Nor did he try to accomplish everything which, in time, the church would have to undertake. The apostle's task was to lay foundations, to establish communities that would serve as lights, as salt and leaven in the midst of the city, as Zion's representatives in the Babylons of the day.

The Witness of the Laity

It is important to observe Paul's typical approach to a city. He was concerned to search out active collaborators, not passive recipients. It was on people like Aquila and Priscilla, to whom religion was not a mere appendage, that the gospel made its greatest impact. Paul was a trainer and coach as much as he was a church planter.

The spread of the gospel, in Paul's estimation, was not a responsibil-

14. Grassi, *World to Win*, pp. 21–23.

ity resting mainly on the shoulders of outsiders like himself, but a joint effort among all of Christ's disciples and a local responsibility. Paul never left the impression that the evangelization of a city or an entire region was his task alone. On the contrary, his converts were told to tell others, win others, and continue what the missionary had begun.

Carl G. Kromminga provides a thorough treatment of the subject of communicating the gospel through personal witnessing to one's neighbors. In it he sums up the New Testament evidence for the obligatory nature of lay witnessing:

> The examination of all these passages in the New Testament shows clearly that believers were actively engaged in the communication of the Gospel to others, to those with whom they came in contact in the conduct of daily affairs. The Lord and his apostles repeatedly taught that those who are citizens in the Kingdom of Heaven, those who share in the new life and the new order, are to love their neighbors without reservation. The Lord and his apostles also clearly taught that it is the obligation of those who share in redemption to confess openly the lordship of Jesus Christ and all that this implies. In obeying these commandments, believers follow in the footsteps of the Lord and his primary ambassadors. The manifestation of love for neighbors and the open confession of Christ's name are acts of obedience to the requirements of citizenship in the Kingdom. . . . Concern for the salvation of others comes to expression in concern for the weak, the penitent, the fallen, the apostate, and those outside the Church.[15]

There is ample evidence throughout the New Testament that believers were active in propagating the faith. The new churches established by Paul and others, and the members of older congregations who were scattered by persecution, all brought the gospel *by both word and deed* to those around them.[16] In other words, the professionalism so characteristic of modern missions and the institutional church was not characteristic of the Christian movement in the first century.

This fact is worth pondering; indeed, modern urban workers wish they knew more about how the apostles passed on their personal evangelistic zeal to others. At least part of the answer is found in Romans 16, where Paul's "fellow workers in Christ Jesus" are listed. There is Phoebe, "a great help to many people, including me" (v. 2). Priscilla and Aquila are there, of whom Paul says, "they risked their lives for me" (v.

15. Carl G. Kromminga, *The Communication of the Gospel Through Neighboring: A Study of the Basis and Practice of Lay Witnessing Through Neighborly Relationships* (Franeker, Netherlands: T. Wever, 1964), p. 66.

16. Ibid.

3). Mary, "who worked very hard for you," is greeted (v. 6). And so the list goes on: Andronicus and Junias, kinsmen of Paul and fellow prisoners, who "are outstanding among the apostles" (v. 7); Urbanus, "our fellow worker in Christ," and Stachys "my dear friend" (v. 9); Tryphena, Tryphosa, and Persis, three women who "worked very hard in the Lord" (v. 12). All of these people had been recipients of Paul's labors and were the beneficiaries of his sacrifices. But that is not why Paul remembers them, nor does it explain why their names are recorded. They are named because they labored—"fellow workers" is their title—and here lies the secret of the gospel's early spread. Conversion was enlistment, and missions meant everybody.

Someone may raise the objection that I am reading between the lines and claiming too much for the early Christians and their willingness to be colaborers in evangelism. But there is a strong argument in defense of this interpretation. The New Testament contains many direct instructions concerning loving one's neighbor, avoiding sexual impurity, speaking the truth, and being honest. But nowhere do we hear the apostles pleading for missions, urging Christians to bear witness to their neighbors, asking for help in evangelizing the Roman Empire. Why this silence on a subject which obviously was very dear to the apostles, and about which today we feel compelled to say so much? The answer, I believe, lies in the fact that the congregations back then were spontaneously carrying out their missionary obligation and needed no urging or correction on this matter. With respect to ethical conduct the situation was different, and that is why the apostles wrote numerous injunctions on that subject. But when it came to mission endeavor, the apostles needed to say nothing.[17]

On this subject of lay witnessing, churches in Western countries must learn from Southern World churches. Whatever strengths the Western churches possess, they are weak in the area of practical discipleship and lay witnessing. Mainline Christianity in the West has become so intellectualized and institutionalized that most of the fire has died out. It was not always that way: there was a time in the early days of the faith when Christianity was not a largely middle-class affair, but rather had its greatest following among the working classes. During the first few centuries, the gospel was spread mainly by lay evangelists, by women and men and even by children.[18] But by and large that day has disappeared, and professionalism now characterizes most missionary

17. Ibid., pp. 66–67. The same argument appears in Roland Allen, *The Spontaneous Expansion of the Church and the Causes Which Hinder It* (London: World Dominion, 1956; Grand Rapids: Eerdmans, 1962).
    18. Green, *Evangelism*, pp. 175–76.

endeavor in and from Western churches. The contagious spontaneity of yesteryear is generally gone. Even when laypersons are encouraged to become more involved in evangelistic outreach, we design training programs and seminars to give their witness at least a smattering of professionalism.

In Southern World countries, however, a revolt against this kind of professionalism is in full swing; prime examples are charismatic churches in Africa, Latin America, and Asia. Western-oriented missionaries stand amazed at the vitality and appeal of movements that want nothing to do with the professionalism we hold in such high regard. Generally these movements don't want to have much to do with our mission organizations and the church structures we produce and control. The issues argued over in the Western church, for example, the role of women in evangelism and church development, are largely irrelevant to these dynamic independent movements. They enlist their women, assigning them roles that are culturally appropriate and open-ended in the possibilities they offer for the full use of women's gifts. Their leaders are chosen on the basis of spiritual authority, not ecclesiastical privilege or educational superiority. And the pastors, like everyone else, must find remunerative employment to support themselves until the churches are able to supply adequate salaries.

The masses clearly prefer to express key doctrines, maintain church life, provide leadership, and spread the faith in ways different from those followed in traditional Western churches.[19] This is as true for ethnic groups in Western cities as it is throughout the Southern World. The forms and values they prefer hark back to the early days of the Christian movement, with its emphasis on a common anointing of the Holy Spirit which equips for ministry, on a leadership chosen on the basis of gifts instead of formal education, on lay participation and witness, and on egalitarian church life. That is why it is generally a mistake for Southern World churches to bind themselves too closely to Western church patterns, which invariably means limited growth and impact on the culture. Their cause is better served by intense study of the New Testament Christian movement and how the church grew back then.

---

19. The term *masses* here refers to the common working people and the poor, in distinction from the classes who live more comfortably and enjoy a greater measure of wealth, power, and influence. Historians have pointed out that religious movements usually enter society among the masses and work their way up. The importance of this fact has been brought home to missiologists through the writings of Donald A. McGavran and C. Peter Wagner.

Lay Preachers

The cities of the first century heard the gospel largely through the witness of lay preachers. The late Dutch missiologist J. H. Bavinck called attention to the repeated references in the Book of Acts to the part played by unofficial lay preachers.

> After the persecution following the death of Stephen, refugees went through the land preaching the gospel (Acts 8:4). Some were apparently driven to Phoenicia, Cyprus, and Antioch (Acts 11:19). Among them some began to preach the gospel to the Greeks (Acts 11:20). . . . We gain the impression that an intense role was played in the missionary activity of the early church by many men and women who held no other office than that of a believer. To the extent that these lay preachers were on their own, they were in danger of becoming involved in all sorts of confusion, and as a matter of fact this is just what happened. It is, however, the great strength of Paul that he did not suppress this spontaneous spreading of the gospel, but utilized and organized it instead.[20]

The ministry of the lay apostolate, of men and women alike, was at the heart of church expansion in the first century, and it explains much of what is happening wherever the gospel is spreading today. Laypeople, when unleashed, have a capacity for evangelistic accomplishments which the clergy are hard pressed to match. That truth, which to many ears sounds radical and revolutionary, has been highlighted recently by Frank R. Tillapaugh in his book *Unleashing the Church*.[21]

How ironic it is that among the less educated masses in the cities, both in the Northern and Southern worlds, God is today raising up churches which enjoy a lay apostolate far in advance of that experienced by older denominations with all their traditions and accumulated wisdom. Nevertheless, many people in the older churches are seeking an effective lay apostolate, and that gives hope, for as Hendrik Kraemer observed a generation ago:

> Of all the voices that are raised around the laity, the call for the lay apostolate is the strongest. The Churches, rediscovering their missionary obligation and suddenly becoming aware of the hugeness of the task, turn to the laity with the argument that every Christian is *eo ipso* a witness and a missionary: to discover next that a laity which has been so long neglected and left ignorant is in its majority unable to respond to such a

---

20. J. H. Bavinck, *An Introduction to the Science of Missions*, trans. David Hugh Freeman (Grand Rapids: Baker, 1960), pp. 39–40.
21. Frank R. Tillapaugh, *Unleashing the Church* (Ventura, Calif.: Regal, 1982).

demand. But it is also true that in many parts of Europe new experiments of evangelization, which often show great originality, daring and inventiveness, are being tried.[22]

The parachurch mission agencies have been raised up to provide structures and vehicles for the ministry of the lay apostolate. In places where ecclesiastical structures had become rigid and evangelism professionalized, groups such as Campus Crusade, Youth with a Mission, and a host of smaller lay-run mission organizations were formed to teach laypeople that evangelism is every Christian's business and that they too, equipped by the Spirit, can share the gospel and advance God's kingdom. These lay-run mission organizations almost always have a clearer grasp of the world situation, and of how Christians should carry the gospel to the non-Christian masses, than do the leading thinkers and administrators of denominations who have many other things to occupy their attention. Until we discover how to bring the church and mission to embrace one another and work together more effectively, a major part of the responsibility for evangelizing cities will continue to be borne by parachurch agencies.

An Apostolic Legacy

Urban society in the Roman Empire was scarcely less threatening and complicated than our own, especially for those who were socially and economically disadvantaged as so many in the early church apparently were. For these new Christians, Paul and his co-workers did four important things which modern urban missionaries would do well to repeat.

First, Paul and his co-workers taught aggressively a clear and concise body of doctrine centered around the pivotal truth that Jesus is the Messiah and, by his death and resurrection, Savior of the world. Second, they spelled out a moral system of behavior for the discipline of individuals, families, and churches that was centered in the lordship of Jesus Christ and his authority over all areas of life, and that stood in sharp contrast to the values and lifestyle of the world. Third, they promoted through the organization of local churches a high level of cohesion and group identity, centered in a common confession and reaching beyond the local group to include the broader movement of "all those everywhere who call on the name of our Lord Jesus Christ— their Lord and ours" (1 Cor. 1:2). This double identity of the early Christians—local identity in a disciplined confessional community

22. Hendrik Kraemer, *A Theology of the Laity* (London: Lutterworth, 1958), p. 45.

and supralocal identity through the broad network of churches located throughout the empire—proved to be a powerful factor in the New Testament missionary movement.

The legacy of the apostles entailed yet a fourth element of tremendous importance for evangelism and the growth of the church. Stemming from their teaching about the Holy Spirit and the fellowship of the Spirit-anointed, it is well illustrated by an experience I had in Sri Lanka that drove home to me the value of a pivotal element of New Testament church life.

The Fellowship of the Spirit

Seated on the front veranda of our home in Colombo, Sri Lanka, I could observe at close hand the activities of the Fellowship Center, a Pentecostal church of the Bakht Singh movement from India. Entirely indigenous in leadership, structure, and support, the Fellowship Center was a splendid example of the fellowship of the Spirit and of witness.

Services at the Fellowship Center were held almost every night of the week. They were long and sometimes loud, and the overflow crowd often stood in the doorways and at the windows straining to hear what was being said inside. Prayer vigils often lasted all night, and by breakfast time a group was usually gathered for a regular morning prayer-meeting. People came and went at all hours of the day—women in their colorful saris, men in white suits or knotted sarongs, some without shoes, and all carrying their Bibles. Converts from all three of the great non-Christian religions—Buddhism, Hinduism, and Islam—mingled together at the Fellowship Center.

The three pastors of the center sometimes came to me to borrow Bible commentaries and ask questions. Office workers in downtown Colombo, none of them had had formal theological training. They were honest, sincere men who had both passion for the lost and compassion for the poor (of whom Colombo had plenty). The Fellowship Center was always a beehive of Bible study and ministry. The members did not believe in Bible institutes or seminaries, but taught that the church itself is the training school for all its members. Sometimes the lights would be on half the night as one group or another discussed a problem or dealt with some need.

But for all its good points, one thing was a bit irksome about the Fellowship Center. It had nothing to do with the loud singing, long services, and continual traffic in and out. What irritated us as foreign missionaries was that most of our converts ended up, not as members of the denominational churches with which we worked, but of the

Fellowship Center, which had no expatriate missionaries at all. Somehow, their zeal and enthusiasm as new Christians kept them from settling down in our denominational churches. The old-line churches had many fine things to offer, such as large buildings, more clearly defined doctrines, highly trained clergy, impressive liturgy, and prestige. But for some reason new converts inevitably ended up at places like the Fellowship Center, with apologies (sometimes) to the missionaries who had led them to the Lord.

Was there an explanation? Of course there was, and it lay in the nature of the two kinds of churches. The Fellowship Center was precisely what its name implied—a center of fellowship, where the presence and power of the Spirit was recognized and his gifts were enjoyed. Things happened when people worshiped at the Fellowship Center, where the Word was not thwarted by archaic traditions designed to fit another time and place.

In cities people crave the kind of interpersonal relationships that the biblical word *koinōnia* ("fellowship") conveys. Churches were meant to provide fellowship, the fellowship of the twice-born, the temples of the Holy Spirit, God's family in the city. But so much of what passes as fellowship in the churches falls far, far short of the fellowship of the Spirit. At best, it is friendly fraternizing: appealing, but easily duplicated by clubs and associations outside the church. On the other hand, supernatural communion—the intercommunion of the Spirit with God's people, and between themselves as members of one family—is hard to find.

The early church experienced fellowship, not in large auditoriums amid lush furnishings and polished liturgy, but in small groups, in private homes, and oftentimes amid persecution. That is where the growing church in China discovered it too, during more than a quarter of a century of Communist oppression. The fellowship of the Spirit is an atmosphere of growth, witness, and ministry. If the patterns which the Western church has adopted and usually tries to implant around the world do not effectively serve the needs of young churches on the outer edge of the urban frontier, they should be dispensed with immediately. Some patterns of church life and worship stifle the Spirit and destroy fellowship. It is better to look to New Testament patterns than to the traditions of the West, and to growing, joyful, Spirit-filled churches than to tradition-bound structures which have the smell of death about them. The communion of the Spirit—that is the thing to be cherished, for in such an atmosphere churches will grow and converts multiply in the city.

A final word about the urban Christian movement which the apostles of the Lord produced. Its approach to the social evils of the day was characterized more by tension and anticipation of eventual resolution than by direct conflict with specific evils and a fixed approach to dealing with them. The early Christian assemblies included in intimate fellowship persons of a wide range of social classes, with tremendous inconsistencies and unresolved social issues between them. There were masters and slaves, rich people and poor, Jews and Gentiles, males and females. Each of these pairings represents social differences and injustices which eventually the Christian community would have to address. But instead of tackling every problem on the agenda immediately, Paul and his colleagues laid the basis for changes of immense significance. They did this by teaching the Scriptures, building the Christian community, and inculcating into believers' minds a patient reliance on God's power, coupled with a firm expectation of a better world to come. By so doing, they set believers free, free from obsessive concern over present inconsistencies, free to wait for God's judgment in this world and the next, and free to tackle the problems at hand through the leading of the Spirit and the instruction of the Scriptures.[23]

Discussion Questions

1. What makes the story of the gospel's spread in the New Testament period so important for mission strategists today? Why do you think the Holy Spirit chose a person like Paul to provide leadership in first-century missions?
2. Discuss the basic features of New Testament mission strategy. Identify any aspects which you feel are not relevant today.
3. Define "conversion" and discuss its implications for personal behavior, family life, community service, church involvement, and witness.
4. Discuss the lay apostolate in the light of this chapter, your experience, and your understanding of the teaching of Scripture. Is the lay apostolate gender-neutral? How should city pastors view their teaching roles vis-à-vis the laity?
5. What steps should city churches take to enjoy the sense of *koinōnia* which was so characteristic of the early church? Apply your suggestions to your own church, and analyze what it will take to bring about changes that will lead to greater fellowship.

23. For a more detailed discussion of Paul's urban ministry with special application to the cities of Latin America, see Greenway, *Urban Strategy for Latin America*, pp. 71–134.

Antioch: A Biblical Model of Urban Church Development
Roger S. Greenway

Antioch of Syria was a cosmopolitan city, closer in character to a modern metropolis than was any other city in the Roman world. Understanding Antioch is crucial for a biblical perception of urban mission, because patterns were established there that set the course of mission history and changed the religious map of the world. At Antioch the gospel was preached for the first time to people who had no previous connection with the Jewish faith and community. The church at Antioch, by commissioning and sending out the first missionaries to the unevangelized world, became the mother of all the Gentile churches. Furthermore, from the life and ministry of the Antiochan church a man who was destined to become the great urban apostle of the first century learned firsthand what a Gentile church could be. This lesson made an indelible stamp on his career.

Beauty, Idolatry, and Sin

As cities go, Antioch had everything to offer. Under Roman rule, it was the third city of the empire, the capital of the province of Syria, and was governed by a proconsul in charge of two legions of soldiers. Known as "Antioch the Beautiful," the city undertook a tremendous building program, which was financed jointly by Augustus and Herod.

Sections of this chapter appear in the author's earlier book, *Apostles to the City* (Grand Rapids: Baker, 1978).

31

Its athletic stadiums drew thousands to see the annual games. Antioch was the center for diplomatic relations with Rome's vassal states in the East and a meeting point for many nationalities and cultures. It was a place where East and West came together, a truly cosmopolitan center.

Archeological excavations indicate that every religious movement in the ancient world was represented in Antioch. There were cults of Zeus and Apollo and the rest of the Greek pantheon. There were also the Syrian worship of Baal and the Mother Goddess, and the mystery religions with their teachings on death and resurrection, initiation, and salvation. Occultism was common along with magic, witchcraft, and astrology.

Antioch was also known for its immorality. The dancing girls of Antioch were the talk of the Mediterranean world. As a large and rich commercial center, Antioch embodied the voluptuousness and corruption of a pagan society untouched by Christian influence. The city rivaled Corinth as a center for vice, and the Roman poet Juvenal, writing near the end of the first century A.D., charged that the wickedness of Antioch was one of the sources of Rome's corruption.

Despite these negative features, Antioch became the main gateway for the gospel to the Gentile world. It is interesting to note that the New Testament never talks about Antioch's wickedness and idolatry, its culture and beauty, or its importance as one of the great commercial centers of antiquity. In describing Antioch, Luke refers only to the great spiritual events that took place there. Events in Antioch affected the course of the gospel, threw open the empire to evangelization, and molded the character of the missionary enterprise. As for its impact upon the world, Antioch soon came to supersede Jerusalem, developing into the missionary headquarters of the first century.

A Church of Unknown Origin

Just when and how the gospel first arrived in Antioch, no one knows. The Book of Acts tells us that when the disciples of Jesus were scattered because of the persecution that arose in connection with Stephen's martyrdom, some of them came to Antioch. It is possible that there was already a believing community in Antioch before Stephen died. This church, which did so much to change the religious map of the Roman Empire, was founded by some unknown missionary, probably a layperson who, without publicity or recognition, was faithful to the Lord. Maybe it was Nicolas, one of the first deacons at Jerusalem, who came from Antioch and may have decided to return home and spread the Good News among his fellow proselytes (Acts

6:5). In any case, we are not told who it was that first preached the gospel in Antioch, or under what conditions he labored.

Most of the churches of the first century, and all succeeding centuries, were founded by Christians whose names were never recorded in history books. They received no acclaim, on earth at least, for their labors and sacrifices. Some giants of faith and missionary endeavor stand out against the horizons of history, and we all know their names: William Carey, Hudson Taylor, David Livingstone. Their very names call to mind the opening of great areas of the world to the gospel. We thank God for such people, for they were faithful servants and God used them mightily. But at the same time we must remember that the vast majority of converts, and most Christian churches, were the fruits of an anonymous multitude who served God faithfully without earthly acclaim. It was that way at Antioch. We do not know who began the church, but Christians for centuries have benefited from what he or she did.

The Overcoming of Racial and Ethnic Barriers

Luke recorded that when persecution broke out in Jerusalem, the disciples of Jesus were scattered as far as Phoenicia, Cyprus, and Antioch. As they fled, they spoke of their faith to none except Jews (Acts 11:19). We can understand the racial and ethnic narrowness of their evangelism when we remember how reluctant most people are today to bridge the gaps between different communities and to witness cross-culturally, even after nineteen centuries of Christian growth and instruction.

"Some of them, however, men from Cyprus and Cyrene, went to Antioch and began to speak to Greeks also, telling them the good news about the Lord Jesus" (Acts 11:20). That was the breakthrough! The earlier preaching of Philip to the Samaritans and the Ethiopian proselyte, and Peter's encounter with Cornelius the centurion, remarkable events though they were, still were limited to people within the circle of Jewish faith and piety. But at Antioch pagans heard the gospel from Christian lips, and the universal spread of the Good News began.

The cosmopolitan climate of the city was conducive to this kind of breakthrough. Antioch was at one and the same time a Hellenistic city, a Roman city, and a Jewish city. It was a meeting place of Oriental and Greek civilizations. It had a large Jewish population, but many of the Jews were lax religiously, and social barriers between Jews and Gentiles were relatively small. Some of the Jews were engaged in proselyting efforts, and converts to Judaism were numerous. If the gap between the Jewish and Gentile worlds was to be bridged anywhere, it could be expected to happen in this cosmopolitan center.

In his book *Evangelism in the Early Church*, Michael Green reminds us that it was not the official policy of the Jerusalem church to evangelize Antioch. On the contrary, a spontaneous movement arose from Christian people who could not keep quiet about Jesus their Lord.[1] Green points out that Antioch of Syria was a virtual microcosm of Roman antiquity in the first century, a city that encompassed most of the human problems with which the new faith would have to grapple as it moved across the world. Racial and ethnic issues were certainly two of the most fundamental, and in this area the Holy Spirit led the church of Antioch in a direction of highest importance for the spread of the gospel.

Evangelistic Revival and Careful Follow-up

Unnamed Christians, foreigners to the great city, began preaching "Jesus is Lord" with tremendous results. There were many gods and many lords in the Gentile world, but for these followers of Jesus there was only one God, the Maker of heaven and earth, and only one Lord, Jesus Christ, through whom all things were made and who himself had come into the world to reconcile sinners to God. "The Lord's hand was with them, and a great number of people believed and turned to the Lord" (Acts 11:21). All the important things that the Antiochan church did later must be seen against the background of the evangelistic fire that broke out when the gospel of Jesus Christ was first preached to the Gentiles there. Before Antioch reached out in mercy to the needy, or commissioned some of their own leaders to carry the gospel to faraway places, the church learned to evangelize powerfully and fruitfully in its own city streets.

News of these occurrences reached the ears of the church in Jerusalem, which sent a one-man commission, in the person of Barnabas, to find out what was happening. At this early stage in the history of the faith, Jerusalem still had great influence, and we can imagine how the disciples in Antioch felt when they heard that Jerusalem was sending someone to investigate their movement. They probably thought, "Here comes trouble!" Jerusalem was the mother church, the citadel of Jewish conservatism. Things had not gone the same way in Antioch as in Jerusalem: the new Gentile converts brought to the church faces and

1. Michael Green, *Evangelism in the Early Church* (Grand Rapids: Eerdmans, 1970), p. 114.

practices that Jerusalem could hardly imagine. What would Barnabas be like? Would he take back to Jerusalem a negative report? Would he condemn this exciting new breakthrough of the gospel into the Gentile world and oppose its spreading any farther?

"When he [Barnabas] arrived," says Luke, "and saw the evidence of the grace of God, he was glad and encouraged them all to remain true to the Lord with all their hearts. He was a good man, full of the Holy Spirit and faith" (Acts 11:23–24a). What a relief it must have been to the Antiochan church that Barnabas was the kind of man he was! One of the hardest things to understand in religious work is the attitude of some of God's children who, when they see something beautiful happening, oppose it, criticize it, and refuse to have anything to do with it. But Barnabas was not such a person. When he saw the evidence of God's grace at work transforming people's lives, he rejoiced, recognized its potential, and threw his energies into the follow-up program. Barnabas realized that the devil would soon begin to discourage the new converts and lead them back into sin and idolatry. The fruits of the Antiochan revival needed to be consolidated immediately or much would be lost. Barnabas apparently did not even take time to go back to Jerusalem with his report. Maybe he sent the elders a letter, but the Bible does not say. All we know is that he set to work at once and "a great number of people were brought to the Lord" (Acts 11:24).

Church growth can occur in three different ways. First, there is *biological* growth. By this we mean the enlargement of the church through internal growth—children born into Christian homes and brought up in the covenant community to acknowledge God in their whole walk of life. Church growth of this kind represents God's age-old way of dealing with believing parents and their children from one generation to another. The second kind of church growth is what we call *transfer* growth. It takes place when church members move from one location to another and, in the new location, either join an established church or begin a new one. There is no numerical increase in the church of Jesus Christ. Christians have simply transferred their membership from one community of believers to another.

The third kind of church growth is what took place at Antioch. We call it *conversion* growth. Granted, in the beginning there was some transfer growth at Antioch as refugees arrived from Jerusalem, but the really important factor in Antioch was the number of pagans who were converted to Christian convictions and church membership. That is the kind of growth we must look for in evangelism. When, as a result of uncertainty or frustration, people engaged in mission work begin to minimize the importance of winning converts from unbelief to saving faith in Christ, something has gone seriously wrong. The pattern established at Antioch was followed consistently by Paul and the rest of the apostles. They verbally proclaimed the Good News of the Lord Jesus for the purpose of persuading men and women to believe the message and be converted to the Lord. Anything less than this is a serious departure from the New Testament pattern of evangelism.

Barnabas was a teacher and organizer. He recognized what the Antiochan church needed most at that time: encouragement, instruction, and counsel as to the direction they ought to go. Barnabas realized too that the increasing number of converts meant that he could not handle the follow-up alone, so he went to Tarsus to look for Saul, the gifted young convert from Pharisaism whom he had introduced to the apostles at Jerusalem (Acts 9:27). This decision on the part of Barnabas was crucial both for Antioch and for the spread of the faith throughout the empire. Barnabas probably did not realize that he was recruiting for active ministry a man whose preaching, writing, and personal influence would in the providence of God change the course of history.[2]

Paul's experience at Antioch provided him with a model of what the church should be. It was a model that later he set out to duplicate, not rigidly nor without allowance for differences in local customs and circumstances, but still with its basic contours visibly intact. It was in Antioch that he learned what it meant to bring Gentiles to a saving faith in Jesus Christ and to instruct, guide, and work with them until a strong functioning church was established. Antioch did more to mold Paul than most people realize. A great deal of what we have come to recognize as the Pauline strategy of church planting (and the theology that accompanies it) can be traced to his early experiences with the vibrant young church at Antioch.

The Name Christians

In the ancient world, slaves were called by their master's name. That probably explains how the followers of the Lord first came to be called *Christianoi* ("Christians"). Slaves had no right to exercise their own will; they could only obey orders. They could not hold property or leave an inheritance. They were their own masters in nothing, but in

2. The question may be asked whether Barnabas learned of the prophecy made at the time of Paul's conversion concerning his future ministry (see Acts 9:15; 22:21; 26:16–18). If already aware of God's intention for Paul, Barnabas may have recognized in Antioch the very situation that would launch Paul on the Gentile mission to which God had appointed him.

everything they submitted to a higher authority, that of their master and lord.

The Bible does not record the name of the observant critic who first gave disciples the nickname *Christians*. But the name stuck because it fit. Disciples of Jesus regarded him as their Master and themselves as his slaves. "We are not our own," they said, "for we have been bought with a price." Body and soul, in life and in death, they belonged to their divine Master, Jesus Christ. Doing God's will was their chief concern. The sovereignty of God was more than a slogan or a doctrine. It had a decisive influence on their way of life, and the enemies of the gospel took note and called them Christians.

The apostle Paul learned much about the character and purpose of the Christian life by observing and working with the young church at Antioch. He took up the derogatory title given to followers of Jesus and made it his badge of honor. He introduced himself to the Romans as "Paul, a bond-servant of Christ Jesus, called as an apostle, set apart for the gospel of God" (Rom. 1:1 NASB). The bondservant status of Christ's followers echoes throughout all of Paul's writings. Christians have no abiding citizenship or inheritance on earth. Their home is in heaven. The purpose of life is service to God, and whether they live or die, they belong to him. The mark of the Antiochan believers became the definition of discipleship for all times.

Today there is a growing awareness that the major reason for the church's powerlessness in the secular city is the lack of true discipleship on the part of most church members. Few merit the name "Christian, bondslave of Jesus Christ." Materialism has made church members virtually indistinguishable from the rest of humankind. The world's way of thinking and doing has by and large taken over, and consequently the church has little to say, with credibility at least, to the secular city. This is a generalization—thank God, there are exceptions! But no honest and informed observer can deny that the supreme need of the church is a radical rediscovery of what it means to be Christian.

Is it not principally in the teaching ministry that our efforts at evangelism have failed? Significantly, the phrase "the disciples were first called Christians at Antioch" follows immediately after the statement, "for a whole year Barnabas and Saul met with the church and taught great numbers of people" (Acts 11:26). Without a thorough teaching ministry, the Antiochan believers would not have matured into the kind of people their critics dubbed "Christians." And no urban strategy today can be expected to produce great fruits unless it includes in-depth instruction in the Scriptures, Christian life, and discipleship.

Compassion for the Poor

In a sense, all the Christian relief and development organizations at work in the world today date their origins back to the church in Antioch. When the Antiochan Christians were informed of Christians suffering in a faraway place, they responded spontaneously and generously to help meet the needs. Luke recorded that upon learning that a great famine would sweep over the world and that Judea was already suffering, "the disciples [in Antioch], each according to his ability, decided to provide help for the brothers living in Judea" (Acts 11:29). Obviously their teachers had instructed them in the Old Testament precept that among God's people there should be mutual sharing and relief of poverty. They accepted the precept as God's contemporary and unchanging word to them (Deut. 15).

Voluntary sharing between believers had taken place in Jerusalem from the very beginning. Note how Acts 2:44–47 describes the life of the early Christians: "All believers were together and had everything in common. Selling their possessions and goods, they gave to anyone as he had need. Every day they continued to meet together in the temple courts. They broke bread in their homes and ate together with glad and sincere hearts, praising God and enjoying the favor of all the people. And the Lord added to their number daily those who were being saved." Acts 4:32–35 gives a similar picture of compassion ministries in the early church. What is described here was not an early form of communism of the kind propagated by Karl Marx and his followers. Nowhere does the Bible teach that it is wrong to own property, or that the Christian community should take over its members' private possessions and own them collectively. On the contrary, early Christians were free to use their possessions as their consciences directed them. Some felt led to sell their land so that the money obtained might assist the poor. Sales of this kind would not have been condoned if private ownership were wrong in principle. What we see in the New Testament are not prohibitions against private ownership of land and property, but the voluntary sale of excess possessions on the part of wealthier Christians to meet the material needs of their poorer brothers and sisters.

Not only did Paul see what the Antiochan church did, he was part of the team that delivered the gift to Jerusalem. There it was administered to the needy under the supervision of the elders of the church (Acts 11:30). This act of compassion on the part of the Antiochan believers made a great impression on Paul, resulting in the consistent integration of word and deed in his later apostolic ministry. It is significant that when Paul reviews his ministry at Ephesus, he dwells at some length on the example he had given not only of self-support, but of working hard in order to supply the needs of his companions and of helping the weak (Acts 20:34–35). In that context Paul quotes words of the Lord Jesus that are not recorded anywhere else: "It is more blessed to give than to receive." The reference is clearly to benevolent, compassionate giving.

The Antiochan model of compassion ministries is still with us, but I fear that it is not taken seriously enough. While visiting a small chapel in Brazil, I observed the clothing worn by some of the children. It was winter and fairly cold. Toes stuck through the tips of some of the shoes, and a few barefoot youngsters kept their feet curled beneath them, partly perhaps because of the cold and partly out of embarrassment because they had no shoes. These children came from Christian homes—homes where the fathers worked ten to twelve hours a day, six days a week, to earn a living for their families; homes where mothers did everything possible to feed their children and clothe them adequately against the cold. When I looked at the coats worn by the two girls sitting next to me, I realized that my dog at home had better things to sleep on than these little girls wore to church. Are not these God's children? I asked. Why then does the worldwide church allow such cruel disparities to continue between members of God's family who suffer poverty and others who abound in possessions and resources? What would the prophets say? What would Paul and the believers at Antioch do?

Having learned at Antioch what Christians should do in response to human needs and suffering, Paul made it a regular emphasis in his preaching and writing that the support of fellow Christians in need is a primary responsibility, and whenever possible, help should be extended indiscriminately to whoever is in need (Gal. 6:10). In his second letter to the church at Corinth, Paul dedicated no less than two chapters (8 and 9) to the subject of Christian charity toward needy brethren. In Paul's theology and mission strategy, proclamation and compassion went together. He viewed them as inseparable components of both the church's ministry and apostolic mission.

Local Leadership

In his book *Pauline Theology and Mission Practice*, Dean S. Gilliland speaks of Paul's remarkable ability to attract key people, who in turn had the capacity for leadership.[3] Scripture suggests that Paul was a

3. Dean S. Gilliland, *Pauline Theology and Mission Practice* (Grand Rapids: Baker, 1983), pp. 213–22.

natural leader even before his conversion (Acts 9:1–2; Phil. 3:6). Yet it was undoubtedly the case that as far as apostolic leadership was concerned, Paul went through an apprenticeship under the tutelage of Barnabas when they worked together in Antioch (Acts 11:25–30) and during their first missionary journey (Acts 13–14).[4]

Among other things, Paul learned at Antioch that the key to developing strong and effective churches is local leadership. Imported leaders like Barnabas and himself had important roles to play in getting the church started. But then they must move on, leaving the new church in the hands of local believers. At Antioch, Barnabas and Paul invested their talents and energy in the development of local leaders, and the opening verses of chapter 13 indicate that, with God's blessing, the strategy was successful. Exactly how long Paul and Barnabas had intended to continue ministering in Antioch, the Bible does not say. But the Holy Spirit intervened (Acts 13:2) and let everyone know that the time had come for the early leaders to move on, entrusting the care of the young church to local leaders.

I believe the divine intervention recorded in Acts 13:1–3 had a tremendous effect on the apostles' future strategy. From then on, their main efforts were directed toward winning initial converts and developing local leaders. They avoided methods that created long-term dependency on the missionaries. Their consistent strategy from Antioch onwards was to lay a spiritual foundation; enlist and train local leaders (elders) who loved the Lord Jesus, cared for the church, lived moral lives, and were willing to accept the responsibilities of leadership; and then move on. There was follow-up in the form of letters, return visits by the apostles, and short-term ministries by their assistants. But the early leaders did not stay around once there were responsible resident Christians. Nowhere is this strategy described more plainly than in Acts 20:13–38.

The Strength of a Balanced Church

Merrill C. Tenney says that the church at Antioch was the home of great Christian preaching and compassion for the poor, and the headquarters of evangelistic missions. From this city the missionary fire spread across the Roman Empire.[5]

---

4. Ibid., p. 214.
5. Merrill C. Tenney, *New Testament Survey* (Grand Rapids: Eerdmans, 1961), p. 253.

It strikes me that there was remarkable balance in the Antiochan church. Luke wrote that there were "prophets and teachers" (Acts 13:1) as well as members ready for action. In this context, prophets most likely were those who spoke God's truth to the unsaved, to inquirers, and to those who were coming to Christ from Jewish or pagan backgrounds. Teachers were those who deepened the faith of the new believers through instruction and helped them mature in their understanding of the Scriptures and the practice of the Christian life. This balance between evangelistic proclamation and thorough instruction produced the spiritual vitality that made the Antiochan believers ready for action and helped the church to grow. It was characteristic of Paul's later ministry that these same components reappeared everywhere in the converts and churches he produced.

The strength of the church was shown also in its spiritual life and exercises (Acts 13:2–3). Worship, fasting, and prayer were marks of the community which God chose to use mightily for the spread of the gospel. Ever since then, great missionary movements have been traced to people on their knees. There has never been a church that accomplished significant things for God that was not strong in prayer and spiritual devotion.

The clearest evidence of Antioch's vitality was its readiness to be a sending church, the first missionary-sending church of the New Testament era. From Jerusalem witnesses were forcibly scattered abroad (Acts 11:19), but at Antioch apostles were set apart, commissioned, and sent forth to the work (Acts 13:2–3). Such sending was, and still is, the sign of a vibrant and obedient church.

The apostles whom the Antiochan church commissioned never forgot the special relationship they had with this congregation. When their first missionary journey was completed, they came back to Antioch where, Luke affectionately recorded, "they had been committed to the grace of God for the work they had now completed" (Acts 14:26). When the missionaries arrived, "they gathered the church together and reported all that God had done through them and how he had opened the door of faith to the Gentiles" (Acts 14:27). Luke says they stayed a "long time" with the believers in Antioch. Their stay was undoubtedly a great blessing to the church, for it is still true today that when a church adds a global dimension to its ministry by sending and supporting workers in distant places, its spiritual growth, joy, and vitality are greatly enriched.

Without question, Antioch left an indelible mark on first-century Christianity and continues to serve as an instructive model of urban church development. At Antioch was demonstrated what God's grace can do in a highly urban and pagan environment, and through this gateway the gospel went forth to other cities, where the struggles and victories of Antioch were repeated over and over again.

Discussion Questions

1. Compare the essential characteristics of Antioch with those of modern cities.
2. Have we given enough credit to the witness of the laity and the role of lay Christians in evangelism? Identify ways in which laypersons work on the cutting edge of gospel witness.
3. Leadership training is vitally important to church development. Describe the ways in which leadership training is conducted in your church. Suggest some additional ways which might be introduced in order to widen Christian witness and ministry.
4. Think of the last ten persons who joined your church. Did they come by transfer from some other church or through evangelism? Analyze what your church is doing to bring in the unsaved, the unchurched, and the poor.
5. What false assumptions about Christian mission govern congregations that are rich in membership, buildings, outstanding pastors and leaders, programs, and resources, but poor in terms of mission, evangelism, and service? Suggest some ways to turn such churches inside out.

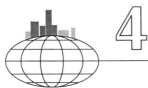

4

Evangelism, Relief, and Development
Roger S. Greenway

The Mahabir slum does not officially exist, but in reality it is home for hundreds of families. There are six hundred communities just like it in New Delhi, India. Because of their tenuous, unofficial status, the residents of Mahabir live in daily fear of being driven off the dusty land on which they've built their shacks.

Recently their worst fears were realized. Police vans appeared suddenly one morning, followed by giant bulldozers. Within a few hours, a large section of the squatter community was reduced to rubble. Along with the houses, a fledgling church and temple were leveled. The residents fought to protect their homes, but police reinforcements were summoned and the resistance was soon over. One man was shot and killed, and twenty people were arrested.

"We always wanted to have a house for our children," said Bhagat Singh, a father of three small children whose cell-sized home was pushed down, its furnishings buried under the rubble. "We paid money for this place," he said, vigorously denying that he was the illegal squatter that government records showed him to be. In fact, he had taken out a loan of more than two thousand dollars for the piece of arid land, a considerable sum for a family earning seventeen dollars a week. Unfortunately, he had bought his plot of dirt from confidence men, who had duped him and his neighbors into thinking they really could become property owners.

Bhagat Singh and his neighbors have rebuilt their shacks of mud and corrugated metal on different plots nearby, hoping this time to be allowed to stay. India has uncounted millions of such squatter families in and around its major cities, where the cramped and chaotic condi-

43

tions are surpassed only by the people's grit and determination to find
work and a better life.[1]

An Overview of the Problem

Biblical solutions to urban needs—that is what Christian ministry
in the urban context is all about. But before we can define solutions, we
must understand the problems. People in Northern World countries,
where a major share of mission effort originates, generally find it difficult to grasp the nature and size of the problems facing the poor in
Southern World cities. They do not realize that the story of Bhagat
Singh is repeated over and over again in dozens of places in Asia, Africa,
and Latin America.

For that reason, in this chapter I will change my approach and
begin by describing what is happening in many countries abroad.
Things are taking place demographically to create conditions that
baffle the most knowledgeable international leaders and cause not a
few of them to be skeptical about the world's future. The data regarding the poor in Southern World countries are such that every Christian should think hard about the Bible's teaching concerning the nature and causes of poverty, the stewardship of resources, our duty
toward the poor, and the kind of assistance that meets the needs of
the poor spiritually as well as physically.

The population explosion and the march to the cities are twin interrelated realities that lie behind the urban slums. It wasn't until
1830—a relatively recent year in human history—that there were one
billion people living together on the planet. But it took only one hundred years to add the second billion, and thirty more years to add the
next billion. In fourteen years, the fourth billion was added, and projections are that by the year 2000 we will add nearly three billion more.
The twenty-first century will in all likelihood begin with a world population approaching seven billion people.

Moving in pace with population growth is the march of the masses
to the cities. In 1800 only 5 percent of the world's population lived in
urban areas. By 1900 the figure had increased to 14 percent. In 1980 it
was approximately 40 percent, and by the year 2000 over half the world
will be urban. By 2050 approximately 79 percent of the world's population will live in urban centers. The Third World accounts for most of
the urban growth. By the year 2050 two-thirds of the world's popula-

1. *New York Times*, July 3, 1987.

tion will live in urban areas of the Third World, and that is where most of the worst poverty conditions are found.

The Frontier of Urban Slums

Nearly 50 percent of the world's population now live in cities, and the majority of them are poor and outside the Christian faith. *The urban poor constitute the largest unclaimed frontier Christian missions has ever encountered.* The urban masses have not heard the gospel of Jesus Christ nor seen it demonstrated in ways that affect their lives. They live outside the normal reach of established churches, and few attempts have been made to draw them into Christian congregations. Their living conditions are largely unseen except in printed statistics and photographs. The causes of their poverty are barely understood by the vast majority of mission-minded Christians. Yet the causes of Southern World urban poverty are not hard to identify:

1. The lack of employment opportunities, particularly among newcomers to the city who lack the skills and the capital required in the urban marketplace.
2. Scarcity of decent and affordable housing. In the Northern World this is seen in the ghettos that form in the old inner-city neighborhoods, and in the Southern World in the squatter settlements that surround the urban centers.
3. Abandoned children by the millions who live in the streets, perpetuating the cycle of suffering, crime, and despair.
4. The gravitation of the elderly to the cities without adequate financial, social, emotional, and religious support systems.
5. The breakdown of family structures, which traditionally have been society's bulwark against spiritual, moral, and material attack.
6. Corruption at all levels of government and society, coupled with callous indifference to the needs of the poor and powerless.
7. Inadequate public services. This is due in part to the precarious financial condition of Southern World countries, and the rapid pace of urbanization which defies even the best efforts of public officials.
8. An abnegation of responsibility on the part of many urban churches, which either relocate at a distance from the poor or refuse to get deeply involved in social ministry.
9. The secularization of many churches in the Southern World,

shown by their concern for self-aggrandizement instead of ministry to the poor, who seem to offer little in return.[2]

Slums, ghettos, and squatter settlements are home to the urban poor. There are thirty cities in the world where over 50 percent of the population live in slums, and this number is bound to increase until at least the end of the century (see table 1). How many people will be numbered among the poor in the year 2000? Table 2 gives estimates for ten of the largest cities.

An additional dimension of the problem is that almost one-half of the population of Third World countries is under the age of fifteen. In Mexico City, about one-half is under thirteen. Tens of thousands of these children live without parental support, shelter, or control.

Both the level of frustration and the potential for revolution of the urban poor are heightened by the fact that cities are cultural and communication centers. The poor are exposed, by television as well as by personal observation, to the wealth and modern lifestyles of the prosperous. The hopes of the common people are stimulated by what they see on the street and on the screen, yet their daily experiences contradict what they see. For vast numbers the hope of self-improvement which first lured them to the city soon is crushed on the pavement.

The pursuit of that hope, however, brings with it an openness to change in a variety of ways. Having broken with tradition and migrated to the city, urban newcomers are often forced to listen and learn just to survive. Lonely and insecure, they display a willingness to experiment with the new and unfamiliar. Change swirls around them, and they themselves are caught up in it. They make new friends, meet new ideas and customs, and take on new jobs.

All this adds up to a remarkable openness to holistic evangelism, making the urban migrant one of the most receptive persons to Christian ministry. On a recent trip through West Africa, I repeatedly asked pastors and missionaries whether tribal people are more open to listening to the gospel in the village or in the city. Without exception the answer was that they are most receptive the first few years they're in the city. The same statement could be made about new urbanites in much of the Southern World.

2. Donald E. Turner, "Draft for a Position Paper on Urban Transformational Ministries," mimeographed (Richmond: Human Needs Ministry Office, Foreign Mission Board of the Southern Baptist Convention, 1986).

Table 1
Percentage of Urban Population Living in Slums and Squatter Settlements

City	Percentage	City	Percentage
Addis Ababa, Ethiopia	90	Lusaka, Zambia	50
Yaoundé, Cameroon	90	Maracaibo, Venezuela	50
Douala, Cameroon	87	Monrovia, Liberia	50
Buenaventura, Colombia	80	Recife, Brazil	50
Mogadiscio, Somalia	77	Guayaquil, Ecuador	49
Ibadan, Nigeria	75	Mexico City, Mexico	46
Lomé, Togo	75	Phnom Penh, Kampuchea	46
Santo Domingo, Dominican Republic	72	Bombay, India	45
Casablanca, Morocco	70	Colombo, Sri Lanka	44
Nairobi, Kenya	70	Tunis, Tunisia	43
Calcutta, India	67	Caracas, Venezuela	42
Chimbote, Peru	67	Barquisimeto, Venezuela	41
Mombasa, Kenya	67	Brasilia, Brazil	41
Izmir, Turkey	65	Arequipa, Peru	40
Accra, Ghana	61	Ciudad Guayana, Venezuela	40
Abidjan, Ivory Coast	60	Istanbul, Turkey	40
Agra, India	60	Lima, Peru	40
Ankara, Turkey	60	Kuala Lumpur, Malaysia	37
Bogota, Colombia	60	Delhi, India	36
Dakar, Senegal	60	Manila, Philippines	35
Kinshasa, Zaire	60	Antananarivo, Madagascar	33
Rabat, Morocco	60	Makasar, Indonesia	33
Blantyre, Malawi	56	Pusan, South Korea	31
Port Sudan, Sudan	55	Cali, Colombia	30
Ouagadougou, Upper Volta	52	Guatemala City, Guatemala	30
Dar es Salaam, Tanzania	50	Rio de Janeiro, Brazil	30

From George Thomas Kurian, *The New Book of World Rankings* (New York: Facts on File, 1984), p. 426. Source: UN Center for Housing, Building, and Planning. The figures are based on 1980 statistics. For unexplained reasons, some cities known to have high percentages of slum dwellers do not appear in the list. Data on these cities may not have been available.

Table 2
Estimates for Ten Third-World Cities in A.D. 2000

	Total Population	People in Slums
1. Mexico City, Mexico	31,616,000	14,543,000
2. Calcutta, India	19,663,000	13,174,000
3. Rio de Janeiro, Brazil	19,383,000	5,815,000
4. Bombay, India	19,065,000	8,579,000
5. Jakarta, Indonesia	16,933,000	4,403,000
6. Delhi, India	13,220,000	4,759,000
7. Manila, Philippines	12,683,000	4,439,000
8. Lima, Peru	12,130,000	4,852,000
9. Bogota, Colombia	9,527,000	5,716,000
10. Caracas, Venezuela	5,963,000	2,504,000

From George Thomas Kurian, *The New Book of World Rankings* (New York: Facts on File, 1984), p. 422.

Has Nothing Been Done?

The minds and hearts of Northern World people have not been alto-gether uninformed about the plight of the Southern World poor, and it would be incorrect to suggest that nothing has been done about it. Pictures on our television screens and in news magazines have brought home the message, and responses have been made. In the past three decades, trillions of dollars have been spent in the form of government assistance, foreign aid, and relief activities, to say nothing of the thou-sands of dedicated lives that have been poured into development ef-forts. But the sad fact is that the results have been meager. In fact, in some parts of the world, such as large areas of Africa, the situation is worsening.

This is due to a combination of political strife and corruption, eco-nomic mismanagement, and hostile weather patterns, as well as a de-bilitating dependence on donations, imports, and foreign aid. In some countries, there has also been a slackening of local agriculture because of a shortsighted dependence on the easy wealth generated by oil pro-duction. All this has frustrated the best intentions and hard work in behalf of the poor and has brought nation after nation to the brink of bankruptcy. Consequently, a large measure of cynicism has developed in some circles, leading people to ask with a shrug, "What's the use?"

The Christian Attitude

A philosophy of development that merits the name *Christian* be-gins with the acknowledgment that the Bible is the source of authority for all thought and action. It is from Scripture that we receive the answer to the fundamental question, What is a human person? What are the nature and the worth of a man, a woman, a child?

Many authors have written about the poor in light of the Bible pas-sages that specifically deal with the subject. I respect their concern for biblical thinking and interpretation. They seek to know and do the full counsel of God. Nonetheless, it seems to me that the basic premise is rooted in Genesis 1–3, where the Bible teaches that the essential na-ture of human beings is the image of God in which they are made. All Christian concern for the poor and downtrodden springs from that premise.

What is a human being, and what value does he or she have? The Bible's answer is that a human being is an image-bearer of God and the most valuable element in God's whole creation. Possessing enormous potentials and designed by the Creator to bring glory to God by exercising dominion over the world and its resources, a human being is of such tremendous value that he or she ought never be trampled upon. God so highly valued human beings that he sent his Son, Jesus Christ, to redeem them from sin and eternal loss.

This biblical assessment of the value of human beings gives the Christian all the motivation required for relief and development ministries. If an image-bearer of God, a person like myself, is poor, oppressed, and helpless, and if I have resources that might lift such an individual out of distress, I need look no further. I have responsibilities toward that person in terms of his or her temporal and eternal welfare. No other motivation is higher nor strong enough to keep the Christian worker from burning out when the going gets rough. As John Perkins has said so often in his speaking and writing, the most important element in Christian ministry among the poor is not our concern for the poor as such, but our love for God and those made in his image.[3]

The Bible teaches a great number of things regarding the poor, the causes of poverty, and the judgment of God against those who oppress the poor. Because there is a tendency in liberal circles to quote Scripture rather loosely on the subject and to romanticize the poor as though their poverty were a guarantee of God's special favor and their own eternal salvation, it is important to comment further on the subject of the Bible and the poor. Whatever strategy we adopt for ministry to the urban poor, it must spring from our understanding of God's attitude toward poor people and what the church must offer them in Christ's name.

There is a sense in which God stands on the side of the poor. The Bible teaches that God is angered when people are oppressed, and in this life or the next he will punish those who are oppressors. The apostasy of Israel is characterized in part in terms of her oppression of the poor (Amos 5:12). The promise of the year of jubilee and the age of the Messiah is portrayed as "good news to the poor" (Isa. 61:1-3; Luke 4:17-21). According to the Book of James, pure religion involves taking care of defenseless widows and orphans (James 1:27). The ministry of Jesus had special significance for the poor and oppressed of his day, for he defined his ministry as preaching the gospel to the poor and announcing freedom for the prisoners, recovery of sight for the blind, and release for the oppressed (Luke 4:17-21).

As we apply this to missions and evangelism, certain clarifications are needed. The Bible does not teach that the requisite for being saved

3. See John Perkins, *Let Justice Roll Down* (Glendale, Calif.: Regal, 1976), and *A Quiet Revolution* (Waco, Tex.: Word, 1986).

is to be poor. Nor does it say that all who are poor will be saved. Instead, the Bible teaches plainly that *all* have sinned; there is no one who does what is right and good (Rom. 3:9–20). If someone who is poor and oppressed does not accept the gospel, he or she will be condemned along with the rich. On the other hand, a rich individual who accepts the gospel and believes in Christ will be saved. It is sheer unbiblical romanticism to suggest that there is a salvific value in being poor, for if that were the case it would be better to leave the poor in their poverty and not try to free them from it.

Moreover, there is a sense in which the materially rich and the materially poor in this world are alike in their bondage to the devil. Hebrews 2:14–15 speaks of the devil as the great oppressor of all humankind. From this slavery Christ is the one and only liberator. The unkindest act of all is to lift a person out of one kind of poverty only to leave him a slave to an oppression of a deeper nature, a bondage which is eternal. God the righteous judge will deal at the final judgment with all who have oppressed and done evil in this life, and he will show eternal mercy to those who, whether rich or poor, have sought salvation through his Son, Jesus Christ. On these issues the Bible is perfectly plain, and its clarity at this point will prevent us from devising an urban mission strategy that might sell short the very people we intend to help.

This leads me to formulate twin propositions that should guide us as we relate urban evangelism to relief and development:

If we wipe out poverty but neglect to tell the poor the Good News about Jesus Christ, we will have failed in our mission.

And if we preach the gospel but ignore the plight of the poor, we are false prophets.

There is ample support for both of these propositions in Scripture, which commit us to a unified ministry of word and deed in Christ's name. There is no point in arguing over which comes first or which has priority. Both are required. The faith by which souls are redeemed and lives transformed, the church is built, and the kingdom advanced, comes through the proclamation of God's grace toward sinners through Christ's redeeming work. That proclamation of the gospel is central to the Christian mission, but it cannot appear without the witness of love in ministries of healing, teaching, and benevolence. These belong together, as they were together in the preaching, teaching, and healing ministry of our Lord. If ever in the missionary enterprise they become separated, serious damage is done to the overall witness of the gospel.

Searching for a Strategy

It is universally recognized by Christians and non-Christians alike that the phenomenal growth of poverty in the world's great cities is a major problem, and that unemployment, or underemployment, lies at the root of the problem.[4] Each day an additional one hundred thousand people enter the work force in the Southern World, yet less than half will find employment that meets their needs. As a result people suffer, and the suffering of the poor is probably more severe in the city than in the countryside. In the city one needs cash, and to get cash legitimately, one needs employment. Yet without skills, and in most cases some capital, the urban migrant has enormous difficulties finding adequate employment.

Relief efforts often take the form of benevolence. To meet unexpected crises, for example, short-term relief ministries are what is needed. When disaster strikes an individual or a community, the Christian response is to take immediate and appropriate action in order to meet the need, as the Samaritan traveler did in the Lord's familiar parable, and as Christ himself did on many occasions by performing miracles. By so doing, Christians bear witness to God's love and mercy. Whenever possible they accompany their good deeds with a verbal witness to Christ, in whose name they perform the relief activities.

But relief ministries do little to alter the long-term problems that beset the cities. Churches and mission agencies that hand out food and clothing month after month and year after year are not really tackling poverty. Things need to be done that will break the poverty cycle for individuals, families, and neighborhoods, and lift people to a level where they can provide for themselves adequately and with dignity. Long-term relief only creates dependency, and dependency is debilitating and dehumanizing. It is tragic that so much of Christian concern for the poor has been expressed in ways that create and maintain dependency relationships. As a consequence, large numbers of poor people have lost confidence in their ability ever to rise above poverty; they have resigned themselves to living off the benevolence of others.

The term *development* is used to describe relief activity that is intended to avoid creating dependency and instead gives the poor the

---

4. "Underemployment" is a term used to describe a common condition in Southern World cities: people work hard at some job, but the remuneration is inadequate to meet their needs. Heads of families in Latin America, for example, who shine shoes ten to twelve hours a day are not unemployed, but they do not bring home enough to provide for their families. As a consequence, all members of the family, including children, must work at something, even though it may pay poorly.

opportunity to earn a respectable living on their own. An old Chinese proverb illustrates the difference between relief and development. "If you give a hungry man a fish, you relieve his hunger for a day. But if you teach him how to catch fish, you relieve his need for many days to come." Applied to an urban strategy on behalf of the poor, this proverb suggests that development rather than benevolence is the route to take. Development protects the dignity of the poor and offers them the chance to rise above poverty and meet their needs on a permanent basis.

Urban Community Development That Is Christian and Holistic

What kind of help should churches and mission agencies extend to the urban poor? What kind of help will fulfil the biblical mandate to evangelize the poor as well as relieve their physical needs? These are fundamental questions which a growing number of Christians are asking. In some places there are strategies in operation from which we can learn important lessons.

Consider the goal of Christian mission. The fulfilment of the missionary mandate requires the proclamation of the gospel of Jesus Christ, the planting and growth of the church, the extension of Christ's lordship over all areas of community life, and the reclaiming of the whole cosmos from the control of Satan and his servants (see fig. 1). In pursuit of this goal, Christ's servants proclaim the gospel of the kingdom of God and bear witness in word and deed to his saving love and compassion. By all that they do, they seek to call forth a saved people, the church, and gather believers into congregations for worship, fellowship, and service. Missionary responsibility does not end when a church is initially planted. It moves on to equip the developing church through instruction, leadership training, and establishment of outreach programs so that the gospel may continue to spread to entire cities and nations. In carrying out this mandate, Christ's servants instruct by word and example concerning the kind of fraternal supportive relationships that should exist between churches and other Christian groups. They thereby testify to their fundamental unity in Christ and their concern for the welfare and growth of Christ's whole body.

When the big picture of God's kingdom is the perspective from which we work, everything which God has made and which affects human life and welfare comes within the purview of Christian mission. From the quality of the air people breathe to the water in the rivers that flow through the city, from the squalor of the slums to the

Figure 1
Urban Mission: *A Holistic Perspective*

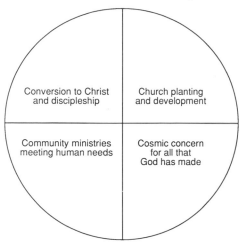

opulent living of the privileged few, from the manner in which the earth's resources are used to the way the city's waste is disposed of, the biblical message of redemption and kingdom stewardship confronts individual behavior and the entire social order. The gospel of the kingdom condemns sin and injustice in every form, and calls for individual and social transformation reflecting God's righteousness and his total claim on all that he has made. The community of believers stands in the city as the showcase of God's kingdom, for it is there that God's Son is loved, his Word is heard and obeyed, and the standards of his righteous rule are exemplified by a people being renewed by the Spirit from within.

Religious belief and level of commitment play a major role in the whole matter of social transformation. As people's religious and moral values change, there generally is progress in social development. This underscores the importance of integrating evangelism with development activities. It is this combination which offers the greatest hope to the poor.

Christian mission with a kingdom perspective is based on, and aims to inculcate, a wide range of moral, religious, and social principles that God has revealed in the Bible. These shape the minds and hearts of those who adhere to them. It is not surprising, therefore, to find a positive relationship between the acceptance of the Christian faith and socioeconomic development. As people adopt a biblical view of God, of themselves, of righteousness, truth, and moral responsibility, they progress in their understanding of God's authority as embracing all of life. They take on attitudes and actions that promote wide-ranging changes in the lives of the poor and oppressed. Attitudinal change is just as necessary for the rich as it is for the poor, both of whom need to have their minds reoriented to focus on the kingdom of God. Failure to bear fruit is the inevitable result when, through selfishness or skewed teaching, Christians fail to adopt and apply kingdom values. Saints who live and operate by God's Word, on the other hand, are the people who can make the greatest difference in the city.[5]

Values to Uphold

Now that the kingdom vision of Christian urban community development has been explained, some of the basic values which undergird that vision should be spelled out. If these values are compromised, the outcome of mission activity will be different and the vision unachieved.

1. From start to finish the ministry must be identifiably Christian. This means that it must be motivated by Christian convictions, conducted by Christian people, identified in the community as a Christian undertaking, and carried out in a manner that demonstrates Christian love and standards of conduct. Besides this, the ministry must fit within the overall goals of the Christian mission, namely, to glorify God through the building of the church and the extension of his righteous kingdom. In all areas, the Bible must be accepted and followed as the self-revelation of the one true God and the norm for all mission activity.

2. Christ's example of blending the spoken word with deeds of compassion toward the suffering must give continual direction to Christian urban-development ministry. Christ preached to the people and, when they were hungry, he fed them. He spoke the gospel of God's forgiveness and raised the sick from their beds of suffering. He did all this through divine, miraculous power, and we do it by the power of the

5. The recognition that there exists a cause-and-effect relationship between conversion to the Christian faith and socioeconomic improvement goes back many years. Missionaries and evangelists have reported it consistently, and so have social scientists. See, for example, Gerhard Lenski, *The Religious Factor: A Sociological Study of Religion's Impact on Politics, Economics, and Family Life* (Garden City, N.Y.: Doubleday, 1961), based on research within the city of Detroit; Emilio Willems, *Followers of the New Faith: Culture Change and the Rise of Protestantism in Brazil and Chile* (Nashville: Vanderbilt University Press, 1967); and the implications of the more recent definition of development in terms of growth with equity, discussed by Charles Wilber and Kenneth Jameson, "Religious Values and Social Limits to Development," *World Development* 8 (1980): 467–79. Equity is more than an economic concept involving the distribution of goods and services; it involves a moral judgment as to the rightness and wrongness of that distribution. The part which religious values play receives fresh attention in this new perception of development.

Spirit, using the means he places in our hands. In either case, word and deed are kept together, as they were in the apostle Paul's ministry (Rom. 15:18). Together they make a mighty witness to the transforming love of God.

3. Christian ministry to the urban poor must follow the principles of indigenization. Indigenization, which is a value long held by Christian missions but not always practiced consistently, is a process leading to local ownership of the church and its ministries. It involves self-government, self-propagation, and self-support. Translated into terms of Christian community development, it means that local Christians will learn to embrace the vision, take hold of the values, practice the skills, and gain control of the ministry so that the church or mission agency which initiated the ministry can withdraw, leaving the local Christians to carry it on and expand it.

The implementation of this principle requires that the development ministry focus on educating and training local Christians. The goal is a compassionate church and a Christian community that recognizes human needs, knows how to meet them, and is motivated to reach out holistically to the city. Dependency on the parent body that initiates the ministry must be as short-lived as possible. Local people and local resources must be mobilized from the outset.

4. Material resources must be used as efficiently as possible. The biblical principle of stewardship needs to be applied in hard-nosed fashion to the ministries we conduct in behalf of the poor, and no amount of missionary romanticism should be allowed to distract us. Management science has a great deal to teach missionaries about goal setting, sound planning, implementation, and honest evaluation.

I am deeply disturbed by the relief work carried on by organizations that year after year bring in money, material, and personnel from places of affluence to places of poverty without accomplishing long-term changes in the lives of the poor. Instead, the poor are kept continually dependent on outside help and are never enabled to meet their own needs. Worse still, since the outside resources are never enough to meet all the needs that exist in the slums, large numbers remain poor and without hope of ever rising to self-sufficiency. There is a better way of conducting development ministry, but it requires a firm commitment to using available resources in the most efficient manner, so that the poor are not merely fed and clothed today, but are empowered to meet their own needs, and the needs of their neighbors, tomorrow.

5. The planting and development of compassionate churches in every part of the city must be the long-term goal. This is the most effective solution to the multiple ills of the urban community. A principle dear to community developers holds that the most effective work is

done through community groups that are taught to identify community needs, practice the basic skills required to alleviate those needs, and take ownership of the program that overcomes those needs. My thesis is that Christian churches, motivated by the love of God and taught the essential principles and values of Christian community development, can become the most effective weapon against poverty and suffering in the city if they are planted and educated in a proper biblical manner.

Evangelism and Development in a Prechurch Setting

Urban ministry is most challenging in places where the church has not yet been established, where few if any mature Christians can be found, and where the evangelist is seeking to announce for the first time the Good News of Christ's power to save and transform life. Under these circumstances, the evangelist is usually surrounded by negative social and religious factors which constantly militate against a true understanding of his or her motives and intentions. In order to communicate the gospel effectively, the Christian worker must know the beliefs, customs, and social patterns of the people and try to avoid the traps that will surely lie in the way. One must always keep in mind that poverty and religious beliefs are deeply interrelated, and that as the gospel of Jesus Christ is addressed to a people, opposition to its acceptance and to the changes for which it calls will surface in a variety of ways.

A familiar trap is the tendency to use relief and development ministries as bait to catch converts to the new religion. From India to Africa, the charge is commonly made that Christians try to buy converts by offering to help the needy. And indeed, some respond to Christianity for no other reason than to gain the benefits and the advantages which come from being identified with a benevolent organization. "Rice Christians" they are called, and every missionary knows that they can be the bane of pioneer church-planting in poor areas. While it is true that some genuine converts may eventually emerge from among those who first come for entirely selfish reasons, a young church composed of such members stands on very shaky ground.

Holistic evangelism in prechurch situations requires great sensitivity to both the needs of the people and the danger of inducing them to accept the new faith for the wrong reasons. The missionary desires to hold up before the community the Good News of what Christ can do to transform their lives and lift them out of poverty, ignorance, and ill health. At the same time the Christian worker must avoid the danger of appearing as a manipulator who takes advantage of their condition in order to foist religion on them.

Accordingly, under such conditions the missionary, whether an expatriate or a national, should avoid starting broad, long-term programs. One should concentrate instead on sowing the seeds of the kingdom by performing meaningful deeds of mercy and at the same time supporting the deeds with a verbal witness to Jesus Christ as the source of total renewal and hope.

At the prechurch stage, the missionary serves as a herald of the kingdom, an announcer of the Good News of Jesus Christ, who came into the world to bring physical and spiritual healing to broken lives and communities. The missionary does everything possible to make it plain that he or she does not serve people on the condition that they become Christians, but deeply hopes that they will. In healing the sick, teaching the illiterate to read, and enabling men and women to earn a better living, the superordinate goal of drawing together a core of believers and planting a church is kept always in mind. Once established, the Christian community will be instructed and equipped to continue and expand the compassion ministries that the missionary began.

Two Models from Sierra Leone

A good way to show how a church-centered outreach program compares to a prechurch holistic strategy is to describe two models currently in operation in Freetown, Sierra Leone. Both are sponsored by a mission organization that shares the values described in this chapter and has as its goal the planting and equipping of compassionate Christian churches that will multiply and minister effectively among the poor. I recently visited these programs and can testify to the quality of their operations.

The first is centered in the George Brook slum community of Freetown, where thousands of African migrants from the villages have congregated, hoping to find a better life in the city. They come from several tribal groups, though there is one that predominates. The missionary in this case is assisting two established churches, one Methodist and the other Pentecostal. All the planning and supervision are carried out through members of these two churches and with the full support of the pastors.

Because the missionary had two good cores of believers to begin with, he had a number of advantages. He could assume Christian values and motivation. He had the approval of the leadership of the two churches and the cooperation of their members. They were poor, but the Holy Spirit had given them a ray of hope that through God's power things could be different. Their prayers blended with the activities right from the start.

The missionary's chosen method is to employ and work closely with a Christian national who knows the area well and lives among the people, to identify specific needs within the community, and to organize groups of Christians that are motivated to attack their problems together. He has helped begin a number of short-term projects among both Christians and non-Christians, but reserves long-term projects for the Christian groups.

"Microenterprises" describes the end results of this method. The missionary helps local Christian groups start or expand small businesses which range from bread shops to market stalls to hand manufacturing of buckets.[6] Working as a development team, the missionary and his national colleague teach the groups management skills so that their businesses will succeed. Small loans (capital) are extended to the groups, which assume responsibility for monthly repayments once the small industries and businesses begin to pay off. The group puts pressure on any delinquent member, because it is the group that has accepted the loan and the responsibility for repayment, and the group receives no further help if their loan is not repaid. Group responsibility and pressure on delinquents make the loan system work. Group members help each other succeed, because they feel they are in the project together.

As a result of the project, several dozen families have emerged out of abject poverty to a level of reasonable self-sufficiency. Moreover, both pastors testify that church attendance has increased by 25 percent since the development projects started. The entire community, composed mostly of animists and nominal Muslims, has a new appreciation for the churches and sees that Christianity really makes a difference in life here and now. On the personal side, Christian mothers working in their market stalls testify with tears running down their cheeks that the help they've been given has transformed their existence, and they praise God for it.

The second model is found on the other end of Freetown, in a slum community that is growing rapidly as villagers pour into the city. In this case, the missionary is helping a young African evangelist who

---

6. For an informative discussion of the microenterprise concept, see Wayne Medendorp, "An Urban Strategy for Addressing Unemployment and Underemployment in the World's Urban Centers," mimeographed (Grand Rapids: Christian Reformed World Relief Committee, 1985).

wants to plant churches among the Muslims and traditional religionists who, in this new urban setting, are particularly open to the Christian message. There is a vacuum in the newcomers' lives that Christ or the devil is going to fill, and the time to reach them with the gospel is now.

The holistic approach to church planting is the same in this area, though the evangelist and the missionary limit the size and scope of the development projects until a solid core of Christians is established. So far they have started nine worship centers, each with ten to twenty-five adults attending regularly. Help is extended in the form of literacy classes, emergency medical assistance, basic health instruction, and a few microenterprise projects. The emphasis is on training local people to help themselves, with as little dependence on outside assistance as possible. By Western standards the amount of help that is given appears trivial, but to the slum dwellers it is impressive.

The testimony of one man in this community illustrates the impact of this word-deed program. I asked a fifty-five-year-old African, the first of his family to become a Christian, what it was that initially attracted him to Christianity. He replied that two things had struck him. First, he observed that the Christians who came visiting his home seemed willing to help anyone, even Muslims. "Muslims will help Muslims," he said, "but these Christians were willing to help anyone. They cared about us, and that raised my curiosity. I listened to what they were saying, and I asked questions. What made them do this, I wanted to know.

"The second thing that struck me," he continued, "was the answer they gave to my questions. They told me that God cared, and that he cared enough to send Jesus to save his people by dying for their sins. That made me think, and after a while I started to believe that Jesus died for my sins too. That's when I became a Christian, and now my four married children and their families are Christians too."

When evangelism, relief, and development are joined in that fashion everywhere, there will be hope for the cities and a bright new day of church growth.

Discussion Questions

1. In what ways is God using the urbanization process to produce breakthroughs for the gospel?
2. Identify and describe the basic Christian motive for ministry among the poor. How would you explain it to a non-Christian who questioned your motives?

3. Discuss the twin propositions presented in this chapter as guide-lines for relating evangelism to relief and development. Try express-ing the biblical balance between word and deed in some better way.
4. Describe the neighborhood surrounding a church you are acquainted with, and suggest ways in which the church can and should impact its neighborhood holistically.
5. If you were a missionary assigned to work in an urban slum where no church exists, what would you do?

The Ends of the Earth Have Come to Town

Roger S. Greenway

For almost a century, Christian congregations have sung fervently William H. Doane's great missionary hymn, "The Ends of All the Earth Shall Hear." The peoples and kindreds of the earth seemed far away one hundred years ago. The church's task was to send missionaries to find them and tell them the gospel. To a large extent, that task remains today, but something new has been added. People from all nations are coming to America. They crowd our cities. In short, the ends of the earth have come to town. And many of them know little or nothing about Christ and salvation.

This situation is now provoking a very significant change in the church's understanding of its global mission. As we see Muslims, Buddhists, Hindus, Jews, and adherents of other religions walking our city streets, we realize that the missionary task begins very close to home. It starts in our cities. Here is our Jerusalem—our Judea and Samaria. We cannot talk credibly about winning distant people to Christ if we neglect the unsaved and unchurched close by. In some cases, people who were unreachable in their homelands are now accessible in North American cities. God is doing an amazing thing. He is bringing all the kindreds of the earth to our doorstep that his name might be honored through their salvation and worship.

The shift to urban and ethnic missions is probably the most important development in denominational and interdenominational home-mission activity in the closing years of the twentieth century. It narrows the distance between home and foreign missions. It changes our ideas about preparation for home missionary service, the training of pastors, the importance of research, and the need for multiplying

Figure 2
The American Mosaic

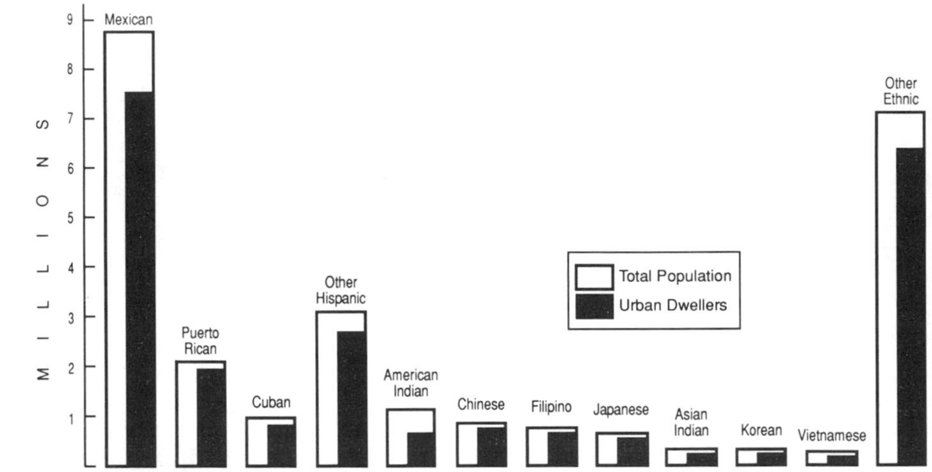

	Mexican	Puerto Rican	Cuban	Other Hispanic	American Indian	Chinese	Filipino	Japanese	Asian Indian	Korean	Vietnamese	Other Ethnic
Total population	8,740,439	2,013,945	803,226	3,051,063	1,364,033	806,040	774,652	700,974	361,531	354,953	261,729	7,041,401
Urban dwellers	7,659,104	1,954,524	785,323	2,734,977	719,047	781,798	716,128	643,081	334,683	329,746	249,674	6,353,550
Percentage of urban dwellers	87.6	97.0	97.8	89.6	52.7	97.0	92.4	91.7	92.6	93.0	95.4	90.2

Source: U.S. Census Bureau (1980)

churches. Because of the current migration of people, Christian missions will never be the same again. We have begun the exciting era of truly global witness.

The Ethnic Mosaic in North American Cities

In Philadelphia we have the saying, "Walk our streets and you tour the world." The same can be said of most North American urban centers. In the United States, daily newspapers are printed in more than forty-five different languages, a fact that says a lot about the nature and size of the ethnic mosaic. The mosaic is composed of at least two hundred different groups of foreign origin in addition to some Native American groups. The ethnic mosaic is not only big, it is growing. Much of the growth is due to continued immigration, 80 percent of which comes from Asia and Latin America (see fig. 2).

Los Angeles public schools daily try to educate children coming from homes where any one of eight-six different languages is spoken. Los Angeles is called the Vietnamese capital of America. It is also the second largest Hispanic city in the Western Hemisphere, surpassed only by Mexico City. Obviously, any Christian ministry that reaches Spanish-speaking people in Los Angeles or any other North American city will provide an important springboard for reaching Hispanics in other lands.

On the other side of the North American continent stands New York City, the great magnet which never stops drawing people from all over the globe. In a special issue of *Time* magazine (July 8, 1985), it was pointed out that New York City has 350,000 Dominicans, which is more than any city other than Santo Domingo. New York City has 225,000 Haitians, more Haitians than anywhere but Port-au-Prince. Of New York's 7,000,000 residents, over 2,000,000 are from overseas (30 percent), and immigrants from almost anywhere can find a community of their own kind in which to live in New York.

Finding people of one's own kind is an important factor that does much to explain the pattern of immigrant settlement in cities. The urban ethnic community offers almost everything immigrants are looking for: stores that sell familiar foods, landlords who speak their language, neighbors who can answer questions and help them find jobs, and religious and community centers much like those they left behind when they immigrated.

Moreover, large cities like New York and Los Angeles offer the immigrant a feeling of acceptance, of living in a place where being different is the norm. Where almost everyone is an alien, no one is an alien. These factors combine to produce the unique flavor of the large city and its power to attract a potpourri of different peoples.

Europe is experiencing much the same thing. Recently I spoke with an Anglican minister from Liverpool who said that in his parish twenty-two different languages are spoken. Thirty years ago, only one language was spoken in that part of the city, and the Anglican church had eleven congregations and eleven parish ministers there. Today, with twenty-two languages spoken in the area, there are only two Anglican clergymen left, and those two are struggling to hold together the few small congregations that remain. How much this says about the demographic changes taking place in cities and the broadening scope of the church's home-missions challenge!

Recently I spent some time in the country of my forefathers, the Netherlands. While there I was invited to preach in Spanish to a congregation composed of people from a dozen different Spanish-speaking countries. The largest number was from the Dominican Republic, a circumstance which struck me with special force because one of our daughters and her husband are foreign missionaries to the Dominican Republic. Yet there in Amsterdam I could preach the gospel to immigrant Dominicans who, along with their friends from other Latin countries, seemed particularly receptive to the biblical message. I had uncovered another new frontier of Christian missions.

When we trace the history of North American cities, we find that they have always drawn immigrants. Like the recent newcomers, most of the earlier immigrants were poor when they arrived. During the last half of the nineteenth and the early decades of the twentieth century, tens of thousands of immigrants came from Europe—Poles, Italians, Greeks, Germans, Jews, and a host of others. They settled in America's growing cities and found jobs as factory workers, craftsmen, and neighborhood merchants. Until the end of World War II, America's urban centers were dominated by white middle-class citizens of European origin. Today we commonly refer to them as the old ethnics.

The immigration picture has changed dramatically in the past few decades. The vast majority of today's foreign immigrants no longer come from Europe. Now the streets of major North American cities are filled with the sights, sounds, and smells of dozens of different cultures—Asian, African, Latin American, and Middle Eastern. Furthermore, cities have received thousands of internal immigrants, especially black Americans from the South. Large areas of today's cities are composed predominantly of blacks who migrated there before or shortly after World War II.

Immigration patterns are important to watch. If current trends continue, at some point in the next decade Hispanics will surpass blacks as the largest minority group in the United States. By the middle of the next century, the Asian population could be as large as the Hispanic. The Chinese are presently the largest Asian ethnic group in the United States, accounting for 22 percent of all Asian-Americans. Filipinos are expected to outnumber the Chinese soon.

Cities will probably remain the focal point of the ethnic mix in the foreseeable future. The suburbs, however, will increasingly feel the impact of foreign cultures. This means that America as a whole must come to terms with the new reality of a widely heterogeneous, multicultural society. Cultural pluralism will touch every segment of national life in the years ahead. No corner will remain unaffected.

English will remain the predominant language, but other languages and the cultures they represent will find their places alongside it. As the entire makeup of the nation is affected, our perception of ourselves as Americans will be altered. Each immigrant who arrives contributes something new to our national life and consciousness. Each person makes a difference, and as ethnic pluralism becomes the watchword of tomorrow, America as a whole will be different. Nowhere will this be more evident than in the cities.

The causes of these demographic changes are worth noting. In the eyes of much of the world, America represents freedom and opportunity. Those are the values that brought immigrants from Europe to

America years ago, and they remain the primary reasons why people from around the world want to come to this country.

But there are other reasons too. The political and revolutionary turmoil in which a number of countries are caught forces many people to leave their homelands in search of places of freedom and refuge. Conflict and war in Southeast Asia brought thousands of refugees to our country. Most of them settled in cities. Political and religious conflicts in the Middle East have brought thousands of immigrants. The same is true of Central America. From Mexico thousands of immigrants, documented and undocumented, keep pouring across the border, driven by the painful economic realities of their homeland. In view of the facts that Mexico has one of the fastest-growing populations in the world and that there is no way to fence off the two-thousand-mile border between our two countries, we have to expect the stream of immigrants from Mexico to continue for a long time.

The Sanctuary Movement

The sanctuary movement deserves attention at this point. There have been a rash of cities in North America that have declared themselves sanctuaries for illegal immigrants from El Salvador and Guatemala. The sanctuary movement appeared at first to be limited to such intellectual centers as Berkeley, Madison, and Cambridge. But then New York, Los Angeles, and San Francisco joined the group. There are now more than a dozen cities of refuge offering protection to aliens victimized by oppression. Cities differ in the wording of their resolutions, and some offer less than others. The Los Angeles sanctuary resolution is so open-ended that presumably it embraces every group from Filipinos to Haitians and Colombians.

The motives behind the sanctuary movement vary according to the individuals and politicians involved. For many it offers an opportunity to condemn the foreign policies of the federal government, particularly in regard to Central America. For others the foremost reasons are humanitarian. Many of the aliens who come here are victims of terrorism and oppression. If they were deported to their homelands, they would probably be killed.

City officials have additional reasons to support the sanctuary movement, as they see the welfare of the aliens and their municipalities intertwined. A city suffers if aliens, for fear of being apprehended and deported, fail to report crimes, consumer fraud, housing or health-code violations, and safety hazards in the workplace. It is to the disadvantage of all urban dwellers when some residents go uneducated, unprotected from crime and exploitation, or untreated for illness. Officials know they are largely helpless to stop the incoming flow of aliens, but by declaring their cities sanctuaries they hope to avoid, at least temporarily, the worst features of the dilemma.

Churches are frequently involved in the sanctuary movement. Their properties are used to harbor illegal aliens seeking refuge. Breaking the law of the land and defying the federal Immigration and Naturalization Service are serious matters which no Christian wants to become involved in unnecessarily or without the most serious thought. As with protests against legalized abortion, Christians may differ as to their reasons for and their methods of protest against such an evil. But certainly the refugee situation and the victimization of thousands of innocent men, women, and children by dictators on the one hand and terrorists on the other are serious issues that no Christian should avoid addressing. Because refugees invariably end up in cities, they present a problem that urban churches especially face. Given the social, political, and economic upheavals likely to occur throughout the world in the next decades, we can expect to face the questions over and over again.

The Challenge to Missionary Strategy

The demographic changes taking place in Western countries present to churches, denominations, and all branches of Christian ministry a challenge which can hardly be underestimated. To a large extent, the future shape of Western civilization will be determined by the response Christians make and the missionary strategies we adopt.

In his book *Understanding Tomorrow*, Lyle Schaller points out that to a substantial degree the religious bodies that will grow during the next dozen years will probably be those that affirm the legitimacy of ethnic churches, that encourage multilingual approaches to preaching the gospel, that are able to affirm a variety of lifestyles, and that are not locked into ordination procedures that effectively exclude ethnics from the highest levels of church leadership. Growing churches will be those that accept ethnic congregations, allow them space to develop their own styles of worship, leadership, and activity, and make the fullest possible use of the laity in the ongoing life of the denomination.[1]

Schaller's observations, if they prove correct (and I think they will), have wide-ranging implications. Churches that keep going in a traditional direction, either ignoring the new elements in society or refusing

1. Lyle E. Schaller, *Understanding Tomorrow* (Nashville: Abingdon, 1974), p. 75.

to allow them the free exercise of their gifts, will fail in large areas of their mission. They will miss the benefits newcomers bring, and as churches and denominations they will not grow.

The increasing number of ethnics in America, particularly in its cities, represents a major challenge to the nation as a whole and to the leadership of the Christian community. For college students and seminarians, it is an important subject to be considering now. A wide array of issues and questions immediately spring from this new reality:

Will Christians meet the newcomers with open arms, or will they view the immigrants as foreign invaders and relocate their homes and churches in distant suburbs, as was the pattern when American blacks moved to the cities?

Public schools in major cities are crying for bilingual teachers, tutors, and administrators. Ethnic neighborhoods require workers who can communicate with the residents. Are the schools, colleges, and seminaries that train Christian leaders willing to require that students learn to speak a second language as part of their training for ministry in a pluralistic society?

How will churches respond to the evangelistic opportunities among the new immigrants from Africa, Asia, Latin America, and the Middle East? Will churches rise to the challenge of developing a multicultural denominational life?

Fundamentally, can we Christians accept the new reality as coming from God, who is moving dramatically across our nation and the world, bringing people from faraway places to our doorstep? Do we see what this can mean for world evangelization? The mission frontier begins at our doors! Do we recognize it?

Discovering Who Lives in the City

Like most large cities, Philadelphia contains a wide variety of ethnic groups drawn from every corner of the globe. Some groups have strong evangelical churches, but others have hardly been touched by the gospel.

A few years ago, Harvie Conn and I initiated a research project in connection with the urban-mission courses we were teaching. The purpose of the project was to uncover valid and useful information about the ethnic groups of Philadelphia. In the process of gathering the data, we would be training our students in the basic techniques of urban demographic research and showing them how such research can help them to develop strategies for Christian ministry. We later shared the fruits of the research with churches and mission agencies located in the Philadelphia area with a view to their making use of the data in their outreach programs.

In the beginning we looked upon the project as being helpful at least for training urban workers and potentially valuable for informing local churches and mission groups. But when news about what we were doing became known, we received numerous requests to share the research form we had devised and the practical lessons we were learning through the project. (The survey form we used can be found at the close of this chapter.) Inquiries from as far away as Taiwan, the Philippines, and the Ivory Coast convinced us that urban workers need help in the area of mission-oriented research.

Working usually in teams, our students compiled reliable surveys on more than two dozen ethnic groups in Philadelphia. Some of their reports are thirty to forty pages in length. Because the research was done with a broad missionary focus, the information gathered goes beyond what is available from census reports and government offices. Here are some brief statements from a few of the reports:

> *Vietnamese:* There are 6,000 or more in Philadelphia, mostly located in West Philadelphia and the Italian Market area of South Philadelphia. There is only one Vietnamese Protestant congregation, with an average attendance of about 50 people.
>
> *Chinese:* There are 10,000 in the area, including 6,000 Cantonese-speaking and 4,000 Mandarin-speaking. Mandarin speakers are located mainly in the Valley Forge area. An estimated 5 to 8 percent of the Chinese are Christians, with higher figures among students (perhaps as high as 25 percent). There are two Chinese evangelical churches ministering among the 10,000.
>
> *Laotians:* There are over 2,000 in the Philadelphia area, located mainly in two districts—46th Street and Walnut, and Chestnut Street in South Philadelphia. Some diaconal ministries are conducted among Laotians by a few small groups, but no Laotian church is being planned. They appear to be open to the gospel.
>
> *Russian Jews:* There are 240,000 Jews in Philadelphia, and a high percentage of them come from Eastern Europe. There is a heavy concentration of Russian Jews in the northeast section of the city, and there are increasing signs of openness to the gospel.
>
> *Thais:* There are 500 Thais in Philadelphia and its suburbs, but no location patterns are discernible. Buddhism is their professed religion, but it appears to be weakly practiced. Nobody is working with the Thais in their language with a view to church planting.

This is merely a sampling. The reports are rich in sociological and religious insights which any church or mission group can use to begin a ministry among a particular ethnic group. The important thing about research of this kind is its eventual use for the furtherance of the gospel.

Research is never an end in itself, nor should reports be written and then left on the shelf. Demographic research is hard work, but it is well worth the effort when it facilitates effective Christian mercy. Every mission agency should invest time and energy in research, and the schools that train missionaries should provide instruction and hands-on experience in research procedures. Research can remove much of the mystery and frustration so often associated with urban ministry.

Mission agencies should also consider training their overseas candidates by sending them first to North American cities with immigrant populations from the countries where they hope to work. There they can begin their cultural introduction to the people and establish valuable relationships. I know of a missionary candidate expecting to go to Haiti who came to Philadelphia for additional seminary education. He has developed a part-time ministry in a Haitian church among the five thousand Haitians living in the city. By so doing, he has begun to master the language, learned much about the Haitian culture, become identified with an evangelistic Haitian church, and gained the respect of its leaders for his sincerity and hard work. By the time he leaves for Haiti, he will have established a whole network of relationships which will stand him in good stead when he begins work in the Caribbean.

A Sample Ethnic Survey

The purpose of an ethnic survey in a particular city is to build a complete and accurate data bank with a view to evangelization, church planting, and Christian ministry. The data collected are made available to churches and mission organizations desiring to reach unevangelized ethnic groups.

Identification of the group

Population total of the group in this city

Population total in the USA, in Canada

Population in the country of origin

Other countries where they are found

Other places where they are found in North America

Language(s) used

Literacy rate

Circumstances of immigration to North America

Religion(s)

Agencies in this city working with them and services offered
(precise names and addresses)
Governmental agencies
Other secular agencies
Religious agencies

Basic needs which can be identified
Physical
Psychological
Educational
Occupational
Other

Evaluation of the degree to which the needs are being met

Christian presence and ministry in the group
Percentage that is Christian
Churches, denominations, agencies at work (names and addresses)
Pastors serving the group (names and addresses)

Evaluation of the strength of the Christian community
Evangelism
Individuals and organizations carrying on the work
Methods being used
Evaluation of the group's receptivity
Growth rate of the churches (if any)
Evaluation of the group's potential for evangelization
Availability of Bibles and Christian literature in the language

Cults that are at work among group members

Organized expressions of non-Christian religions

Places of non-Christian worship in the city (addresses and information concerning the size and condition of the worship centers)

Non-Christian religious leaders working with the group (names and
addresses)

Major festivals, ceremonies, and customs related to the culture or
religion

Evaluation of the apparent strength of the religious commitment

Evaluation of the changes taking place as a result of immigration
and other factors

To conduct this survey a minimum of ten interviews is required, as is personal observation of at least one cultural or religious event of the group being studied. The survey should conclude with the names and addresses of the persons interviewed as well as the time and place of each interview. The interviews are to include representatives of three agencies—one governmental, one secular (other than governmental), and one religious—and seven private parties, at least five of whom are members of the ethnic group. Casual conversations during the cultural or religious event(s) attended should also be mentioned.

Discussion Questions

1. What's new and different about the recent immigrants to North America? Hasn't America always been a haven for immigrants and refugees?
2. How do people you know feel about immigrants moving into their neighborhoods and attending their churches? What has your church done for the newcomers, particularly those of another race?
3. What are the differences and similarities between ministry to Haitians in Haiti and ministry among Haitians in Philadelphia? What does this say about the traditional distinction between home and foreign missions?

Barriers to Reaching Urban Ethnics

Roger S. Greenway

I have never met a Christian who argued against the evangelization of the new ethnic populations in American cities. Anyone with a basic knowledge of Scripture realizes that God wants all peoples to know his Word and believe in his Son. Undeniably, that requires the evangelization of an ethnic population that is unsaved and unchurched.

Likewise, the importance of directing the human and financial resources of Christian missions toward the cities appears obvious. We would expect, therefore, to see Christians spearheading efforts to recruit and train missionaries for the new urban ethnics. We would expect established churches to reach out and welcome ethnics who already have an interest in the Christian faith and prefer to affiliate with a church within the majority culture. Certainly we would expect to see many new church-planting initiatives among the unreached and under-evangelized, as well as serious attempts to encourage the growth and development of ethnic congregations that already exist.

Some of these things are happening, and we are grateful for that. The Southern Baptists, for example, have launched a major effort to plant and multiply ethnic churches in cities all across America. They encourage existing churches to sponsor new ethnic congregations, and they are developing educational and evangelistic materials in a number of languages other than English for ethnic mission work. The Southern Baptists are investing heavily in urban and ethnic research in order to pinpoint specific ethnic groups for ministry. They call their program "Laser Thrust" because, like a laser beam, it scans a broad area and then focuses on a specific group selected for closer attention.

Across the board, however, the needs and the opportunities among urban ethnic populations far exceed the degree of interest being shown. Almost everyone agrees that ethnic evangelism on a large scale is needed urgently. But powerful forces still militate against it. In this chapter we will take a careful look at factors which divert Christians' attention away from city populations and ethnic evangelism.

Ambivalence toward Immigrants

It seems that Americans in general alternate between attitudes of hospitality and paranoia in regard to new immigrants, particularly immigrants of different racial and ethnic groups. On the one hand, we have the Statue of Liberty as a favorite national monument, with its kindly words to the foreign masses yearning to breathe free. On the other hand, we fear what the newcomers may bring and the changes they may produce in the American way of life.

These attitudes are not restricted to the white community. Many American blacks resent the newcomers just as much. They see them as unfair economic competition and a threat to their own social welfare. Because ethnic newcomers generally settle in poor urban neighborhoods, hostility and even violence between the established residents and the immigrants are common. The attention and benefits extended by government agencies to immigrant refugees are viewed very negatively by native Americans who are trying desperately to pull themselves out of poverty.

Christians find themselves with the same kind of ambivalence. We hold the basic conviction that all are equal before God and thus we owe it to our neighbors to be open and hospitable. Yet we are also torn by the common fears about jobs, competition, and the unseen effects newcomers may have on our lives. We know we should love them, but we'd rather do so from a distance.

As for the churches, we subtly prefer to keep them homogeneous, that is, composed of people like ourselves. We may disguise our feelings, but newcomers catch on. People know when they are wanted and trusted. They sense too if church leadership will ever be opened to members of their group. Among all the barriers to reaching urban ethnics, the matter of attitudes is the most formidable.

The Negative Image of the City

When it comes to fostering the growth and influence of Christian churches, cities have a poor reputation. Historically, Protestantism has not fared well in American cities. This goes hand in hand with its dismal record for assimilating the waves of new immigrants settling in urban areas. Studying the history of old churches in places like New York and Philadelphia, one discovers that, from the mid-nineteenth century on, countless church buildings were abandoned when the members moved away from the foreign immigrants pouring into the old neighborhoods. The pattern of churches running away from new ethnics has, unfortunately, a long and painful history in America.

Connected with this is the fact that neither Protestant nor Catholic churches have been able to make many profound and lasting changes in the moral climate of American cities. It is true, of course, that cities benefited enormously from certain great ministries in the past. This fact must not be forgotten nor minimized. But even the most devoted city-lover must admit that Christianity has not done especially well in the great urban centers in terms of making a lasting moral and religious impact on the society, its politics, schools, and economy. In part, the churches themselves are responsible for this, and hard questions need to be asked about a religion that sounds great inside church buildings but has little transforming impact in the markets and the streets. But there are other factors too, forces that the churches can do little about. The net result has been the city's negative image. Cities are seen as too big and bad to be redeemed.

Americans hate failure and adore success. We tend to set goals for our lives and ministries that aren't easy to achieve in cities. This may explain why so many of the more gifted ministers and ambitious workers look elsewhere for their challenges. Our view of cities needs to be changed before this barrier disappears. At the same time our definitions of success, discipleship, and fruitful ministry need serious overhauling.

Fear of the Social Gospel

The multiple social problems associated with cities have bewildered, angered, and isolated conservative American Protestants from urban life for over a century. In the minds of many church leaders, anyone who gets involved in urban ministries and starts clamoring about urban issues is dangerously close to falling into the worst of errors, the so-called social gospel.

To deal with this charge and the formidable barrier to urban missions that it represents, we must look back in American history. Around the turn of the century, the social gospel arose as urban Protestantism's response to social problems in the cities. Many of those problems had their roots in the great influx of foreign immigrants and the conditions they encountered and exacerbated. The theology on which the social gospel rested was, from an evangelical viewpoint, liberal and weak. But the movement itself had features that have value and relevance even today. In the context of horrendous urban problems, human suffering, and exploited people, the social gospel was a genuine attempt to deal with the problems, heal wounds, and denounce the perpetrators of wrong against other human beings.

Because Protestant churches grew and multiplied fastest on the frontier, North American Protestantism has traditionally borne a rural stamp. In the nonurban setting, the problems and issues were different from those in the cities. As a result, Protestant churches developed an outlook on moral and social questions that was shaped largely by their rural experience. They were totally unprepared to deal with the issues raised by the continuous waves of immigrants flooding the cities.

Rural Protestants looked at the theology associated with the social gospel and wisely rejected it. They saw that it had cut itself off from solid biblical and doctrinal foundations, and that it was moving its followers to serve humanitarian causes that lacked a biblical message or the redemptive power to make a lasting difference in their beneficiaries.

But along with their rejection of the social gospel, American Protestants by and large turned their backs on the burning social problems of the cities. They closed their eyes to nearly everything the proponents of the social gospel had been saying about poverty, suffering, dreadful housing conditions, and exploitation of workers. Instead of taking up the urban challenges and dealing with them biblically and courageously, American Protestants opted for a theological platform that left the big social issues until the millennium. Urban evangelism was reduced to rescue missions, benevolence, and the periodic city-wide crusade.

Lost in this process was the key premise which the social gospel had defended and with which all Christians ought to agree: people in society stand under the judgment of God and his Word, and the standards of Christ's kingdom are applicable here and now to all areas of life, to society and its structures as much as to individuals. Had that premise retained a prominent place on the evangelical agenda, the history of American Protestantism and the development of our cities might have been very different. But because it was lost, there emerged an urban secularism which sees no place for religion in public and economic life, and deals with major social issues without reference to Christian values.

White Flight to the Suburbs

Through the years American white churches have responded to the influx of immigrants in various ways, but the most common response has been flight. Churches consistently relocated when new people moved into the neighborhood. Since World War II, the flight of white churches to the suburbs has been motivated largely by the perceived encroachment of immigrants from the American South and from overseas. Insofar as suburbia arose as a reaction to the city and its people, suburbia is an attitude, a mind-set, as much as it is a geographical entity. This fact has not escaped the attention of urban dwellers. They generally have strong feelings about the white Christians who fled when people of color moved into their neighborhoods.

The American church historian Martin E. Marty has commented that by 1963 the white flight from the city was in full swing. Between 1963 and 1983, the membership of white churches in the city plummeted. Great old churches were closed as members drifted away. Suburban churches benefited from the shift, of course, and many new suburban churches were started. But significant numbers of members were lost in the shuffle. Roman Catholic churches generally held on in the cities, though with severe losses in membership.[1]

As a result of white flight, the religious map of most cities has changed dramatically. The largest and strongest city churches today are black. At the same time, cities are dotted with small, struggling white congregations surrounded by new neighbors with whom they don't communicate.

Consequently, white Protestants find themselves in a very disadvantageous position for ministering to cities. White Protestantism's base is outside the city, in suburbia and small towns. Consciously or unconsciously, white Protestants know that cities are not their turf. If they want to enter the main arenas, where the fiercest battles for minds and hearts are being fought, they will have to work very hard to regain lost ground and establish their credibility in the city.

"Pith Helmet" Stereotype of Missions

Another obstacle to urban evangelism concerns the image church people generally have of missionaries. They think of them as very special individuals who travel long distances to reach exotic people

---

1. Martin E. Marty, "Devastating Decline in White Peoples' City Churches Continues," *Context* 17.2 (Jan. 15, 1985): 5.

living in thatched-roofed villages, suffering from malaria, and paddling canoes. As often as not, they don't wear many clothes, and the women carry baskets on their heads. The courageous souls who work among such people are the real missionaries, the ones worth supporting because obviously they are fulfilling the Great Commission.

The tight hold which this old image of missions has on American Christians can be seen in the photographs published by mission agencies to advertise their work. Invariably they emphasize rural efforts. Secular journalists have a similar perception. A fairly recent cover of *Time* magazine (Dec. 27, 1982) carried a picture entitled "The New Missionary." The picture showed a tall, white, North American missionary, open Bible in hand, surrounded by short, dark-complexioned New Guineans. Inside were a lead article on modern missions and many photographs of thatched-roofed huts, native villagers, remote places. The artist who prepared the cover astutely conveyed the prevailing attitude in American missions. But I suggest that the title was mistaken. In view of contemporary movements and the monumental growth of cities globally, what *Time* depicted was not the "new missionary," but the *old* missionary, representing yesterday's mission situation more than today's or tomorrow's.

Why are church members more willing to support missions to faraway places than missions to the unreached people-laden cities of their own country? Why this absorption with scattered islands while unevangelized and unchurched people are packed together in great numbers in cities throughout the world? What mysterious barrier prevents us from seeing unreached people here at home? They aren't hard to find if we have our eyes open. In the Logan section of Philadelphia where my wife and I once lived, there are thirty-two different ethnic groups. And Logan is just one of two dozen sections of the city! We could not travel three blocks from our home without passing at least one Muslim, Buddhist, or Hindu. City neighborhoods like this are microcosms of the whole world.

In the cities, unreached people are pressed together in towering apartments, huddled in slums, playing games in crowded schoolyards, and carrying briefcases to work on buses and subways. Some are rich, others are poor. Some live on welfare, and others earn high incomes. Many of them come from foreign countries and speak languages other than English at home. Without Christ, the urbanite is just as lost and in need of evangelization as are people living in thatched huts beneath swaying palm trees! Let's take our blinders off and see through this barrier.

Cultural Inflexibility

The next obstacle is more difficult to describe. It has to do with the unwillingness of established American churches to deal openly and flexibly in intercultural matters. Overseas missionaries have faced intercultural differences for years. They have had to learn to adjust to other cultures and not to expect things to go exactly as they do in the States. In doing this, overseas missionaries have had the advantage of working at a distance from the supporting churches back home, where openness to intercultural adaptations might not be understood or approved. Missions to unreached ethnics here in North America, however, confront the mother churches with intercultural issues. Many of them are not ready for this, and that is why cultural inflexibility is a serious barrier to the free flow of the gospel and the development of ethnic churches.

Is it unrealistic to expect traditional, conservative churches to stretch their rules to include, or at least approve, new patterns of worship, discipline, pastoral leadership, and training in order to promote the spread of the gospel among ethnics in our cities? This is one of the greatest challenges facing any church or denomination desiring to work effectively in ethnic evangelism. The danger of cultural imperialism in missions is very real. It appears in the form of imposing on new believers and smaller groups the majority group's way, or the mother church's traditional expression of the Christian faith and life. It inevitably paralyzes the gospel's growth.

Since most American Christians have only the foggiest notions about intercultural communication and adjustment, people who give leadership in ethnic missions must also work harder to educate traditional Christians as to what is going on and why. Rank-and-file church members need to be informed about intercultural differences and some of the splendid things the Holy Spirit has taught other branches of Christ's body. They must learn what it means to respect all parts of the Christian family and allow each part the freedom to develop its own unique expression of the faith. When this occurs, intercultural differences will no longer loom as barriers, but will be regarded as further opportunities to grow in our love and mutual understanding.

An Inadequate Theology of the City

The final barrier has to do with our failure to develop a theology that deals effectively with a multitude of cultures and the social dynamics of great cities. Until there are enough people who have prepared themselves for urban mission by gaining a firm hold on an adequate theology for the city and a biblical understanding of ethnicity, evangelistic efforts among urban ethnics will continue to be weak and faltering. Most of America's evangelical schools are located in suburbs and small towns. Many have intentionally relocated their campuses away from ethnic neighborhoods and urban congestion. Is it any wonder, then, that the Bible is read and theology is discussed in ways that filter out the city with its pressing social issues, poverty, suffering, and maze of people? Does it surprise us that we find it difficult to address the city's problems from well-developed theological perspectives?

Bible scholars and theologians must return to the city. Evangelical schools need extension campuses there with urban-mission study programs. Reaching cities for Christ takes training and special people. Until those who are our leaders, our thinkers, and our interpreters take the cities seriously, there will continue to be theological and professional barriers hindering our mission.

Discussion Questions

1. Do you see evangelicals becoming more (or less) concerned about the poor and about ministry among them? What are the reasons for the change?
2. What does your church do to motivate its members to become actively involved in intercultural ministry? Is the church itself becoming more racially and culturally diverse?
3. What do you think God has in mind in bringing Muslims, Buddhists, Hindus, and Jews to this country? If it is to expose them to the gospel, what should we be doing about it?
4. Describe two or three basic biblical truths which have bearing on intercultural mission.

Goals of Urban Ethnic Evangelism

Roger S. Greenway

Having surveyed the field and examined the barriers to ethnic evangelism, we now set about to define its goals. The ultimate goal is the advancement of Christ's kingdom among all peoples in the city. The planting and building of the church is always "unto the kingdom," that is, for the purpose of extending the reign of Jesus Christ in truth and righteousness in the hearts and lives of people. Only then can we expect to see city streets cleansed in relative measure from violence, injustice, poverty, and greed. While looking for "the city that is to come" (Heb. 13:14), God's servants are to pursue their urban pilgrimage as ambassadors of King Jesus in the cities of humankind. The task is never easy because Satan, the great opposer, relinquishes nothing without a struggle. Conflicts, disappointments, and setbacks are to be expected. But the relentless pursuit must continue until "the city of the living God" (Heb. 12:22) appears from heaven.

Goal 1. The Evangelization of All Urban Ethnics

The objective of evangelizing *all* ethnic peoples within our cities calls for the concerted efforts of city churches, urban-suburban church coalitions, mission agencies, intercultural workers, and service organizations. All are needed in one way or another. Alongside them there must be schools, colleges, and seminaries, enlarging their perspectives to include training for, and the education of, urban church leadership. The goal of this coordinated effort is the winning and discipling of urban ethnics, building churches within each linguistic, cultural, and ethnic community, helping young Christians mature in the faith, and raising the masses out of poverty, isolation, and marginal positions to active Christian roles in society and increased contribution to the welfare of the city.

Christ commanded the church to make disciples of *panta ta ethnē*, all the peoples. Not to Anglo-Americanize them or make them behave like white middle-class Protestants, but rather to disciple them within their cultures, transformationally, until all areas of their lives have been leavened by the gospel. That is a big order, and it will take all the resources the church can muster.

The first step toward implementing this goal is prayer. Nothing good will happen without it. Prayer must be mobilized throughout the Christian community, prayer that all the ethnic peoples whom God is bringing to America will hear the gospel in their own languages and cultures and bow before the Lord. Let thousands of pulpits sound this petition, and it will echo in prayers in the homes. Then watch what happens.

Second, specialized materials must be prepared to facilitate the evangelization of urban ethnics. For example, the Home Missions Board of my own denomination, the Christian Reformed Church, has developed a Materials Resource Department for Asian Literature. Materials such as Bibles, books, tracts, Bible-study suggestions and study plans, hymnbooks, and cassette tapes are available in the Cambodian, Hmong, Lao, and Vietnamese languages. Also available are a *Guide to Refugees' Culture and Religious Background*, a booklet called "How to Reach Them," and a glossary for interpreters.[1] Other boards and agencies are preparing similar resources, and their availability should be publicized.

Goal 2. The Compilation of an Information Bank

The compilation of a complete and up-to-date information bank on all existing and emerging ethnic groups in every city and the agencies working among them is essential. This calls for city-by-city research, cooperation and sharing of information between churches and agencies, and the networking of Christian ministries. No church or agency can do it all, nor should any attempt to do it alone. Cities require something better than lone-wolf operations.

My old neighborhood in Philadelphia will illustrate what I have in

---

1. To obtain a list of available materials write to Home Missions, 2850 Kalamazoo Ave. S.E., Grand Rapids, MI 49560.

mind. The Logan section is multiethnic, roughly 70 percent black, 20 percent Asian (mainly Korean, Vietnamese, Indian, and Chinese), and 10 percent elderly white. It once had a largely Jewish and Ukrainian population, but all except the oldest of these have left. The largest institution in the community is the Albert Einstein Medical Center, a Jewish teaching hospital which covers several square blocks. Einstein is staffed to service patients in twenty-eight languages, reflecting the multiethnic character of the city. This speaks well for the hospital and its administrators. They intend to serve patients effectively, which requires that communication barriers be overcome. If patients cannot explain their symptoms to the medical staff, and in turn cannot understand what is said to them, good medicine cannot be practiced. Therefore, the hospital found out which languages are used among their potential clientele, staffed accordingly, and let the community know it is prepared to serve them.

Unfortunately, Christians engaged in church work in the Philadelphia area have not yet learned this lesson. Einstein works in twenty-eight languages, but at least one-third of the languages used in Philadelphia are neglected by the churches and their missionary outreach. In fact, Christian workers currently lack as basic a tool as a directory containing information on all the ethnic groups in the city and ongoing ministries among them.

Recently in Philadelphia a tragic episode occurred involving the Hmong people, refugees from Laos. The Hmong were primitive farmers in their home country, yet they were resettled in the inner city, in Southwest Philadelphia and Logan, which are mainly black neighborhoods. The Hmong are Buddhist and largely illiterate. Hard work is their principal asset, yet in Philadelphia they were threatened and bullied by neighborhood residents who resented their presence. Ultimately most of the Hmong felt compelled to leave the city. Philadelphia's Hmong population was reduced from thirty-five hundred to six hundred overnight when violence broke out against them and they migrated en masse to Minnesota. At the height of the crisis, churches tried to step in, but they were ill prepared to minister to the Hmong in their language and culture. They had hardly been noticed until the trouble began. As is often the case in the city, the Catholic church was the most directly involved; priests and nuns consistently showed up at the neighborhood meetings held to discuss the Hmong issue. This episode made abundantly clear the need for a data bank, professional in quality and kept up-to-date, from which all religious agencies can obtain information and assistance in planning ministry strategies.

Goal 3. The Development of Specific Strategies

We must also develop strategies to reach specific ethnic communities and multiply churches among them. We noted earlier that prayer is an essential part of a Christian strategy for the city. We should remind ourselves here that every step in urban mission has to be bathed in earnest prayer.

One thing we must realize is that the shotgun approach to mission work in the city generally misses ethnics and special language groups. Cities, as we have seen, are not single homogeneous units but conglomerates of different groups and subgroups, many of which require a specially designed missionary strategy. The unreached in the cities must be identified, studied, and described before effective mission strategies can be developed to evangelize them. Many people have remained untouched by Christianity for years simply because they were insulated by language and cultural barriers, and nobody took notice of them.

The first step in reaching a hitherto unreached ethnic group is to find out what is already being done by churches and mission agencies. Here and there someone may be doing something. In Philadelphia, for example, a small inner-city Lutheran church began holding English classes for Hmong people at least a year before the trouble started. Despite language barriers, they had built up a degree of rapport with the Hmong community on which something more substantial might have been built. Another avenue is to find out what churches in other cities are doing and to network with them. They might have a worker to spare who knows the language and culture. Contacts should also be made with former missionaries and foreign-mission agencies that have had experience working with the particular ethnic group overseas. In other words, we must do our homework. We must read all we can about the ethnic group we're interested in, and contact people who can be of help.

The second step is to lay plans that include three distinct yet closely related thrusts:

1. *Assistance* to existing churches of the targeted ethnic group by offering encouragement and sharing resources even though the churches may be of a different denomination or theological tradition. At this point one's allegiance to the kingdom of Jesus Christ, which is above and beyond denominational loyalty, comes into focus. In the city we must have the broader vision.
2. *Outreach evangelism* through existing neighborhood churches—whatever their racial or ethnic makeup—to the non-Christians of

the ethnic group targeted. We must never overlook the strong churches that already exist in the cities, particularly in the black, Asian, and Hispanic communities. They must be incorporated into the strategy and their leadership acknowledged, for they are at home in the city and they can teach us a great deal. There are some ethnic and minority people, especially those emerging from their strong ethnic identity, who may desire to join churches with a heterogeneous makeup. They are ready for assimilation and may prefer to affiliate with an English-speaking congregation instead of forming one of their own.

3. *Recruitment and training* of intercultural evangelists and church planters. In many cases, language acquisition is as much a requirement for urban ethnic ministry as it is for work overseas. Nobody should think that he or she can make the transition from a typical Protestant congregation to ministry among urban ethnics without extensive retraining and orientation.

In this connection, we would do well to make contact with leaders from overseas churches. Their experience and expertise can inform our efforts to evangelize people from their race, language, and culture who are now living in North America. In a similar way, we would also benefit from the wisdom of former overseas missionaries, who know the language and culture of a particular people in their native setting. The knowledge they have acquired can be a tremendous asset in the new era of missions, where the sharp distinction between home and foreign missions is bound to be erased.

Goal 4. The Establishment of Relief and Development Ministries

We must set up relief and development ministries that are clearly Christian, convey the gospel in word and deed, and are appropriate to the needs and cultures of ethnic people. The kingdom of Jesus Christ is to be advanced in the urban ethnic community through actions that are identifiably Christian in content and style and that bring overall health and healing to people in need.

Obviously, agencies besides the church are involved here; it would be poor stewardship for the Christian community to duplicate services that are already rendered in a satisfactory way. Rather than assuming the roles of government and community organizations, Christians should do all they can to promote the effective operation of these organizations and confront them when they fail. When needed services are not delivered or are rendered in a way inconsistent with Christian convictions and the recipients' needs, appropriate action to relieve suffering and assist ethnic people in their own development certainly is in order.

In such cases, the "let the government do it" syndrome must be broken. Otherwise, human needs will remain unmet, and the term *compassion* will lose credibility. It is, of course, an essential part of urban mission to seek to influence public policy for the welfare of minority groups. Much more of this needs to be done. But we must also realize that there are built-in limitations to the standards and the effectiveness of public services; many areas cry out for direct Christian action. When supplementary or alternative programs of a long- or short-range nature are needed, urban and nonurban Christians should stand together in their support of appropriate ministries.

It would be tempting at this point to digress and discuss the need for the urbanization of relief and development ministries in overseas countries. In many places, the worst suffering is not in rural areas but in the cities, where cash is king and newcomers lack the skills to earn a living wage. The poverty and suffering in the slums of cities like Bombay, Lima, and Mexico City are indescribable, and compassion ministries of many kinds are sorely needed. But in this chapter we are dealing primarily with urban ethnics in North American cities, and I will limit myself to that concern.

Refugees in general place high value on the education of their children. And it is precisely there that they run into serious difficulties in the city. City schools are notoriously poor, and ethnic children come with the added disadvantage of hearing and speaking a foreign language in the home. Their parents may encourage them to study, and in fact often push them hard to do well in school. But because of language and educational differences, the parents cannot assist the children with their studies nor help them overcome the handicaps they experience in the classroom.

Nonurban people often do not understand the difficulties confronted in city schools. Some schools are excellent, to be sure. But many are poor, inadequately equipped, and inefficient. Some grades have only a single set of textbooks for five or more classes of students, and many of the textbooks are outdated.[2] Since the inability to read and write goes hand in hand with poverty, unemployment, and crime, any proposed solution to these problems must take into account the educational system.

Illiteracy is a recognized problem in American cities. Though it is

2. *Philadelphia Inquirer*, October 29, 1984.

not easily solved, some things can be done to alleviate it. Part of the problem is due to the fact that a language other than English may be spoken in the pupil's home. The best solution involves tutoring, private classes, and a great amount of compassionate one-on-one instruction. Could anything be more made-to-order for churches and Christian organizations? A language tutor builds trusting relationships with pupils and their families and demonstrates love. Through tutoring, the love of God can readily be shown and spoken. Tutoring meets a need felt by parents, builds relationships with ethnic people, and facilitates evangelism. It also opens the door to progress, escape from poverty, and eventual service to the community.

A good illustration of a church-based urban educational program is found in the Spirit and Truth Fellowship in Chicago's Humboldt Park neighborhood. Humboldt Park is a predominantly Hispanic community. The percentage of Hispanic young people who graduate from high school is notoriously low, and far fewer go on to college. Motivated by these facts and the desire to help Hispanic youth break out of the poverty-and-dependency syndrome, the Spirit and Truth congregation offers personalized tutoring to individual students, an alternative Christian school for elementary pupils, and a college-preparatory program for Hispanic high-schoolers. By addressing spiritual, social, and educational needs in an integrated fashion, the church is changing the lives of its youth and impacting the community at large. The program is clearly contextualized to meet the Hispanics' needs and at the same time uses the services of church members from the Anglo community.[3]

In the Philadelphia area, a question facing some Christian-school administrators is whether or not to enrol Muslim children. Muslim parents, many of them refugees from the Middle East, value quality education for their children; they know the children's future in America depends on it. Disgusted by the low quality of the education offered by the neighborhood schools, and fearful of the violence their children frequently meet there, they are willing to pay the high tuition charged by Christian schools and run the risk of exposing their children to Christian influences. Administrators of the Christian schools have told me that almost all the Muslim children have problems with English because Arabic is spoken in their homes. In response to this, one Presbyterian church in the area has launched a tutoring program for Muslim children and thus opened up scores of homes to Christian witness.

---

3. The Spirit and Truth congregation (1847 N. Humboldt Blvd., Chicago, IL 60647) is affiliated with the Christian Reformed Church in North America. Its creative approach to contextualized Christian education for the inner city is the product of the leadership of the former pastor, Manuel Ortiz, and his staff.

What this clearly indicates is that tutoring and, in some cases, alternative Christian schools are an appropriate expression of Christian concern for the needs and wants of ethnic people. It is not the whole answer; indeed, tutoring can help only those who are motivated enough to take advantage of it. But for those who want to rise out of poverty and marginality to successful, productive lives, education with a Christian heart is certainly one answer. And it is a direct avenue for evangelization.

Goal 5. New Approaches in Theological Education

Theological education that trains leaders to minister beyond the traditional white middle-class church and is adaptable to the needs of ethnic congregations must be developed and expanded. This calls for new approaches to theological education, drawing from the best in the traditions of both the majority and the minority communities without enslavement to any one model.[4]

The church's ability to minister in and to the city is determined to a large degree by the schools that train the church's leaders. These schools shape and inform the people who will give direction to the church's mission tomorrow. A month or more of urban internship during the formative years of education will have gigantic effects even on those students who never will actually minister in the city and on the suburban or rural churches and agencies they will eventually serve. And it will bring results in the neighborhoods of the city where the poor and the ethnics live.

Here is a possible agenda for seminaries and Christian colleges desiring to pursue urban relevancy:

1. Develop a biblical theology that deals adequately with the city, ethnicity, and the many things the Bible says about the poor, the sojourner, the refugee. Mission, after all, springs from theology and biblical understanding.
2. Encourage students to focus their church-history and biblical-studies assignments on themes relating to the city, urban minis-

---

4. Two of the best programs are those of the Missionary Internship (36200 Freedom Rd., Farmington, MI 48024), which utilizes inner-city Detroit to train candidates for overseas missionaries; and the Seminary Consortium for Urban Pastoral Education in Chicago (737 N. LaSalle St., Chicago, IL 60610).

tries, the poor, minorities, and the multiracial character of the church.

3. Invite guest speakers from foreign communities and inner-city ministries on a regular basis, make attendance at their lectures mandatory, and encourage them to speak freely about the matters that affect their people.

4. Insist that faculty and students become involved with ethnic people, inner-city churches, and the poor. Perhaps suburban churches can develop vital connections with city churches through the seminary.

5. Expand field-work positions and internships in city churches and urban-mission programs. This will give students practical experience in working with different races and cultures.

6. Add required courses designed to introduce nonurban men and women to urban issues and ministries.

7. Establish an urban campus in a multicultural setting where all students will take at least some classes, with the urban atmosphere as part of the learning experience. It is one thing to theorize about contextualization, quite another thing to *do* it. I doubt whether contextualization can be done outside the actual context.

8. Encourage students to live in interracial communities and to involve themselves as much as they can in neighborhood life.

9. Incorporate into courses on cults and non-Christian religions actual face-to-face confrontation, dialogue, and evangelism on the street. That can be done easily in the city, where alien cultures and adherents to other faiths are met not in textbooks, but in flesh and blood. There one quickly learns that Buddhists, Muslims, and Jews are real people, and that is exciting. After reading about them and their beliefs, the best education is to meet them personally and engage them in serious conversation.

Another dimension of our fifth goal is still to be discussed. It has to do with educating leaders for the ethnic churches themselves. This education must be adapted to their needs, financial resources, time schedules, and valued traditions—in other words, a theological education that is appropriate to ethnic cultures and differs from training designed exclusively for white middle-class church leaders.

A crucial distinguishing characteristic of ethnic churches is that age and maturity are usually required before one can assume pastoral leadership. The individuals who pastor large, thriving inner-city churches seldom have academic degrees, but invariably they have climbed a long ladder of ministry experience in order to arrive where they are.

Ethnic people generally want as their spiritual leader a seasoned person rich in practical knowledge of the Christian faith. In contrast to the prevailing white American culture that prizes youth so highly, many ethnic communities respect age. Gray hair elicits trust and confidence. Theological education that is appropriate to such cultures will blend serious study with a large amount of practical experience. Training will be spread over a longer period of time than most seminaries are set up for, and the ethnic students will generally be older and already proven for their sincerity and effective ministry.

The Center for Urban Theological Studies (CUTS) in Philadelphia is a contextualized program offering college and seminary education for inner-city church leaders. The average age of a CUTS student is forty-two, and every enrollee must already be actively engaged in church ministry. The courses offered bear the same names as those in suburban and small-town schools, but the style of teaching and the expectations of teachers and learners are quite different. Since the culture is predominantly oral and less book-oriented, reading assignments are shorter, but intense discussion takes place at each class session.

In teaching at CUTS, I cover the same material as I do on suburban campuses, but I communicate the material differently. The content I intend to present in a given hour often comes out in response to students' questions rather than in the traditional lecture format. I can expect to be questioned and challenged immediately to prove that what I have said is true and relevant. Theory is tested at once, because the students are thinking about next Sunday's sermons, the problems they face in counseling and evangelism, and maybe the grieving family they will visit after class. Students don't take many notes, because they want to be free to discuss. I have never been surrounded by so many tape recorders and microphones as at CUTS, and I know what I say will be replayed in students' homes and cars. A class session in this context is live drama, and it is not uncommon for class to end with group prayer and spontaneous singing. When students shake hands with me after class, thanking me for the help they received that hour, I know the teaching was effectively contextualized to meet urban people's needs.

Are there other worthy objectives to be identified and pursued in urban ethnic missions? Certainly, and new ones will appear as time passes. From the ethnic communities themselves will emerge creative approaches which God will use to expand his kingdom and bring renewal to North American Christianity.

This is what is occurring in other parts of the world as the churches of Asia, Africa, and Latin America add their contributions to the richness of the Christian faith. The older churches of the West now find themselves receiving as well as giving. The twenty-first century may well see the North American continent stronger in the faith and in a better position to advance Christ's kingdom throughout the world precisely because the goals of Christian mission were pursued with zeal and energy close to home.

Discussion Questions

1. Discuss the spiritual warfare going on in cities, and identify the major combat zones between Christ's kingdom and the forces of evil and idolatry. How can prayer be mobilized more effectively against these evil powers? Mention specific things to pray for.
2. Think about the school(s) you know best and suggest changes that would urbanize the curriculum and better equip students for intercultural ministry.
3. Make inquiries as to the ethnic composition of the city where you live and try to discover how well the Christian church is represented among each group. Then discuss the goals presented in this chapter in the light of your local situation.

A Model of Church-centered Ethnic Outreach

Roger S. Greenway

Revere, Massachusetts, is one of the oldest communities in America. First settled in 1626, it became part of Boston in 1632 and was later named Revere in honor of the American Revolutionary hero, Paul Revere. First Congregational Church was started in 1710 and is one of the oldest churches in the United States. The sanctuary now in use was erected in 1849. In the nineteenth century the church was known as the orthodox church, because it had broken away from its mother church when the older congregation became Unitarian.

First Congregational's apex came in the 1940s when it had about four hundred members. Between the two world wars, the population of Revere had begun to change from homogeneous white Anglo-Saxon Protestant to a high percentage of Roman Catholic residents. Even bigger changes occurred after World War II. Revere's demographics shifted radically as Italians, Jews, and other foreign-born people moved in and traditional residents moved away or died. Today, 60 percent of the population is Italian, served by six Catholic churches; 15 percent is Jewish, served by three synagogues; 10 percent is foreign-born and represents various non-European racial and ethnic groups, including more than a thousand Cambodians.

Twenty years ago a demographic analysis was done of Revere by a church-sponsored agency. The predictions made at that time have almost all come true. It was predicted that major demographic changes were coming for the community and that its religious makeup would be sharply altered. At that time there were thirteen Protestant churches in Revere. Those churches were warned that they would have to make major adjustments if they wanted to survive. Most of the churches ignored the warning and subsequently died. They died because they did not care to follow their departing members to other communities nor to assimilate the new ethnics arriving in Revere. What is more, they did not know how to evangelize people unlike themselves.

The same fate nearly befell First Congregational. When Pastor Nickolas Granitsas arrived in 1974, fresh out of Gordon-Conwell Seminary, the church had 157 adult members, almost all of them elderly. Sunday worship saw forty to forty-five persons in the pews. "Young people" were members in their sixties. The church had the options of moving away from Revere and starting over somewhere else, closing down entirely, or shifting the ministry to reach the new residents of the community. The community had now become overwhelmingly Italian and Jewish, but the church had only one Italian member and no Jews. Yet it did have a core of faithful people who wanted the church to stay and be God's servants in Revere. On that basis and with the hope of seeing things turn around, Pastor Granitsas had accepted the call to First Congregational.

In one month of his early pastorate, four of the key members died. The deacons who ran the church met only once a year. The annual budget was a mere fifteen thousand dollars. Worst of all, a survey of the community showed that most residents thought the church was closed! The building looked drab and ill-kept, and there never seemed to be any activity around it. The common opinion in the neighborhood was that First Congregational really did not exist at all.

The First Step: Day Care

Pastor Granitsas laid plans to turn the church around slowly. He discussed with the remaining members the basic biblical goals that every church should have: to be a worshiping community, a praying people, witnesses and servants to the neighborhood, students of God's Word, and leaven in the city. Besides its small but faithful core of believers, the members agreed that First Congregational had one major asset—its building. After repainting and clearing out the facility (the basement had become the repository of a century-old junk collection), the blue-collar congregation began to examine the needs of the community outside its doors.

The most pressing need was day care for the children of single parents. There was not one day-care center in the city at that time, while there were plenty of working mothers who urgently needed help with their children. First Congregational decided not to service the wealthy, but to show their particular concern for the children of the poor.

At first, starting a day-care center appeared impossible because of the mountain of government regulations. The book of regulations was thirty pages long! However, when the community at large heard about First Congregational's intention, help came from unexpected sources. The government regulator proved to be personally interested in helping the church get started. He advised them as to how they might comply with the regulations without going beyond their limited budget. In 1976 the center opened with one teacher and two children. After a year of hard struggle and the growing support of local residents, enrolment jumped and the difficulties with the government subsided. Today the day-care center services thirty-seven children, twenty-four of whom are state-supported. Three of the twenty-four are cases of abuse or neglect sent to the center by the courts. The day-care center's budget now exceeds that of the church.

The staff is composed entirely of Christians. Most of the children are from non-Christian homes. The children are taught the Bible every day, hymns and choruses are sung, and there is regular tactful witness to Christ and God's Word. There is also personal work with the parents. "We witness to the total child," says Pastor Granitsas. "In this operation there is no sharp line between ministry to the soul and service to the mind and body. The center offers a complete program, a full kindergarten, with music, games, art, cooking, and medical services nine hours a day, soon to be increased to ten."

The benefits to the church have been numerous. Some mothers have become members, while other parents have been spiritually renewed and either have joined other congregations or become active once again in their former churches. In addition, the day-care center has made the church known to its neighbors as an institution that seeks to be relevant to the needs of the community. No longer does anyone think First Congregational is out of business. The center has also stimulated church members to think about people and needs that had previously gone unnoticed. It became the catalyst for a host of other services, involvements, and relationships.

"I wouldn't call day care the number-one way to church growth," says Pastor Granitsas, "but I can tell you that many solid new members came in through day care. They wouldn't be here if it weren't for this ministry. One mother came into my office, and the first thing she said to me was, 'Tell me more about Jesus. My daughter has never been the same since she started coming to your day-care center.' That woman and her daughter are now in church every Sunday." Nine Jews have become members of the church. One of them was formerly the director of the Jewish Community Center, and her daughter works for the day-care center.

The day-care center was just the beginning of the outreach ministries in which First Congregational is now engaged. There is a food pantry which serves as the food depot for all the churches in Revere. "Nobody has to go hungry in Revere," says Pastor Granitsas. "If they come to us, they are serviced. We counsel them as to the government assistance that is available to them. We supply them with good food on an emergency basis. The pantry has never run short because we get gifts of food, money, and grants to keep the pantry supplied. We buy our supplies at the Boston Food Bank, where everything from beef to rice goes at twelve cents a pound. We service street people, ex–mental patients, and a wide variety of destitute individuals every week. Thank God, we have women in this church who use their gifts and talents in tremendous ways to serve people in Christ's name."

First Congregational has its own weekly half-hour cable-television show, with church members in charge of designing and presenting the programs. The broadcast includes testimonies, Christian music, discussions of religious and moral issues, and Christian teaching. "It doesn't reach beyond Revere," says Pastor Granitsas, "but Revere is our target area, and these are the people we want to reach." The church also sponsors a weekly television show called "L'English," directed by a woman of the church and designed especially to help people learn English. Since there are many refugees from Southeast Asia in Revere, as well as many Italian immigrants whose English is limited, "L'English" had immediate appeal from the day it started in 1984. "L'English" uses children, often Cambodian children, as the actors in a format that makes viewers feel comfortable about their inability to speak English and willing to follow the steps and exercises the show presents.

Refugee Ministry

First Congregational's refugee ministry is the program that excites Pastor Granitsas most. In 1975, during the early days of struggle at the church, the pastor and his wife sponsored a Vietnamese refugee family, Nhien Nguyen and her three children. "The presence of this family with us gave the church a good taste of a totally new thing. It's had many benefits," he says. "Our blue-collar membership did not have much of a world awareness, and just having this Vietnamese family in our midst and seeing their faith in Christ develop was a wonderful eye-opener." In 1979 the church as a whole sponsored a family, and since then the refugee program has grown by leaps and bounds.

"There has been a lot of prayer at every stage," says Pastor Granitsas. "One answer to prayer which we never expected was the gift of a nine-room, six-bedroom house to serve as a 'Refugee House.' " Spiritually, the church has seen amazing things happen. Some refugees were Christians when they arrived; some became Christians through the ministry of the church in Revere; others moved away, often to join relatives in California or elsewhere. The congregation learned to leave to God the results of their witness and service.

Between 1980 and 1985 the church sponsored two hundred refugees, mostly from Cambodia, though some were from Vietnam and a few were Russian Jews. In 1981 the Lord provided a Cambodian pastor to lead the Cambodian ministry. Though sponsored by First Congregational, the Cambodian congregation chose to affiliate with the Christian and Missionary Alliance denomination. Sharing the building with the English-speaking congregation, the Cambodian church now has sixty adult members and many children. The Cambodian congregation is sponsoring sixty refugees on its own.

Renewal Through Outreach

Because of a variety of outreach ministries, the median age of First Congregational's members has dropped from sixty-five to a little over thirty in a decade. One of the most effective outreach methods used by the church was a coffee house operated in the late 1970s in the church basement. "The thing about the coffee-house ministry was the effect it had on the people who learned to trust Jesus there," Pastor Granitsas reflects. "They brought new life to the congregation as they went on to create new ministries when the coffee house itself had run its course and was closed. These people literally emerged from the basement and took to the streets. Lots of things we have going now stem from the vision that got started in the coffee house."

Home Bible studies and a weekly prayer meeting in a member's home are the backbone of the evangelistic outreach of First Congregational today. Four home Bible studies are conducted each week, and many of the converts come through them. "Forty-five percent of the people who have joined our church have come through the home Bible studies," says Pastor Granitsas. "When I started here a decade ago, we didn't have four visitors a year. But once we began the home Bible studies and the coffee house down in the basement, the flow of visitors never stopped. The public doesn't come in off the street to attend worship services. The new faces I see on Sunday are there because they've been introduced to the Lord and to our members in the home Bible studies. Here in Revere, if a nominal Christian or a Jew decides to attend a religious service, he or she will drift into a mass or attend a synagogue, not an evangelical church like ours. We have to get them through things like home Bible studies."

Outreach to the new ethnics in the community has brought overall renewal to the church and a vision for evangelism that is embraced by the entire congregation. Through First Congregational, hundreds of lives are being affected.

Discussion Questions

1. Do you know of an old urban church that has been declining over the years and now faces an unfriendly neighborhood? Describe the church, the membership, the neighborhood, the pastor, and the dilemmas it faces in trying to minister.
2. How do you feel about the ministries conducted by the church in Revere? What attracts you to such a model? What prevents other old urban churches from following the model?
3. What can be done to encourage traditional Anglo churches to welcome people from other races and cultures and to adapt their styles of worship and church life to a more intercultural mode?
4. What kind of leadership does a multicultural church require? How can such leadership be developed?

Soaring Populations in the Southern World

Timothy Monsma

When I visited the city of Enugu, Nigeria, shortly after the Nigerian civil war (1967–1970), devastation could be seen on every hand. Buildings lay in ruins, goods were in short supply, and young men who had lost arms and legs attempting to defend Biafra from the superior Nigerian armed forces were begging in the streets. Enugu had been declared the capital of Biafra and had undergone heavy bombardment from Nigerian artillery before it was captured.

Nonetheless, now that the war was over, the pounding of hammers and other sounds of construction could be heard everywhere. Before the hostilities Enugu had been the capital of the Eastern Region of Nigeria. It was now the capital of East-Central State, controlling a territory only about one-third the size of its original domain. But no one doubted that Enugu was to become a growing city once again. In fact, Enugu grew from a population of 62,764 in 1952 to over 165,000 by 1977.

Enugu's story is the story of the entire developing world. It is in this part of the globe, which is also called the Third World or the Southern World, that traditionally most mission work has been done. Figure 3 shows steady growth in cities of the Northern World (Europe, North America, the USSR, and Australia/New Zealand).[1] It shows meteoric growth for the rest of the world (Africa, Latin America, and Asia, including the South Pacific islands). Already the total population in Southern cities has outpaced the total in Northern cities.

While Northern cities continue to grow, the pace is slow and orderly

1. Although Australia and New Zealand are in the Southern Hemisphere, they represent Northern or Western culture. Japan and China are included in the Southern nations.

Figure 3
The Growth of Cities in Our World

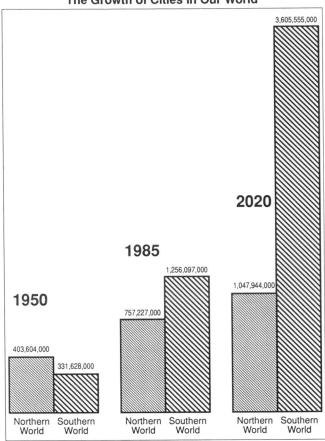

Total Urban Population			
	1950	1985	2020
Africa	32,899,000	177,402,000	821,471,000
Latin America	67,707,000	279,675,000	615,036,000
Asia	230,835,000	797,630,000	2,164,383,000
Pacific Islands	187,000	1,390,000	4,665,000
	331,628,000	1,256,097,000	3,605,555,000
Europe	219,162,000	360,587,000	444,996,000
North America	106,105,000	195,654,000	286,248,000
USSR	70,772,000	184,583,000	292,175,000
Australia/New Zealand	7,565,000	16,403,000	24,525,000
	403,604,000	757,227,000	1,047,944,000

Source: United Nations, Department of International Economic and Social Affairs, *Estimates and Projections of Urban, Rural and City Populations, 1950–2025: The 1982 Assessment*

Figure 4
The Ten Largest Cities in the World
(population in millions)

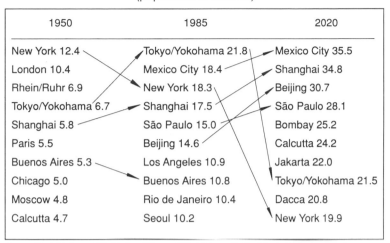

1950	1985	2020
New York 12.4	Tokyo/Yokohama 21.8	Mexico City 35.5
London 10.4	Mexico City 18.4	Shanghai 34.8
Rhein/Ruhr 6.9	New York 18.3	Beijing 30.7
Tokyo/Yokohama 6.7	Shanghai 17.5	São Paulo 28.1
Shanghai 5.8	São Paulo 15.0	Bombay 25.2
Paris 5.5	Beijing 14.6	Calcutta 24.2
Buenos Aires 5.3	Los Angeles 10.9	Jakarta 22.0
Chicago 5.0	Buenos Aires 10.8	Tokyo/Yokohama 21.5
Moscow 4.8	Rio de Janeiro 10.4	Dacca 20.8
Calcutta 4.7	Seoul 10.2	New York 19.9

Source: David B. Barrett, *World-Class Cities and World Evangelization* (Birmingham, Ala.: New Hope, 1986)

when compared to that of many Southern cities. The growth of New York City as shown in figure 4 is typical of most Northern cities. New York was the largest city in the world in 1950. During the next thirty-five years it grew from 12.4 million to 18.3 million—a respectable increase. Nonetheless, it was surpassed by both Tokyo and Mexico City. During the next thirty-five-year period, New York will continue to grow. Projections call for it to reach almost 20 million inhabitants by the year 2020. Nonetheless, it will probably be at the bottom of the list of the ten largest cities in the world. All the other cities on the list will be from the Southern World. (Note that figure 4 lends credibility to figure 3. Figure 3 is based upon data submitted by the various nations, and their definitions of "urban" differ.[2] But Figure 4 is a nonsubjective chart of the very largest cities in the world, which David Barrett calls supercities and supergiants.[3] Both figures, of course, illustrate a meteoric population increase in the cities of the developing world.)

It is predicted that by the year 2000 half of the world will be living in cities. As centers of power, cities have always had a disproportionate influence on national cultures. Now we have an added reason for turning our attention to cities: this is where most of the people of the world

2. In some definitions towns of twenty-five hundred are classified as urban.
3. David B. Barrett, *World-Class Cities and World Evangelization* (Birmingham, Ala.: New Hope, 1986), p. 8.

will be found from the year 2000 onwards. Accordingly, we Christians must attend to the growing cities of the Northern World. And even more important, we must greatly increase our efforts in the cities of the Southern World if we are ever to keep pace with the urban explosion now under way.

Urban Growth in the Southern World

This chapter will examine the scope of urban growth throughout the Southern World, a subject that will have a major bearing on mission strategy for decades to come. We will look briefly at the three continents involved and then discover that there are sound reasons for the overwhelming urban expansion. We begin with the leading urban continent, both historically and in absolute size and numbers.

Asia

When urban missionary Viv Grigg visited one of the 771 squatter areas in Dacca, the capital of Bangladesh, he happened upon a mother and two malnourished children living in a hut four feet by six feet, with walls made of mud brick. She had come to the city seeking work, but had found none. In his book *Companion to the Poor*, Grigg reminds us that in most cities of Asia there are vast slums and shantytowns in which more and more of the new migrants to the city are living. Such migration presents tremendous problems to urban planners who work on severely limited budgets. But it also presents a tremendous challenge and opportunity to Christians, who are called to display the love of Christ to all strata of urban society.

The history of cities in Asia goes back a long way. Many of the leading cities of antiquity were located in the Fertile Crescent, the area that stretches from the Mediterranean Sea to the Persian Gulf. Damascus, the oldest city in the world, is located here. Islam, the dominant religion in the Fertile Crescent today, is largely a faith of urbanites and prospers in urban environments. Several Muslim cities of the Middle East are taking their place among the largest cities of the world.

Many cities of India and China also go back to ancient times. While urban growth in these two nations is reaching proportions never before seen in history, both have had cities of more than one hundred thousand inhabitants for many centuries.

For our purposes, the vast continent of Asia (excluding the USSR) can be divided into four cultural areas: the Middle East, South Asia, Southeast Asia, and the Orient. Figure 5 indicates that the cities of the

Figure 5
Urban Growth in Asia
(population in millions)

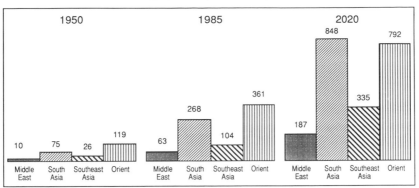

Source: *Estimates and Projections, 1950–2025* (UN, 1982)

Figure 6
The Seven Largest Cities of Asia in 2020
(population in millions)

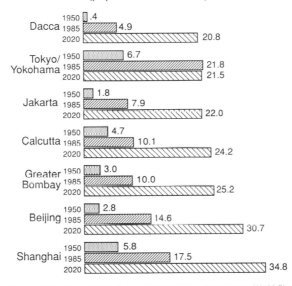

Source: *Estimates and Projections, 1950–2025* (UN, 1982); Barrett, *World-Class Cities*

Middle East and Southeast Asia will experience steady growth, but the cities of the Orient and South Asia will experience phenomenal growth. In 2020 six of the ten largest cities in the world—Shanghai, Beijing, Bombay, Calcutta, Tokyo, and Dacca—will be in these parts of

Asia. Figure 6 illustrates the actual and potential growth of these six cities as well as Jakarta, the capital of Indonesia, which will also be among the ten largest cities in the world.

The reason for this phenomenal growth is clear: the Orient and South Asia have greater population density over wider areas than do any other parts of the world. One in every four people in the world is Chinese. Even though the Chinese government stringently promotes birth control and has been emphasizing agriculture in order to discourage urbanization, the pressures for urbanization are inevitable. Modernization and industrialization (two goals in contemporary China) both stimulate the growth of cities.

Some writers have stressed the percentage of urban dwellers versus the percentage of farmers in Asia. Viewed from this angle, urbanization does not seem overly intense. Table 3 gives the figures for China and India. It might be argued that in 1985 only one-fourth of the people in India were living in cities, and even by 2020 only half of the people will be living in cities. Therefore India, and certainly China, are and will remain primarily agricultural countries for some time to come.

But we must ask if looking at percentages gives us a true picture of urban growth. Patrick Johnstone reports in the fourth edition of *Operation World* that urbanization in the Falkland Islands is 50 percent.[4] Yet these islands have only one city, Stanley, with a total population of fifteen hundred. On the other hand, a populous nation like Nigeria, with a capital city (Lagos) of five million and several other large cities, is reported as being only 28 percent urban. If we are to obtain a true picture of the magnitude of urbanization within a country or region, we must look at the population totals for the metropolitan areas. That is what has been done in the various graphs that appear in this chapter.

A basic reason why percentage is not a good gauge of urbanization is that the size of farms and ranches varies tremendously as one moves from one part of the world to another. In many parts of the developing world, farms are small because they are very labor-intensive. A large number of farmers may be crowded together in a small area. If the farms should be mechanized to any extent, many farmers will be thrown out of work and will stream into the cities. When we look at percentages, this potentially volatile situation escapes our attention. According to United Nations projections, four of the ten largest cities in the world in 2020 will be in China and India (Shanghai, Beijing, Calcutta, and Bombay). This is the type of information we need as we pray and plan for the future.

---

4. Patrick J. Johnstone, *Operation World*, 4th ed. (Pasadena: William Carey Library, 1986), p. 172.

Table 3
Percentage of Urban Dwellers
in China and India

	1950	1985	2020
China	12.20%	21.04%	41.56%
India	17.25%	25.51%	49.81%

From a mission perspective cities are important, first because they are centers which tend to dominate the entire society, and secondly because of the sheer numbers of people living in them. This applies with special force in Asia. Asia is much larger and more diverse than Latin America and Africa. Oriental cities are as different from Middle Eastern cities as they are from African cities. Consequently, it is hard to generalize regarding Asian cities and to formulate an overall mission strategy for them.

Viv Grigg has directed our attention to the shantytowns that surround many Asian cities. These are built on undesirable (usually public) land on the outskirts of giant cities by migrants who cannot afford traditional housing. (Shantytowns surround many Latin American and African cities as well.) Grigg feels that the shantytowns are more fertile areas for church planting than are the slums (dilapidated housing occupied by longtime city residents), because the shantytowns are usually occupied by recent migrants who display some hope of upward mobility and openness to change. Accordingly, they tend to be more receptive to the gospel than are longtime residents.

While opportunity beckons in every social stratum of Asian cities, the shantytowns must certainly be a focal point of any comprehensive mission strategy. It is especially here that today's missionary has opportunity to live out the words of him who said, "As you did it to one of the least of these my brethren, you did it to me" (Matt. 25:40 RSV).

Latin America

Acapulco, Mexico, is world-famous for its divers, some of whom plunge from rocky heights over one hundred feet above the ocean into water so shallow that the dive must be timed with an incoming wave to make sure that the diver is not harmed. Before the diving begins, these young athletes carry flaming torches reminiscent of ancient Greek and Roman traditions. Yet on meeting the divers in person, one quickly realizes that their hereditary background is mostly New World Indian.

There is a restaurant in downtown Acapulco called the Portafino, adorned with statues copied from ancient Greece. On the street in front of this restaurant, Indian women sell clothing and jewelry to tourists.

In Latin America, two distinct cultures have met and blended, one from Europe and one indigenous to the New World. The country of Mexico is more self-consciously aware of this blend than are other Latin American nations. Chile, Argentina, and Uruguay seem least aware of any blend, for their Indian populations are small. In any case, Latin America is not simply a repetition of Spain and Portugal, nor are the cities of Latin America duplications of Lisbon, Barcelona, and Madrid. They are products of a history all their own. Mexico City was founded by the Aztecs long before the Spanish came to the Western Hemisphere. The Incas of Peru also had urban settlements, although Lima was founded by the Spanish.

Even if one were to consider urbanization as originating with the coming of the Spanish, one must remember that Columbus discovered the New World before Luther nailed his ninety-five theses on the church door at Wittenberg. The Spanish and Portuguese were building and rebuilding cities in Latin America before the English and the French became involved in North America. The oldest city in the United States, St. Augustine, Florida, was founded by the Spanish. Numerous place names in the southwestern United States, such as Santa Fe, San Diego, Los Angeles, and San Francisco, also testify to their Spanish origins.

But the long history of Spanish and Portuguese involvement in the Western Hemisphere does not account for the stupendous urban expansion during the closing decades of the twentieth century. Figure 7 illustrates the projected growth of Central America and the Caribbean in comparison with the rest of Latin America, namely the entire continent of South America. It is interesting that although Central America contains what will be the largest city in the world, Mexico City, South American urban population will outstrip Central American urban population in raw numbers. This is partly due to the fact that Mexico City will be the only giant city in all of Central America, whereas South America's urban population will be spread over several giant cities. The fact that South America's total land mass and overall population exceed Central America's is another factor.

Figure 8 displays the projected growth of the four leading cities of Latin America. In the history of Western countries, large-scale urbanization has gone hand in hand with industrialization. To this day, most Westerners who move from farm to city seek employment in industry. Industrialization in Latin America does not as a rule reach the level found in most Western countries. But even without heavy industrialization the cities are growing rapidly. Many new migrants are finding

Figure 7
Urban Growth in Latin America
(population in millions)

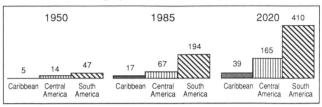

Source: *Estimates and Projections, 1950–2025* (UN, 1982)

Figure 8
The Four Largest Cities of Latin America in 2020
(population in millions)

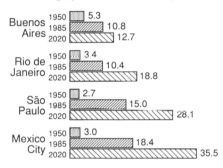

Source: *Estimates and Projections, 1950–2025* (UN, 1982); Barrett, *World-Class Cities*

work in service jobs, and others become street vendors. Still others find no work and end up sleeping on the streets.

At an international conference in early 1987, Luis Ortiz Ramirez, the deputy commerce secretary of Paraguay, spoke of "uncontrolled urban growth" and "poverty in rural areas."[5] There is an obvious relation between these two phenomena. As long as poverty continues in rural areas, people will be enticed to take their chances in the city because they have little to lose. Some have tried to improve the quality of life in rural areas. This usually involves making farming more efficient or less labor-intensive. But the more farming is mechanized, the fewer farmers will be needed, and the more the cities will grow.

Demographers agree that further urbanization is inevitable in Latin America regardless of whether cities have the economic vitality to sustain it. Christian compassion must see beyond physical need to the

5. *Mexico City News*, January 20, 1987, p. 4.

tremendous spiritual need tied up with Latin American urbanization. New migrants to the city are usually most open to the gospel message shortly after they arrive. But how many migrants come to the city and are not confronted with the claims of Christ on their lives even within five years of their arrival? Research has just begun to find the answer to that question for every leading city in Latin America. But even now it is safe to say that there are many who meet new sights and sounds in the city, but who do not meet Jesus Christ in the person of his ambassadors.

Africa

Recently, as I walked the streets of Lagos, Nigeria, the largest black metropolis in the world (five million people in 1985), I was reminded of the time my wife and I had spent there in 1974 in the home of a Nigerian Christian. More roads and bridges have been built since then. The outskirts of the city are now much farther from the downtown area. But living conditions have not changed much.

We had stayed in a building that would probably be called slum housing by *The New Book of World Rankings*. For Ibadan, Nigeria, is classified therein as 75 percent slum,[6] and living conditions in Lagos are similar to those in Ibadan. There were eight apartments in the building in which we stayed. For these eight apartments there were one water faucet, two stalls where one could bathe with a bucket of water, and two pit latrines. One resident had a television set which the others were invited to watch from time to time. Surprisingly, the various tenants seemed to get on with one another, despite such hassles as having to wait one's turn at the water faucet. The landlord followed a policy of mixing the ethnic groups that stayed in his building because he did not want the residents to join together to plead for lower rents or more amenities.

Although such housing in Western cities would be called a slum, this designation is not appropriate for Africa. In Africa there are shantytowns, but this was not a shantytown. It was African middle-class housing. The residents had meaningful work. Some of them owned cars or motorcycles. My host worked as an engineer for the Nigerian railroad. Even some wealthy Nigerians who could afford to live elsewhere choose to live in this part of Lagos, called Yaba, for a variety of reasons.

Africa has been called the least urbanized of the major continents. This is true, but the situation has begun to change rapidly. According

6. George Thomas Kurian, *The New Book of World Rankings* (New York: Facts on File, 1984), p. 426.

Figure 9
The Four Largest Cities of Africa in 2020
(population in millions)

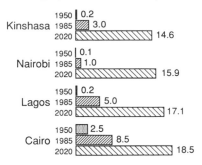

Source: *Estimates and Projections, 1950–2025* (UN, 1982); Barrett,
World-Class Cities

Figure 10
Urban Growth in Africa
(population in millions)

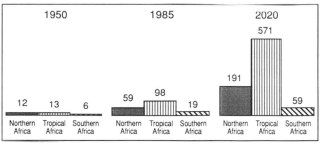

Source: *Estimates and Projections, 1950–2025* (UN, 1982)

to United Nations projections, Cairo will have a population of 18.5 million by 2020. Lagos, Nairobi, and Kinshasa will not be far behind (see fig. 9). Figure 10 indicates that most urban growth will take place in tropical Africa. Northern Africa is controlled by people of Arab background and is mostly desert. A large portion of Southern Africa is controlled by white settlers. The situation there is so volatile that the future is hard to predict. But tropical Africa, the home of about two thousand black ethnic groups (formerly called tribes), each with its own language and culture, is the garden in which urbanization will flourish.

Why should that be? Writers on urbanization have pointed to a rule of thumb which on the surface appears contradictory, but in reality is very logical: urbanization flourishes wherever agriculture flourishes. Most large cities are located in rich farming areas. Urbanization became possible in ancient Egypt and Babylonia when people gave up hunting and gathering in favor of farming. Chicago grew to prominence because of its proximity to agriculture in the heartland of America. Cities depend on farms for food, and farms depend on cities for manufactured products. Using a term from biology, one can say that the relationship between farm and city in contemporary society is symbiotic; the one cannot exist without the other.

Most Africans today are farmers; and unless drought or war throws everything into confusion, Africa can be self-sufficient in food production. This circumstance points to an exploding urbanization. Moreover, with minimal medical help the traditional African ideal of a large family is now within reach. The average woman in Kenya gives birth to eight children. Even when warfare decimates the male population, the custom of polygamy allows childbirth to continue with minimal interruption.

A given piece of land can conveniently support only so many people, even if the farming methods are very labor-intensive. The surplus population inevitably drifts off to the cities and towns. Others are attracted to the city even when there is plenty of land for them to farm. Farming is thought appropriate work for those with minimal schooling; it is assumed that secondary-school graduates and college graduates will seek their fortunes in the city.

Here, then, is the challenge for Christian missions at work in Africa today. Do churches and missionaries see that the future of Africa lies in its cities? This is where the majority of its people will be living. Surely this is where those who formulate public opinion will be living. A relevant witness in Africa today must include the great and growing cities.

The Dynamics of Urbanization

In this chapter we have considered the magnitude of urban growth worldwide, and especially in the developing world. Analyses of cities in Asia, Latin America, and Africa have revealed that although there are significant differences among these continents, they have this in common: their cities are growing rapidly and will continue to grow for the foreseeable future. Let's consider now the reasons for urbanization.

Cities are centers of service and dominance. That is to say, cities arise and grow because they serve the towns, villages, and farms that surround them. This activity takes various forms; some cities emphasize one more than the others. But as a city grows larger, it tends to serve and influence its hinterland in at least eight major areas. People who live in towns and villages expect these services and would be disappointed if cities failed to perform them. It is worthy of note that each of these services requires personnel to run them, and therefore each contributes to urban growth.

1. *Government.* Many ancient cities began as centers of government. All modern nations need not only national capitals but regional capitals as well. Government covers all people whether they live on the farm or in the city.

2. *Education.* We are all familiar with university towns. Most schools of higher education are in cities, which offer libraries, part-time work for students, and easy access from the surrounding area. This is especially important in the developing world, where people rely more heavily on public transportation than they do in the West.

3. *Health care.* While some medical care may be available in rural areas, more-specialized care, especially surgical procedures, can be obtained only in large-city hospitals. Thus health care is a key factor in Third World urbanization.

4. *Information.* People, even those who are illiterate, want to be informed about the world, and especially about their own nation. Information is provided by radio, television, newspapers, magazines, and books. All these avenues of information originate in the city. The sphere of influence of a given city probably extends as far as its radio waves. Radio and television place virtually everyone in immediate contact with the city, and at least one radio can now be found in most Third World villages.

5. *Entertainment.* The culture of a nation is embodied in its cities; cities usually set the pace and initiate trends. Whether it's through the fine arts, sports, rock concerts, or some other form of relaxation, people go to the city to enjoy themselves. They expect the city to provide cultural leadership.

6. *Trade.* In the days when people were more dependent on shipping goods by water than we are today, cities grew by the riverside or where there were deep harbors. Later, cities grew where railroad lines and roads intersected. Now airports (or the lack thereof) affect urban growth. Commerce and the transportation that it involves contribute mightily to the growth of cities.

7. *Industry.* Manufacturing has given tremendous impetus to the growth of Western cities (and some cities in the developing world). Westerners are therefore surprised when cities that have minimal manufacturing nonetheless achieve world-class status (a population of one million and direct ties with the world beyond national borders). But there were cities in the ancient world and in India and China long before industrialization took place. The other causes for urbanization

listed in this section help explain how cities grow and why they will continue to grow even without heavy industry.

8. *Warfare.* Some cities began as military camps. This is the history of Ibadan, Pittsburgh, and all the cities whose names begin with "Fort." The need to set up military camps and defense plants encourages urbanization during wartime. Many young men in Africa and Asia first left their home village in order to join the army. Once they had seen the world, there was no way to get them to settle back in their home village again.

We should also mention at this point those dynamics which urbanologists term "push-and-pull factors." When there is not enough farmland to go around, people are pushed off the farm. And when there is drought or a drop in farm prices, or when landlords ask too much from their tenants, people are pushed off the farm. On the other hand, the city attracts. The younger generation especially is attracted by the entertainment, the excitement, the jobs, and the ambiance of the city. One must remember in this connection that most villages and farms in the developing world are still without electricity, running water, gas stoves, and other amenities, but these conveniences are available in the cities.

Missions as a Factor in Urbanization

Missionaries also have made a decisive contribution to Southern World urbanization through their ministries. Mission efforts in the area of education are one example. Whether they have reduced a language to writing and taught people how to read it, or whether they have established and maintained primary and secondary schools, missionaries have provided many of the students who eventually attended schools of higher learning in the city. In fact, the modern city could not function without a large population of literate men and women.

Missionaries, both Protestant and Catholic, have also made a decisive contribution in the area of health care. In many countries where 50 percent of all children died before they reached five years of age, missions have worked on public-health campaigns to prevent disease, and in hospitals and clinics to forestall the mortality that accompanies it. In many areas the compassion of a loving God was first observed in the persons of medical missionaries, and indigenous solutions to the problems of sickness and death (together with their animistic connotations) became passé. Medical missionaries, together with fantastic advances in medical care and government-sponsored health programs, are now contributing to a population explosion such as the world has never seen.

Even in the areas of information, entertainment, and the other factors that encourage urbanization, the missionary influence is inevitable. J. H. Bavinck once wrote, "[The missionary's] sole purpose there is to preach the gospel, but in order to preach he must exist, and this very existence involves him in all sorts of activities. . . . Everything that the missionary does, even if it is quite customary to him, is a force which radically affects life."[7]

Missionaries live in glass houses. Their example affects life around them. If missionaries living in remote areas nonetheless treasure the education, information, medical care, and entertainment that originate in cities, many with whom they work will begin to treasure such items as well. The seeds of further urbanization will have been sown.

Missionaries are instigators of social change, whether that is their goal or not. Missions ought to accept full responsibility for their role in the tremendous urban growth taking place in our generation. Then they ought to do something about it. They ought to target cities as one of the prime areas in which new mission projects will be launched. As the Christians of Asia, Latin America, and Africa see Western missionaries moving in this direction, they too will wish to be involved. And the claims of Christ on city residents the world over will take root and grow.

Discussion Questions

1. The cities of the Southern World have become an urban planner's nightmare. What are some reasons for this, and how might a Christian witness to the city speak to these problems?
2. Why should we pay special attention to the shantytowns that surround many cities? What are some ways a word-and-deed witness could be demonstrated there?
3. Why does urbanization flourish wherever agriculture flourishes? Some have wanted to slow the pace of urbanization by emphasizing rural development. Is this feasible?
4. What attracts people to the city, and how have mission efforts promoted urbanization (or at least contributed to its growth)?

7. J. H. Bavinck, *An Introduction to the Science of Missions*, trans. David Hugh Freeman (Grand Rapids: Baker, 1960), p. 110.

The Intersecting Veins of the City

Timothy Monsma

Veins of gold lie buried deep in the earth in places scattered around the globe. The gold is there for the taking, but one must dig for it in order to obtain it!

There is gold for the Lord in the cities of the world. But one must work for it too! Strip mining is not sufficient. One must locate the veins, which are the various kinds of people groups in a city. These veins run in many directions and often intersect. The missionary's challenge is to know enough about each vein to mine it appropriately and extract the priceless ore of human souls to add to the treasury of the King.

Cities are complicated. One or two levels of analysis are not sufficient to understand them. But cities are not incomprehensible. Some guidelines can be given to urban missionaries, along with the promise that their labors will be worth the effort. The gold in the cities of the world is precious in God's sight. And our labors in the city have implications beyond its boundaries. We must remember that as the city goes, so (usually) goes the nation.

Ethnic Groups

Ibu is a young man in his early twenties. He left his home in Ghana to seek work in Abidjan, the capital of the Ivory Coast. Because of his limited knowledge of French, no firm was willing to hire him. But he found work in the home of a wealthy lawyer whose wife works as a part-time teacher. Ibu cares for the yard, mops the floors, and runs errands. He hopes that someday he will become a chauffeur and find a wife to live with him in Abidjan.

Ibu is one of about two hundred thousand Ghanians who have moved to the Ivory Coast to take advantage of Abidjan's relative prosperity. They are three steps removed from the average resident of Abidjan: their ethnic group is different from any of the ethnic groups of the Ivory Coast, they are not citizens, and they do not speak the national language, French. If they know French at all, it is only conversational French.

People like Ibu have been neglected by the traditional missions in Abidjan. Protestant missionaries and evangelists have had all they can do to reach the French-speaking population. This has left them no time for a concerted outreach to smaller groups, such as the one from Ghana.

Ethnic groups constitute some of the veins of gold awaiting discovery by urban missionary-miners. It is vital to identify which ethnic groups living in a city are being reached with the gospel and which are not. In most major cities today, even those that appear to have many churches, there are pockets of people who are neglected because of their ethnic identity, linguistic problems, or other cultural barriers.

In one predominantly Muslim country there is a city of one million people with seventy churches. On the surface it appears that Christianity is making great strides there. But when one examines the ethnic composition of these churches, one discovers that their members are not indigenous to the area. There is one small denomination for the two indigenous ethnic groups, and that church is shrinking rather than growing. Until a city is analyzed in terms of its ethnic composition, such information does not come to light, and the missionary may be misled by appearances.

Recent missiological thinking has emphasized the need to identify "unreached people groups." Frequently these are ethnic groups. A group is considered unreached if in its midst there is no vigorous church capable of bringing the gospel to the other members of the group. As soon as a vigorous and growing church has been planted in the midst of a group, it is considered reached.

Many have thought that the emphasis on unreached people groups is an emphasis on rural evangelism, for it appears to focus on isolated tribes to whom no missionary has yet been sent. But there are unreached peoples in cities as well. Members of many isolated tribes have already made their way to the cities. And this raises a new question: Is it better to approach a people group in the city first or in the hinterlands? The answer will depend on the circumstances of each individual group. In some cases, groups that are highly resistant to the gospel in their homelands may be very open to the gospel in an urban environment.

Most urban immigrants preserve numerous ties with their kin back in the countryside. There is travel back and forth for holidays and other special occasions. Food is sent from the rural area to relatives living in the city, while those in the city send items that cannot be purchased in the village except at a very high price. Public transportation is continually used to convey children, money, animals, food, and manufactured goods back and forth between town and country.

Public transportation between town and country also conveys the news, sometimes very rapidly. After a church service in Lagos, for example, someone said to me, "I hear that a child of one of your missionaries died yesterday in Gboko." Gboko is eight hundred miles away, but the overnight bus service between Gboko and Lagos had already carried the news.

Because of such relationships the symbiosis between city and hinterland extends beyond the realm of formal business matters. For the social ties between the members of a particular ethnic group who live in the country and those in the city also help to spread new ideas, including religious ideas. It is not preposterous, therefore, to evangelize the countryside by evangelizing the city or, conversely, to evangelize the city by evangelizing the countryside.

In the city there are various social groupings other than ethnic—people of one ethnic group may be separated from one another by class distinctions. Nonetheless, they often have a sense of cohesion and unity that transcends social barriers. This is especially true of relatives. Those within an extended family feel obligations toward one another in spite of social barriers. I have observed illiterate peasants staying with wealthy and cultured relatives in the city, at least temporarily, simply because they were family.

As we seek to measure the progress of the gospel among various groups, the most natural approach to the city is to classify its residents on the basis of their ethnicity. But for the cities of Japan and Korea, where virtually everyone is of the same ethnic stock, such a division is not useful. And in cities where an ethnic group is so small that its members prefer to worship with some other group or groups, the ethnic criterion also loses its value. But in most cases ethnic divisions are most useful for evaluating the progress of evangelism in the city.

Jakarta, the capital of Indonesia, is a city of churches. Out of a total population of eight million, about one million identify themselves as Protestant Christians. Someone might argue that there are enough Christians in Jakarta to evangelize the rest of the city. And from a strictly numerical point of view, this argument seems valid. But if we think of Jakarta as a gold mine with many intersecting veins, we will realize that there are numerous Christians in some veins, while other veins contain virtually no Christians at all.

We can identify the ethnic groups among whom Christians are few and far between. There are, for example, the Sundanese, a group twenty million strong living on the western end of Java. The Sundanese are committed Muslims and not very willing to give the Christian faith serious consideration.

The Javanese form another large ethnic group in Jakarta. They make up the bulk of the population of Java, a heavily populated island of almost one hundred million people. The Javanese are more willing than the Sundanese to consider various religious options. Some of them in Jakarta profess faith in Christ, but a strong Javanese church has not yet arisen.

Then there are those groups that have migrated to Jakarta from the outlying islands. Some of these islands are predominantly Christian, and it is from there that the majority of the Christian population of Jakarta have come. But other islands, such as Sumatra, are predominantly Muslim, and their people have also moved to Jakarta in large numbers. People from the island of Bali remain Hindu.

One ethnic group in Jakarta that has been reached with the gospel is the Chinese. Although the majority of them are still Buddhists, there is a vigorous and growing Christian church among them. Indonesians of Chinese descent are busy evangelizing their own people, and God is blessing their efforts.

By dividing the population of the city into ethnic groups, we get a better idea of the evangelistic task that remains. It probably will not be possible for foreign missionaries to spread the gospel to the as yet unreached groups in Indonesia, because the government is not granting visas to new missionaries. But Indonesian Christians are able to shoulder this burden. They have already made some efforts in this direction, and they will become more vigorously involved in cross-cultural evangelistic activity as fellow Christians from outside the country remind them of these God-given opportunities.

This writer is convinced that ethnic groups in the cities of the world must be identified by the Christian community. If someday every tribe, tongue, people, and nation are to be gathered before God's throne (Rev. 5:9), then they must hear and believe the Good News about Jesus before he returns. Mission scholars have identified many ethnic groups that do not yet have a church in their midst. When these groups have been identified, missionaries and evangelists can prepare to go to them with the gospel.

Increasingly, unreached ethnic groups are represented in cities. In some cases, they have traveled such a distance that they form a totally new group within their chosen city. This happens especially when they cross international borders. But whether they constitute a newly formed group in a foreign country or have remained in their homeland, every urban ethnic group must be reached with the gospel.

Anyone who wishes to investigate a specific city is advised to draw up a list of ethnic groups within that city and to identify those that already have living, growing churches in their midst. In this way one will, by a process of elimination, be able to target those groups still in need of a vital witness. A person who has lived in a city for some time will have contacts who can assist in drawing up the list. But someone who is new to a city will have to prevail upon Christians who are already there to help in this effort. They will probably be willing to do so, provided one does not take up too much of their time.

Once the list has been drawn up, one must determine which of those ethnic groups still in need of a vital witness constitute what missions literature calls "people groups." An urban ethnic group is a people group if one can contemplate planting a church or a worshiping congregation just for them. A given ethnic group may be so similar to other ethnic groups that one church can serve them all in culturally appropriate ways. Or an ethnic group might have so few members in a given city that it would be preferable for them to worship with other Christians in a common language or in the national language of the land.

There is a special advantage in identifying people groups in cities, especially groups that have been resistant to the gospel in rural areas. Sometimes village life is woven so tightly that no one is able to step out of line. No one dares accept a new faith such as Christianity. In extreme cases, those who do may be killed. But in the city there is greater freedom. The social controls of the village are gone. There is less danger of losing one's job when one changes religions in the city. Here there is often a community of Christians who can help new converts make the necessary adjustments.

Social Groups

At the beginning of this chapter the city was called a gold mine with many intersecting veins, some of which are the ethnic groupings we have been discussing. We might picture them as vertical veins running through the city. Just as important in many cases are social distinctions, which we might picture as horizontal veins.

We were in a crowded upper room of a warehouse in Jakarta. The men and women in the room were of all ages and various skin colors. When the chairman asked for a show of hands to determine the islands from which these people had come, it became apparent that there was great ethnic diversity in the room. Yet they all had one thing in common: they were all seamen or the relatives of seamen, and they were all comparatively poor.

Now it is a fact that schooling, occupation, and wealth (or lack of it) tend to determine one's social status. But within the broad categories of upper, middle, and lower class, there are subcategories that group people in terms of how they view themselves or how others view them. The seamen of Jakarta are a case in point. While many others might have an income in the same range as theirs, they would not feel an affinity for each other because their lives revolve around entirely different occupations. That street vendors and seamen have the same level of income does not automatically place them in the same sociological group. In the case of the seamen, the method of earning a living determines the cohesiveness of the group. As a matter of fact, their shared occupation appears more important than their ethnic identity. This, then, is their primary group, the people group among whom we may expect a church to arise.

In the city there are other such occupational groupings that appear to bind their members so closely to one another that they override all ethnic considerations. These occupational groupings tend to cluster both at the top and at the bottom of the socioeconomic scale. Thus corporation executives, actors, top-level civil servants, and high-ranking military officers might feel an affinity for one another that overrides the ethnic pull. Toward the bottom of the socioeconomic scale, pimps and prostitutes, drug dealers, beggars, thieves, and scavengers might feel close to one another and rather distant from their own ethnic groups.

We may need a different evangelistic strategy for each one of these groups, for each group may have its own set of needs and interests (although they all need salvation through Christ). For example, what evangelistic strategy would one use with prostitutes? We sense immediately that it will have to differ from that used with women who are wives and mothers, or that used with women who are office workers, nurses, telephone operators, or attorneys.

Simply to tell prostitutes that they are sinners will not make much of an impression, because they know that without being told. Those who have worked with prostitutes in various countries tell us that a holistic approach is needed. Many became prostitutes because they were desperate to find work or because they were duped by someone. Now they cannot get out even if they want to.

Prostitutes must be shown that there is a viable way out. They must be protected from the pimps and brothel owners who may try to reclaim them. Commitment to Jesus Christ must become for them the beginning of a period of cleansing and renewal in body and spirit. It may also involve further education so that they can find their places as useful members of society once again.

The fact that prostitutes require a special evangelistic strategy, however, does not mean that they are a people group so distinctive that a church can and ought to be planted just for them. If every occupational class were a people group as that term is presently used in missions literature, then there would be virtually no end to the number of people groups in the world, for new occupations are always appearing. Then, too, the people-group concept could not be used effectively as a measure to determine the progress of the gospel in the world. It is better to recognize that within every people group there are subgroups requiring special evangelistic strategies. From the point of view of good evangelism, each subgroup, and finally each person, must be taken into account.

The cities of Japan, Korea, and Sweden are, except for foreigners in their midst, made up of people of one ethnic group speaking the same language. In such cities the sociological groupings become very important, for ethnic distinctions are virtually nonexistent. Christian workers will classify such urbanites on the basis of income, education, status in society, and possibly the neighborhoods in which they live. People with similar income levels might be placed in different groups if their occupations and lifestyle so warrant. The number of groups found will reflect the number of different churches needed to minister effectively to all of them.

Cities contain areas for the wealthy, the middle class, and the poor, although sometimes middle-class people are mixed in with the wealthy or the poor. While in Western cities the poor tend to congregate in the inner cities and those with means tend to flock to the suburbs, in the developing world these tendencies are often reversed. Those with means live in the central city not far from the downtown area, while the poor live in shantytowns built on the hills and in the ravines that surround the city. In the West the poor generally live in slums (formerly good housing that has deteriorated over time). There is slum housing in cities of the Southern World as well, but in addition there are shantytowns built by people who have recently moved to the city. The residents often experience upward mobility as they find meaningful work and as city governments, recognizing their existence, provide them with electricity, water, schools, and other services.

Many Southern World cities are experiencing chaotic growth, and shantytowns are multiplying. Alongside some upward mobility there is also desperate poverty. Fernando Silva Pontes, who is both a physician and a priest, reports concerning a shantytown of Itapipoca, a city of northeastern Brazil: "All they have is farinha and beans, and some mothers are too sick to supply milk. In one house a baby was crying and crying. The mother was in tears. I told her to give the baby milk, but she didn't want to and I almost forced her. And then I saw the baby suck blood from the mother's breast."[1] In *Companion to the Poor*, Viv Grigg describes his similar experiences as a Protestant missionary in a Manila shantytown.[2] (For case studies of Grigg's work in Manila and of efforts in a shantytown of Nairobi, see pp. 158–59, 163–65.)

These examples are mentioned to highlight the fact that in most of the metropolises of Asia, Latin America, and Africa, there are extensive residential areas for the very poor. These areas continue to grow rapidly as the poor are forced out of rural regions and into the cities. We must carefully plan our approach to this large group of people. Will we plant churches among them that cater to their ethnic origins, or is their poverty so pervasive that it is the chief determinant of the type of church which will arise in their midst? On-site research, city by city and area by area, is needed to determine the type of people group most significant to the poor and the shape of the church which will emerge among them.

In compiling a list of the people groups within a city, there is the possibility of including the same individuals twice: first as members of an ethnic group and then as members of some sociological group. For example, a person (P) might be viewed as a member of ethnic group Y and social group X (see fig. 11). To complicate matters further, P might also be a member of group Z, which intersects with the others diagonally. Group Z might be a veterans' organization, a mothers' group in a specific neighborhood, or a religion.

For the purpose of measuring the progress of the gospel, P should be regarded primarily as a member of ethnic group Y unless there are very good reasons for identification with a sociological group. In general we will assign persons to the group whose church we expect them to attend after conversion to Jesus Christ. But evangelistic strategies may differ widely, depending on people's interests and needs when they are first approached.

1. Prut J. Vesilind, "Brazil, Moments of Promise and Pain," *National Geographic* 171.3 (March 1987): 258, 360.
2. Viv Grigg, *Companion to the Poor* (Sutherland, Australia: Albatross, 1984).

Figure 11
People Groups Within a City

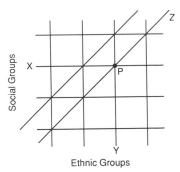

The City as Organism

The city is a gold mine. It has prominent ethnic (vertical) veins. It has prominent sociological (horizontal) veins. And it has other veins that run at will in all directions. This image is useful in helping us schematize and also simplify in our own thinking a complex evangelistic task. But there is yet another level of complexity to be examined. The city and its suburbs are more than a static entity to be charted in one way or another. The city is also an organism that is constantly on the move. This movement is not random like the movement of atoms within a molecule. It is concerted and interconnected, like that of an animal or a human body. Without losing sight of the intersecting veins, we need also to see the city as a giant organism pulsing with life.

As the first rays of sunlight stretch across the eastern sky, every city is like a giant arousing from deep slumber. In house after house, the lights go on. Soon the streets are filled with people on their way to work. As the sun rises higher, children make their way to school; trucks, trains, and airplanes ply their routes; and shoppers begin to crowd the markets and stores.

The various occupational groups that live in the city are dependent on one another. This interdependence might be called the essence of urban life. Teachers depend on cobblers to repair their shoes, who call on mechanics to repair their cars, who buy food from women at the market, who need nurses when they are sick, who are licensed by the government, which uses secretaries and computer operators to keep track of all its business. One could go on and on.

The point is this: urban life is the opposite of life in isolated and self-contained societies where virtually every member does *all* the tasks traditionally assigned to his or her sex. Urban life breeds interdependence whether urban residents like it or not.

In 1 Corinthians 12 and Romans 12 the apostle Paul compares the Christian congregation to the human body. Each member of the body has its own unique function that the other members cannot perform, be it seeing, hearing, talking, or walking. The members depend on one another and cooperate with one another so that the body achieves its goals. It would be ludicrous for the members of the body to fight with one another.

The congregation is an organism because all its members are joined to Christ and find unity in him. The city is an organism because all its residents depend on one another for their well-being. The city is an organism in spite of all the ethnic and sociological diversity described earlier in this chapter.

While evangelism must take urban diversity into account, spiritual care leading to growth in Christ must work for Christian unity. It can do so by keeping in view biblical passages like Paul's description of the church as a body. In addition, the very structure and interrelationships of the city can be used as a model for Christians of various ethnic groups and social strata to follow in developing spiritual interdependence. If there is interdependence in the workplace, surely there is need for interdependence within the body of Christ.

When one thinks of the city as an organism, one can't help noticing that most people who live in the city interact with one another through a web of interlocking relationships. This web of relationships is called a network by social scientists. The following account, which is a composite story drawing on my firsthand observation of urbanization in Nigerian cities, will serve to illustrate.

When George Aduku graduated from secondary school and did not pass the university entrance exam, he decided to go to a city in order to find work. He had an uncle living in Kaduna, over four hundred miles from his home. So George took a passenger truck to Makurdi and from there traveled by train to Kaduna.

When George arrived in Kaduna, his uncle and aunt welcomed him into their home and provided both food and lodging at no charge, because George was their nephew. The next day George went out looking for work. For an entire week he searched for a job. He could have taken temporary work cleaning up the market at the close of the day, but felt that such a job was too low-paying and demeaning for a high-school graduate. In any case, he was looking for permanent employment.

After one week, George's Uncle Samuel came home with good news. A fellow worker at the textile mill had told him that the ordnance factory in Kaduna would be hiring clerks and supervisors the following day. A cousin who worked in the personnel office would put in a good word for George if Uncle Samuel recommended him without reservation.

As a result, George Aduku found meaningful work in Kaduna before many others with the same qualifications. By the time he received his first paycheck, he had sensed that his aunt was growing weary of having him around the house and that it would be good for him to move into an apartment. A workmate from his own ethnic group invited George to move into the apartment he shared with another young man. Although this workmate was Catholic and George was Protestant, he felt that their shared tribal identity would prevent any problems.

George and his new friend were now both workmates and roommates. They sometimes played together as well, although George slowly developed other friends whose tastes in recreation were more similar to his. He began saving money for the time several years away when he would be able to pay the price for a bride from his ethnic homeland and bring her to live with him in Kaduna.

To accomplish his goals, George and his uncle made use of several networks. George started with the network already in place when he arrived in the city, his relatives. His Uncle Samuel in turn activated another network, that of his workmates. Once George had work, he also could use this network to find a place to live. And when he had a place to live, a third network emerged, that of his neighbors. From his workmates, his neighbors, and possibly other relatives in the city, he could develop his playmates, those with whom he pursued recreation.

Notice that we have already mentioned four networks: relatives, workmates, neighbors, and playmates. The members of George's church or his fellow believers might constitute a fifth network. The term *fellow believer* is used because if George were a Muslim, he might find help at the mosque rather than at church.

I was in the city of Zaria in Nigeria when a Christian man was hit by a triple tragedy. First he lost his job, and then his ten-year-old daughter died while his wife was in the hospital with a terminal illness. His wife was so sick that no one dared tell her about the death of the daughter. Fellow Christians rallied around the man; many attended the daughter's burial, at which I was asked to officiate.

When the wife also died, the Christian community put forth more strenuous efforts to help. One church member arranged for the wife's body to be kept refrigerated in the hospital morgue, while another, who was with the police force, used the police radio to notify relatives back home. This made it possible for them to arrive in Zaria in time for the burial. Generous gifts were also donated to the widower to tide him over until new work could be found. He had a network that sustained him in time of tragedy—the members of his church.

Such networks could be called homogeneous networks because the people involved in them have something in common. They are joined to one another by (usually) several webs of common interests and mutual benefits.[3] Donald McGavran wrote and spoke about "homogeneous units" and "webs of relationships" long before the term *network* became common among social scientists. Such relationships do not disappear in the city. In some cases they are strengthened there. The fact that they are informal and are often invoked in an ad hoc manner to deal with specific problems does not detract from their helpfulness.

Both flexible and productive, these networks can be used as an avenue for the spread of the gospel. People tend to trust those who are members of their networks not only for information about where to find work, medical help, or good housing at a reasonable price. They also lean on network members for advice on deeper needs, such as whom to marry, how to deal with marital problems, and how to handle depression. Among these deeper needs is one's religious allegiance. When people recommend Jesus Christ to other members of their networks, it is a potent endorsement.

Networks can facilitate the spread of the gospel within a people group. For example, Tiv people living in the cities of Nigeria have used their networks to spread the Christian faith. During the Nigerian civil war (1967–1970), many Tiv young men who had been involved in Christian work as laymen went off to join the army. In the army they continued to witness to their fellow Tiv about Jesus Christ, even though they now received no payment for this witness and no church was supervising them. Workmates (in this case soldiers) witnessed to their fellows and thus spread the gospel. The wives and children of married soldiers also became involved. And so the network of workmates was extended by adding a network of relatives. The result was the spread of the gospel among Tiv soldiers and their families both during and, most notably, after the war.

In addition, a network of workmates often becomes a bridge for the gospel to pass from one people group to another. When the Nigerian civil war was over, I spoke to Tiv soldiers and their families at the Rainbow Army Camp at Port Harcourt. Hausa-speaking soldiers were also present, and whatever I said in Tiv was translated into Hausa. Tiv soldiers who were Christians had told their fellow Hausa soldiers that a missionary was speaking in the army chapel that evening. They too

3. For a fuller discussion of homogeneous networks, see the June 1987 issue of the *International Journal of Frontier Missions*, pp. 45–52.

came to participate. Joint service in the Nigerian army created a bridge from one group to another.

But the same networks that serve as a bridge for the gospel can also present obstacles to its spread. Some people may hesitate to declare faith in Christ because they fear ridicule from others in their network(s). Others may fear the loss of the support of their network(s) if they make a firm Christian commitment. Or one might feel free to talk with fellow workers about Jesus Christ, but be reluctant to approach relatives, who may disparage anything to do with Christianity. Playmates might not disparage Christianity, but present so many tempting alternatives to the Christian life that the growing seeds of faith are choked.

Christian workers who recognize and understand these networks will wish to utilize them for the spread of the gospel, and will try to minimize any detrimental effects. They may also assist new Christians in finding new networks if this is necessary.

In addition to networks there are what Kenneth Little describes as "voluntary associations."[4] Voluntary associations differ from networks in that they are more formalized. They are organizations that one can join. By joining, one comes to participate in both the benefits and the obligations of membership. Little mentions tribal associations, mutual-aid societies, recreation societies, Christian clubs, syncretistic cults, and cultural societies, all of which seek to benefit both their members and others in various ways. Scholarships, funeral expenses, and civic improvement in the home area are among the common benefits provided by such associations. Although Little wrote about West Africa, evidence suggests that helpful voluntary associations are a worldwide urban phenomenon. Together with networks, they help to ease the stress of urban life and even to make such life enjoyable.

The church as an institution (formalized and organized under officers) is like a voluntary association; the church as the people of God out in the world is more like a helpful network of fellow believers. It is often difficult, however, to tell where the voluntary association stops and the network starts.

Discussion Questions

1. This chapter suggests that a people group is a collection of individuals whose distinguishing common traits and numbers warrant the

4. Kenneth Little, *West African Urbanization* (New York: Cambridge University Press, 1970); *Urban Life* (New York: St. Martin's, 1980), pp. 120ff.

establishment of a worshiping congregation just for them. In what other ways can a people group be defined?

2. For the city you know best, list the ethnic groups and social groups present and some of the more prominent networks and voluntary associations. What evangelistic efforts and churches are effective among these groups? How do you account for their success?

3. Give examples of ways in which your church functions as a network and as a voluntary association. How successful is your church in using these dual roles to reach other ethnic and social groups?

Research as a Tool for Evangelism

Timothy Monsma

Many groups are beginning to see the value of research for evangelism and church growth. This writer would not be surprised if several years from now, of a total worldwide work force of more than one hundred thousand cross-cultural Protestant missionaries, several hundred are involved in periodic on-location research in many nations. Research in cities will surely promote effective metropolitan evangelism and spiritual growth.

Research, says James Engel, is simply "the gathering of information for use in decision-making."[1] A glance out the window to check the weather before getting dressed is one kind of research. When Paul walked through the city of Athens and observed all the objects of worship (Acts 17:22–23), he too was conducting research. Most research is more complex than these two examples. But the principle remains the same: one gathers sufficient information so that intelligent decisions can be made.

In the first part of this chapter I will describe how I became acquainted with formal research in missions. Lessons I learned, both positive and negative, will be brought out. I will then more formally discuss the uses for and major steps in good research.

---

1. James F. Engel, *How Can I Get Them to Listen?* (Grand Rapids: Zondervan, 1977), p. 13. The entire text of Engel's book was reprinted in the classroom syllabus prepared by Harvie Conn and given the title *Urban Church Research: Methods & Models* (Philadelphia: Westminster Seminary, 1985).

Getting Started

I was a missionary teaching at a Nigerian theological college when I decided to pursue doctoral studies at a major seminary in the United States. I wrote to the dean, stated the topic on which I wished to write my dissertation, and asked if I could do the basic research for the dissertation while I was still in Nigeria. The seminary agreed to this arrangement and assigned a professor who had served in Africa to be my mentor. He was coming back to Nigeria for a visit. I met him in the city of Jos and discussed with him the form and method of the research to be done. I had in mind a study of eight major cities in Nigeria: Lagos, Ibadan, Port Harcourt, Enugu, Kaduna, Zaria, Kano, and Jos. There were people of the Tiv tribe living in all these cities, and I wanted to research their relationship (or lack of relationship) to Jesus Christ, to the church, to one another, and to other groups. Inasmuch as printed material about these cities was rather scanty, it was quickly determined that I would need to do considerable research from the bottom up.

My mentor suggested that I use questionnaires and assistants in order to gather information. Each assistant would be assigned to one of the cities and would ask four people presently living there to write an autobiography in an exercise book similar to, but longer than (about forty pages) the bluebooks used by American college students for writing exams. In addition, a professor of demography from Belgium who was on vacation offered valuable suggestions as to how I should gather information for my project. Among other things, he urged me to use more questionnaires than I had originally planned.

I visited the bookstore at the University of Lagos and purchased a small book entitled *Survey Research Methods for West Africa*.[2] While several books published in North America describe procedures for conducting a survey, certain standard procedures in the United States and Canada cannot be used in developing nations. The use of telephones or even telephone books is not appropriate in Nigeria, since such a small percentage of the population have their own phones. Street names and house numbers are often nonexistent. Other strategies must be used to gain a representative sampling of the people whose ideas and experiences one wishes to survey. In this respect the small book written for West Africa was very helpful and could prove helpful in many other cities of the Southern World as well.

2. Margaret Peil and David Lucas, *Survey Research Methods for West Africa* (Lagos: University of Lagos, 1972).

I selected eight of my students at the college and made arrangements for each one to do six weeks of field work in one of the eight cities that I had chosen for study. The synod of the Protestant Church Among the Tiv People, which I served as missionary, agreed to pay half the stipend that each student would receive if I paid the other half. My financial investment entitled me to give instructions to the eight students before they left on their assignments.

Each student was given two hundred schedules. (In the technical jargon of the world of research, a *schedule* is filled out by the researcher or an assistant, while a *questionnaire* is to be filled out by the informant.) On a school vacation I had pretested fifty such schedules in the city of Kaduna with the help of one of my students. I felt at the time that very few adjustments needed to be made on the original schedule. The people who were interviewed seemed to understand the questions and gave appropriate answers.

It was only after I was back in the United States to write up the results of my study that problems began to surface. The biggest problem was that I had asked too many open-ended questions for a study of this magnitude. When one is dealing with hundreds of schedules, one should be able to tabulate the answers systematically. If the question allows for, say, four possible answers, the results can be readily calculated by punch cards or computer. But an open-ended question allows for infinite variety in the answers. One must either divide the answers into categories and thus quantify them, or simply read them over to gain a general impression. Both solutions are time-consuming, and accuracy is difficult to achieve.

When the eight seminary students returned, their enthusiasm was almost as great as that of the seventy who returned to Jesus, saying, "Lord, even the demons submit to us in your name!" (Luke 10:17). The need to find two hundred ethnic Tiv to fill out two hundred schedules had forced them to get out among the people. The questions on the schedules provoked discussions with the Tiv people that otherwise might not have taken place. This gave the seminary students excellent opportunities to offer pastoral care on a personal basis, a rarity in many African cities. When all two hundred schedules had been filled out, some Tiv who had not been interviewed felt slighted. A couple of the student pastors got around this problem by duplicating copies of the schedules so they might conduct additional interviews. These students turned in close to three hundred completed schedules.

Neither were people hesitant to write their autobiographies. (Those who did were rewarded with a new hymnbook or a Bible.) In keeping with the Tiv inclination to be frank and open, many of them wrote very candidly about temptations that were too much for them and about other difficulties they were facing.

In reviewing the work of my assistants, I discovered a few problems. Some of them had used the forms as questionnaires rather than as schedules. That is, instead of conducting personal interviews, they had simply asked the people to fill out the forms. As a result, not all the questions were fully understood by all the respondents.

Another problem lay in the area of quota sampling. This involves dividing the group being studied into categories, and then interviewing a certain number of individuals in each category. The purpose of this is to make sure that all strata of the group have been reached.

I had instructed my assistants to interview about fifty people from each of four categories: women, church members, church attenders, and non–church attenders. Inasmuch as it was easier for the assistants to interview people who came to church, they were lax in finding people who did not. I'm sure such individuals were around, but they were harder for my assistants to locate. In this respect the completed schedules were deficient.

Personal Involvement

After I had reviewed the completed schedules and the autobiographies, I prepared to visit each of the eight cities personally. A professor from a Bible college in the United States had volunteered to teach my courses at the theological college for one semester. His coming enabled my wife and me to travel to the eight cities under study.

We began by spending several days in library research at Ahmadu Bello University in Zaria. By this I mean that we read all the books, periodicals, and other printed material available on our chosen subject. All research ought to begin by uncovering information that others have already reported. During the course of library research, one may also come across ideas to be checked out and hypotheses to be tested. I was able to locate some information regarding the history of every city on my list. However, there was little or no information in the libraries regarding the spiritual history and present religious status of these cities. My work was cut out for me.

When we went from city to city, we practiced the technique of "participant observation," although I didn't know the term at the time. Participant observation involves joining (or at least being physically present) with the subjects in all their activities in order to observe what they do and why they do it. In each city my wife and I requested lodging with the people we came to study. We did this partly as an economy measure and partly because we wanted long conversations with them in the evening. This tended to increase my work load, for many people came to me for counsel. But even the counseling sessions were a learning experience for me.

I had a notebook with a separate section for each city. I took notes whenever I could, sometimes in the presence of people and sometimes after they had gone. I also had with me a cassette recorder, which was used to tape the formal interviews I conducted. These were always held in the Tiv language even if the informant knew some English. I cannot recall that any Tiv person—even those who were not Christians—refused to participate in a taped interview.

Since I traveled to the eight cities after my students had been there, I was able to investigate tendencies which they had discovered but on which information was lacking. To compensate for a weakness in the schedules, I made a special point of interviewing Tiv who were not Christians. Then, too, the schedules from Enugu led one to believe that the only Tiv there were soldiers and their families. Upon investigation I found Tiv people working in the market and on the police force as well. In Kano I sold Tiv Bibles to the prostitutes with whom my assistant had been working. While we were in Kaduna, a child died, and I was asked to lead the graveside burial services.

Aside from what I had recorded in my notebook and on tape, many impressions were stored in my memory. These impressions still inform my thinking about urbanization in Africa. And when my memory fails, I consult my wife, who shared many of these experiences with me.

Organizing Data and Writing a Report

After two years of graduate study at an American seminary, it was time for me to write my dissertation. I needed to organize the data I had collected two years earlier. I was advised that this could be done on a computer or by way of punch cards. In those days personal computers were not yet in use. Since I was planning to move to another state, I decided to use punch cards, the principle behind which is similar to the binary system used by computers.

I had in my possession more than twelve hundred completed schedules. Each schedule allowed for more than fifty different answers. Thus I was dealing with more than sixty thousand variables. This was too much even for a doctoral dissertation. I began a process of cutting down. The questionnaires from Port Harcourt and Enugu were excluded because virtually all of them had been filled out by Tiv soldiers or their wives. A truly representative survey would include civilians as well as soldiers. (Later I decided to include Enugu in my dissertation, but without using data from those questionnaires.)

It had been my intention right from the start to use the quota-sampling method. But too few of the schedules returned to me were from non–church attenders. On the other hand, there were too many schedules recording the answers of church attenders. In order to eliminate the surplus schedules, I resorted to systematic random sampling. The idea here is that one surveys a representative sample of a larger unit. If the sample is truly representative, the researcher will have a good idea of what the entire unit is like. Pollsters use systematic random sampling to predict election results long before the election is held, and they are usually accurate.

But how does one know that a sample is truly representative of the entire unit? The first principle here is that the sample must be random. That is to say, a researcher must not select people simply because they are acquaintances or because they are ready at hand. If the selections are made on that basis, the sample will not be random nor the group truly representative.

The second principle is that the selection must also be systematic. Suppose a researcher decides to select at random a given number of names from one page of the telephone book. Suppose also that our researcher happens to open the book at a page of names beginning with the letters Van. "Van" is the Dutch word for "from." Most of those whose names begin with "Van" are of Dutch descent. If only people of Dutch descent are interviewed, the researcher will obtain the views of only one ethnic group in a city that comprises many ethnic groups. It would be better to say, "I'll select the fifth name on every page of the book." The choice of the fifth name is random; the choice of every page in the book is systematic.

In many cities of the world, however, most residents do not have their names in telephone books. Other means to obtain a systematic random sampling must be devised. For example, because there were far more schedules from women than necessary, I simply decided to choose every other one. I describe this procedure in an appendix to my dissertation:

> Even after the schedules from Port Harcourt and Enugu were laid aside, more questionnaires were on hand than were needed for a good sampling. In any city, therefore, where there were more than fifty schedules for one category (as women, attenders, men members), half of the questionnaires

were eliminated by a systematic random sampling method. In this way a little over 600 schedules were eventually used.[3]

Once the data from the schedules had been transferred to punch cards, I drew up twelve tables of statistics. On the basis of these tables, charts and graphs were prepared so that readers could visualize the information conveyed. The graphs were used in the dissertation, and later some were also used in the book *An Urban Strategy for Africa*.[4] Most people find tables of statistics very boring. But conversion of statistics into a bar graph, a pie graph, or a line graph will arouse the interest of readers and help them catch the point.

A good report does much more than present data in an interesting and readable way, however. It evaluates the data; it correlates numerical data with information gained in other ways (such as participant observation); it contrasts one city with other cities and one nation with other nations. It relates the information discovered to similar information obtained by others, and it evaluates the whole in the light of Scripture and biblical principles. In addition, if one is writing a report for a specific mission or organization, the report will likely contain recommendations for action on the basis of the information that has been brought to light.

I discovered that the discipline and labor involved in bringing all these elements together into one dissertation were good preparation for other projects that I would later undertake. Here in this type of creative activity, as in all of life, practice and experience enable a person to gain in speed and efficiency.

Uses for Research

Research is growing in popularity in the evangelical Christian community. Yet research means different things to different people. There are many different types of research and many different goals that a researcher might have in mind. In this section we will consider various uses for research.

3. Timothy Monsma, "African Urban Missiology: A Synthesis of Nigerian Case Studies and Biblical Principles" (Ph.D. diss., Fuller Theological Seminary, 1977), p. 399. For additional information on other sampling methods see Engel, *How Can I Get Them to Listen?* pp. 58–69.

4. Timothy Monsma, *An Urban Strategy for Africa* (Pasadena: William Carey Library, 1979).

Determining the Location for New Work

A church or mission may wish to open a new urban work but be unsure of which city to choose. Even if a city has been chosen, an agency may not be sure in what part of that city the work ought to begin. In either case, research may be necessary to resolve the problem.

My wife and I once traveled from coast to coast in Africa in order to survey six cities personally. The mission agency that sponsored this research wanted to compare these six cities in terms of missionaries and churches already present, unreached people groups, opportunities for witness to Muslims, opportunities for medical work, and the attitude of the national government. Eventually a city was chosen as a new site for missionary endeavor on the basis of my written and verbal report.

Research within the boundaries of a city is equally important. Because of the distribution of ethnic and social groups, a missionary or evangelist might find one area of the city resistant to the gospel, while another area might be very open. Research determines where the various groups are living and what their attitudes are, so that when the work begins, the workers know both the challenges and the opportunities they are facing.

Understanding the Audience

Who are these people to whom we hope to present the gospel? What are their present religious beliefs? What is their ethnic identity? What is their socioeconomic status? How do others perceive them? How do they perceive themselves? What are their rules of etiquette?

There are 101 questions that might be asked regarding a group with whom one hopes to work. As a general rule, the more answers one can find, the more effective one will be in working with the group. Research helps a person to avoid the pitfalls and to know what must take place in a society if its members are to embrace Jesus Christ as Savior and Lord.

While research is helpful for all Christian workers, including those who labor in villages and rural areas, it is especially critical in the city. Here the various groups live side by side and interact with one another during the normal course of urban life. A message that is appropriate for one group might be totally inappropriate for another group found nearby. Urban research promotes increased discernment so that the message of Christianity is communicated effectively.

Take, for example, the soldiers of the Nigerian army. Nigeria has a rather large army because of the civil war and its aftermath, and the need to assist in keeping the peace in other African nations. As noted earlier, many Nigerian soldiers are of the Tiv tribe. I made acquaintance with a large number of them as I carried out my urban research. Before I got to know these soldiers as individuals, I might have assumed that they were a tough group with little compassion for others and consciences that were dormant. If this assumption were correct, any Christian leader wishing to communicate Christian ideals to them would have to devise some very innovative methods.

Research revealed, however, that many Nigerian soldiers have both consciences which accuse them of past sins and compassion for civilians. They feel a need for assurance that God abundantly pardons all who repent. They also feel a need for guidance in facing the tough ethical choices that are bound up with army life. Equipped with this information, I knew what type of messages they needed to hear.

The research methods used were participant observation (including public question-and-answer sessions as well as private counseling) and short autobiographies. Participant observation disclosed the interaction of soldiers with their wives and other relatives. It revealed their desire for instruction in the Christian faith and for harmony among the various ethnic groups that make up the army.

The autobiographies, which were written in the Tiv language, spoke of the difficulties of trench warfare, the loneliness of isolation from friends and family, and the temptations that come to soldiers in such environments. One soldier wrote:

> During the time that we were there, one day I gave the women who were working with us some food. A girl saw me and liked me, and I didn't know it. When we were finished I went to where they sold beer. When I went there she and her sister followed, bought a soft drink and gave it to me. I asked her if we could return home together. She agreed quickly as if this is what she had been planning to do. My heart accused me but I was alone and I was young. There was no one to strengthen my heart. So I began to do much evil.

The autobiographies helped me to get behind the uniforms worn by the soldiers and understand their longings, their fears, their temptations, and their latent idealism. Church leaders in any part of the world could address the needs of their people with much greater precision if only they had similar autobiographies in hand. Research helps urban pastors to understand city life and the involvement of their people in it. Such knowledge in turn will improve their ministry.

Measuring the Effectiveness
of Evangelistic Methods

In a book entitled *The Master's Plan for Making Disciples* Win and Charles Arn report on a survey of how fourteen thousand Americans became Christians (see table 4).[5] There is a problem with this study in that it does not distinguish internal (or biological) growth from conversion growth. That the largest category ranges from 75 to 90 percent also causes one to wonder about the accuracy of the survey. Nonetheless, the report is worthy of attention in that it calls into question certain notions that many Christians have regarding evangelism in America. If only 0.5 percent of American Christians came to Christ through evangelistic crusades, including radio and television programs, these methods are much less effective than many think. The authors also suggest that networks of human relationships are more effective evangelistic tools than is generally realized. If nothing else, the publication of these survey results calls for further research either to verify or to disprove the impression they give.

Harvie Conn reports on research which reveals that numerous evangelistic films used in Africa are unsuitable because the viewers do not understand them.[6] He reports on Bibles mailed out and then promptly thrown away because the recipients are culturally conditioned not to value items that come in the mail. Research brought this situation to light. Research also discovered that comic books are effective with the average person in Brazil and Korea, while ordinary texts are not.

We cannot assume that our work is effective just because we love the Lord and want to do well. Research provides objective tools for evaluating the effectiveness of our work. Missionaries might receive a temporary shock early in their careers if research reveals that most of their work is going down the drain. But better for them to find that out early while there is opportunity for some mid-course corrections than to wait until retirement and then discover that most of their efforts were in vain. The principle of good stewardship as taught by our Lord does not allow us the luxury of closing our eyes to results and plunging ahead blindly.

Steps in Good Research

1. Establish Reasonable Goals

The goals of one's research should be written out and clearly understood by all concerned. Students should have their goals approved by

5. Win Arn and Charles Arn, *The Master's Plan for Making Disciples* (Pasadena: Church Growth, 1982), pp. 43–45.
6. Conn, *Urban Church Research*, p. 3.

Table 4
Agencies of Conversion

Special need	1–2%
Walk-in	2–3%
Pastor	5–6%
Visitation	1–2%
Sunday School	4–5%
Evangelistic Crusade or Television Program	.5%
Church Program	2–3%
Friend or Relative	75–90%

their professors, if at all possible, before serious research is attempted. In other circumstances, a church or mission agency may hire a consultant to research specific items on their behalf. If the two parties (the mission agency and the consultant) do not agree from the beginning on the goals of the research, disappointment may follow.

For example, a mission agency may be trying to decide in what city or neighborhood to open a new work. This calls for "geographical research," gathering data on specific locations. A consulting agency may, however, assume that it is being asked to study the culture of a people, including their religious allegiance. This is usually called "ethnographic research" by social scientists, although the research in a missions context is more specific than in most anthropological studies. The research methods, the number of personnel, and the time and money required will differ according to the goals in view.

The goals that are set should be a reasonable reflection of the time and resources available to do the job. If it appears that the goals may not all be met, they ought to be prioritized so that those that are logically first are tackled first. The other goals on the list can be addressed in a later study if necessary.

If a researcher discovers that a mission agency is unclear about its goals, the researcher can suggest various alternatives or ask questions designed to clarify the options. When clarity has been achieved, the researcher can proceed with confidence, knowing that he or she is gathering information that will be of value to the initiating body.

2. Design a Strategy to Achieve the Goals

When we know what our research is supposed to achieve, we can decide what type of research is needed. We can also decide about the personnel and time required. This in turn will have an impact on the funds that are needed. Wise planning will save time once we are on location. And common sense tells us that the more numerous and the more diverse the goals, the more difficult it will be to devise a simple strategy to meet them.

Geographical research begins with library and statistical study. The statistics may be found in books or be available from government agencies. Some government agencies may also have useful maps for sale.

Such initial research ought to be followed by interviews with Christian leaders if possible. They can explain where their people and their churches are located. By a process of deduction the researcher can gradually determine the localities (whether entire cities or sections of a city) where Christians are few and far between.

Prepared schedules are useful for interviewing Christian leaders, who are generally sympathetic with the researcher's goal. They will understand that the interview is not finished until the schedule is completed. Another advantage of using a schedule is that one obtains the same type of information from every person interviewed.

But if it is necessary to interview non-Christian leaders, it is generally best to leave the schedule at home or in the car. One can fill it in as soon as possible once the interview is over. Some of the information will be lost, but using a schedule or tape recorder might antagonize the respondent and terminate the interview prematurely.[7]

If one's goals call for cultural or ethnographic research, the methods used will probably vary from the suggestions given above. To study the culture of a people, including their worldview and their religious allegiance, one may wish to use research assistants. Research assistants in this context are people hired locally by a researcher in order to conduct a survey. They may be asked to interview people and fill in a schedule. They may be asked to distribute questionnaires, encourage people to fill them out, and then collect them. They may be asked simply to count or observe.

A very important part of ethnographic research is participant observation, described earlier in this chapter. Participant observation is especially important in the first stages of a project. It is beneficial while one is still learning the language or the vocabulary of the group under study. Participant observation will give the researcher relevant questions to ask in the next phase of research and may also help determine the right people to interview. Participant observation is most productive if arrangements can be made to stay day and night with the group being studied.

Participant observation should be followed by (and often blends into) informal interviews. An informal interview is a conversation with in-

---

7. For more information on using questionnaires in interviews see Engel, *How Can I Get Them to Listen?* pp. 71–93.

formants who may not be aware of their status as such. They may simply feel that the researcher is curious. In an informal interview, the informant does most of the talking and may also choose the subjects for the conversation, which takes place in casual situations like drinking a cup of tea, riding a bus, or watching a sports event. Sometimes the conversation is recorded by the researcher for later analysis, sometimes not.

Informal interviews are generally followed by more-formal interviews, which may have to be scheduled in advance. Researchers will likely come armed with a note pad or a tape recorder, and will ask questions about specific items that are on their agenda. The respondents for formal interviews must be chosen with care: in addition to time to spare, they must have knowledge on the subject and a forthright character.

Formal interviews can be used to test the hypotheses that researchers developed during participant observation and informal interviews. Michael Agar puts it this way, "There must be a set of responses that informants can give that prove you wrong."[8] One's ideas can be tested by persuading a few informants to act out a simulated situation, to comment on a hypothetical state of affairs, or to complete a sentence. The accuracy of hypotheses is best checked with informants other than those who provided the information in the first place.[9]

3. Do the Research on Location

The best research is done on location. Barring accidents or other unforeseen developments, the researcher who has prepared carefully will likely find such work challenging and enjoyable. Most people are willing to talk, and some will even go beyond the call of duty in order to help.

Perhaps the most annoying problem that one encounters while on location is the language barrier. While some developing nations use English as their national language, others use French, Spanish, Portuguese, or something more obscure to us. Even in those nations that use English there are often numerous vernaculars, and many people know a vernacular better than they know standard English. This requires patience. It may sometimes be necessary to ask a respondent to repeat a question to make sure it has been understood. Using interpreters is not ideal, but may sometimes be unavoidable.

8. Michael H. Agar, *The Professional Stranger: An Informal Introduction to Ethnography* (New York: Academic, 1980), p. 133.
9. For additional helpful suggestions see James P. Spradley, *The Ethnographic Interview* (New York: Holt, Rinehart and Winston, 1979).

In nations where Christians are a small and persecuted minority, researchers may have to go about their work very discreetly. I know of one group of researchers who walked through a Muslim city with no tablet or other recording device in hand. Because of government hostility they recorded their impressions only after they had returned to their rooms. It is advisable to inquire about government regulations and then abide by them as much as possible.

4. Draw Up an Evaluative Report

The final step in good research is to draft an analysis of what has been achieved. Student researchers will write up their report under the guidance of their mentor. But those who do research by contract or under some other sponsorship may be given considerable leeway in preparing their reports.

The report should be long enough to cover the subject but not so long that it becomes tedious. Interesting details that would make good copy for a promotional brochure will not necessarily impress busy mission executives. They will expect the report to get to the point and demonstrate to them how the goals of the research project have been achieved. In case any of the goals were left unaccomplished, a brief explanation is appropriate.

A good report will not only present the data; it will also analyze the data and bring out the conclusions to which they lead. In this connection, charts and graphs can be very useful. A report which thus draws together the pertinent information in concise and arresting fashion, evaluates it in the light of Scripture, and comes up with concrete recommendations will prove invaluable for urban evangelism and church planting.

Discussion Questions

1. How do you reconcile the planning and devising of a strategy of research with the desire to be yielded to God's sovereign will?
2. American missionaries are sometimes accused of skewing their God-given task by using too much business expertise and pragmatic techniques. Is this a valid argument against research?
3. What sorts of strategic errors can prior research help a missionary to avoid? What sort of errors are beyond the scope of research?

The Stages
of Church Development
Timothy Monsma

Some missionaries fail in the city because they have no specific plan of action. Whether one is working alone or with a team, one must have a strategy in mind. It is wise to put this plan down on paper even if the missionary is accountable to no one else. This will help to define goals and to plan the way in which these goals will be met.

If missionaries are working together as a team, the need to put the plan in written form is beyond question. Such a step will prevent or settle disagreements as the strategy unfolds. In fact, many mission boards require their missionaries to develop their strategies in this way.

This chapter will outline the stages in the birth and development of urban churches. The guidelines presented are general and will need occasional adjustment because individual cities differ and the developing churches within them will differ from each other too. Four stages of church development will be considered: preliminary groundwork, formal organization, the small church, and the large church.

Preliminary Groundwork

Most cities are so large and diverse that any attempt to evangelize an entire city at once will lead to great frustration. In the city there are many different people groups. One must decide first of all which of these groups is to be the object of one's efforts.

140

Choosing a Specific Group

One of the goals of research as described in chapter 11 is to assist missionaries and evangelists to make wise choices regarding the group to which they will direct their attention. It is necessary to make these choices in all missionary work, but in the countryside they are simplified because the people of a specific ethnic or social group tend to be concentrated in a geographical area. In the city, on the other hand, the various groups are intermingled with one another. Many neighborhoods have a mix of ethnic and social groups. People of different ethnic groups may work side by side in the same factory or the same store. Informed discernment is needed first to delineate the groups and then to choose the group that will become the object of ministry.

In choosing a people group with which to work, one should ask what kind of church will develop as the people of this group turn to the Lord. Will it be a self-sustaining church, or will it be continually dependent on outside help because of the extreme poverty of its members? Will it be a church with capable leaders, or will there be an absence of leaders?

Let us say, for example, that a person decides to work only with street children or only with prostitutes. Will a church consisting only of children be viable? Can they be ordained as church officers? Can former prostitutes be ordained as church officers if the sponsoring mission feels that only men should be ordained? Although street children and prostitutes are very real subgroups in many societies, they are not people groups in the sense that we ought to establish congregations just for them. Biblical congregations are always made up of men, women, and children; and there are no special advantages in departing from this pattern today.

In other words, the group with which a person decides to work should be large enough to include both sexes and all ages. With this in mind, one might designate all the street people, all those engaged in antisocial behavior, or all the poor in a given area as the group with which to work. If one chooses to concentrate on witnessing to a subgroup, they should be funneled into a larger homogeneous fellowship as they profess their faith in Christ.

Studying the Group

The rule of thumb, as suggested in chapter 11, is to begin with library research. There is no point in rediscovering what someone else has already discovered. Foreign missionaries can sometimes begin their research even before they leave their home country. Library research can also be done in the city in which they intend to minister. Government and university libraries will probably prove the most helpful for this type of work. Journals should be consulted as well as books. Local newspapers may afford valuable data about the group chosen and should be scanned daily for helpful bits of information.

The next step is to become involved in participant observation with the chosen group. The best approach is to actually live with the people. This gives the advantage of twenty-four-hour contact. It also eliminates the need to invent an explanation for each visit. Some experts go as far as to contend that only those who are willing to live among the urban poor can work effectively with them.

There is no doubt that taking up permanent residence in the area is the most desirable way to work among the urban poor, and some missionaries do so with great success. But not all missionaries are able to live on a continuing basis among the very poor. It may, for example, necessitate voluntary celibacy or postponement of childbearing for married couples. Even those who advocate permanent residence recognize that it is difficult for Westerners to raise a family in the midst of a shantytown or slum where childhood diseases are endemic and violence is near at hand. In addition some missionaries have chronic health problems before they leave for work overseas. Insisting that such individuals live permanently among the poor might force their return to the relative safety of home.

Those who find it impossible to live permanently among the poor can still be involved in participant observation. Some may be able to live temporarily among the poor. Married couples may choose to take turns living among the poor: one spouse is free for full-time work while the other stays with the children in another part of the city. Missionaries who have some special service to render, such as medical help or vocational training, may commute daily and still be welcome.

Missionaries who say that they have come to a neighborhood in order to observe the people will likely receive a negative reaction. But those who say that they have come to learn the language, to render a service, or even to sell something that the residents desire, will likely be received with a minimum of questions. The announced reason for their presence will result in a measure of acceptance, even though their hidden agenda is participant observation. In such cases, participant observation will advance to informal interviews as the missionaries get to know the people and an atmosphere of trust develops.

Addressing Needs

All people have two kinds of needs: those they feel and those of which they are unaware. Their spiritual needs often fall into the latter category. It may be very plain to an evangelist that a person's most profound needs are spiritual, yet that person may be oblivious to them. He or she may be concentrating entirely on certain specific physical needs, or possibly some emotional ones.

Good missionary strategy begins with the needs that are felt or admitted, and gradually works from them to the deeper needs that have often been repressed. Jesus worked this way with the woman at the well in Samaria, and we can learn from his example.

Among some groups there is such hunger for the gospel that one can begin rather directly with its verbal proclamation. With other groups, however, there is resistance to the gospel for various reasons: the audience may be deeply involved in another religion, the occupations or lifestyle of the audience may be at variance with Christian morality, or the audience may take a secular view of all religions because of communistic or some other ideology.

In dealing with resistant groups, it is especially important to begin with felt needs. Felt needs can be addressed in a verbal message. I once spoke to a group of Nigerian soldiers a few months after the conclusion of the Nigeria-Biafra civil war. Some of them had used their guns to kill civilians as well as soldiers. They felt an overwhelming need for forgiveness. In another situation a Nigerian seminary student who spoke to prostitutes quickly realized that their felt needs were not just for forgiveness, but for a way out of the bondage in which they found themselves.

It is said that there are more conversions to Christianity in Iran under Ayatollah Khomeini than there were under the shah. Khomeini's tactics have caused people to feel a need for peace, harmony, and forgiveness. They perceive that Christianity offers these blessings and are attracted to it.

Often the felt needs are physical, and acts of charity are required to meet them. But Christian charity ought not to be practiced simply to gain a hearing or to attract converts to the Christian faith. It should be available to all who are in need even if there is no sign that it will lead to conversion. While Christian charity begins with the household of God, it does not end there. It is universal in scope.

Medical needs and the desire for academic or vocational training are commonly felt in both the rural areas and the cities of the developing world, but the problems of unemployment and underemployment are especially acute in the city. While governments become involved in huge development projects—many of which fail to accomplish their goals—Christians can be involved in a meaningful way by encouraging and enabling small-scale businesses. This addresses the problem of unemployment and also the need for a self-sustaining church as the number of believers increases in a given locality.[1]

Announcing Conversions—The Need for Caution

People who see the power of Christ at work in the lives of God's children often become interested in the Christian faith. A conversation about spiritual matters may lead to the decision to follow Christ. At this point care must be exercised. Rural people are connected to family and neighbors by a web of relationships, and urban residents are involved in similar networks. Questions ought to be asked about the impact of conversion on the various networks in which the new Christian is involved. When the hazards and the potential are clearly understood, the path to follow will also become clear.

Premature public declarations of the desire to follow Christ may shut new believers off from the others in their networks. In highly closed societies they might have to flee for their lives or they might even be killed before there is a chance to flee. In more open societies new Christians might simply be ostracized so that an effective barrier is raised between them and the people who might benefit from their witness. A new Christian may also become fainthearted and return to former ways. And so while commitment to Christ must be encouraged and the work of the Holy Spirit in a person's heart must always be given full recognition, the missionary or evangelist must be highly sensitive as to how and when a person's conversion is best made public.

Utilizing Home Meetings

A key factor in planting new churches is the home meeting. In some cases home meetings will precede conversions. In other cases they will begin after one or more commitments have been made. Usually these meetings are held in the home of a new or potential convert. In cities where receptivity to the gospel is high, the group of interested individuals might be so large right from the start that it is not possible to use a home. In such cases other facilities must be found. Even so, there is value in home groups. The largest church in the world, pastored by Paul Yonggi Cho in Seoul, South Korea, makes extensive use of home groups. They are often the only means for Christians in a very large church to get to know other Christians in a personal and intimate way.

---

1. Wayne Medendorp has written a brief and helpful guide on this subject—"An Urban Strategy for Addressing Unemployment and Underemployment in the World's Urban Centers" (Grand Rapids: Christian Reformed World Relief Committee [2850 Kalamazoo S.E., Grand Rapids, MI 49560], 1985).

Home meetings are especially useful when the group is too small to merit hiring an auditorium or the people do not have the funds to build a church. The chief activity is a study of the Bible. This is helpful both to potential converts and to new Christians who wish to grow in their faith. Other activities may include singing, praying, and sharing of needs.

Formal Organization

Three Options

Believers need nurture and fellowship with one another. Home meetings serve to fill these needs. But these groups should be encouraged to evolve into a congregation or a more formal fellowship of believers. What shape should this organization take? Three options come to mind.

The first option is to work toward the planting of congregations with their own church buildings and the other ecclesiastical trappings seen in most Western nations today. The second option is to promote house churches with little structure or church government and no ordained church officers. The third option is a compromise between these two extremes. For example, one might encourage house churches in conjunction with a central church that meets once a week or once a month. One might also advocate the ordination of church officers provided they do not receive a salary.

The New Testament evidence points in the direction of flexibility. There were house churches, or at least home meetings, from the early days of the church in Jerusalem onwards (Acts 2:46). Evangelistic meetings were held in homes (Luke 19:1–10; Acts 10:24–48; 16:32–34). The Epistles contain references to the churches in various houses (Rom. 16:5; 1 Cor. 16:19; Col. 4:15; Philem. 2).

On the other hand, Christian gatherings were not limited to houses. The Christians in Jerusalem continued to meet in the temple (Acts 2:46). Paul was content to use synagogues until he was thrown out. After he withdrew from the synagogue in Ephesus, he used the hall of Tyrannus (Acts 19:8–10). When forced out of the synagogue of Corinth, he chose to use the house of Titius Justus, located right next door; this indicates that he would have preferred using the synagogue (Acts 18:4, 7) if that had been possible. And, too, the "upstairs room" (Acts 20:8) used by the church in Troas must have been much more than a bedroom in a private residence.

In regard to the ordination of church officers, there are many examples and commands scattered throughout the New Testament. It is more difficult, however, to demonstrate from the Scriptures that these officers worked full-time at their assignments or that they were paid for their work by the church. The evidence is mixed. Paul made tents, but he and many others certainly used far more than their spare time to promote the gospel.

Persecution: A Milieu for House Churches

In recent years house churches have thrived in Communist China. The number of Christians there has grown from a few million at the time of the Communist takeover to more than fifty million today—largely because of house churches. House churches are useful in all lands where Christians are a small and persecuted minority, for instance, in Muslim countries. They often escape the attention of officials, and governments find them difficult to control. House churches also eliminate the need for heavy financial investments in places where Christians are poor or the future of the church is uncertain.

But house churches are not the perfect answer for every Christian need. They encourage the rise of lay leaders who may be skilled at witnessing to those outside the faith, but who lack the background to instruct new believers. Whole areas of Christian truth may be neglected by them, and misinterpretation of Scripture is a real possibility. Many house churches in China have faced this problem, which is made worse by the fact that Bibles and Christian literature are scarce there.[2]

Inasmuch as the New Testament approvingly describes both large assemblies of believers as well as small assemblies in private residences, Christians today ought to consider using both. The mix and the emphasis will depend on the circumstances. If the number of Christians is large and persecution is minimal, the primary emphasis will be on large assemblies. But if the number of Christians is small or persecution is intense, small assemblies and house churches will likely prevail.

Adoption of house churches as the primary form of Christian fellowship should not in itself preclude the selection of leaders. Even a service in a house requires someone to be the master of ceremonies, so to speak. And while house churches deemphasize structure, it is desirable that they be linked to one another in at least a loose confederation. A federation of house churches is able to provide for the training of leaders and teachers. It is significant in this connection that although house churches were used rather extensively in New Testament times, there were still the apostles, the evangelists, and other ordained offi-

2. See David H. Adeney, *China: The Church's Long March* (Ventura, Calif.: Regal, 1985), pp. 158–60.

cers in the church. Contemporary churches in all nations ought not abandon this model unless persecution forces a group to abandon it on a temporary basis.

Facing Hostility

The issue of persecution raises the question, How should the church deal with hostility? The word *hostility* is used here in a broad sense. Persecution is the outward display of hostility. But people often have hostile attitudes toward Christians without allowing these attitudes to develop into overt persecution. Those who harbor such hostility may be thereby prevented from seriously considering the Christian message as a message for them, and may be motivated to try to block the advance of the gospel in subtle ways that fall short of outright persecution.

In some areas those who are turning to Christ are mainly from the younger generation. This may enlarge a rift that is already present between them and their elders. Older persons may feel that life is falling apart because children no longer respect the ways of their parents and others who have gone before.

Young Christians can do much to preclude a rift of this sort by continuing to respect their parents and other elders. It should be remembered that Peter instructed Christian wives to be submissive to their pagan husbands as a means of witness to them: "Likewise you wives, be submissive to your husbands, so that some, though they do not obey the word, may be won without a word by the behavior of their wives, when they see your reverent and chaste behavior" (1 Pet. 3:1–2 rsv). If the faithfulness of wives can be used to win pagan husbands to the faith, surely the faithfulness of children, even those already out of the house, can be used to influence their parents or others of the older generation.

In some situations, of course, complete submissiveness is impossible because it goes contrary to Christian principles. A Christian employee may be asked to demand a bribe from those with whom the firm does business. The understanding is that the bribe will be split between the employee and employer. Though aware that it is wrong, the Christian employee may feel that the boss must be obeyed in this matter because failure to comply will mean loss of the job.

Innovative Christians may be able to find functional substitutes for that which they, for ethical reasons, cannot do. They may be able to do their work so well that the employer simply cannot afford to do without them. Thus the quality of their work substitutes for the immediate financial gain that might come from bribes. Or, because of their Christian connections, they may be able to bring to the firm business that would otherwise go elsewhere.

On the other hand, Christians may at times have to confront the powers of evil head on, as Gideon did when he tore down the altar of Baal (Judg. 6:25–32). This type of encounter is hazardous for Christians. They may end up in prison, as Joseph did when he refused the temptations of Potiphar's wife (Gen. 39:6–20). But in time God may honor them as he did Joseph. Even if they suffer martyrdom, it should be remembered that martyrs' blood has often encouraged church growth.

Another method of dealing with hostility is deeds of kindness to the poor and helpless. Christian kindness made an impression in the Roman Empire in ancient times and is making an impression in certain Muslim lands today. Mission organizations often serve as vehicles through which local Christians can both meet immediate crises and establish development projects to meet long-term needs.

Last but not least, the power of prayer to overcome hostility must be remembered. The early Christians used prayer to overcome Jewish hostility (Acts 4:24–31). Stephen prayed for those who were stoning him (Acts 7:60), and a short time later Saul was converted. Prayer is also a powerful weapon in the hands of Christians in mainland China today. It has often opened the hearts of reluctant city officials so that rallies could be held, property obtained for building churches, and broadcast time made available on local radio and television stations.

The Small Church

In Western nations parents often tell each other, "Enjoy your children while they're young. They will grow up before you know it." These parents know that the teenage years can be turbulent. Teenagers often discover a conflict between the subculture of their peers and the subculture of their parents. While on the one hand they wish to assert their independence, on the other they are financially dependent and lack emotional stability. There may be conflict over moral issues as well. Yet parents want to see their children grow. So they accept the problems of adolescence as part of the maturing process.

Missionaries and evangelists may have similar feelings in regard to the groups of believers they have nurtured. As the groups grow, problems emerge. But these problems are a necessary step on the road to maturity. Let us look at some of them.

Language

Language differences are usually not a serious problem in rural areas because ethnic groups tend to cluster. A church in a given area will use the language of that region. In the city, however, various language groups are often intermingled. Several different languages may be spoken by the members of one church. Which language ought to be used for church gatherings, and how does one satisfy those whose language is not selected? If the missionary decides at the outset to work with a single language group, the language problem in its severest form can be prevented.

But in urban congregations the language problem often comes in another form. A congregation that uses the language of a given ethnic group often finds, with the passage of time, that the children and young people prefer to study and worship in the national language of the country. This may be a language of European origin or an indigenous language that is promoted by the government.

The best way to handle this situation is to have two services in the same building, one using the ethnic and the other the national language. The services may be held concurrently or at different times. Joint services ought to be held from time to time to express the unity of the congregation. At such joint services both languages should be used. It is also important that representatives from both language groups serve on the administrative councils of the church.

Leadership

It is usually not difficult to determine who ought to lead a group of Christians. Leaders naturally emerge as a program develops, and the local believers themselves will tell the missionary whom they trust and who can provide the type of leadership they need. An informal election is thus taking place.

The question of adequate training for such leaders is more difficult. The New Testament emphasizes the need for study of the Scripture and for instruction in the Christian faith, especially for those who are leaders (James 3:1; 2 Tim. 2:2). How can such instruction be given in an urban environment? One possibility is Theological Education by Extension (TEE). The initial goal of TEE was to train Christian leaders in their home villages rather than in a boarding school in the city. Yet TEE is also an excellent method for training lay leaders who live in the city. If the city is large, the instructor might teach in a different section of the city three or four evenings per week.

TEE has a distinct advantage over correspondence courses in that the weekly meeting allows emerging leaders to encourage one another.

Direct contact between teacher and student is also desirable for both parties. Other possibilities for instructing lay leaders such as evangelists, elders, and deacons are week-long educational retreats or weekend seminars.

Most missions and churches still prefer traditional schooling for those who seek ordination to full-time leadership positions. TEE depends on Bible schools or seminaries to anchor its program. By teaching in these institutions many missionaries have given fruitful service long after their other duties have been phased out. As soon as church planters in urban areas begin their work, they should ask how leaders will be trained. They cannot expect the work to prosper unless provision is made for this key ingredient.

Finance

A problem that many missionaries face is the extreme poverty of urban Christians. Coupled with this problem are (1) the danger of establishing a relationship of continuous dependency, and (2) the high cost of urban property and buildings, which often precludes a permanent edifice for the church.

The early Christians of Antioch and Corinth showed concern for their poorer brothers and sisters in Jerusalem by sending them financial aid. These gifts flowed across ethnic boundaries from Gentiles to Jews and fulfilled Paul's command to show charity "especially to those who belong to the family of believers" (Gal. 6:10). It is fitting today that Christians in wealthy nations follow this example and show concern for fellow believers in the poorer nations. This aid should be given in such a way that it attacks the root of the problem, not just its symptoms. Many urban-shantytown residents who are receptive to the gospel are poor because they do not have the skills and the training to obtain meaningful work. To give them food, clothes, or money, or even to build them a church edifice, does not attack the root of the problem.

To attack the root, one must assist the urban poor in finding meaningful, adequately paid employment, either working for someone else or managing their own small businesses. They need practical vocational training. Their children may need schooling, for many city governments do not provide schools for shantytowns. Some urban poor may need a loan in order to begin a small business. Notice that the suggestions given here do not foster continuous dependency, but are intended to help people to help themselves. They are in basic agreement with the principle that a truly indigenous church is, among other things, self-supporting.

A major obstacle faced by urban Christians in their bid to be self-supporting is the steep prices for property and buildings. Poor people in rural areas can often build their own church structures. In many parts of Africa, rural land is free for those indigenous to the area. But in the city, land must be leased or purchased, often at an exorbitant price. Even middle-class Christians in many cities of the developing world struggle with this problem. Sometimes an old building can be bought at a reasonable price and renovated for use as a church, but in the city there are often building codes to contend with. If a church is built in a shantytown so that it blends in with the rest of the neighborhood, this problem may be avoided. House churches may also form a temporary solution. But sooner or later, a permanent and respectable structure will likely be desired and needed.

Some missions have established revolving loan funds to be used by city churches in obtaining land and erecting buildings. The churches are under pressure to repay their loans—if they don't, others will not be able to borrow from the fund. This appears to be the best solution to the problem of land and buildings.

Another solution that is sometimes helpful is for a church or mission to obtain land in a newly developing area while the price is still reasonable. In some areas the land may be free if dedicated to religious use. Once the land has been obtained, efforts to build a congregation can begin, using private homes or rented facilities as need may require. If a congregation does not develop, the land can always be sold or donated to another group. But in most cities where even a modest amount of church growth is taking place, this rarely happens.

Relationships Between Church and Missionary

When there are only a few scattered believers in a city, they usually enjoy good relationships with the missionary or missionaries. But when the number of believers grows, tensions often develop. There are several reasons why this happens. If the missionary has a higher standard of living than do the other Christians of the city, there is often jealousy, which may show up in arguments over things not directly related to the perceived affluence. There may also be misunderstandings because the culture of the missionary is different from the culture of the new Christians, especially if there is a language difference as well. Moreover, there is the question of how soon a church ought to be self-governing, and there are differing perceptions of which sins are really serious and call for confession and which sins are less serious and ought simply to be overlooked.

There are several ways in which these problems can be prevented or solved. Missionaries (or evangelists) should strive for a simple lifestyle.

While they and their families want to be comfortable, healthy, and happy in their work, they surely do not need to display wealth in order to achieve these goals. And whatever good things missionaries do have ought to be shared with their fellow Christians in appropriate ways. Church leaders should always be welcome in the home and at the table of a missionary family. The missionary who has a car should be willing to take the church leaders to meetings. Indeed, all those with whom the missionary has contact can benefit from the use of the car in emergencies, even if this means taking a sick person to the hospital in the middle of the night. People can live with some variation in standards of living, provided missionaries do not hoard all their good things to themselves.

Missionaries must also be ready to relinquish control as the church develops. As soon as there is a small group of Christians and worship services are held, a steering committee ought to be chosen to assist the missionary in making decisions. The members of the committee will thus gain valuable experience. Once the church has been formally organized, the missionary can still advise, but must be ready to accept the decisions of the ruling body. Pastors in Western nations don't always agree with their elders, deacons, or congregations on specific issues; they must nonetheless live with these decisions or seek another church. The same applies to missionary pastors overseas.

In any case it is often wise to move missionaries around from time to time. We see much movement by the apostles and evangelists in New Testament times and considerable movement by pastors in Western nations. This custom might be effectively followed in non-Western cities. When people know each other too well, certain annoying habits or tendencies may hinder fruitful relationships. And a missionary who is new on the job in a given city will be less likely to take charge than one who has been there for many years.

Many problems are caused by the overassertiveness of the missionary, but occasionally it may be necessary to take decisive action. While ever respecting the opinion of fellow Christians, the missionary may have to mediate when they fail to agree among themselves. Sometimes a pastor who has arisen from among the people becomes dictatorial and is resented. Here the missionary may be needed to mediate between the pastor and the congregation. Missionaries should also be alert to protect the rights of minorities and the underprivileged within the church, who might be neglected by the majority.

If there are church leaders from within the country who can serve as mediators, it is usually preferable for them to handle disputes. Sometimes, however, missionaries are the mediators of choice simply because they are from outside the country and may view matters more objectively. I lived in Nigeria during the troublesome days preceding the Nigeria-Biafra civil war. Other missionaries and I tried to mediate on the local level as certain problems developed. One pastor later suggested to me that mission organizations should have tried to mediate on a grander scale, and that such mediation, if successful, might even have prevented the war and all its waste and bloodshed. Who is to say whether he may not have been right?

The Large Church

If the Lord prospers his work in a city, small churches will grow into large churches. But how large ought a church to be? Is it better to have one large church for an entire city or several smaller churches scattered throughout the city?

The New Testament Model:
A Two-Tiered Structure

During the first century the Jews met every Sabbath in their synagogues. Synagogues were also used for instruction in the faith during the week. In addition to the synagogues there was the temple in Jerusalem, at which sacrifices and other rituals were performed under priestly guidance. The synagogues emphasized instruction, while the temple emphasized communion with God through worship. The practice of Jewish religion, then, had a two-tiered structure.

The practice of the Christian faith in Jerusalem also had a two-tiered structure. The early Christians often gathered in Solomon's Porch (Acts 5:12), which was part of the outer court of the temple. They also gathered in private homes: "And day by day, attending the temple together and breaking bread in their homes, they partook of food with glad and generous hearts" (Acts 2:46 RSV).

It appears that the practice of the Jerusalem church spread to other cities as well. In his farewell speech to the elders of Ephesus, Paul mentions that he had taught them "publicly and from house to house" (Acts 20:20). Moreover, Paul addressed many of his letters to the church or to the body of Christians in a given city, but in these same letters he makes reference to the churches (or congregations) in people's houses (Rom. 16:5; 1 Cor. 16:19; Col. 4:15; Philem. 2).

It is important to recognize that in New Testament times it was not a matter of having either house churches or one large church for the entire city, but of having both types of churches concurrently in the same city. That the Greek word for church (*ekklēsia*) can more accurately be translated "assembly" or "congregation" allows us to view the smaller churches as subdivisions of the large church in a given city.

The Value of Flexibility

The New Testament gives the impression that, within certain limits, there was considerable flexibility in the organization of the early church. R. C. H. Lenski, in his commentary on Hebrews 10:32–34, argues strongly that there were two churches in Rome, one primarily for Gentiles and the other primarily for Jews.[3] If this is so—and I agree with Lenski—each of these ethnic churches may have been subdivided into various house churches or synagogues scattered around the city.

The flexibility in the organization of the New Testament church will serve us well as we ask about the ideal for city churches today. When the government bore down heavily on the church in Communist China, only the house churches survived. As the pressure eased, the house churches excelled in evangelism, and today the great majority of Christians in China are in the house-church movement. At the same time, China watchers have observed weaknesses in the house churches: a lack of qualified leaders and difficulty in forming a network of relationships between the churches.

House churches are presently forming in certain Muslim lands as well. These churches may in time experience the same weaknesses as do their counterparts in China.

At the other end of the spectrum are the superchurches with thousands of members. It is easy for a person to be a member of such a church and remain anonymous. Any specific problems experienced by such an individual will go undetected by the leadership of the church. In such cases, small-group meetings or house churches in which the participants get to know, trust, and sympathize with one another are crucial. Some churches have tried to alleviate the problem by forming groups that cater to people in specific circumstances, such as unmarried adults, the widowed and divorced, and the handicapped. But it is, of course, impossible to create groups that address every need, especially if the needs are spiritual.

What about the medium-sized churches—churches with one hundred to four hundred adult members? Such churches are too large to be called house churches, yet they are small enough that the pastor knows all the members by name and they also know one another. It may not

3. R. C. H. Lenski, *Interpretation of the Epistle to the Hebrews and of the Epistle of James* (Columbus: Wartburg, 1956), pp. 362–67.

be necessary to subdivide the congregation into smaller groups, but a few group meetings geared, for example, to young adults or to people who have recently migrated from a rural area to the city, are highly desirable. In this way the medium-sized congregation will be able to combine the various strengths of small and large churches.

Discussion Questions

1. What factors influence the form a new church takes? What are the essentials for a worshiping Christian community regardless of structure?
2. Of the four stages of church development mentioned in this chapter, which one is the most difficult for the average missionary? Why?
3. In what ways can a missionary's cross-cultural perspective be of help to a new church? What guidelines should missionaries establish for themselves to be sure that their counsel is not culturally, but biblically based?

13

Great Models
from Three Continents
Timothy Monsma

Do the principles set forth in the previous chapters really work in practice? Who has tried them, and how have they fared?

In this chapter we will take a quick tour around the world. We will visit cities on three continents to observe what God has done through his servants in the past few years. As we move from continent to continent, we will observe very large churches as well as smaller ones. We will see what they have in common and where they differ.

Expanding Urban Churches in Asia

The Yoido Full Gospel Church (Seoul)

The Yoido Full Gospel Church began in Seoul in 1958 under the leadership of Paul Yonggi Cho. Starting with just a few members, today this church is the largest church in the world with a membership of over five hundred thousand. What is the secret of this rapid growth? Can it be copied by pastors and churches in other parts of the world? To answer these questions, let's examine three factors that have encouraged the growth of this church and then consider the flexible structure that promotes its continued advance.

First of all, the Full Gospel Church is growing because it was established in the midst of a responsive population. Many churches are growing in South Korea. The largest Presbyterian church in the world is also found in Seoul. This is the "fullness of time" for Korea; indeed, if a Korean church is not growing, we ought to ask what is wrong.

In the second place, the Full Gospel Church is growing because of prayer. God has prepared the Korean people to be responsive to the gospel during the latter decades of the twentieth century. God will also assist his servants to gather in his harvest as they, through prayer, acknowledge their dependence on him. Paul Cho is a man of prayer, and he has encouraged his people to pray with him. He has built grottos on a hillside called Prayer Mountain. In one year 630,000 people came to pray at this sanctuary.

Cho stresses the need for prayer to overcome the problems of destitution and illness. He cites many examples in which prayer has made a difference. One wonders, however, how he and his people deal with "unanswered" prayer, that is, situations in which God's answer is either postponed or negative. We can assume, for example, that many South Korean Christians are praying for political stability in their nation and freedom in North Korea, but at this writing God has postponed granting a favorable answer. On this point those of us who are not charismatic (Cho is mildly charismatic) feel that we are more realistic than those who report only favorable answers while ignoring the unfavorable ones. At the same time, we all must acknowledge that our God is a God who hears and answers prayer, and if we desire churches to grow, we must be praying daily.

A third factor that contributes to the rapid growth of the Full Gospel Church is the compassion displayed for the needy by its members. They don't just pray for people in need; they do what they can to help them. In the 1950s Seoul was devastated by the Korean War. Poverty was endemic. *Ora et labora* ("Pray and work") became the unspoken motto of Cho and his followers as they took steps to relieve the suffering of those around them. The physical display of concern for others made a deep impression on many. Then and there the church began to grow, and that growth has been sustained ever since.

When structures grow, they can easily become top-heavy and eventually fall under their own weight. So far, the Full Gospel Church has avoided such a crisis. The organizational structure of a central church combined with numerous house churches or cell groups allows the congregation to continue growing at the fringes without becoming ossified at the center.

When in 1964 Cho's church grew to about two thousand members, he was overworked. One Sunday he collapsed on the platform. During his recovery he decided to promote home meetings as a means for pastoral care and evangelism. Eventually these groups met in locations other than homes as well. The meetings are led by deacons and deaconesses. (Church elders may also be involved, but Cho does not mention them in this connection, possibly because there are only fifty elders and more than eighteen thousand weekly cell meetings!)

The cell movement began under the leadership of deaconesses. Cho struggled with the question of female leadership from the point of view both of biblical directives and of Korean culture. A careful reading of Scripture alleviates much, if not all, of the problem. Paul writes, "Let your women keep silence in the churches" (1 Cor. 14:34 KJV). Cho contends that what Paul has in mind are assemblies of the entire church in a given area (1 Cor. 14:23). Silence in these large assemblies does not preclude speaking or leadership in cell meetings.

Cho deals with 1 Timothy 2:11–12 by encouraging women to teach other women. Meetings of men, on the other hand, are to be led by men. The basic principle here is that the cell groups are homogeneous while the church as a whole is heterogeneous. It includes people of all ages, sexes, and socioeconomic strata.

There is a vigorous system of training for cell leaders. Cho is himself in charge, offering weekly "personal" training to all eighteen thousand cell leaders by the use of videotapes. He also makes reference to a school where they are instructed.

While the cell groups meet during the week, the entire church gathers at a central location every Sunday. Ten thousand people jam the auditorium for the seven services held each Lord's Day. Thousands more watch by closed-circuit television in adjacent rooms. Even then it is evident that not all members make it to church every Sunday. But the Full Gospel Church is doing what it can to minister to a very large flock.[1]

Santa Maria Christian Fellowship (Manila)

Viv Grigg, a bachelor from New Zealand, had a vision to plant a church among the very poor in a shantytown of Manila. He found a couple of rooms in a shantytown which, to protect those who found the Lord through this ministry, we shall call Santa Maria. After staying in Santa Maria for three months Grigg was joined by a dedicated Filipino couple, Jan and Milleth Paragas. The three of them lived and worked in the squatter settlement. They initiated Bible studies for people enslaved by gambling, drinking, thievery, and prostitution. Acceptance by the community did not come overnight. Grigg and his companions had to earn respect with patience and kindness. They prayed for those who were sick and demon-possessed, and they witnessed cases of remarkable deliverance.

Grigg saw the dire need for employment, both for the unemployed

---

1. See also Paul Yonggi Cho, "Reaching Cities with Home Cells," *Urban Mission* 1.3 (Jan. 1984): 4–14; idem, *More than Numbers* (Waco, Tex.: Word, 1984).

and for those caught up in sinful pursuits. A system was developed by which revolving loans were made by a diaconal committee to assist people in initiating their own small businesses on the street and to promote small-scale cottage industries with products for sale outside the shantytown. Ninety-five percent of the loans were repaid.

Slowly a fellowship of believers began to emerge. Filipino middle-class Christians and other missionaries came to assist. Four years after Grigg completed his book *Companion to the Poor*[2] and left the area, a fellowship of seventy-five to one hundred believers has survived; it is called the Santa Maria Christian Fellowship. The middle-class leaders who became involved are now establishing churches for poor people in other squatter areas.

The Santa Maria fellowship experiences one continuing problem—the lack of leadership from among the poor. It is difficult to find strong church leaders among those who in their past lives have given in to temptation time and again. Yet without strong leaders from their own group new Christians cannot be stabilized in the faith and may fall away. Furthermore, management skills are not well developed among the poor. An additional factor is that Christian leaders who are adept at bringing others to faith in Christ may not be adept at leading a flock of more than one hundred believers. The problem of leadership in Santa Maria is similar to the problem encountered by Ray Bakke in his work among the poor in Chicago. We trust that in time God will lead to an acceptable solution.

Although problems remain, the experience of Viv Grigg in Manila holds several lessons for us: (1) It is possible for a Western missionary to live and survive in a shantytown of the developing world. (2) There are potential Christians in such locations; they are waiting for someone to show the way. (3) When Christian witness is combined with economic help, human betterment results. (4) There is a great need for people to give their lives to the task of training leaders for Christian movements among the urban poor, who constitute 40 to 50 percent of Asian cities.

Expanding Urban Churches in Latin America

Lima al Encuentro con Dios (Lima)

A Christian and Missionary Alliance Church was begun in 1958 in central Lima with twenty-five members. The congregation purchased an old mansion on a major thoroughfare to use as a church building. An

2. Viv Grigg, *Companion to the Poor* (Sutherland, Australia: Albatross, 1984).

evangelistic campaign that doubled the membership of the group in its early years was forgotten until 1970, when a number of events led the church to step out in faith with a renewed evangelistic program.[3]

When the congregation decided to enlarge their building to a seating capacity of five hundred, an American businessman persuaded them to enlarge to a capacity of one thousand. An evangelistic program named *Lima al Encuentro con Dios* (LED—"Lima Encounters God") was initiated. Ten years later over thirty-five thousand decisions for Christ had been recorded, and membership in the Alliance churches of Lima had grown to over five thousand.

Fred H. Smith lists the factors contributing to this growth:

1. The entire church program was geared to evangelism. Sermons, classes, and church organization all had evangelism in mind.
2. Prayer cells were formed to pray for blessing on the evangelistic efforts. Prayers were offered while evangelistic services were in progress and were terminated only when the prayer warriors were needed to counsel new Christians.
3. Provisions were made for sound leadership. A pastor was called from Argentina, and later a Bible institute was founded to train Peruvian nationals. Experienced evangelists were invited in to lead the campaigns.
4. Two weeks of evangelistic campaigns alternated with two weeks of instruction for new converts. A Bible academy was established at which six to eight courses leading to church membership were offered.
5. All church members were asked to get involved. This drove some members away, but those who remained became a powerhouse for good, and the church took in many more members than it lost.
6. Highly visible, attractive church buildings were encouraged. It is a fact that many people simply aren't interested in house churches or storefront churches.[4]

In addition, there were various issues that had to be faced lest they inhibit growth. First, the church had to deal with financial problems. It takes money to bring in evangelists, to teach new converts, to erect buildings, and to hire pastors for new congregations. Much of the start-up money was donated by Christians from another country. It was

---

3. Fred H. Smith, "Growth Through Evangelism," *Urban Mission* 1.1 (Sept. 1983): 19–28.
4. Ibid., pp. 21ff.

donated with the understanding that it either be repaid or reinvested in new projects in Peru. Thus money from outside sources became (for the most part) a revolving fund that was used again and again. While this arrangement did not free the Lima congregations from all financial worries, it did provide enough money so that the expansion could continue.

Secondly, the church had to provide for sound leadership. Although sound leadership was cited as one of the factors contributing to growth, more than once the entire project was in danger of foundering because of a lack in this area. When the quality of leadership that was needed could not be found within Peru, the church obtained first a pastor from Argentina and then four other pastors from outside the country. When over sixty newly converted young people expressed the desire to carry the gospel to others, the Alliance Bible Institute, which was not part of the original plan, was founded. In time this Bible institute furnished the indigenous leaders needed for the movement to prosper.

Thirdly, middle-class Christians had to find a way to bridge the gap between themselves and the poorer classes of Lima. Smith observes that churches sprang up in lower-class barrios such as El Agustino, La Tablado, San Juan de Dios, and Comas. The move into these barrios was facilitated by the financial support of the middle-class church. One wonders if the middle-class churches did not provide most of the leaders as well.

While evangelistic campaigns have been held in many cities, LED proved particularly successful because commitments to Christ were followed by pastoral care in the classes of the Bible academy. And good pastoral care was possible first because the churches went outside Peru to find new pastors, and secondly because a Bible institute was founded to train national pastors.

Mission to the World (Acapulco)

Somewhat later than the efforts in Lima just described, missionaries from the Presbyterian Church in America (PCA) initiated work in the rapidly growing city of Acapulco. This project placed greater emphasis on a cluster of congregations, which in the Presbyterian system is called a presbytery, than was the case in Lima. Consequently, the individual churches in Acapulco are smaller, although the leaders in the movement are optimistic about future growth.[5]

It all began in 1978 with a small church of nineteen members and

5. Richard Dye, "Church Growth in Acapulco: Planting a Whole Presbytery," *Urban Mission* 3.3 (Jan. 1986): 34–39.

about fifty attenders. When the pastry chef of the most prestigious hotel in Acapulco (the city has been built around tourism) turned to the Lord and gave a sterling testimony, numerical growth increased markedly. By the fall of 1980 there were about two hundred members. By 1984 Richard Dye and the other missionaries on the Acapulco team were ministering in nine preaching centers to almost one thousand people. Pastoral training through Theological Education by Extension (TEE) was also well under way.

By 1987 two of the preaching centers had been closed, but of those remaining, three had become organized churches. A presbytery was officially established in 1989, with ordained pastors for the young congregations. The missionary team left Acapulco in 1988.

The Acapulco project has certain distinctive features. Mission to the World, the PCA's mission arm, began the effort by sending a team of three couples and two singles to work together in Acapulco. Their assignment was to plant several churches which could be formed into a presbytery with its own officers within a few years. It was thought that the team members could strengthen one another for the work, and, in the end, the goals would be achieved more rapidly than if each missionary was working alone. To sum up the distinctive features of the project:

1. A team of missionaries was sent to accomplish the work.
2. This team planned to withdraw from Acapulco and go on to church planting elsewhere within a specified period of time.
3. The team's goal was a cluster of churches called a presbytery rather than one large central church.
4. The missionaries regarded leadership training (largely through TEE) as a key to the success of the project.
5. The target audience was the middle class. Hotels were used for special meetings and sometimes for weekly worship services.

Although there were problems, Mission to the World was so pleased with the results that Acapulco became their model for what they wished to do elsewhere.

The fifth feature of the Acapulco project calls for additional comment. The majority of migrants to the cities of the developing world are very poor. They live in the shantytowns that surround the cities. They are often receptive to the gospel. It has proven difficult, however, to build up self-sustaining and self-governing churches among them. Accordingly, Mission to the World has chosen to target middle-class citizens and eventually to use them to minister to the needs of the poor. They project a church made up of middle-class and poor people, with the middle-class members placing their gifts and resources at the disposal of the poor. Richard Dye explains:

> We reason that if the gospel can penetrate the richer classes with the biblical teaching concerning justice, compassion, and concern for others, then the middle and upper class believers will use their positions of power and influence to change the way things are done in the city. They will remove the abuses and support the ministries that will help the poor. . . . The skills and resources of the middle and upper classes, once they have been committed to Christ's cause and kingdom, will be of great value in ministering among the poor and establishing churches.[6]

Not all Mission to the World missionaries in Acapulco, Nairobi, or elsewhere are convinced of the wisdom of this approach. However, the trickle-down theory of urban church planting appears to be working: two of the congregations formed in Acapulco are in the poor sections of the city. More experience and more case studies are needed before an approach emerges on which there is general agreement.

Expanding Urban Churches in Africa

The Redeemed Gospel Church of Mathare Valley (Nairobi)

Founded by the British in 1899 as a depot for the Ugandan Railway, Nairobi became the capital of Kenya in 1905. Its present population of 1.6 million is expected to swell to 4.9 million by the year 2000. At an elevation of 5,600 feet, its temperate climate has attracted many international organizations, including church and mission agencies. Although 11 million Kenyans identify themselves as Christians and there are over 750 churches in Nairobi, there is still room for more. Some sections of the city have no churches whatever.

In contrast with mission experiences in other cities, two respected writers have encountered difficulties in maintaining house churches in Nairobi. J. Philip Hogan speaks of up to twenty people crowded into "dimly lighted rooms about 8 feet by 10 feet in size."[7] Jimmy Maroney is more explicit: "In East and West Africa, the typical African desires to worship in the conventional western-type church building. They will meet in a house or a community building for a short period but expect

6. Ibid., p. 39.
7. J. Philip Hogan, "The Assemblies of God in Nairobi, Kenya," in *Guidelines for Urban Church Planting*, ed. Roger S. Greenway (Grand Rapids: Baker, 1976), p. 40.

to move into a more conventional church within a few years. In the house churches we started in Nairobi, this was a continuous problem."[8] Even in the shantytowns of Nairobi, house churches are not recommended. The houses—if one can call them that—are small, and the crowds are large, almost right from the start. By contrast the Redeemed Gospel Church of Mathare Valley is an example of the type of approach which does succeed in the poverty-stricken areas of the city.

Although Nairobi might be called the tourist mecca of East Africa and parts of the city compare favorably with many American cities, about one-third of the population live in squatter settlements or shantytowns. Of the various shantytowns on the outskirts of the city, Mathare Valley is "the largest, filthiest and most crowded." The population of Mathare Valley (over 100,000 according to the 1979 census) "survives almost entirely through prostitution and illicit brewing of alcohol."[9]

The Redeemed Gospel Church began a ministry in Mathare Valley in 1974 with seven adherents. By 1982 the congregation had six hundred members, with another three hundred attending a branch church in another part of the valley. The charismatic orientation of the Redeemed Gospel Church does not prevent its members from taking a hard look at physical needs and specific social problems. The church ministers to the whole person as a demonstration of Christ's love. While not regarded as bait to catch converts, the church's social ministry has influenced many in their decision to follow Christ. An example of such concern could be seen the morning after a fire in Mathare Valley had spread quickly from shanty to shanty, rendering ten thousand families homeless. With help from World Vision the church distributed blankets, cooking utensils, cooking oil, flour, and milk. Later, building materials were supplied which were not as flammable as those that had burned so rapidly.[10]

As in Manila, the churches of the poor in Nairobi need more leaders and self-sufficiency. A few Western organizations are working with local Christians toward this goal. Construction of churches has been financed by a fund from the Netherlands. World Vision is assisting people in their search for respectable work, and eventually they may be self-supporting. It appears too that leaders are developing in the

8. Jimmy Maroney, "Urban Ministry in Third World Cities: Three Examples. Nairobi," in *An Urban World: Churches Face the Future*, ed. Larry L. Rose and C. Kirk Hadaway (Nashville: Broadman, 1984), pp. 126–27.

9. "Relationship Between Evangelism and Social Concern," interview with Wilson Kiilu, in *African Pulse* 15.2 (Aug. 1982): 2.

10. Joseph Machunn, "A Kenyan Remembers," *World Vision* 28.9 (Dec. 1984–Jan. 1985): 10–11.

churches of the shantytowns, as the members of the younger generation from these areas pursue formal education to prepare for Christian
service.

In Acapulco the strategy has been to build churches among the middle class, who in turn can help the poor. In Nairobi the middle-class
Redeemed Gospel Church has established a branch in Mathare Valley
and poured in time and resources with help from Western agencies.
They have been able in this way to assist a larger number of poor people
faster. But are they creating rice Christians in the process? The emphasis on helping people to help themselves would seem to minimize this
possibility. The Nairobi experiment is worth watching in order to observe what permanent benefits emerge.

The Tiv Church (Kaduna)

Kaduna was founded by the British as a military encampment on the
Kaduna River in 1912 and became the capital of the Northern Region of
Nigeria in 1916. The city really began to grow only after the Second
World War, when it became the headquarters of the Nigerian army as
well as the home of several textile factories and other industries. By
1972 Kaduna had a population of one hundred fifty thousand. Today
three hundred thousand would be a more accurate figure.

While there are several Protestant churches in Kaduna, this study will
focus on what is popularly known as the Tiv Church.[11] This group of
Christians began as a congregation within the union church in Kaduna,
which consisted of all churches established by the various branches of
the Sudan United Mission. Whereas most of these churches worshiped
in the Hausa language, the group we will be considering used the Tiv
tribal language. The group gradually drifted apart from the others until
1970, when it struck out on its own. By 1977 there were fifteen hundred
adherents worshiping in nine different locations throughout the city. By
1987 there were over two thousand communicant members in two organized churches, each with its own pastor. We will describe the development of the Tiv Church in Kaduna up until the time that it split into two
congregations.

There are four distinctive characteristics of the Kaduna church that
may serve as models for others, at least in Africa (for not all models
apply with equal validity in every part of the world):

11. Most of the material in this section arises out of the author's doctoral research—
"African Urban Missiology: A Synthesis of Nigerian Case Studies and Biblical Principles" (Ph.D. diss., Fuller Theological Seminary, 1977). A summary of the dissertation is
found in An Urban Strategy for Africa (Pasadena: William Carey Library, 1979). The
author last visited Kaduna in 1985, staying for two nights in the home of the pastor.

1. *The Tiv Church was completely self-supporting from the start.* Many missions have a revolving loan fund to assist their city churches; some will roof a building if the people will put up the walls. But the Sudan United Mission gave no financial help to Tiv city churches. (It would take us too far afield to delve into all the reasons for this official policy of neglect.)

Being without funds from outside sources, the Tiv Christians contributed toward building the union church. Then they left and erected their own building in another section of the city. The majority are middle class by African standards. They hold meaningful jobs in the city. The men among them have gone to primary school, and some have gone further. In their view, a person with no schooling might as well stay on the farm because he cannot better his lot by moving to the city.

These middle-class Tiv Christians gave sacrificially to build their own central church that could seat about eight hundred people, several branch churches in other parts of the city, and a parsonage for the pastor, whom they fully supported. It is noteworthy that, like the Tiv Church, many African independent churches are city churches, and they, too, not only survive, but often prosper without external funding.

2. *The Tiv Christians established a central church and several branch churches.* Whereas the Yoido Full Gospel Church in Korea has a central church and cell groups, and the emerging Acapulco presbytery is composed of several smaller and equal congregations, here in Kaduna we see a third possibility. Specialists in church government would call the Kaduna arrangement a collegiate church because, until it split, it was governed by one council of elders. All the members of the Tiv Church in Kaduna, regardless of what branch church they ordinarily attended, were invited to come to monthly meetings on a designated weekend of the month. These monthly meetings were usually held at the central church. Having one ordained pastor for the entire city, one council of elders and deacons from throughout the city, and the monthly meetings tended to promote unity among the various branches.

It is obvious that the one pastor could lead only one of the nine services on a given Sunday morning. So the Tiv Church, following the example of its rural counterparts elsewhere in Nigeria, made extensive use of lay leaders. Evangelists and elders were freely invited to lead the various services, and this they gladly did without financial remuneration.

This arrangement also solved the transportation problem. To have to come to one central location every Sunday would have been a burden for many members, for although they were middle-class by African standards, most did not own cars. They would have had to rely upon public transportation which could prove costly and time-consuming to a family. Almost everyone, however, could reach one of the branch churches on foot or by bicycle not only on Sunday, but also during the week.

The pattern of a central church and branch churches continued even when the church split in two. Now there are two central churches, each with its own pastor and several branches. Although the strict collegiate pattern is no longer followed in that there is no longer only one central church for the entire city, a looser collegiate arrangement is still in effect.

3. *The church has remained culturally indigenous.* The language used for worship and instruction is Tiv, as are the musical instruments that accompany the singing—drums, chimes, and rattles. City dwellers who rub elbows with people from many different cultural groups during the week feel that they are back home as soon as they step inside a Tiv house of worship, for everything used in the service (Bibles, songbooks, liturgy, etc.) is identical to that used in their home church.

The Tiv Church in Kaduna, therefore, has tremendous potential for evangelizing the Tiv in the city who are not yet Christians. As a matter of fact, a majority of the members of the Tiv Church had not known Christ as their Savior until they were attracted by this cultural oasis in the city. It's a place where the homesick can feel at home. Even Catholics are attracted to these Protestant services, for the local Catholic services are interethnic and do not use the Tiv language.

But that which nicely equips this church to evangelize and disciple other Tiv also prevents it from evangelizing Nigerians of other tribes. Recently a sister church in the city of Jos began to sponsor worship services in English as well as in Tiv. The purpose is to reach the intellectuals who may prefer to worship in English, and also to reach out to other Nigerians who are not Tiv. This does not solve every problem, for many Nigerians do not know English well enough to worship in it. But this is at least a step in the right direction, and someday other Tiv urban churches, including Kaduna, will follow the Jos example.

4. *The Tiv Church in Kaduna handled the land problem with foresight and ingenuity.* In his discussion of Nairobi, Jimmy Maroney mentions the high cost of property and the virtual impossibility of obtaining a grant of land from the government.[12] House churches do not solve the problem, for Africans have come to expect to worship in public buildings, not private homes. By contrast, during the 1970s the Tiv Christians of Kaduna wisely used their ethnic and social networks to acquire land for religious purposes. We have already mentioned that

12. Maroney, "Urban Ministry," p. 126.

many of the Tiv who move to cities become policemen or soldiers. The uniforms they wear can sometimes be used to advantage to get things done without the payment of bribes. In this particular case, a Tiv government official who was Catholic helped his Protestant brothers to obtain the land on which the central church and parsonage now stand.

The history of the preaching center called Television (the name derives from a television transmitter located nearby) is especially interesting. In 1974 the Tiv Christians learned of plans to build a Peugeot plant in southern Kaduna. They knew that the area would be growing rapidly. Anticipating the building boom, they obtained a plot of farmland at a fraction of what it would have cost them later. The Peugeot plant was built, and so was the branch church called Television.

Many urban churches in the developing world do not have friends in government circles who can assist them in obtaining land at reasonable prices. They may need help from missionaries or other outsiders. Innovative solutions must be sought. The possibilities include buying old buildings and renovating them for use as churches, using a houseboat for worship, or meeting in the open air until the funds for erecting a building can be obtained. It is vital that the church find some means of quickly establishing a presence in burgeoning areas, as the Tiv Christians did in southern Kaduna. Quick action is necessary not only because land prices will rise rapidly, but also because the people who will soon move there are the most likely to be open to the gospel.

Discussion Questions

1. What are the benefits of a church the size of the Yoido Full Gospel Church? Is a church this size feasible in all contexts—in shantytowns, for example? Why or why not? How might the model be adapted?
2. What social and economic factors cause the ideal size of a church to vary from culture to culture and from city to city?
3. In your opinion, what ideas and models contained in this chapter are the most helpful for the spiritual and numerical growth of churches in metropolitan areas?

The Urban Poor in "Christian" America

Roger S. Greenway

My experience living among the working poor in a North American city has intensified my distress that among middle-class Christians discussions about the poor generally bog down at the level of principle. The debate usually focuses on the relation between evangelism and social action and right priorities in Christian ministry.

In many ways, that is yesterday's dilemma, a question based on a theological perspective that has been properly rejected by many evangelicals. Needed right now are creative strategies to minister to the urban poor in North America in ways that combine evangelism, church planting and development, and effective long-term relief of the conditions that haunt the poor. These strategies must have theological integrity, which means that biblical scholars and street workers must begin talking to one another. So often we seem to work on opposite ends of the block.

In chapter 4 I dealt with the question of evangelism, relief, and development, giving special attention to the Southern World and its enormous numbers of poor people. In this chapter I intend to discuss the subject of the urban poor in so-called Christian America, the part of the world from which most evangelical missionaries come and where hard lessons have yet to be learned concerning ministry among the poor. If we do not learn these lessons here, I doubt that we will do much good among the poor in other parts of the world.

I am extremely concerned about North America and the attitude of most middle-class Christians toward the poor. On the other hand, in some circles it seems that the conscience of the church has been pricked, and more attention is being paid to the poor. But there are also danger signals, and the progress of recent years seems to be slowing down as a new wave of religious and social narcissism is emerging.[1]

How deep does the concern of middle-class North American churches for the urban poor really go? I include in this question all churches, Protestant and Catholic, charismatic and evangelical, and congregations of all races. Do Christians really want to engage in the kind of ministry that might bring the urban masses storming through their church doors? Or is this frontier of missions, the frontier of the urban poor, too wild and forbidding for the church to enter with more than words and gestures?

I want to raise some tough issues. Who are the poor, and why do their conditions persist? Where are the poor—are they only in Addis Ababa, Calcutta, and Mexico City? What can the Christian poor teach us about God, faith, perseverance, and discipleship? Are there chapters in theology that no textbook contains because traditional scholars can't write them? How do middle-class churches appear to the poor? Are there good reasons why they avoid them? How is the biblical concept of the kingdom of God understood in a slum? Might the "neighborhood of God" convey the same truth better?[2]

Classifications of the Urban Poor in North America

Who are the poor in American cities? Compared with New Delhi, Santo Domingo, and Lima, Western cities seem wonderfully free of poverty. Except for the bag ladies and vent people, the welfare system appears to be working quite well. But appearances are relative and they can be deceiving.

According to the government's official definition of poverty, there are approximately thirty-five million poor in the United States. There

---

1. A danger signal which struck home to me occurred in San Francisco in December 1983 at the four-day conference called "Christ and the City" sponsored by Inter-Varsity Christian Fellowship. Approximately one thousand young people attended, and many of us who were there rejoiced that genuine holistic concerns were expressed by speakers and workshop leaders. But a disturbing thing happened at the conference. Of the fifty-three urban issues around which sessions were planned, sixteen had to be dropped because of lack of interest. Most of the dropped subjects had to do with urban social problems. They included unemployment, immigrants, the elderly, drug and alcohol abuse and treatment, the poor, racial prejudice and its consequences, urban health problems, and public welfare ("San Francisco A.M.," a bulletin of Inter-Varsity's Conference on Christ and the City, December 27, 1983).

2. Philip Morris, "Mission and the Poor—Some Further Agenda," *Gap* 1 (1983).

are another twenty to thirty million people who have incomes that place them above the official poverty line but are insufficient to raise them to a level where they cannot reasonably be called needy. The fact that a nation as rich as the United States has so many poor people is a social and moral scandal that cannot be ignored.

It should be pointed out that the poor fall into several different categories. First, many people are poor because they are physically or mentally incapable of working at a normal level. Many others are in the category of the working poor. They are employed, but as a result of poor education, low skill levels, or racial factors, they do not earn enough to rise above poverty. The third group is relatively small (though middle-class Americans often regard it as the largest group), consisting of the lazy people who would rather survive on welfare than find a job and go to work. The fourth group is growing rapidly, especially among blacks, and it bodes ill for the future. It consists of women who are heads of households with dependent children. Without Aid to Families with Dependent Children (AFDC) they would be in a perilous condition. Then there are the elderly poor, often found in old, depressed neighborhoods, who have only Social Security and small pensions to live on. Finally there are people who are poor because of alcohol or drug addiction or some other self-destructive lifestyle.

While writing this chapter, I took a break to walk my one-hundred-pound Rottweiler in the park near our home in Philadelphia. Three black boys came along and stopped to admire the dog. After making sure she was friendly, they started to ask questions: "Man, she's big . . . could she kill a pit bull? How often do you feed her? Once a day, twice? What kind of food does she eat?" The questions mostly had to do with food, and as the boys moved away I heard one of them say wistfully, "Man, I bet she never goes hungry."

What kind of boys were these? From appearances they were not poor. They wore good jackets and shoes. But being from this neighborhood, they probably were acquainted with periodic poverty. Folks around here fall into and out of poverty. Their situation at any given moment depends on unpredictable employment opportunities, conditions at home, and the avoidance of emergencies that drain resources.

These were black boys; in America 30 percent of the poor are black. In large cities some 40 percent of black children come from homes where mothers are single parents. Even when someone in the family has a job, wages are usually low. Without a wage earner, welfare is an off-and-on thing. Therefore, the boys probably had good reasons for asking me about the food my dog ate and for admiring her girth and shiny coat. On a day-to-day basis, she very likely eats better than they do.

The number of new poor is a growing worry for many Western cities. Homeless people are flowing into urban areas at an increasing rate. Some are transients between jobs and soon will be reabsorbed into the economy. But various signs indicate that many of them will become a permanent part of the urban landscape. They can be seen by the thousands in most cities of Europe and Great Britain, and their numbers are swelling in America. The unique characteristic of the new poor is that they come from all walks of middle- and working-class life. Most of them once held jobs and lived respectable lives. But because of changes in the economy and other factors, their lives fell apart. Now they are waiting in line at soup kitchens, sleeping in rescue missions, and reinstituting a social class once famous in France, *les miserables.*

Poverty in Terms of Human Loss and Suffering

Who can estimate the amount of human suffering in the city and the dreadful loss of human talent and potential? The list of problems with which the poor must contend is endless. Among the most serious: unemployment, or underemployment, with all its dehumanizing consequences; poor housing, or no housing at all; lack of good food, sanitation, medical services, and quality education for children.

The poor depend on public transportation, but this is often costly and unreliable. The systems are designed primarily to serve the upper classes and seldom meet the needs of the poor. Where there is poverty, crime is rife, which combines with violence to produce fear and insecurity. Worse perhaps than the physical suffering is the mental and emotional anguish, the sense of helplessness in the face of overwhelming problems.

The Bible and the Poor

Charles Troutman once observed that it is extraordinarily difficult today for Christians to be biblical with regard to the poor. North Americans, on the one hand, find it almost impossible to understand either the massive poverty of the Third World or the teaching of the Bible that the chief cause of poverty is oppression, not laziness or underdevelopment. Christians in the Third World, on the other hand, are tempted to rely too much on the only current ideology apparently sympathetic to their tragic condition, Marxism.[3]

What we need is a biblical theology of wealth and poverty untainted by the popular biases of either the political left or the right. What does it mean to think as a Christian in a world polarized between capitalism and communism with a vast number of poor people caught in the middle? The cause of Christ is not served by naively adopting the slogans of either side, nor by the faddish exegesis of certain biblical passages.

Two things stand out in my mind as needing clarification. First, the Old Testament has a great deal to say about the poor, and a careful examination of the Hebrew words translated "poor" reveals a much wider meaning than we might have expected.[4] The poor are those who are forced into submission, reduced to subservience—the oppressed and violated. The poor are powerless, weak, and rendered helpless. Poor people have no social or political clout with which to free themselves from need. The poor are destitute, bereft of life's necessities, and dispossessed. In short, they are the wretched of the earth. Injustice is the predominant cause of their wretchedness. From the biblical point of view, they are powerless and poor because the powerful and rich have structured the social order to favor themselves. But God knows the causes, and he judges the perpetrators.

Old Testament Israel, we must remember, was a theocracy, a covenant people ruled by God according to his revealed Word. The social system laid down in the Bible had a theology behind it, the theology of a God who loves and cares for the poor among his people (Deut. 10:12–22). In the affairs of the theocracy, God's attribute of love took social form and shape. Israel was to emulate God in caring for the poor and destitute within its borders. The ideal was the total elimination of poverty in Israel (Deut. 15).

Outside Israel, where other gods were worshiped, different social values would be practiced, and poverty and oppression might be the norm. But in Israel such things were not to be. Israel's witness before the nations was to be in terms of justice, righteousness, and compassion for the poor as well as in worship and proclamation.

The theocratic character of Israel and its special relationship to God

---

3. Charles Troutman, commenting on Thomas D. Hanks, *God So Loved the Third World: The Bible, the Reformation and Liberation Theologies* (Maryknoll, N.Y.: Orbis, 1983). Hanks is professor of Old Testament at the Latin American Seminary, San Jose, Costa Rica.

4. For a helpful examination of the Hebrew words, see the Appendix in "Thailand Report: Christian Witness to the Urban Poor," *Lausanne Occasional Papers* 22 (Wheaton, Ill.: Lausanne Committee for World Evangelization, 1980), pp. 22–35.

and his Word must be kept in mind when we apply Old Testament Scripture to the worldwide situation today. It is seriously misleading to take every Old Testament text dealing with Israel's poor and apply it universally to today's poor throughout the world. Yet to do so is commonplace in much of today's mission literature. For that reason I raise a note of caution. Yes, the church has a big responsibility toward the poor, but that responsibility begins with the poor and oppressed who are Christians.

Before an uncaring and unjust world the church must be a showcase of Christ's righteous kingdom. Among Christians it must be visible that where God reigns and his Word is heeded, the needs of the poor are met and oppressions are removed. The church is a spiritual theocracy, a covenant community, and to that community the Scriptures speak first of all.

Compassion, like judgment, begins with the house of God. For that very reason the diaconate is one of the church's essential ministries and is ordained as one of its offices. God has mercy on his people; he is concerned about the poor, and this principle of divine compassion shines through in the church. This has, it seems to me, tremendous implications for a diaconal ministry among the urban poor.

The second point that needs to be emphasized is the basic truth that the weak and the poor, just as much as the rich and the powerful, need to hear the gospel, repent, believe in Christ, and be saved. The poor are not exempt from this requirement, as if their poverty somehow atoned for their sins. Central to every strategy must be the proclamation of Jesus Christ and his redemptive work for sinners.

The Model of Jesus' Ministry

In Fyodor Dostoevsky's classic novel *The Brothers Karamazov* there is a powerful chapter concerned with hunger. Ivan, the intellectual, is conversing with Alyosha, his saintly brother. He recalls a parable he wrote as a very young man. It describes the second coming of Jesus; Jesus is proclaiming his original message, "Man shall not live by bread alone." However, this time the church, which is personified by the Grand Inquisitor, joins Satan and the world to tempt Jesus into reversing his priorities, to make his main mission turning stones into bread.

The Grand Inquisitor, representing an apostate church, argues that there is no crime and no sin, only hunger. He warns Jesus that the hungry mobs will turn against him with greater ferocity this time unless their hunger is satisfied. "Feed men first," he warns, "and then ask them to be good!"

Hunger then, and hunger now, seems so urgent, so primary a need, such an absolute condition, that nothing else, not even the eternal state of one's soul, compares with it in importance. Which comes first, feeding the stomach or feeding the soul?

In the life and ministry of the Lord Jesus Christ, what has often appeared to Christians as a dilemma finds a resolution. Jesus' ministry is a model of the way the Christian's twin responsibilities of evangelism and social involvement are to be integrated. Jesus preached, taught, and healed. His concern for the physical needs of people flowed from his love and compassion for them as people, image-bearers of God, who are burdened down by sin and its consequences, hurting, hoping, seeking, dying. His healing ministry served as a bridge to his preaching ministry, as he blended concern for the temporal and eternal dimensions of human existence.

Christ's compassion was holistic compassion, concerned for sick bodies, empty stomachs, and perishing souls. Out of compassion for a leprous man he reached out and healed (Mark 1:41). Moved with compassion for people without spiritual direction, he set aside plans for a restful retreat and taught a multitude (Mark 6:34). When people were hungry and had no food left, Jesus used his power to feed them (Mark 8:1–10). Both his words and his works were expressions of his compassion for people.[5] In the prayer Jesus taught us, he kept humankind's two essential needs together—daily bread and the forgiveness of sins.

Christian Responses to the Urban Poor

White middle-class churches are in a weak position to minister to the urban poor, but the situation is not hopeless. With commitment and sacrifice, many good things can be done to effect lasting changes in the city. I suggest that churches and denominations take seriously the following agenda for involvement with the urban poor.

1. Seeing, Learning, and Loving

The gap in understanding and communication between the poor and the middle class is a large part of the problem. Effective Christian responses to the urban poor are frustrated at every level because the poor and their conditions are not understood. In his book *Urban Ministry*, David Claerbaut refers to this problem as "invisibility." He points

---

5. Bong Rin Ro and Gottfried Osei-Mensah, Preface, in *Word and Deed*, ed. Bruce J. Nicholls (Grand Rapids: Eerdmans, 1985), p. 8.

out that it is difficult for Christians to become concerned about problems with which they are not personally confronted. In cities the poor are segregated from the higher classes, and a person can live for years in an urban metropolis without ever driving through a poor neighborhood or becoming acquainted with one poor family. When poverty is an abstraction, says Claerbaut, it is exceedingly difficult for most middle-class people to believe that there can be as many as thirty-five million Americans living below the poverty level.[6]

The poor are relatively immobile and tend to stay within their own neighborhoods. Middle-class people do their best to avoid these poor areas. The result is that neither understands the other. The beginning of a Christian response to the poor in the city, therefore, must take the form of planned visits, the development of trusting relationships, the exchange of ministries and resources, and growing demonstrations of Christian love. I suggest that every suburban or small-town church make a long-term commitment to building meaningful relationships with a church in a poor city neighborhood. In some places, churches are alread doing this, and they have discovered what an uplifting experience it can be.

To facilitate these kinds of exchanges, people who are known and trusted by the poor and by middle-class church leaders are needed to serve as bridges. Bill Leslie, pastor of the LaSalle Street Church in Chicago, is one of these persons. He has developed many ministries which help the poor in Chicago. One of them, which is called "bridging," links the needs of the poor with the resources of middle-class churches. To get something started, Leslie suggests that middle-class churches begin once-a-month discussion groups to talk about the city and its needs. By inviting resource people to speak and by visiting various places in the city, the group can serve as the information channel and motivator for the entire congregation.

2. Presence Among the Poor
and Sharing Their Needs

Traditional denominations find it difficult to make a mark in the city because they generally lack a strong, locally rooted Christian presence among the groups society has left without power or voice. As a result, the relationship between the urban poor and Christianity is generally weak, tenuous, and unhealthy. How tragic it is that where the needs are greatest, the church is weakest. Where the voice of Christ ought to be heard the loudest, there is awesome silence.

6. David Claerbaut, *Urban Ministry* (Grand Rapids: Zondervan, 1983), p. 69.

For that reason John M. Perkins, founder of Voice of Calvary Ministries, has been pleading for years in behalf of his Three Rs for the city: Reconciliation, Relocation, and Redistribution. Perkins has spent twenty-five years in this ministry and believes that the key to helping people is to bring them into a right relationship with God and then to assist them to recognize their God-given potential. Perkins senses that all people must see their true worth as God's creatures and God's children before they can love and reach their own human potential. Perkins pleads for Christians to relocate their homes, invest their lives in service to and among the poor, and change a city neighborhood for Christ and its residents.[7]

That is a tough agenda to consider! To walk the streets of poor neighborhoods, live in low-income housing, and identify with the underclass in everything one does represent more than most Christians are willing to consider. The whole movement of population is away from the slums, and only a rare kind of person is willing to reverse the direction. A new voice is being heard, however. It is coming out of the Philippines, and more recently from California and Calcutta. It comes from Viv Grigg, a New Zealander who has lived among the poor in a Manila slum. His book entitled *Companion to the Poor* describes how he established a Christian church among some of Asia's poorest people, the slum dwellers of Manila. He did it by living among them in a shack, identifying with their conditions, and treating their spiritual needs and their physical conditions together. Grigg is calling for a new wave of Christian workers to enter the slums and live there with the people. He says we must stop treating the urban poor as objects of charity and relief, begin to understand them as they are, and deal with spiritual and social needs together in genuine integration of word, deed, and life. Our mandate is to bring these slum communities under the authority of the kingdom of God.

> Our methodology is that of preaching the good news of Jesus, teaching the whole counsel of God and establishing disciples in worshipping, economically stable fellowships.
>
> Let us trust God to provide converts, disciples and leaders. We need to see churches properly nurtured, squatter discipleship and vocational training strategically placed and effectively led, and the gospel free to transform the economic, social and political life of these slum areas.
>
> Economic transformation is an immediate pastoral concern. Compassion demands that we not only pray for but also *give* to the poor. Evangelism cannot be done outside of compassion. Economic programs on their

---

7. John M. Perkins, *A Quiet Revolution* (Waco, Tex.: Word, 1976), pp. 215–24.

own, however, do not appear to extend the kingdom when used as a basis for evangelism. On the other hand, the discipling process involves dealing with a person's environment, as well as with his personality. It is insufficient to save people's souls when their environment forces them back into spiritual slavery. . . . It is insufficient to develop economic projects while ignoring issues of oppression, exploitation and injustice.[8]

Viv Grigg's vision gave impetus to the founding of Servants Among the Poor, a missionary organization whose American base is in Pasadena, California.[9] It prepares, sends, and sponsors missionaries to live as poor people among the poor of the world, following the life and incarnation of Jesus Christ as the model for their ministry. The goals and methods of Servants Among the Poor deserve very serious consideration, for they may be the missing key to effective ministry among the urban poor. Grigg himself has moved to the slums of Calcutta.

3. Urban Diaconal Task Forces

Neither a deed-only nor a word-only strategy is adequate in the city. Poor people need more than bread and more than verbal truth if their lives are to be changed and made whole. The lie of the Marxists is that people need and want only food. The mistake of some evangelists is to think that words alone are enough. Both approaches ignore the example of Christ, and both are inadequate for cities.

Nowhere is genuine diaconal ministry more needed than among the poor in large cities. But it must be genuinely Christian diaconal ministry, in which service among the poor is never separated from the gospel and its communication. Diaconal ministry requires sound theological principles undergirding it. Otherwise, forces in the city are likely to tear it from the gospel and send it careening in wrong directions.

Here are some of the principles by which an urban diaconate must be guided:

a. The goal of all Christian ministry in the city is the glorification of God through the salvation of sinners, the building of the church, and the extension of the kingdom of God. The pursuit of this goal is carried on in different ways, but the goal does not change. Everything done in the name of mercy must be evaluated in terms of its contribution to the accomplishment of this goal.

b. Central to the task of the church in the city is the proclamation of

8. Viv Grigg, *Companion to the Poor* (Sutherland, Australia: Albatross, 1984), pp. 22–23.

9. The U.S. address of Servants Among the Poor is 1240 North Garfield, Pasadena, California 91101.

the gospel (Matt. 28:19–20; Rom. 1:1–16). This task never competes with diaconal ministry, but accompanies it, complements it, and becomes the driving force of diaconal concern (1 John 3:16–18). Whenever, in the course of events and relationships, the ministry of the Word and the ministry of mercy proceed down separate streets and appear even to be in conflict with one another, immediate efforts must be made to examine the difficulties and to rectify them.

c. Diaconal ministry in the city begins with the poor among believers, for they are the church's first responsibility (Gal. 6:10). But it does not end with them. It extends to every needy person whom God makes our neighbor (Luke 10:29–37). The implication here is that the stewardship we exercise as Christians is a corporate matter involving all members of Christ's body. This should lead to mutual sharing between the diaconates of richer churches and those of poorer congregations in the city. Nonurban churches should be moved to diaconal action by the news that some of their city brothers and sisters are suffering. Mutual concern and love for one another are vital to the church's witness before the world.

d. Diaconal evangelism in the city is a natural outcome of a biblical understanding of the breadth of human need and the depth of God's provision in Christ. It recognizes that the ultimate need of every person is saving faith and reconciliation with God. Through the life and words of Christ's diaconal representatives, the eternal Good News comes to the poor in unique and powerful ways. Those whose special gifts lie in management, organization, training, or distribution must not be silent about their faith. Giving a cup of water in Christ's name (Mark 9:41) involves more than merely mounting a text on the office wall or stamping the logo of a religious organization on boxes. It involves using every appropriate opportunity to tell people the story of the God who cared so much for poor sinners that he gave his best, his only Son Jesus, at Calvary. Only when immediate and ultimate needs are met through Christ in the ministry of his servants will the wide spectrum of human exigencies be adequately addressed in the city.

c. Diaconal ministry among the urban poor must be holistic, going beyond temporary relief to treating the long-range causes of poverty and the resulting conditions. Given the facts behind poverty, political involvement cannot be ruled out.

In his article "Justice for the Poor: The Political Problem of Poverties," Jasper Lesage makes the point that poverty is a complex problem, and in actuality there is no such thing as simple poverty. There are many poverties, each requiring concentrated study and appropriate remedies. Lesage makes a number of suggestions which any urban diaconate might follow. He underscores the fact that most poverty situations are the result of some form of injustice and require political action and changes in government policies. "What is called for is a complex political response to a complex set of social problems," Lesage says. "If the problem of poverty were to be attacked solely by promoting Christian charity through private agencies and individuals, the problem would remain insoluble. It is simply too complex and vast a problem on a national scale, disregarding the international problem, to be handled completely outside of government agencies."[10]

But on a simpler and more local level, a great deal of holistic, neighborhood-changing ministry can and should be done. Evangelical churches still have a great deal to learn about urban community development and the ways in which changes can be brought about in poor and distressed neighborhoods. This area provides a major challenge for the next decade.

4. Educational Training for Ministry Among the Poor

The fourth item I want to propose relates to Christian educational institutions and the kind of training given to future leaders. In this area I work with several assumptions: (a) a large share of our past failure to minister effectively among the poor stems from the way we train church leaders, and even the way we read the Bible and study theology; (b) the church in most countries possesses tremendous resources which could make substantial differences in the lives of the poor if congregations were mobilized to carry out the needed ministries; (c) when we learn to help the poor and speak Christ's message to them meaningfully, we will learn also how to communicate to the nonpoor, and our message will bear a stamp of credibility which so often now is missing.

On my list of urban giants is Harv Oostdyk, who worked for thirty years in the ghettos of New York City and more recently in Dallas and other cities. Oostdyk understands God's heart towards the urban poor and the conditions that prevail among them. In his book *Step One: The Gospel and the Ghetto* Oostdyk suggests eight specific applications of biblical principles for ministry among the poor:

1. Place special emphasis on the family of God. The church which ignores the plight of believers in the slums is disobedient to the Scriptures and insensitive to its responsibilities to help the Christian poor.

---

10. Jasper Lesage, "Justice for the Poor: The Political Problem of Poverties," *Pro Rege* 14.2 (Dec. 1985).

2. Maintain a close relationship between evangelism and helping the poor. Christ wants his Word spoken in the pulpits of churches and also in the marketplaces of the city. "People with their hands dirty have more of a ring of truth in their voices." Evangelism happens in the midst of deep social involvement.
3. Go and love a poor person. If all Christians would try to love one poor person, the face of poverty would be drastically altered.
4. Pray for the poor. Cities need our prayers. Every Christian, even the elderly and bedridden, can through prayer be involved in urban ministry.
5. Recognize that part of any concern for the poor must be institutionally expressed. We live in an institutional society, and despite the number of its members the Christian church cannot make the impact that is needed unless it organizes institutionally in behalf of the needs of the poor.
6. Support local urban ministries. Most Christian urban workers are walking alone, and they desperately need the support of the Christian community. The slum, the ghetto, is a very lonely place unless one knows there are dedicated people spiritually, if not physically, alongside.
7. Minister to the urban poor locally as a means of promoting world evangelism. The Great Commission to the world is the Great Commission to our home community. Our opportunities overseas are staked to our domestic responsibilities.
8. Rely on God's grace to bring help to the poor. Claiming God's grace is essential for urban ministry.[11]

Oostdyk insists that before evangelical churches can be expected to turn in any significant degree toward the cities and the poor, something must take place in Christian colleges and seminaries. The Bible, he says, must not only be understood in its original languages and translated properly, it must also be applied to the needs of the contemporary poor. This is where the intellectual leadership in the evangelical tradition has failed.

Very few pastors and professors, says Oostdyk, have even basic urban experience. They are experientially deprived. Most of their time is spent in suburban churches and classrooms; hardly ever can they be found in the streets of the ghetto. If every Christian scholar, student, and preacher, challenges Oostdyk, spent just one month living among the poor, no church or school would ever be the same. Ministries

11. Harv Oostdyk, *Step One: The Gospel and the Ghetto* (Basking Ridge, N.J.: SonLife International, 1983), pp. 223–36.

would be changed overnight. The neighborhoods of the poor would be changed, too.[12]

I think Oostdyk is correct, and I suggest that every training institution take his agenda for the urban poor seriously. There is no time to lose. The poor in the city cannot wait until the slow wheels of old bureaucracies turn in their direction. A new generation of evangelical leaders must be raised up quickly for daring frontier ministries in the world's cities.[13]

Discussion Questions

1. Enumerate some of the reasons commonly given by middle-class people as to why some people are poor. Evaluate these reasons.
2. Why does the subject of poverty and ministry to the poor so often become controversial in evangelical churches? Describe some of the debates you have heard on the subject and analyze the positions.
3. Express in your own words the position of John Perkins and Viv Grigg regarding ministry to the urban poor and dealing with the poor person's social and economic environment. How do you feel about relocating your residence and living among the urban poor?
4. Design a ministry to the poor which a church you are acquainted with could conduct if properly motivated. Use the principles presented in this chapter. Consider presenting your ideas to the church.

12. Ibid., pp. 190–91.

13. Tetsunao Yamamori, president of Food for the Hungry International, recently pleaded with Christian educational institutions to do more to train the kind of workers needed for service among the poor. "Evangelical relief and development organizations are having problems finding qualified personnel," said Yamamori. "We're wondering where we can go, what we can do to find good, adequately prepared personnel. Right now, it seems we have to go to seminaries and Bible colleges to find people with the theological qualifications of missionaries, but we have to go to secular schools to find people with the professional skills of relief and development specialists. If we are to be effective, if we are to fulfill our biblical mandate, we need people with both sets of qualifications" ("Training for Relief and Development: A Task for Christian Higher Education?" *Mission Frontiers*, Aug.–Sept. 1985).

Ministering to Street People

Roger S. Greenway

There are an estimated four to five million homeless people in the United States, and most of them live on the streets of our large cities. They are the poorest of the poor, the destitute, the unwanted. They can be spotted picking through garbage cans, huddled in doorways at night, and sleeping over steam vents on the sidewalk. Children are among them, too; and in growing numbers whole families drift from one temporary shelter to another or make their home in the cities' welfare hotels.

Homeless street people are a nation's most visible social failure. Certainly they are one of the most serious challenges to our moral sensitivity. If we fail to see or care about the homeless and destitute at our doorstep, we dare not talk about our concern for the poor anywhere else.

In North America the problem of homelessness is scarcely understood. The number of street people is greater and their plight more serious than at any time since the Great Depression of the 1930s. With the growing number of homeless families and small children on the street, most Americans feel bewildered by what they see or read about, and they are at a loss to know how to respond.

Street people used to comprise what were known as Skid Row bums, bag ladies, drifters, or tramps. Today, however, entire families make up a large proportion of the homeless; and the parents, especially single mothers, must struggle not only with finding food, shelter, and protection, but also with finding schools for their children, whose only address is a temporary shelter.

The purpose of this chapter is to create an awareness of the nature and causes of this urban social problem and to suggest specific ways Christians can minister to street people. The problem exists in abundance in other parts of the world as well as in North America; but if we learn to understand it close to home, we will likely be able to deal with it appropriately in other places as well.

Churches and independent Christian organizations can make a big difference in meeting the needs of the homeless, and some are doing a great deal already. If the Lord were here physically, I believe he would minister intensely to street people. They are the most visible modern example of what Jesus called "the least of these my brothers." Our response to their needs may just be the acid test of the social conscience of American Christianity.

Who Are the Street People?

"Street people" is a broad term that covers a heterogeneous population with one thing in common: its members are homeless. A wide variety of individuals is included: runaway boys and girls, displaced families, legal and illegal refugees, prostitutes, alcoholics and drug addicts, the aged and senile, and the mentally retarded. The median age in many cities is thirty-five, and it is dropping dramatically. Some are homeless only temporarily, but for many others it is a chronic condition ended only by death.

In the last few years, "shelter children" have replaced latchkey children as a leading concern in regard to the young. Latchkey children are those who return from school and let themselves into an empty home because their parents are at work. Shelter children have no home to return to and sometimes no school to attend. The plight of these children is the saddest aspect of the street-people phenomenon. Most of them go to school only sporadically. They move from school to school as they move from shelter to shelter. Uprooted again and again, they are never part of any community. Given the corrupting environment surrounding them, only the hardiest will escape permanent membership in the growing underclass that lives on welfare or crime or both.

One-third to one-half of the homeless are mentally ill. They are on the streets because of a process in America known as deinstitutionalization. It was started about thirty years ago, when the development of psychotropic drugs (tranquilizers) suggested that even serious mental cases could be treated chemically on an outpatient basis, and there was no reason why thousands of hospitalized persons should not be returned to the general population. At first, deinstitutionalization was hailed as a major reform of the mental-health-care system. But that isn't the way it turned out. Thousands of patients were released from mental hospitals, but most communities were not willing or ready to accept them. Nor were the patients themselves, in many instances, able to fit into normal family or community life. The results have been disastrous.

The resident population of large mental hospitals in America has been reduced by 75 percent in the last thirty years. But local mental-health-care systems have not been able to cope with the influx of people needing treatment. Underfinanced and understaffed, private and community mental-health programs have borne the brunt of deinstitutionalization, and admittedly they have failed. Skid Row is where many patients end up, particularly when they are given a treatment known as bus therapy, which consists of bus fare from the mental hospital to a city, where they are left to fend for themselves.

Diverse Causes of Homelessness

Besides the deinstitutionalization policy, changes in the nation's economy have forced a great number of people out of jobs and onto the streets. Coupled with this have been cutbacks in government programs that benefited the poor. Robert E. Jones, president of the Philadelphia Committee for the Homeless, pointed out that reductions have been made in a variety of programs designed to help the elderly, the families and children of the unemployed, the sick, and victims of alcohol and drug addiction. Jones added another factor contributing to homelessness: the razing of old downtown buildings and inner-city houses as part of urban renewal, and the process known as gentrification. The poor depend on old buildings for cheap housing, and when these buildings are replaced by hotels, convention centers, and condominiums, poor people lose the only homes they can afford. The shortage of houses available for those at or near the poverty level is a critical problem seldom understood by middle-class citizens. In cities like New York, a family currently housed in a temporary shelter has almost no chance of finding affordable permanent housing. As the stock of low-income housing continues to decrease, more and more families will be forced onto the street.

Substance abuse is another major cause of homelessness. It is estimated that alcoholics and drug abusers represent up to 40 percent of the homeless population in this country. Because of their addiction, these people cannot get or hold a job, they cannot pay for decent housing, and they are not mentally alert enough to make adequate use of available community services. If substance abuse is combined with mental disability, diagnosis and regular treatment are doubly difficult.

Besides the mentally ill, the unemployed, and the drug and alcohol abusers, there is an assortment of other people on the street who have no place to go. They may be runaways, refugees from Central America, illegal immigrants from Mexico, or Native Americans recently arrived from the reservations. They share the same suffering, the wind and cold of winter, the danger of robbery and attack, the soup lines, the scarcity of public bathrooms, the humiliation, and the gripping hopelessness of the streets.

Solutions Worth Pursuing

Rescue missions of various kinds have been working with the homeless for years. The Salvation Army must be credited for its outstanding record of providing food, shelter, and Christian counseling to the homeless in the city.

Downtown churches in growing number have been opening their doors in winter to provide temporary lodging for the homeless. This is not a small step for a church to take, as it entails certain sacrifices which not every congregation is willing to make.

Very recently, advocacy groups have been formed in some cities on behalf of the poor and homeless. They consist of professional people who believe that state and local officials ought to be doing more to find structural solutions to the problem of the homeless. They have used the news media effectively, and as a result of their efforts, a number of new facilities for the needy have been opened in large cities across America.

These steps have not been achieved without opposition. Shelters and soup kitchens attract the poor and destitute, whom merchants regard as threats to their businesses because frightened customers stay away. Similarly, neighborhood residents resist the establishment of shelters and halfway houses because they fear the criminal elements commonly associated with the homeless.

In a democracy such as ours, citizens can pressure the government to help supply human needs that are not being met by private or local groups. Only the government is powerful enough to turn back the process of deinstitutionalization, or at least to modify it enough so that mental patients receive the care and protection they need. Legislation aimed at correcting the defects of deinstitutionalization has been introduced in Washington, and it merits support. Aggressive citizen groups like the Coalition for the Homeless in New York provide leadership in such areas.

Obstacles to Helping the Homeless

Experienced street workers can tell us a host of reasons why it is difficult to help the chronically homeless, and why anyone interested in getting involved had better count the cost before beginning. The first problem to be faced is that of *transience,* which is particularly characteristic of the mentally disordered. Various terms used to describe strect people (e.g., "truckers" and "road people") point to the fact that the homeless person seldom spends more than half a year in any one place. People with long-standing mental and emotional problems don't like to make commitments or be held to obligations they feel they can't meet. Getting out of town is the easiest way to leave failures behind and avoid the consequences of behavior they aren't proud of.

Once the wandering pattern is established, it further impoverishes the individual in a number of ways. It leaves the drifting young person, for example, without any sense of roots or of belonging, and often leads to crime, prostitution, or drug peddling as a means of income. Homelessness further undermines the effectiveness of any help that churches or other institutions might try to give the transient person.

A second obstacle has to do with the *isolated lifestyle* of many of the homeless and socially marginalized. One of the first lessons street workers are taught by the Philadelphia Committee for the Homeless is to respect the homeless person's turf, the little circle of space where he or she guards a few meager possessions. The worker must not come too close, especially at first. Talking too loud or coming too close will cause the person on the pavement to move away. Such people, remember, spend their whole lives in physical and emotional isolation from others. Even the most well meant offer of food and assistance, not handled tactfully, may be viewed as a threat to the small bit of security they feel. With them, relationship building is a slow process, and any bond that may form always remains fragile.

The third obstacle is *failure.* Working with the homeless is filled with frustration. Seldom does the street worker enjoy the feeling of success and mission accomplished which can be expected regularly in other kinds of service. Disillusionment is a constant threat. It is true, of course, that some street people can be helped and rehabilitated in lasting ways, but for those with chronic mental disorders there is little ground for optimism. Given the present limitations in the mental-health profession, it must be assumed that most of those who have been deinstitutionalized will remain marginal for the rest of their lives. Some will follow the familiar pattern among single homeless men, who in late-middle age become less transient and less volatile, and settle down on the park benches of some community. What will happen to many others is hard to predict. With these obstacles to face, it is no wonder that burnout is frequent among street workers.

The fourth obstacle is *violence,* the fear of which keeps most people away from work with the homeless. There are places on the street where it is almost impossible to stay for any length of time without being mugged, robbed, or stabbed. The uninitiated worker is especially vulnerable. Being viewed as a do-gooder invites attack. "Get a police whistle," advises a Philadelphia street worker to new recruits, "and always have it on a string around your neck; but be sure the string is breakable so you won't get strangled."

Effective work among the homeless requires personal involvement and relationship building. This means running the risk of facing violence. Many ex–mental patients are harmless. But there are also the unpredictable ones with a propensity to violence. Furthermore, because so many street people are addicted to drugs and alcohol, attack and robbery are constant dangers to be reckoned with.

The fifth obstacle is the attitude of *indifference* toward the plight of the homeless poor and the mentally retarded. Most people try not to see the problem or quietly sweep it under the rug. There was a time when the mentally retarded and even the indigent poor were stored away in big state institutions, safely out of sight of the mainline community. The government's policy of deinstitutionalization has not been a total failure in that it allows some of the mentally impaired to find a place in society. To this extent the policy has put an end to the kind of public irresponsibility that warehoused society's misfits and tried to forget they existed. But what are we prepared to do for the bag ladies, the homeless men, the runaway young people, and the families with small children that walk the streets and sleep in the alleys of American cities? How many more people must freeze to death before public attitudes change and national mental-health policies are altered or expanded to meet the needs of the homeless?

The Churches' Expanded Role

Let the churches become the conscience centers of the nation in behalf of the homeless poor. Urban and suburban churches can share their resources and convictions in this common cause. They must be willing to care enough and to risk enough to reach out in love to the lowest of the low and to work in an often hostile environment.

Actions must be taken at many different levels. First, there is a need for Christian leadership in organizations like the Philadelphia Committee for the Homeless, which unites the efforts of concerned profession-als. Its purpose is to seek an understanding of the problems related to the poor and the homeless, to support the civic and private organiza-tions working with that population, and to develop and sponsor direct services to the homeless on the street. Every city needs such a group. It is the best way to channel effort and to influence and inform in all directions.

Secondly, churches must be prepared to respond to the needs of homeless people who may show up at their door at any time. As the number of the homeless grows larger in America, no church anywhere can consider itself too far removed from the city to escape this chal-lenge. A homeless family may appear unexpectedly in a church service or the pastor's study, or be found sleeping in the doorway when the janitor arrives on Sunday morning. Should the police or the deacons be called? One church I know of on Long Island played cat and mouse with a drifter for almost a year. He would sneak in through unlocked doors during the day and sleep in closets, under pews, or behind the organ until the next morning. Because such things can happen any-where, it's important that pastors prepare themselves mentally for sit-uations which might arise and in which they must give leadership to their congregation vis-à-vis homeless people.

Third, I hope we will see very soon a growing number of Christians from many denominations committing themselves to mission careers among the homeless. There is very little how-to literature available on the subject, but on-the-job training is available for those who sincerely want it. Rescue missions and rehabilitation centers of various kinds are generally understaffed, and they welcome volunteers who can learn while they work. My advice to potential street workers is to read widely and ask lots of questions. In this field there aren't many experts.

Starting out, street workers need to get to know the people, the soup kitchens, the cheap hotels, and the alleys where the homeless sleep. They must gain a thorough acquaintance with the welfare agencies, the community-health services, and every available resource, public and private, that helps street people. A week living in a temporary shelter or welfare hotel is an educational experience, too. Workers must know who the street leaders are, for on the street, as everywhere else, there are the leaders and the followers. After building up trust with the leaders, it is easier to work with the ordinary people. The leaders will either back up or stamp out the street workers, so it is essential to build strong relationships with them.

Recognizing that some groups are more apt to respond to both the gospel and assistance than are others, the street workers' next step is to target a specific group to deal with. Goals and objectives should be defined in the light of the target group's needs and expected responses. It is important to avoid groups that will prove difficult to handle, such as the gays, prostitutes, and potentially violent ex–mental patients, who should be left to others with special calling and skills. There are refugees and families on the street, as well as youthful runaways and old people closeted in cheap hotels. It is better to begin by developing fruitful ministries with them. Ability to deal with the tougher cases will come with experience.

Working with the homeless will uniquely challenge the novice street workers' ability to tell the gospel. The first day on the street they will confront situations for which Bible college and seminary never prepared them, and they will be humbled by their own awkwardness when they try to draw from all they have learned and to communicate it meaningfully. On the street God's fathomless truths and promises have to be distributed in spoonfuls, in the simplest words and the most concrete ways. And the message must be delivered in doorways, in dimly lit, stinking hotel corridors, to people whose minds may be only half there and whose only emotion is despair. One has to surrender a lot of oneself to be a street worker.

Street People and the Churches

Relating the homeless and the poor to established middle-class churches is not easy. In some cases it is impossible. Some very high barriers stand between them. For one thing, poor people naturally feel uneasy in most churches. They know that their clothes are shabby and dirty, and they haven't been able to take a bath in weeks. They probably can't read the bulletin someone hands them, nor can they follow music. Besides, they may have had some bad experiences with churches years ago, and there may be shadows in their lives which church people have a way of calling back.

On the other side of the aisle, middle-class church members often feel awkward and apprehensive when they see a street person in the pew. The stranger's behavior may be alarming, and some other factors may frankly irritate. Except for good and well-intentioned acts of be-nevolence, most church members are not equipped to handle street people or minister to them in the way they require.

Having said this, however, I want to encourage churches not to avoid such ministry if the Lord sends street people their way. I've seen some beautiful things happen in congregations that opened their arms and hearts to people from life's fringes. There are many kinds of people among the poor and homeless. They are not all inclined to violence.

Some would hold a job if they could get one, and many have serious physical problems which they themselves are powerless to solve.

The middle-class church should get involved but be prepared for surprise and disappointments in enormous sizes. The family a church has helped and helped may suddenly disappear, leaving behind a pile of bills and a torn-up apartment. Maybe the family will never be seen again, or maybe they'll show up months later in worse condition than before, asking for more assistance. Consider the case of two former parishioners of mine in Michigan. The street walker they housed at their home and counseled for many hours, who they felt was beginning to move toward Jesus, ended up floating in a river. They may never find out whether it was murder or suicide, but they know she left behind a two-year-old child whom she wanted and cared for very much. Churches that get involved with street people can expect to do a lot of spiritual growing, but they must also be prepared for heartaches along the way.

Lessons from the Street

Five things stand out in my mind as I reflect on ministry to street people. First, God is mighty, and his grace proves itself over and over again as able to change the most degraded individuals. Often he does it through the feeblest of means and most awkward of his servants. I learned that lesson years ago in a small mission when, after a stammering seminarian had finished his sermon, a self-confessed murderer of two persons—mentally retarded and built like a bull moose—stumbled down the aisle and poured out his heart before the Lord and a stunned audience. And he was genuinely converted.

Second, it requires great measures of love and perseverance by the workers to build positive long-term relationships with street people. Not every Christian can handle this kind of ministry. It is a calling reserved for the best.

Third, Christian optimism must be tempered by realism as to how much improvement can be expected, especially in the case of the mentally retarded. If we expect that everyone who proclaims trust in Jesus is going to straighten out and resemble a white middle-class suburban church member, we are set up for some shocking disappointments. Many of the changes we work toward and pray for don't happen in this life at all. From some bondages, deliverance comes only in the next world, and we have to accept that.

Fourth, the street is not a place where long-term spiritual and moral growth can be expected to occur. The street has too much evil, too many influences that entice, enslave, and beckon back. It's a place where Christians can make contact with the destitute and homeless, show them love, build relationships of trust, and introduce them to Jesus. But after that, the homeless should be taken to a rehabilitation center where their lives can be reordered under the care of Christian disciplers. This kind of ministry is absolutely essential if street work is ever to be freed from the revolving-door syndrome. Christian rehabilitation centers deserve the loyal support of churches.

The fifth lesson I've learned from street ministry is that like everyone else street people need pastors. A pastor's job is fourfold: to feed the sheep, to defend them, to guide them, and when they stray, to seek them out. Of all people, street people need pastors.

Preaching to street people takes on many forms and shapes. Their context requires its own medium, but the gospel is the same. Conversion to the Lord Jesus Christ is the essential heart-changing experience which the body of Christ alone, among all the agencies and groups at work on the street, represents and proclaims. That message must never be diminished, nor the presenting of it slighted.

To the outsider it may come as a surprise that religion is a subject of considerable interest among many street people. It always amazes me how a simple message from the Bible attracts listeners. Despite serious handicaps, its power gets through. I once baptized a woman who had worked the streets of Los Angeles until her pimp nearly killed her. But by God's grace, in a small, love-filled women's Bible study, she was turned around, became an active church member, and later a wife and mother. Not all cases turn out that way, but the ones that do make all the effort worthwhile.

It is this pastoral dimension that needs to be enlarged in order to get us beyond the band-aid approach to Christian street work. Without the holistic pastoral approach, the whole endeavor may be discredited. Illustrating this is a letter I received recently from a Christian woman who works in a church-sponsored shelter for homeless people in a Midwestern city. Her letter is filled with brief accounts of the people to whom she ministers as a counselor and unofficial Bible teacher. She considers the ministry of the shelter to be effective as far as it goes, but she pleads in the letter for pastors. Street people's lives are so messed up that their need for pastors is greater than anyone else's. They need pastors with big hearts, sharp minds, lots of street savvy, and a firm knowledge of God's Word.

"Feed my sheep," said Jesus. Sometimes pastors must find the sheep before they can feed them, just as Jesus did. I know where some torn and battered sheep are right now. They are scattered among the homeless on city streets, waiting for someone with a shepherd's heart to reach them.

So churches should seriously consider adding a street pastor to the list of workers they support or to their own ministerial staff. This is a vital part of our global mission. It won't be easy work, nor glamorous, and applicants for the job won't be lining up at the door. But it may just be the Lord's way of testing whether our Christianity is for real.

Discussion Questions

1. Have you ever encountered a street person? Describe the encounter. Evaluate your interaction with the street person and reflect on how you might have served the person's needs more effectively.
2. What is the likelihood that your church would be willing to become a conscience center in behalf of the homeless poor? How would the suggestion be received? How would it affect your church's image? Its growth?
3. Role-play an attempt to help a street person. (The type of person can vary from an elderly bag lady to a mentally retarded middle-aged male to a homeless young mother with two small children in tow.)

16

Ministry in the
Red-Light District
Roger S. Greenway

Prostitution can be found in varying degrees in all countries of the world, in all cultures, and especially in places where the population is dense, the poor are numerous, and money flows freely. Despite the efforts of national and international organizations to curb prostitution, it continues to spread and is in fact increasing. For example, in one country where the three factors mentioned above are all found, the proportion of women between the ages of fifteen and thirty who are caught up in prostitution is about 10 percent. In another country, the proportion of prostitutes among the female population of the capital city is over 13 percent. Even more alarming is the fact that prostitution is beginning at a younger age and increasingly involves preadolescent children.

Much that has been said and written about prostitution in the news media has focused on the wrong people. Treatment of the subject by Christians and secular writers alike has been superficial and sporadic, usually more sensational than substantive. Consequently, the public is largely ignorant of the causes and forces involved in prostitution, and efforts to reduce it have been frustratingly ineffective.

Most people cannot imagine how sordid the prostitution industry really is, or how desperate is the situation in which millions of women and children are caught. The purpose of this chapter is to bring these matters to the attention of Christian leaders. We will examine prostitu-

A major source of information for this chapter is Jean Fernand-Laurent, "Report . . . on the Suppression of Traffic in Persons and the Exploitation of the Prostitution of Others," in *Activities for the Advancement of Women: Equality, Development and Peace*, United Nations Economic and Social Council, E/1983/7 (March 17, 1983).

tion on a worldwide scale, analyze the way it operates, and suggest ways in which Christians can combat the industry and rescue some of its victims.

The World of Prostitution

To begin with, we need to know something about the way the world of prostitution operates. To state it simply, three parties are involved: the client, the prostitute, and the pimp or procurer. It is the client's desire for illicit pleasure that creates the market for prostitution. There would be no prostitution if there were no clients willing and able to pay.

The prostitutes are usually women. Considerably more is known about them because a number of studies on prostitutes have been made in various parts of the world. The findings show that most prostitutes come from broken homes, and a large percentage of them were victims of rape or incest early in life. The specific reasons for their involvement in prostitution are varied. Some prostitutes are addicted to drugs or alcohol, and prostitution is the means they use to support their addiction. Others suffer from emotional frustrations; they've been deserted by a husband or lover, or their homelife was a mess and they are rebelling against their parents. Worldwide, extreme poverty is the single greatest cause. Thousands of girls in poverty-stricken areas of the world are annually sold into prostitution before they reach adolescence. Indifference to moral values characterizes everyone involved in prostitution.

The third party involved is the procurer. He comes in various guises: pimp, recruiter, brothel owner, or operator of a massage parlor, topless bar, or adult movie theater. Nine times out of ten, prostitution involves a third party of this kind. Procurers, usually men, recruit women for prostitution and organize the market professionally. In most cases procurers are involved in the larger world of crime. They make big money, for they keep almost all the prostitutes' wages, and they use a variety of coercive methods to keep the women working for them.

What holds a prostitute in bondage to the procurer? That is a familiar question, and it has a number of answers. First of all, procurers are as clever as they are cruel. Their most common method is to get a woman in financial debt to them and then force her to try to repay it through prostitution. For example, if they can get a girl hooked on drugs, they can force her into prostitution to support her habit. Most prostitutes are in financial debt to their procurers; though the prostitute may not know the exact size of the debt, the procurer constantly uses it as a weapon against her.

Procurers employ very effective disciplinary techniques on the victims. They may alternate between wooing like a lover and brutalizing a girl half to death. The net effect is a kind of psychological conditioning much like brainwashing which renders the woman physically and emotionally dependent on the procurer for as long as he wants her. Procurers sometimes sell their women to other procurers. Through violence, threats, and isolation from anyone who might help them, prostitutes are reduced to the point of having lost all self-esteem, even their personal identity. Their procurers are their masters, and they are the slaves. Prostitution scars a woman's character so deeply, and creates such a gap between her and society, that few ever manage to escape.

Numbered alongside the pimps and brothel owners are the people who produce and sell pornographic literature and films. They are as deeply involved with prostitution as are the owners of topless bars. Pornography and prostitution complement and reinforce each other; it is not by accident that the streets where the sex shops are located are generally the places where prostitution is heaviest.

Sexual Slavery—An International Business

The International Criminal Police Organization (Interpol) has uncovered the existence of a number of international networks involved in buying and transporting women and children for sexual exploitation. In other words, sexual slavery is conducted on an international scale. According to Interpol reports, traffic in women and girls flows from Latin America to southern Europe and the Middle East. Another network operates from Southeast Asia to the Middle East and central and northern Europe. There is a regional European market: French women are exported to Luxembourg and the Federal Republic of Germany. Some of the richer countries of West Africa are supplied by Europe, and a regional market exists in the Arab countries. Hardly any country is free of the international traffic in women, and even underage girls are moved from one country to another for sexual exploitation.

On October 7, 1983, the television program "20/20" presented a documented report on the importation of prostitutes from Korea. American soldiers, reported "20/20," are frequently approached in Seoul with offers of large amounts of money in return for marrying a Korean girl, thus securing the girl's entry into the United States. After she arrives in this country, the soldier is told (falsely) that he has no legal obligation to her. Thousands of dollars are offered, and some soldiers jump at the opportunity. This illegal procedure is being used to supply topless bars and massage parlors all across America with Oriental women who are kept as prostitutes. The girls are heavily in debt to the procurers who bought their plane tickets and got them to the United States through fraudulent marriages and illegal immigration procedures.

Once they are in the United States, the women become merchandise in the sex market. They are exploited in every way, often brutalized, and sometimes killed. If the police raid the places where they work and arrest them, their procurers quickly move them to some other city before their cases are investigated or brought to trial. Hardly ever are the women sentenced or deported. Nor do they ever get out of debt or sexual slavery.

Sex tours are another form of international traffic in women and children. Package tours take clients to overseas sex centers where the most degrading kinds of sexual exploitation are carried on. Organized sex tourism is practiced on a large scale in the Caribbean, Southeast Asia, and parts of Africa. Young boys as well as women and girls are caught in this vice market. In fact, one of the main attractions of sex tourism is the availability of young children. Sex magazines sold throughout Europe and America advertise to pedophiles the availability of young boys and very young girls in the large cities of Southeast Asia and Africa.

Young people, especially girls traveling alone, are favorite targets of certain procurers who use seduction, guile, and trickery to obtain their human merchandise. Sometimes procurers use force and simply kidnap their victims. But generally they use more subtle methods, at least in the beginning of the seduction process. They offer assistance to stranded female travelers. To a young tourist suddenly out of money, procurers offer temporary lodging, transportation, or assistance in finding a job. Promises of exciting art tours, film auditions, and free trips abroad are among the ruses they use. All of these lead eventually to houses of prostitution, threats, beatings, gang rape, and sexual enslavement. Bus stations, airports, and train depots are places where procurers are likely to be on the prowl for naive young travelers.

Children of the Poor and Prostitution

In many large cities, children by the thousands survive by picking through garbage, begging, stealing, doing odd jobs, or becoming prostitutes. Pedophiles and procurers take advantage of these children. Most tragic of all, some parents are so poor that they are willing to sell or rent their children to procurers in order to pay debts they cannot otherwise meet. The pornographic industry currently is taking advantage of parents who need money and are willing to rent out the services of their defenseless children to photographers. In Latin America, the prostitutes most in demand are between the ages of ten and fourteen. According to reliable estimates, some five thousand boys and three thousand girls below the age of eighteen work as prostitutes in Paris. Studies in Brazil indicate that the traffic is high in very young girls. A girl of twelve can bring in more money in Brazil than an adult man can earn by working full-time in a factory. Many families depend for their entire living on the prostitution of their minor children.

In the United States there are at least 264 magazines specializing in child pornography. No wonder, then, that stables of child prostitutes have been discovered in Chicago, New York, New Orleans, Dallas, and Los Angeles. In other countries, cities such as Rio de Janeiro, Abidjan, Dakar, Istanbul, and Hammamet are known for the children of both sexes that are available to pedophile tourists. Colombo was recently reported to have two thousand small boys in prostitution. The literature advertising these children is readily available.

Poverty, whatever its nature or source, has driven more women to prostitution over the years than has any other social factor. In the ancient world, prostitutes were slaves, chattel at the disposal of their owners. Today slavery takes other forms but is no less binding on the victims. In Hong Kong and Bangkok, girls just a few years old are handed over to procurers for the equivalent of a few American dollars. In Macao, girls can be bought for one hundred to two hundred dollars. A variety of explanations can be given for this heinous business; high on the list is the low regard for females in those cultures. But along with the cultural factors, poverty remains a major element. In the industrialized nations there are high-class prostitutes who appear to be prostitutes by choice. But studies show that such women are relatively few, and hardly any would remain in prostitution if they were genuinely free to leave.

In cities of Asia, Africa, and Latin America, masses of poor migrants huddle in crowded squatter settlements. Millions cannot find adequately remunerative employment. Women from rural areas, unskilled and often illiterate, are offered few alternatives. Factories exploit young women by making them work long hours for low wages. Domestic employment as maids in the homes of wealthier citizens, if available, is poorly paid. If a woman has dependents to provide for, prostitution may seem the only alternative to starvation. Meanwhile, the demand for prostitutes—the younger the better—keeps growing, fueled by the advertising media, pornography, sex tours, and male chauvinism. No wonder prostitution is one of the leading growth industries of the world.

Pornography and Violence Toward Children

Speaking to the National Consultation on Pornography in September 1985, Surgeon General C. Everett Koop underscored the fact that pornography is a contributing factor to certain mental disorders leading to serious antisocial actions, including violence against children:

> Men who see or read *sexually violent material* over a period of time tend to have a higher degree of tolerance for sexual violence and acts of sexual degradation. And we suspect that for men who are even slightly predisposed to such behavior, this material may push them from the unreal world of fantasy over into the real world of overt action.
>
> A second area involves both the use of children as subjects in pornography and the use of such *child pornography* to arouse children and adults to engage in illicit and often violent sexual acts. Lately, we've been learning just how devastating the long-term effects of this kind of pornography can be upon the physical and mental health of the victimized children.
>
> We also are discovering that many children exploited by the pornographer soon become victims of the even more frightening world of child prostitution. And there is growing evidence that child pornography stimulates some adults into sexually abusing defenseless children.

When adult bookstores, X-rated movie theaters, sex by telephone, and sleazy videos are seen in this light, the damage they do to society becomes obvious. They deserve the active opposition of every citizen concerned about decency, the family, the dignity of womanhood, and the protection of children. War against pornography is war against prostitution, injustice, and the worst forms of cruelty known on earth.

Christian Responses
to the Prostitution Underworld

When the facts are presented, a haunting picture emerges of gross exploitation, intense cruelty, and the worst forms of sin. Next to willful abortion and murder, it is the ugliest scar on humanity's face. Nothing could be more obnoxious to our holy God than the prostitution of his image-bearers by the sex industry. Prostitution is a far broader and more sinister evil than most people imagine. Certainly most Christians have only a limited understanding of how enslaving this vice really is. Because powerful people, from local politicians to international crime syndicates, are involved in the prostitution industry, any individuals daring to oppose it must expect rough going. They will be the objects of intimidation and even violence. There are some Christians already taking these risks, and they are setting victims free. I am confident that new and even more aggressive efforts will be organized by Christians in the future.

My suggestions for concerted opposition to prostitution are arranged around the three groups of people involved in the sex industry. First, the prostitutes themselves, whom I consider largely to be victims of exploitation, need our compassion, the message of the gospel, and adequate rehabilitation. Second, there are the procurers, the callous exploiters of the poor and defenseless, and the publishers, landlords, and merchants who in every conceivable way promote sexual exploitation. They deserve public condemnation and every form of righteous opposition that can be mustered. Third, the clients must be dealt with, anonymous as they tend to be, because deeper maladies are at work here than most people recognize. In all these areas, churches, schools, and committed individuals have important roles to play.

To the Prostitutes

First, in regard to the prostitutes themselves, traditional attitudes need to be reevaluated in the light of the Bible and the real situation in the underworld. In view of what we have said about the causes of prostitution and the slave conditions produced by it, how should the Christian regard the hooker on the corner or the waitress in a topless bar? Fallen women they may certainly be, but not irredeemable!

God's righteous indignation against adultery is clear throughout Scripture, but so is his power to forgive and restore public sinners. There were plenty of prostitutes in Palestine in Jesus' day, and their unrighteous activity placed them far outside the kingdom of God. But the Gospels tell us that prostitutes and sinners went out to hear the preaching of John the Baptist, and many responded (Matt. 21:32). There were fallen women among the converts of Jesus, and to one of them, a Samaritan, Jesus taught deeper truths about God than are found almost anywhere else in the New Testament (John 4:7–29). On one occasion Jesus said that through repentance and faith more prostitutes enter the kingdom than do religious leaders whom everyone considers respectable (Matt. 21:31).

In the light of what we know about prostitution and its bondage, we can better understand Jesus' compassion for the woman caught in adultery. After dispersing the Pharisees who had accused her, Jesus said to the woman, "Neither do I condemn you. . . . Go now and leave your life of sin" (John 8:11). My colleague at Westminster Seminary, Harvie Conn, worked for several years as a missionary among prostitutes in Seoul. He reports seeing many Korean girls come out of prostitution after hearing the story of Jesus and this woman. Don't we have here an indicator of the direction in which evangelism should go?

Few women today, and certainly no children, can escape the bondage of prostitution without adequate outside assistance. Here is where bands of trained and committed Christians can do significant things. The risks are high, but someone has to take them. There are locations where prostitutes can be talked to and the gospel presented in clear and simple terms. Prostitutes need to hear that caring people are willing to help them get out of prostitution and begin a new life. Homes must be provided for ex-prostitutes, and security for the children involved, as well as job training, counseling, medical care, and a lot of patient, compassionate Christian discipleship. God's grace can transform anybody, so let's allow the miracles to happen. The rehabilitation of public sinners is a noble Christian endeavor.

There are models for this type of ministry. I personally have seen it being done in Amsterdam, where Youth with a Mission owns and operates ministry centers in the heart of the prostitution zone, an area considered one of the worst of its kind in the world. Director Floyd McClung and his family, along with the mission staff, live and work in the center of the red-light area. I have accompanied some of the workers on their night rounds. They know the women's first names, and they speak a word for Christ to one after another. While sipping coffee in dimly lit bars, they counsel troubled waitresses. In dark doorways they offer help and rehabilitation to women who are seeking a way out. It's not what most church people think of as evangelism, but to reach the lowest it is necessary to go where they are.

To the Procurers

Second, Christians should organize to put procurers on the run. If there were fewer procurers, fewer women would be trapped in the underworld and more prostitutes would be able to get out. Combating procurers is not easy, but it isn't impossible either. Politicians may turn deaf ears for a while, but when the pressure mounts and the media are brought in, they pay attention. The police may seem to have other priorities at first, but they too can be pressured. If Christians and others who are concerned for decency and human rights will organize and develop wise strategies against procurers and their accomplices, hard blows can be struck against the sex industry. Not just the pimps must be targeted, but the owners and managers of topless bars, massage parlors, and houses of prostitution, and the publishers and merchants of pornography. And the businesses that cater to sex tourism must not be forgotten. They are all just as guilty as the hookers on the street.

When I say that Christians should organize against these social vices, I mean precisely that: organize! Individual Christians can help a single prostitute, but tackling the procurers requires coordinated effort. The city and the community need to be educated as to what is going on. Before political pressure can amount to anything, there must be an organization of concerned and vocal citizens. Rehabilitation programs require the help of many workers, including specialists. Christians have the resources, at least to some degree, to diminish the rising tide of prostitution, but to make an impact they must unite, organize, and be willing to take risks for the cause of righteousness.

What a testimony it would be if the churches of Colombo would regularly organize public protests against the sexual exploitation of the thousands of small boys and girls known to be used in the brothels and massage parlors of the city! And let them make sure that the media people are present with their cameras!

Think of what the four thousand churches in Seoul could do to change its image from one of the world's worst sex capitals to a city of righteousness where so many people are hearing the gospel and being transformed by God's grace that the entire urban area is feeling the impact and the brothels are going out of business. Korean Christians could organize boycotts of any business or hotel that caters to prostitution. They could turn out in the tens of thousands at the airport to protest the arrival of sex tours, and later carry their protest to the hotels where the groups stay. Korean churches have the resources to establish rehabilitation programs for prostitutes and advertise these programs throughout the red-light districts, some of which are directly adjacent to churches.

Christians in all large cities where prostitution thrives could set up employment agencies, job-training programs, and referral services between rural and urban churches so that young girls coming to the city in search of work would not fall so easily into the hands of the procurers. Much can be done, but it requires leadership, motivation, and the kind of faith that translates creeds into actions.

To the Clients

Finally, there are the clients, without whom there would be no prostitution industry at all. When we examine this group, we discover maladies far deeper and broader than most people want to acknowledge. For prostitution strikes at the very worth and dignity of human beings.

What sexist and racist attitudes lie beneath the unabashed sexual exploitation of Oriental women in America and Europe as well as in Asia? An American army chaplain told me that 99 percent of the American soldiers stationed in an Asian country where he once served were sexually involved with local women on a regular basis, and his efforts to counsel against such behavior hit a brick wall. If, as is reasonable to assume, half of the men came from Christian homes and churches, what does this say about the moral upbringing they received? In cities throughout Europe and America the sexual exploitation of foreign women, especially poor women from Asia, is practiced daily in brothels, massage parlors, and bars. Is it ignorance or a deeper and more sinister malady that keeps upright citizens from denouncing such social rot?

I think we have to press the diagnosis all the way to the human heart and the subconscious attitudes that produce and condone the sexual exploitation of women. In varying degrees, societies all around the world value women far less than men. It is this underlying sinful attitude that keeps the prostitution industry going.

To those who regard women as objects designed for men's pleasure, use, and disposal, prostitution makes sense, in a warped sort of way. This attitude lies behind the sale of female children in Asia and Latin America, the growing number of female infants allowed to die in China where limits on family size are enforced, and the worldwide commerce in women for prostitution. It is likewise evident in Western media advertising, where female nudity is the most common device for inducing customers to buy a product.

The only cure for all this is the heart-and-life-changing leaven of the gospel, the message and morality of the kingdom of God. The false image of women must be eradicated and the biblical image established in its place. The Bible teaches that women of all races and nationalities are made in God's likeness, and as such they are equal in value and dignity with men. Any attack on, or exploitation of, women and girls is a serious affront to God as well as an ugly blemish on human society.

Prostitution is not a necessary evil in society. It is rather the most degrading activity devised by Satan against womanhood. *Let these women go!* That ought to be the church's cry against prostitution in all its forms. We should shout it so loud that hell shudders.

Testimony of a Missionary

The red-light district of Manila is notorious the world over. Within a three-block area there are nearly one hundred bars which attract customers from every part of the world. Americans, Europeans, Japanese, and Australians walk the streets in search of erotic pleasure. By official count, the district offers one hundred thousand registered call girls, though the actual number is probably much higher since many of the women are unregistered and simply come and go. Besides these, there are an estimated twenty thousand child prostitutes and thousands more male prostitutes of all ages.

Several years ago, an attractive American woman in her mid-twenties by the name of Robin Haines arrived in Manila on a photojournalism assignment to cover the work that Action International Ministries was doing among prostitutes. Her job was to get the pictures and cover the story, not to get deeply involved in the ministry. But to her own surprise, the work among prostitutes intrigued her. She saw a challenge in Manila's massive red-light district, a place from which most Christians could be expected to turn away. She's been involved part-time as a volunteer missionary ever since. She shared the challenge of ministry to prostitutes in an interview with Timothy Monsma, as reported in the August 1987 issue of *City Watch.*

TM: What leads these girls into prostitution?

RH: I have found for the most part it's strictly economic. Now the homosexuals and the male prostitutes are a different story. But for the women, a lot of them have families. Some are women with children and no husband to support them. Many of them are young village girls who have been tricked into prostitution. They left their rural areas after being promised jobs as waitresses in the city, but when they arrived, they were tricked into prostitution. Many of them are picked up at the bus depots when they first arrive in the city and taken to some place where they are repeatedly raped. Then, through the humiliation and shame, they become prostitutes. This happens to very young children as well.

TM: You mentioned that some of them are mothers and have families to support. The people who are brought in against their will, are they able to support their families back home?

RH: Yes. They continue to send the money back home, and most often their families have no idea what trade the women are actually in. But because the family needs the money, the women have to continue working.

TM: How can you help these people?

RH: We have a twenty-four-hour counseling center right in the heart of the red-light district. The center is called The Lighthouse. It's run by our staff. We have Bible studies and various outreach programs. We organize field trips for the girls. Sometimes we take them to the beach. They really love this because they actually live in the bars and they can be there seven days a week without ever leaving that raunchy area.

Sometimes we get a huge bus, load up a bunch of girls, and take them out to the beach for a day off. This gives them a chance to get away, hear God's Word, have a good time, and enjoy nice surroundings. We have also started a vocational training center, and we currently have fourteen girls enrolled in the first class. We teach them tailoring and cosmetology. Both of these trades are very viable in the Philippines. The girls who are getting out of prostitution also need a new place to live, and therefore we are now looking for a house that will serve as a living center.

TM: How many people are on the staff of The Lighthouse?

RH: There are approximately ten Filipinos who live and work there regularly. We would like more foreign missionaries to work among them. I'm currently the only one, other than visitors that come through. I'm working as a volunteer. My forty-hour-a-week job is media. In my free time, when I go out to evangelize, I work with the team of The Lighthouse. Foreigners are desperately needed in this kind of work because in the Philippines people are very attracted to foreigners. I am the only white woman I've seen down there. They come up and talk to me, and then I invite them to come to our Lighthouse center. We work as a great team together, myself and the Filipinos. They do the intensive Bible study and counseling, which I can't do because I'm not fluent in the language.

TM: You are a white woman. Do you ever feel afraid to work in that environment?

RH: Yes!

TM: How do you handle that?

RH: I think for my first year I was riding on a wave of naiveté—extreme boldness. Therefore I did not feel threatened. But now, the more I learn the language, and the more I know what's going on, the more threatened I feel. I always have a bodyguard or a partner with me. When I'm threatened, I run. Threats come from pimps or from drunk men who think that I'm a white prostitute. But most of the people who work in the bars—say the vendors, the doorkeepers, or the policemen—know who I am. I've let people know that I'm a missionary.

TM: If someone would like to begin working with prostitutes, how would you suggest he or she begin?

RH: I have found that the most effective technique is friendship evangelism. They don't want to be bombarded with the gospel. They know they're sinners. They need someone who truly cares about them. They need to know the true love of Christ. They don't know what love really is. And when someone shows them what true love is, it breaks their heart. And because they're hurting so much inside, they're going to try you and reject you for a while. It's because they feel the pain of your love for them. That's why a missionary working with prostitutes has to be someone who's going to hang in there through a lot of disappointments and not expect results real fast.

TM: For the women who have come to the Lord as a result of your work, how many months did you know them before they actually made that bona fide decision and said, "I'm going to serve the Lord"?

RH: Well, some of them come to the center, and they immediately give their lives to the Lord. Maybe they've received a tract that's been passed out, and on the back they find our address. They come and that same day they give their lives to the Lord. Sometimes we don't even know them until they walk into the building. One of the girls that I've been working with is like that. I don't know when she gave her life to the Lord, but I know her conversion is real. She feels now that God has called her to minister among the same group of people that she came from. So she's now enrolled in a discipleship training school conducted by Youth with a Mission, and she is leading Bible studies with bar owners.

TM: What's the place of male workers in this whole endeavor?

RH: Men are needed. In fact, I really wish we had a man right now who'd be down there, helping me work with bar owners. If I had a man down there who would lead Bible studies, and even just have friendship evangelism with the bar owners, it would help a lot. We had a male missionary for a year, mainly working with bar owners. He did incredible work in that area. And we need more people like that, people who are willing to spend a great amount of time making friends and evangelizing them.

TM: In your experience, are women best qualified to work with women in this particular kind of ministry?

RH: Yes, women with women. We do have a large pastoral staff of men working in the counseling center with women, but I think a foreign man should not work with women. The chief ambition of many of the women is to marry a foreign man, so there will always be problems if male missionaries work directly with women.

TM: Is there a message that you would like to get across to Christians in every part of the world concerning work among prostitutes?

RH: Yes, there certainly is. They are an extremely needy and largely unreached people. If God lays on the heart of some Christian an interest in ministering to prostitutes and others who live and work in the red-light districts, I would urge them to give it a try. I'd say to them, come to a place like Manila and work with us for a few weeks. That's the best way to discover if this is where God is calling you.

I would add, however, that anyone who becomes involved in this type of ministry had better be sure about his or her own life, making sure they can maintain their own purity while working in a very unholy environment. If you have serious moral problems in your own life, this isn't the place for you to be.

TM: What prayer requests do you have for all of us?

RH: First, pray for the safety of missionaries and national staff who work in the red-light districts of cities like Manila. Second, pray that the governments of these countries will crack down on the big international organizations that control and profit from the sex business. Third, pray that the girls and the young children will commit themselves to Jesus Christ and have their lives changed.

Discussion Questions

1. What surprises did you discover in this chapter? How has it reshaped your attitude?

2. Evaluate the suggestions made in this chapter as to organized opposition to prostitution. Will they work? Are they sufficient? Will Christians dare?

3. What connection do you see between the deeply ingrained evil of sexism and the exploitation of women through pornography and certain kinds of commercial advertising? How should we personally and individually attack this evil in society?

Church-State Relationships
Timothy Monsma

W hat ought Christians to do when their churches and property are destroyed by Muslim gangs? Should they fight fire with fire? Should they counterattack, destroying mosques and Muslim property?

This was the question faced by the Christians of Kaduna State in northern Nigeria after extensive rioting in their cities in March 1987. The rioters managed to destroy 151 churches (111 of them in the city of Zaria), 155 houses, 169 hotels and restaurants, and 95 vehicles. Two Christians were killed. A pastor was knifed to death, while a deacon was doused with gasoline and, with a tire around his neck, burned to ashes inside his church.

The fighting had begun in the town of Kafanchan. When it spread to the cities of Kaduna and Zaria, the Christian young men of these cities went to the church leaders and said, "What shall we do? If the police and the soldiers do not protect us, we are prepared to fight or to counterattack to defend our lives, our property, and our honor." Since Christians in Kaduna State outnumber Muslims, they might have been able to even the score or to inflict more damage than they had sustained.

Jabani Mambula, executive secretary general of the Fellowship of Churches of Christ in Nigeria, reviewed many of these events in a sermon given in Cameroon the following November. The sermon was based on Matthew 10:16–23 and especially verse 16, which reads, "Behold, I send you out as sheep in the midst of wolves; so be wise as serpents and innocent as doves" (RSV). Mambula explained how wolves will readily attack sheep, which have no way of defending themselves. He then applied the text to the situation faced by the Christians of northern Nigeria the previous March. The church leaders had advised the young men that counterattack was not the Christian way. There are times when Christians must accept and endure persecution without seeking revenge. They must, however, also be "wise as serpents." The Christians proclaimed seven days of fasting and prayer. Not one Christian renounced the faith because of Muslim pressure. On Sunday they gathered for worship in roofless buildings, and the crowds were greater than ever. This was recorded on television for the entire nation to see. All Christians, both Protestant and Catholic, felt a sense of unity with one another such as they had never felt before. Donations poured in from Christians living in other parts of Nigeria. And a number of Muslims, upon seeing the tremendous contrast between their own people, who used violence to gain their way, and the Christians, who turned the other cheek, chose the religion of love and peace. They too became Christians, a result opposite from what the Muslim gangs had intended.

Renouncing violence does not preclude *legal* means of self-protection. One large church building in Kaduna was saved because teams of Christians guarded the structure day and night. Later, when the government held an inquiry into the disturbances, the Christians prepared their case. When a young Christian lawyer faltered because of fear of the authorities, a girl still in her teens took the witness stand. The judge accused her and others of proclaiming the gospel to Muslims. She boldly responded that this was done in obedience to the command of Christ given in Matthew 28:19, a higher authority. In the end, several Muslims were jailed while the Christians were exonerated.

Furthermore, the Christian Association of Nigeria, an organization formed to promote Christian interests in a nation divided into two major religious groups, lodged a protest with the federal government and called for the removal of the governor of Kaduna State. While this request was not granted, the Muslim leaders learned that Christian restraint is not to be interpreted as a weakness to be exploited. They learned that Christians will use every legal means they can find to protect their interests.

In Nigeria the ratio of Christians to Muslims is about fifty-fifty. If, therefore, Nigeria is to have peace and security, these two religious groups must learn tolerance for one another. When conversions take place, it may be necessary for the government to enforce this tolerance.

In other countries, however, Christians find themselves in a definite minority position. Minorities can sometimes appeal to government to protect them from persecution by a majority. But sometimes the government itself joins in the persecution or promotes it. What should Christians do in such circumstances? Or, to state the issue in a more general way, How ought the church of Christ to relate to secular governments? For the last two millennia Christians have asked this question. But it must be asked afresh as the church spreads all over the world and comes into close contact with other religions and blatantly secular ideologies.

The question of church-state relationships is especially prominent in those cities that serve as national or provincial capitals. Here the two entities of church and state rub shoulders with one another. But the question can quickly spring up in any city where government officials are present. In the countryside, on the other hand, people generally have greater freedom to go their own way because of the absence of government officials. Coups take place in cities, not in rural areas.

Models from the Bible

Daniel and Esther

To deal with the issue of how a Christian minority should relate to secular government, we turn to the Bible. The examples of Daniel and Esther are especially instructive. For both Daniel and Esther were members of a minority group in an environment hostile to their faith.

The Jewish nation had been defeated and humiliated by the superior numbers and military might of Babylon. The temple dedicated to their God and their capital city lay in ruins. Most Jews had been deported and were thoroughly demoralized. They lamented, "How shall we sing the LORD's song in a foreign land?" (Ps. 137:4 RSV). Add to this the fact that, in the view of the ancients, the god of a victorious nation was stronger than the god of a vanquished nation. If Babylon could defeat one nation after the other, surely her gods were the strongest of all! How could these impoverished and humiliated Jewish captives "sing praises to [God] among the nations" (Ps. 108:3 RSV)?

A few of the captives had opportunity for advancement. They were, no doubt, tempted to practice their religion in private lest their convictions prevent their advancement or cause them to fall from the favor of their superiors. They might have argued that it was expedient for them to compromise their religious scruples in order to accomplish a greater good, the honor and protection of the people of God. But Daniel and Esther were able to maintain their religious integrity within a hostile environment.

Some might counter that the example of Daniel does not apply to contemporary confrontations because we cannot presume that Christians will receive the miraculous protection that Daniel and his friends enjoyed. It is plain, though, that Esther did not receive miraculous protection in the sense that God set aside the normal course of nature. The story of Esther does not even mention the name of God nor the miracles that God is able to perform. And as for Daniel and his friends, they had no assurance beforehand that God would intervene in their behalf. This is especially clear in the narrative about the giant image that all were commanded to worship. Shadrach, Meshach, and Abednego said, "Our God whom we serve is able to deliver us from the burning fiery furnace. . . . But if not, be it known to you, O king, that we will not serve your gods or worship the golden image which you have set up" (Dan. 3:17–18 RSV). They were prepared to lay their lives on the line.

It should also be remembered that both Daniel and Esther were an encouragement to Jews during the intertestamental period when many died for their faith. These Jewish martyrs were not deterred by the fact that they sealed with their death a witness that Daniel sealed with his life. And in much the same vein Hebrews 11 tells New Testament Christians to take instruction from the faithful of Old Testament times. Should the perseverance of Christians in this age of greater knowledge be weaker than the perseverance of those whose knowledge of God's future redemption was clouded and incomplete?

Moreover, God may still show his power in miraculous ways as he did in the days of Daniel. We hear stories of miraculous intervention in Communist China and other nations where Christian progress is impeded by powerful forces. In 1965 there was an attempted Communist coup in Indonesia. The missionaries of the Christian and Missionary Alliance in Jakarta were ordered to dig a trench in front of their mission, which was located next door to the Communist Party headquarters. The trench was intended to be their grave. But the attempt by Communist forces to take over the government was foiled, and the hand of Christians in Indonesia was strengthened rather than weakened. Some, myself included, would call this a miraculous deliverance. We have no right to declare arbitrarily that the power of God is limited in this age. But the point is that we ought to follow Daniel's and Esther's examples regardless of whether God will miraculously intervene to secure freedom and long life for his people.

Implications for Today

What implications do the stories of Daniel and Esther have for Christian workers in Bagdad, Cairo, Lagos, Buenos Aires, and Hong Kong today? The most important lesson is that Daniel and Esther did not withdraw from the world in order to practice their faith in private or in an isolated community. We can sympathize with the desire of the Essenes and the Jewish monks at Qumran to withdraw from the world in order to practice godliness. We understand why Christian ascetics of ancient times and the monks and nuns of the Middle Ages lived in caves and monasteries far from urban life. But the best model of godliness is not found in isolation from the world. It is found in those who remain loyal to God while they rub elbows with those who reject him. We learn this from Daniel and Esther even if we learn nothing else.

When Daniel and his friends were given special training to prepare them for royal service, they did not reject out of hand the idea of serving a pagan king and the preparation that this entailed. But they made sure that in their eating they honored the Mosaic legislation (Dan. 1). They agreed to serve King Nebuchadnezzar, but not his golden image (Dan. 3). Their unabashed testimony in the course of their work made an impression on the king (Dan. 4). Later, when called to interpret the writing which appeared on the wall during King Belshazzar's feast, Daniel gave a straightforward interpretation, even though it spelled disaster for the king, who might well have responded by killing Daniel on the spot (Dan. 5).

The final story of the book is especially instructive. Daniel's enemies "could find no ground for complaint or any fault, because he was faithful, and no error or fault was found in him" (Dan. 6:4 RSV). They concluded, "We shall not find any ground for complaint against this Daniel unless we find it in connection with the law of his God" (Dan. 6:5 RSV). And when the pressure was on, Daniel refused to hide his religious practice simply to avoid persecution.

Christians today who work for adherents of another faith are sometimes tempted to neglect their work in order to spend more time with their families (a good goal) or in order to go out and witness. Daniel witnessed by the way he did his secular work, and the message came through loud and clear to friends and enemies alike. Babylon (and later Susa) was his home, but he lived there as a citizen of Jerusalem. He had a dual citizenship, just as all Christians, who are in the world but not of the world, have dual citizenship today.

The story of Esther contrasts sharply with the story of Daniel. While Daniel was a man of the Jewish nobility, Esther was a nobody. She was a woman in a man's world. She was orphaned at an early age and brought up by her cousin. Her beauty was an asset, but would have counted for little if she had not been a woman of character and personality, for there were many beautiful women within the far-flung Persian Empire.

Esther was taken to the king's harem without regard to her personal wishes. But she made the best of the situation, obtaining first the favor of Hegai, who had charge of the women, and then winning the favor of the king himself. Neither she nor her cousin Mordecai considered such cooperation to be contrary to their Jewish faith. But when the survival of the Jews hung in the balance, Mordecai persuaded her that she must speak out boldly. And she did so at the risk of her life, although she took every precaution humanly possible to assure the success of her venture.

Both Daniel and Esther were in the world but not of it. They both knew where to draw the line between cooperation with the world in nonessentials and confrontation with the world in essentials. Their examples, together with other examples and instructions in the rest of Scripture, are our models for service to God in the cities of the world.

Guidelines for Church-State Relationships

Respect, If Possible, the Government in Power

What guidelines are available for Christians as they live for Christ under a variety of governments (some hostile and some not) in the urban centers of today's world? It is essential to note, first, that Jesus said, "Give to Caesar what is Caesar's" (Matt. 22:21). Similarly Paul wrote, "Everyone must submit himself to the governing authorities, for there is no authority except that which God has established" (Rom. 13:1). And Peter said, "Submit yourselves for the Lord's sake to every authority instituted among men: whether to the king, as the supreme authority, or to governors" (1 Pet. 2:13–14a). In each of these cases the authority to be honored was pagan. God has provided governments to maintain law, order, and the welfare of the people. We should back these governments even if their leaders are not Christian and we think their policies unwise.

Missionaries and church leaders have demonstrated loyalty to governments by flying the flag and by accepting invitations to government functions, even if they are only social affairs. It is my conviction that missionaries and church leaders ought also to refrain from demonstrations against the government and from party politics. For those who work in places where government policy promotes a religion other than Christianity (or a distinctly different form of Christianity), there are two rules of thumb: (1) Try to obey the law if at all possible, and (2) Refrain from needless provocation.

In order to obey the law, one must first know what it says; then one must try to live within the limits it imposes. Now it is a fact that most governments which proscribe certain activities at the same time permit others. Christians ought to focus on what they are allowed to do rather than testing the government to see how far they can go in doing what is not permitted. For example, some governments ban outdoor Christian meetings. In such situations, one may have to hold all meetings indoors. Expatriate Christian teachers in Communist China are not allowed to speak of their faith openly in the classroom. But they can give witness when students ask them privately about Christianity. They can also speak about it freely in the privacy of their own homes or apartments.

To refrain from giving needless provocation, Christians must be keenly aware of local sensitivities. The word *crusade*, for instance, has negative connotations in the Muslim mind because of the wars over the Holy Land during the Middle Ages. Missions that work in Muslim countries ought therefore to avoid the word *crusade* in describing their work.

Similarly, many governments in Latin America are suspicious of anything associated with liberation theology. So missionaries and churches involved in helping the poor there ought to avoid the term *liberation* in describing their ministry. I am not suggesting that Christians avoid ministries to the poor or muffle the liberating effect of the gospel. But we should avoid using terms that are provocative in and of themselves.

Some Christians invite persecution by foolish behavior. In ancient times, Origen wanted to die a martyr's death along with a number of Christians who were to be executed in the town square. But his mother wisely hid his clothes. Not wishing to appear naked on the streets, Origen stayed home, and his considerable talents were spared for later use in God's service. Daniel and Esther, by contrast, did not invite persecution. They did not needlessly provoke government officials or adherents of other religions. If persecution does come, let it come for the right reasons!

Assert the Right of the Church to Worship and Instruct

Jesus said, "Give to Caesar what is Caesar's." But when Peter stood trial before the Sanhedrin, he told that body, "We must obey God rather than men!" (Acts 5:29). Where is the line between respect for lawful authority and the need to ignore certain laws because they are not in harmony with God's will?

The Bible indicates that Christians are entitled to worship God not only in the privacy of their own homes, but also in corporate services. Along with worship goes instruction in Christian teachings. The apostles were meeting with other Christians in Solomon's Porch, which was part of the outer court of the temple (Acts 5:12), when they were arrested by the Jewish authorities. It was on that occasion that Peter made his statement about serving God instead of men.

Christians need the fellowship of other Christians. In lands where they are persecuted, they often meet secretly in each other's homes or in other nonpublic locations. They find this essential for their Christian development. Accordingly, any law that tries to prevent Christians from meeting with one another for instruction and worship is not to be obeyed.

Though the early Christians honored the Roman government in other respects, they defied its ban on worship by meeting in the catacombs. The house-church movement in modern China is largely responsible for the growth of the Chinese church from a few million members when Communism came to power to over fifty million members today. House churches are used in various lands where Christians are persecuted. Recently, small groups meeting in closed countries that would never grant visas for Christian teachers from abroad to minister openly and freely within their borders have started to use videotapes of well-known Bible teachers.

At times the church may have to be aggressive in defending its right to worship or in defending its members from government harassment. Christians in Indonesia are a minority, but they are a minority recognized by the government. When the Muslim majority becomes too bold, Christians find it necessary to defend their rights by appealing to the government policy. In Nigeria the number of Christians and the number of Muslims are about equal. When Muslims act as if they are the majority, Christians find it necessary to protest, lest they find themselves living in an Islamic state.

Christians should not hesitate to go to court if this is the only way they can obtain their rights. In the early sixties, the headmaster of a mission school was beaten so badly by the Nigerian police that he later died. (The police had been provoked by the murder of two policemen and took out their frustrations on whoever was handy.) Some Nigerians suggested that the Christian mission take the case to court. But the mission took no action, fearing no doubt that some or all of their missionaries would become *personae non gratae* with the Nigerian government. When the family tried to take legal action, people were reluctant to testify and the case was dropped.

In my view, the mission made a mistake in failing to pursue justice in the courts. Suppose that the mission had brought the case to court, and one or more of their personnel had been deported. They could have been replaced, and the Christians of Nigeria would have learned that there are times when they must stand up for their rights. As it turned out, there was a military coup shortly after these events. The new military government would have looked with favor upon a mission that had stood up to the officials of the old regime.

Instruct, but Do Not Intervene

The people of God living out their individual Christian lives in the marketplace are the church of God, but in this section we have in view the church assembled, the church in its official capacity, organized for instruction and worship under its officers. Jesus commanded this church to "make disciples of all nations, baptizing them in the name of the Father and of the Son and of the Holy Spirit, and teaching them to obey everything I have commanded you" (Matt. 28:19–20). Here Jesus gave his apostles a discipling, baptizing, and teaching ministry. It is plain from other parts of the New Testament that the church is also obligated to care for the poor. But the church is not given a mandate to correct all the ills of society, to determine foreign policy, or to overthrow corrupt governments.

The organized church is not a political-action group or a political party. At times the church may wish to address the government on pressing moral issues. But it will do so only if its leaders are agreed that cardinal biblical principles are being violated. The church might wish, for example, to say something about abortion and the sanctity of human life because the sixth commandment clearly says, "Thou shalt not kill." But it would be foolish for a church to try to tell the government where a new highway ought to be built, for there are no biblical directives on which to base such advice.

While the church is not a political party, it does have a teaching ministry that touches all of life. It must teach its members the full counsel of God for every area of life, as taught throughout the Scriptures. This includes the biblical concern for the poor and the downtrodden, who sometimes suffer because of government policies. Recently an Indonesian Christian publisher said to me, "We need more Indonesian Christians who are Josephs or Daniels." This was an apt comparison, for these two men stood up for the Lord in the midst of a pagan society, and they were, or became, government officials.

Does the church of Christ around the world teach about Joseph, Daniel, and Esther? Or are many pastors content to proclaim only the way of salvation Sunday after Sunday while they avoid the thorny issues involved in living for the Lord out in the world? Do we sometimes preach Jesus Christ as Savior but omit to mention that he is to be the Lord and King of our lives?

A good teaching ministry tackles the hard issues that arise for Christians in the workplace and in politics. It provides instruction on biblical ethics so that Christians, when they must make crucial decisions, can do so confidently, knowing that they are guided by the Word of

God. Church leaders will also want to pray individually with their members as they face critical issues, and to engage in private counseling regarding specific problems.

Bribery

We conclude this chapter with a problem that arises frequently for Christians in developing countries—the problem of bribery. The Bible clearly states that bribery is wrong (1 Sam. 8:3; Amos 5:12). Yet there are certain nations where it is virtually impossible to do business with the government or in the private sector unless some bribery takes place. A bribe is here defined as paying in advance to receive a service or a contract to which one is entitled. People who take bribes place that money in their own pockets rather than in the account of the government or the company for which they work.

A Christian approach to this problem distinguishes between demanding a bribe from others and paying a bribe to someone who forces it from you. Christians who are given positions of authority sin against the Lord if they demand bribe money from others. On the other hand, Christians may sometimes find it necessary to pay bribe money in order to accomplish their objectives. It would be wrong, of course, for them to bribe in order to receive positions, promotions, or contracts to which they are not entitled. But usually the one who sins is the one who demands and takes the bribe.

When the church of Christ observes bribery, nepotism, corruption, and blatant disregard for the rights of the poor, it may be tempted to intervene by way of political action. It may wish to sponsor demonstrations, call for a general strike, distribute arms, or engage in subversive activities. Individual Christians may and ought to be active politically. But political activity was not on the list of obligations given by Christ to the organized church and its officers. Full-time church workers do well to refrain from running for political office while they remain church employees, so that it is clear to everyone that worship and party politics are two separate spheres of life.

The church's concern for the poor can be directly expressed in diaconal work among them. As the church cares for its own poor and reaches out to others, it becomes a model in miniature of what society ought to be like. It has often happened that works of charity first begun by the church or by a Christian society were later assumed by a government agency, as government officials felt an obligation to carry forward what Christians had begun. Often the people of God have been in the vanguard of social change. Even when governments assume responsibility for relief or development programs formerly administered by the Christian community, there are always other areas of need not yet touched by the government in which Christians can and should be active.

Christians who live in metropolitan areas will face many problems that are not specifically mentioned in this chapter. A whole book could be written on this subject. For now, however, I have sought to give some guidelines that might be applied to a variety of specific problems.

It is important that we continue to study Scripture for guidance on specific issues and that we do so communally. The difficulties are too imposing for Christians to face in isolation. But in fellowship with other Christians who discuss the problems in the light of Scripture, we may expect divine guidance (John 14:26). We may also look forward to the joy and satisfaction of being light and salt for the Lord in a dark and suffering world.

Discussion Questions

1. List some specific problems in state-church relationships that are not discussed in this chapter. What guidelines given in this chapter are relevant to these problems?
2. In addition to Daniel and Esther, what other Bible characters furnish examples for contemporary Christians to follow? Explain their significance.
3. Do you agree with the author's belief that full-time Christian work ers should not run for political office? Discuss your reasons.
4. Think of reasons why a Christian group that has been wronged might not seek to obtain justice in the courts, and evaluate the arguments pro and con.

18

Raising a Family in the City by Choice
Roger S. Greenway

Twenty-four wives and mothers helped me prepare this chapter. All of them are raising, or have raised, their children in large cities for the sake of Christian ministry. That is, these families intentionally chose to live in the city for the sake of serving the Lord and building his kingdom in the urban context. All twenty-four families presently live in North America, though some have had overseas experience. They represent a variety of churches and mission organizations, and not all of them are Caucasian.

For many young couples the chief obstacle to urban mission is the thought of having to raise their children in what is perceived as a hostile environment. My wife and I know from experience that the city can be hostile and that the decision to live there with a family should not be treated lightly. In the course of raising our five children, we lived in several large cities: Colombo (four years), Mexico City (seven years), Fort Worth (two years), and a medium-sized city, Grand Rapids (ten years). By the time we moved to Philadelphia in 1982, our children were grown and had left home. Nevertheless, there were much prayer and soul searching before we decided to move into an inner-city neighborhood which had a generous share of problems.

As I look back over the years of child rearing in major urban centers, I recognize that our family did a number of things to cope with the realities of the situation. We faced the problems of home and family security like everyone else, and we struggled over the issue of proper schooling for the children. We did the same things that hosts of other people did every day. The only differences were that as Christians and as missionaries we deliberately chose the city as our arena and we sought to live by kingdom values in the urban milieu. We wanted our children protected from violence and undue temptation and, at the same time, exposed to enough of life's harsh realities that they would mature in their understanding of the gospel of sin and grace and be moved to Christlike compassion for a lost and hurting world. We wanted them to participate in our ministry, part of which was our choice of location and life in the city.

A Questionnaire on Urban Living

In order to test our own experiences and observations against those of others serving God in the city, I prepared a questionnaire which I sent to twenty-five wives and mothers. I solicited the reactions of these women because they carried a major share of the responsibility for raising their children. Often it is said that while the men may enjoy working in the city, their wives don't share the enthusiasm because they have to bear the burdens which come from urban circumstances. Therefore, I wanted to know what the wives and mothers thought. All but one answered my questionnaire, and most sent long, thoughtful responses. Several added personal letters, giving additional thoughts and observations.

Accompanying the questionnaire was the letter which appears on the following page.

Dear _____,

One of the biggest obstacles to urban
ministry for many people is the prospect of
raising a family in the city. For non-urban
people, the thought of bringing children into
city neighborhoods is almost too much to
expect.

For that reason I am doing research on
Christian family life in the city with a view
to uncovering the facts as they are and
helping those who are considering a move to
the city for ethical and religious reasons.

The enclosed questionnaire is being sent to
persons like yourself—Christians who live in
the city by choice and who are raising, or
have raised, a family there.

Please pour yourself a cup of coffee and
answer the questions as candidly as possible.
Some of the issues you probably have thought
about many times in the past, and the answers
are on the tip of your pen. In other cases
you may want to do some fresh thinking.

Your insights and observations are worth a
great deal. The number of people who can help
in this type of research is not great, so I
am depending heavily on your answers.
Together we may be able to increase the
number of servant-families for Christ in the
city.

In the questionnaire I raised six issues and asked for the women's opinions. In the pages that follow I present their thoughts and ideas, generally verbatim but sometimes in summary form.[1] Very often the same idea appeared in several responses; I have tried not to repeat unnecessarily.

1. What were your strongest motivations for choosing to raise your family in the city?

"The desire to be involved with a strong church that was committed to making an impact on society, and whose members lived within a few blocks of one another."

"The desire that our children not be insulated from the problems of our cities, but rather learn to care about and address those problems in the context of a Christian community."

"We never would have chosen the city ourselves! But we strongly believe this is where God brought us and wants us to be. Believing this, we are at peace about it and find joy in living in the city."

"My husband and I started our marriage with the commitment to be salt and light in places where these are needed. We found what we were looking for in the city."

"We enjoy living with a variety of people, cultures, and experiences. City life is so fascinating and stimulating."

"When we came to the city, we hardly knew what we were getting into. Our children were very small, and we didn't know what raising them in the city might mean. But we believe God led us here for ministry, and he will protect and provide."

"We came to the city to serve God in an international neighborhood by turning our home into a discipleship center for different kinds of people. We couldn't do this anywhere else."

"We moved to the city and joined an older church whose members

1. I acknowledge with thanks the following people who responded to my survey and contributed the valuable insights and observations built into this chapter: Debra Algera, Susan Baker, Linda Bobick, Jan Borger, Joan Brauning, Bettina Clowney, Jan Comanda, Anne Corey, Ruth Correnti, Arneda Crichton, Edna Greenway, Judy Hall, Marcia Hopler, Beth Kidd, Mary Krispin, Helen Labosier, Kathy McGovern, Sara Mitchell, Bonnie Negan, Marsha Petty, Millicent Pinnock, Lynn Prontnicki, Charlene Rogers, Barbara Vander Klay.

I also call the reader's attention to Raymond J. Bakke's excellent chapter on this subject in his book *The Urban Christian* (Downers Grove, Ill.: Inter-Varsity, 1987), pp. 158–78. Bakke stresses the point that if "churches are to flourish in our most disturbed urban areas, then Christians must learn to be incomers, living and raising families in them. Without incomers, we cannot expect God to raise up new generations of Christians where there are none now" (p. 160).

were almost all senior citizens. We felt like 'pioneers'; we were the first young white family to move into that neighborhood for years. We were motivated to try something risky for Christ and show other young families that it could be done. We wanted our children to grow up in an interracial community, to develop healthy attitudes toward people who were different from themselves, and to be part of a strong Christian community that struggled with the big issues. And that's exactly what we've found. It's great!"

"Very simply, our motivation came from my husband's clear call to ministry in New York City and the overwhelming need for Christian witness that we've found here."

"First of all, our sense of calling brought us to the city. Since coming we've found the city so challenging, and never boring. Our children's spiritual lives have flourished because of the strong, vital Christian community we're part of."

"We chose the city for ourselves and our children because of our commitment to serving Christ in a place of high need, and also the belief that the gospel is best modeled by incarnation, not by commuting."

"For us, there was no choice. My husband's job is here."

2. What things do you find hardest about raising your children in the city?

"Crime, the traffic, and the litter on the street."

"Minimal yard space for the children to play."

"Poor public-school system. Alternative Christian schools aren't available in this part of the city."

"Being surrounded by so much brokenness and so many hurting people, trash strewn everywhere, marred buildings, while I long for beauty and wholeness for my children as well as myself."

"The constant blaring of disco music, especially in the summertime when the windows are open. You can't get away from it, and it's so loud. It penetrates through the walls of the apartment building two yards from the wall of our house!"

"Our children see so many negative models, hear so much foul language, and see so much immorality. They see drunks, prostitutes, and drug peddlers every day. Yet I know that it makes them learn early to take a stand for Christ."

"We have to use public transportation, and it's so time-consuming. Getting around the big city eats up your day. But our children know nothing different and don't mind it at all."

"Not being able to let the children run freely through the neighborhood because of the dangers involved."

"Having to keep doors locked is a hassle with three kids constantly in and out, especially in summer."

"We live in an apartment. There's no grass, no yard, not even a place to learn to ride a bike."

"I grew up on a farm, and I'm still learning how to live in the city and enjoy it. It's so different. My two children, sixteen and twelve, take the city for granted. But I'm still learning."

"My family is afraid to come here. So they seldom visit us, which means our children miss getting to know their relatives."

"You've got to fight for your rights in the schools and everywhere else. There are so many pressures against everyone."

"I fear that the children will pick up wrong attitudes. There's so much indifference toward basic human values, disregard for God's creation, lying and deception, and the moral degradation you see everywhere. Our children will either grow morally tough, or they are likely to succumb."

"We are minorities in our neighborhood, and we're here to serve others. It's hard for our children to accept this role."

"Our older children spend much time traveling by foot and public transportation. It's sometimes hard for us as parents to keep trusting God to keep them safe and growing morally and spiritually in an environment that is often hostile and violent."

"Our children have often felt as though they didn't fit anywhere, neither with the blacks or whites in the neighborhood because we won't let them do many of the things the neighborhood kids do, nor with their cousins who live in suburbia."

"We fear our children will be catapulted into adolescence and not have a full childhood to prepare them for their teen years. They're exposed to everything so young. As parents, we struggle to find the balance between protecting them and teaching them independence."

3. What advantages have you discovered in raising your family in the city?

"There are many educational, cultural, and recreational facilities, such as zoos, art galleries, museums, libraries, concert halls, science centers, and sport arenas."

"Exposure to a wide variety of people, cultures, races, and economic levels. The children grow up experiencing what the world is like."

"Our church is more vital than most suburban churches we know. The members here really support one another, and we're more aware of the major issues facing the world."

"Because our family is constantly exposed to so many needy people and spiritually lost people, we've developed a deep sense of mission and compassion."

"Living in this big social mix has done a lot for our family. We attend concerts at the Academy of Music and shop for clothes at a thrift store. Our children know all about street beggars, drug addicts, homeless children, and bag ladies. They've learned to love blacks and whites and to pray for a wide variety of people. It's made them learn young how to pray over enormous spiritual and social problems."

"Our children are 'street smart' and know how to handle themselves in a wide variety of situations."

"There are many children close by for our children to associate with. We've become close to many of our neighbors, and since our relatives live far away, these neighbors have become our extended family."

"In the city you can develop your own lifestyle and don't have to 'keep up with the Joneses' who may have more money. There's so much variety here that you're free to design your lifestyle according to your convictions and your income. As for the children, you don't have to remind them of poor people far away. They grow up knowing about the poor."

"Public transportation is great. We don't have the chauffeuring problems that parents in the suburbs have with their kids. Our kids know how to get anywhere using buses, trains, and subways."

"Closeness to stores and services."

"Christian families in the city are closer because you have to look out for each other. Just because it's tough, we lean on each other more. It's not an unhealthy, isolated existence."

"We find it a healthy place to raise kids because we learn to meet problems head on as a family, and to deal with them together. The kids are the beneficiaries as they learn to live the Christian life, and make distinctively Christian decisions, in the context of all kinds of moral, social, and religious challenges."

"Our children have received a first-hand education in terms of sin's reality and consequences without actually being tainted themselves. They've been much more exposed than children in small towns or suburbs, but it's not hurt them a bit. Instead, it's made them stronger, more alert Christians. We praise God for that."

"The development of cross-cultural skills in the lives of our children will serve them well in later life."

"It has made us choose between biblical values and the cultural values and ethical patterns of society in general. The issues in urban society are so large that you can't avoid making decisions. In our case we've made them as a family, and I think it has shaped our children enormously."

"Property taxes are lower."

"Proximity to first-rate medical care."

"Our children will be better prepared for the future, when almost everyone will live in cities."

4. What are the most serious problems in your neighborhood as far as your family and its welfare are concerned?

"Crime and the threat of crime, both petty stuff like purse snatching and major crimes such as murder and rape. We've got all kinds close by, and you always have to be on guard."

"Locks and keys, watchmen and security devices, and still you're never sure you're safe. There are always enough things happening in our building to keep you uneasy."

"The local public school is poor, and as a result the children on our block go to a variety of alternative schools. This hurts the quality of the neighborhood, especially for the children."

"Women and girls can't go out alone at night, because it isn't safe. This cramps our lifestyle."

"Small children have to be watched all the time. The traffic is heavy in front, and there are known abusers in the neighborhood."

"The deterioration of property due to lack of caring. The defacing of walls and buildings with graffiti has a negative effect on people's spirits. It makes it hard to teach children care and respect for property."

"Our particular neighborhood is very mono-ethnic and racist. The children have picked up some of it."

"Drugs are used all the time near our house, but that doesn't affect us directly. For us the most discouraging thing is the trash and broken glass. Litter is everywhere, on the streets and sidewalks, in the parks, and in every vacant space."

"Financially, we find it more expensive to live in the city. Taxes are high, property is expensive and so is insurance. Auto insurance is so high that we can hardly afford to own a car."

"Noise and air pollution. We're accustomed to traffic sounds, but when the neighbors fight or turn the music up at night we can't sleep."

"We find it hectic to always have to schedule the kids' lives so that they don't have to walk alone."

"We have three teenage daughters, and their safety is a constant concern. In our neighborhood, 55 percent of the youth are unemployed, and there's always a group hanging around looking for something to do. Usually what they do isn't good."

"Vulnerability because of the nature of our ministry. We open our door to all kinds of people with a wide variety of problems. Sometimes they are not satisfied with the kind of help we give, and they might take it out on our children. Abuse and violence are quite common occurrences."

"Gangs, and the possibility of being an innocent bystander caught in a gang fight over 'turf.' The possibility of attack and robbery from addicts needing money for a fix is always on our minds."

"Exposure of young children to acts of violence. Street fights, gang violence, family fights, and the mistreatment of animals are things our children see too much of."

"Poor schools, lack of discipline in the schools, and the negative influence of other pupils whose parents neither discipline them nor encourage them to study."

"We have to go outside our neighborhood to find decent medical care, adequate schools, and things for our children to do. Our immediate neighborhood offers almost nothing that we hold dear."

5. Do your children attend public or private schools?

"We teach them at home."

"We were able to get them out of the neighborhood public school and transfer them to an excellent public school in another part of the city. This school offers good education, and it is well integrated racially. Other parents from our neighborhood are trying to transfer their children too."

"Private school, but we're switching to public mostly for financial reasons."

"Private school. It isn't a Christian school, but it offers excellent education, there is discipline, and the basic values of our home are upheld in the school."

"Thank God, a Christian school! We began a Christian school in order to make staying in the city a viable option for young families like ours."

"Public! We believe it's important to be 'in the world,' and we don't want our children growing up afraid of the world. We teach our children Christian values at home, they are active in our church, and for the rest we don't want them surrounded by an overly protective environment."

"We've had them in both public and Christian schools, and there are advantages and disadvantages to both. Each family has to decide. Sometimes being in a more protected atmosphere is more important for one child than for another."

"We're home schooling them for the first few years and then plan to send them to a Christian school."

6. What advice would you give to young couples considering moving to a city neighborhood and raising a family there?

"Live near other members of your church. They will provide you not only with friends and playmates for the children, but also with emotional support and opportunities for shared ministry."

"Realize that your block is your primary neighborhood. Look for a block that is not on too busy a street and where there are other young families and long-term residents."

"Take advantage of the many educational and cultural opportunities the city has to offer, and get involved with your neighbors."

"Be sure the city is where God wants you. That really is the main motivation for being there. And that's the safest place to be."

"Involve your children in your ministry."

"Realize that the frustrations, difficulties, dangers, and problems can be used by God to teach you and your family valuable lessons. The urban environment can be a terrific place to grow spiritually for all of you, but be prepared for spiritual warfare. It's no playground!"

"Plan regular times to get away from it all—from the concrete and the filth, the noise and the traffic, just to be together as a family where it's quiet and peaceful."

"Be sure both parents want to live in the city. Once the decision has been made, decide together on the section of the city and the neighborhood. There's plenty to choose from, and making the choice together is a key to success and happiness in the city."

"Have fairly clear goals as to what you want to achieve by living as a family in the city. For example, what do you seek to accomplish in terms of ministry, church involvement, community participation, and personal witness? You will have to keep going back to these goals to evaluate what you are accomplishing and where you may be failing. You may also want to spell out the things to avoid for the sake of family well-being."

"Make it a matter of serious prayer before deciding to move to (or remain in) the city. Where you live is a religious choice, and it's important to know that the Lord wants you where you are."

"If you are about to move into a large city for the first time, expect some culture shock. It's a lot like moving to a foreign country. Determine to be flexible, and go slowly."

"When choosing a place to live, look for neighborhoods that have some Christians already settled there. Try to pick a neighborhood that has a positive community spirit, or at least the makings of it. Building such spirit may become one of the things you work at."

"Recognize that it takes time to make friends in the city. People here are not as open as they are in small towns and many suburbs. You will have to put forth time and effort to get to know your neighbors and build relationships."

"Don't sacrifice your children unnecessarily. I recommend a Christian school, but in any case you'll have to investigate, monitor, and keep informed of what's happening in your children's schooling."

"Regularly get your family *out* of the city. Take them camping in the woods away from the noise and pressures of urban life."

"In everything you do, keep eternity's values in view. You're called to the city for the sake of Christ's kingdom and his righteousness, so don't allow earthly treasures (or the possible loss of them) to stand in your way. Safety and satisfaction are in and from the Lord, not from communities, comforts, or human devices."

"Set your minds to avoid making comparisons between your own suburban childhood and your children's life in the big city. Comparisons of that kind can have negative effects, especially when you remember only the positive aspects of suburban and small-town life."

"Plant a garden if you have any yard at all, and put up a bird feeder. Keep in touch with nature."

"Make friends of city people; learn to relax and enjoy their company. It isn't good for you or your children always to run off to your suburban friends when you want a good time."

"Consider carefully your motives for living in the city. Are you ready to love city people, open your home and hearts to them, and become one with them? If you choose the city because of the 'glamor' of it, or because you think that somehow you're going to 'save the city,' you are in for a letdown. Come here to learn, to love, and to serve, and you'll find a place and a welcome."

"Be sensitive to the needs of each family member."

"It is easier to move to the city if you are young and your children are small. The children grow up learning cross-cultural living, and they adapt naturally to the things their parents may have to struggle with."

"Finding a community-oriented church is so important."

"Learn the basic rules of safety and precaution, and teach them to your children. Then trust God for your safety, and don't let all the stories you hear scare you away."

"Use the urban environment as occasions to instruct your children about injustice, inequality, and racism. It's hard to learn what these things really are without personal exposure. Let the city become your teacher."

"Be prepared to set aside some of your pleasant old habits, like taking walks at night. But at the same time look forward to the new and exciting experiences the city makes available to you."

"Don't be too idealistic. Moving into a predominantly ethnic neighborhood may not be easy, and you may find yourself becoming more racist than before."

"Analyze your own ability to appreciate people of other races and cultures, and whether you can minister comfortably and effectively among them. Test yourself in these areas before moving into a cross-cultural neighborhood or starting cross-cultural ministry. This kind of life and service isn't for everyone."

"Find a Christian support group as soon as possible."

"While it is true that concerns about the children take top priority, young families living and ministering in the city have to be alerted to other problems too. For one, we've struggled with just plain *burn-out*. There is so much to be done, and fresh needs are always pounding at our door. Second, there's *discouragement* because there's so much failure and so much pain. There's a lot of failure in ministry too, and every inner-city worker I know struggles frequently against a strong inclination to give up and move away. What this means is that living and ministering in the city require a lot of prayer, constant dependence on God's strength, and a faithful support group."

A Strong Recommendation

On the strongly positive side, a mother who is raising five children in the inner city writes:

> Despite its problems and frustration, I highly recommend living in the city. If the main purpose of your life, individually and as a family unit, is to advance God's kingdom, where could you find a more challenging place? Our faith has grown enormously since we moved to the city. We've learned to trust God for our children's safety and education. As a family we've learned to understand the hard realities of poverty, unemployment, and substandard education, and it's helped form in us the compassion of Christ. At the same time, we've come to see the hollowness of many of the goals and values of middle-class Christianity and the extent to which materialism has gained control of many churches. Our own church in the city is a vital part of our lives. So what does it matter if the sidewalks are covered with litter and there's no big yard to play in?

City life is a blessing to us, and we've learned to celebrate God's grace and power here.

Summary Observations

As I review the responses and the frequency with which some of them appear, it strikes me that nearly all the women indicate high Christian motivation and a desire to serve God wherever he places them. Most have chosen the city out of a sense of calling and a desire to do something significant for the kingdom of God. In the process they have come to appreciate the advantages as well as the difficulties of urban living.

Crime and inferior schooling pose the major problems for families. It strikes me that none of the respondents reported actual attacks on her children. God is thanked for that, and almost all mentioned trusting God to protect their families. Schooling is a universal problem, and city families deal with it in a variety of ways, including home schooling, private schools, and seeking a public school that is reasonably good.

The social and cultural advantages of living in the city are recognized by all. Alongside these are the personal spiritual advantages incurred through involvement in vital community-oriented churches and cross-cultural exposure. Some parents see the city as an ideal environment for the development of morally and spiritually tough young kingdom citizens. Cities have everything, and they require adaptability on the part of residents. The variety of cultures and experiences stimulates growth, challenges Christian thinking, and offers a host of opportunities to witness for Christ. It is significant that not one of the respondents suggested that the urban environment had proven detrimental to her family's well-being.

The respondents offer plenty of sober advice to young couples who, for the sake of ministry, are considering moving to a city neighborhood and raising a family there. Everything the respondents say is worth pondering. It strikes me that without exception they find the church in the city to be vital, and fellowship with other Christians an intense and rewarding experience. It seems that the pressures of urban life bring out the need for mutual support among believers.

Finally, borne out by many of the responses is a theory I've had for some time: a child's character development suffers in direct proportion to how *in*frequently he or she is obligated to cope with life's inequities. Please note that I say "infrequently." Sheltered children in affluent homes who are never exposed to some of life's ugly injustices, inequities, and human suffering grow up as *victims of experiential depriva-*

tion. Antiseptic environments are not the best breeding grounds for warriors of the kingdom of Christ. I am not promoting overexposure, nor do I underestimate the danger of sin and temptation. But I believe that if supported by a warm Christian home and vital church, and supervised by prayerful, watchful parents and concerned Christian leaders, children have a better opportunity in the city than in any other social or geographical context to grow up strong and wise in the areas of life that count most and best prepare them for broad and fruitful kingdom service.

Discussion Questions

1. After reading this chapter, how do you feel about the prospects of raising a family in a large city?
2. Do you think it is important to live in the neighborhood (a) where your church building is located? (b) where most of its members live?
3. Compare the temptations experienced by the average suburban youth with those of the big city. Is suburbia really so much safer?
4. Why do you think it is that North American cities generally have more violent crime than do giant metropolises like Tokyo and Seoul?

The Pros and Cons of Church Buildings

Roger S. Greenway

Church buildings are common sights in most cities, reminding us of the presence and sometimes the prestige of organized Christianity. In Western cities we take church buildings for granted. But today the cost of buying property and erecting traditional types of church buildings is staggering. In every discussion of urban mission strategy, the question inevitably arises as to whether we can *afford* to plant churches in major cities. Compared with the funds needed to start rural congregations, church-planting work in the city appears to be more costly than most mission budgets will allow.

This chapter will examine the pros and cons of church buildings in the city and suggest certain guidelines for deciding whether, and what kind, to build. In a personal letter dated May 24, 1985, Donald McGavran raised the question as to whether urban realities require us to reassess the value of traditional church buildings:

> As I look at the amazing growth of house churches in China and remember that the New Testament nowhere records the building of a single building and remember the amazing growth of Yonggi Cho's denomination in Seoul, South Korea, where he has more than 20,000 house churches, I am led increasingly to believe that effective urban evangelization today must mean founding living churches in rented quarters. Perhaps every hundred such churches will erect a central building. But the building must always be regarded as a secondary matter. House churches are led by men and women who receive no salary and who speak about Christ and the Bible in terms understandable to their intimates.

Added to the issues raised by McGavran are questions concerning stewardship and the message conveyed to the poor by the kind of church buildings we typically erect. The lament of the great Japanese urban evangelist Toyohiko Kagawa is highly relevant to today's mission strategists:

> The religion of imposing edifices is a heartbreaking affair. It is the soul's cast-off shell. A religion which builds men rather than temples is much to be preferred. For this reason I reject everything connected with the religion of imposing architecture.
>
> Under the eaves of the cathedral nestle the slums. Before the Vatican Palace mercenary troops stand guard. Nothing is so pitiful as the religion of cathedrals, temples, and stately edifices.
>
> Well would it be if the world's churches and temples were razed to the ground. Then possibly we would understand genuine religion.[1]

The Pros of Church Buildings

Let's examine some specific factors relevant to this discussion. One factor is the long history behind the erection and setting apart of special buildings for church use. People have come to expect them. It can be argued that because the use of specially designed buildings for religious purposes is such a long-standing tradition, there must be some wisdom to it. To break with this tradition of the Christian religion is a risky undertaking.

There are obvious advantages to having church facilities. A building provides a congregation with a fixed address and a place to which people can be referred. A building may help convey a sense of identity to both the members of the congregation and outsiders. An edifice designed or renovated to meet the ministry needs of the church can be a valuable asset. Besides providing an auditorium for congregational worship, there are classrooms and office space. Church buildings are available for use seven days a week, and that is a big advantage. Anyone who has ever lived with the limitations of rented quarters that were designed for other purposes or are available only certain hours a week knows how difficult such arrangements can be.

Another advantage is privacy for worship, for counseling, and for the various meetings of the church. Buildings offer opportunities for creative ministries in the urban context. They can be places for refreshment and spiritual retreat amid the rush and clamor of the city. If used

1. Cited in Cyril J. Davey, *Kagawa of Japan* (New York: Abingdon, 1960), p. 27.

properly, a downtown or inner-city location can make the church building a kind of oasis for spiritual and emotional renewal. Such oases are much more needed in the city than in rural locations.

In the crowded city of Colombo, on one of the busiest intersections, stands the Church of the Open Door, belonging to the Anglican denomination. Two decades ago this congregation decided that the location of its building should be turned into a witnessing opportunity. Thousands of people—Buddhists, Hindus, Muslims, and Christians—passed the church doors every day. Many of them lived under crowded and difficult conditions, and a high percentage had personal and spiritual problems which the church thought they might like to talk about. Why not use the building to good advantage and make it a twenty-four-hour-per-day oasis where people could get away from the rush of the street, pray, talk to a Christian counselor, and be exposed to the values and teachings of Christianity?

A price would have to be paid, of course. If the church were to remain open day and night, staff would have to be present at all hours to watch the premises, deal with difficult individuals, and counsel people who might come seeking help of various kinds. There would be some wear and tear on the building if it were exposed around the clock to people from the street. But the church made the decision to maximize the building's location and use it to minister to whoever would come through the doors. Staff was hired, volunteers from within the congregation were trained and organized, and a vital ministry was begun. Seven days a week and twenty-four hours a day the Church of the Open Door is a spiritual oasis and witnessing center for the southern end of the city.

A Message of Commitment

The erection of a building sends a message of commitment to the neighborhood. It shows that the Christians who are making this investment intend to stay and become part of the life of the community. They say by their investment: "We're here to stay and we mean business. We're not a fly-by-night operation." It may be that in the city, where changes occur so rapidly and people have learned to expect short-term commitments from those who claim they want to help, investing in a building says more than a thousand sermons about the intention of the congregation. That may explain why attendance often picks up when a new building is opened.

Buildings are statements to believers and nonbelievers about the builders (or remodelers) and the concept of ministry which they have in mind. The way a building is designed and the ministry facilities it offers convey a message, and the world hears it.

The commitment of a congregation to a building project also serves to measure the members' loyalty and enthusiasm for the church and its ministry. A building program can spur the development of congregational life because members feel personal ownership of the things they have invested their money in. People are less likely to pick up and leave a church when they've put some of their hard-earned money into erecting or refurbishing its building. If our goal is to make a long-term impact for Christ on a city, making an investment in a building, though it may be a subtle device, is a factor to consider seriously.

In some countries special buildings set apart for Christian worship are required. Services cannot legally be held anywhere else. In Cuba, for example, the law states that all religious activities must take place inside an approved church building. It is difficult to obtain a permit to erect a new church building; the buildings that are approved are under government surveillance and control. Annually, Cuban pastors must submit to the government their church's schedule for the year. The schedule must be posted at the church, and everything the church does must take place in the building. The same is true in many other Communist countries.

In China there is a different situation: there are both underground churches, which technically are illegal, and officially recognized and controlled churches, which occupy designated government-approved buildings. For a quarter century the Christian faith survived and grew through a network of underground churches, while the regular church buildings were kept closed by the Communist government. Today many of the buildings have been reopened for worship, and a great deal of effort is being made by the government to close down the operations of the underground churches. The issue is one of control; by trying to keep everything religious within officially designated buildings, the government hopes to maintain surveillance over Christian teaching and activity.

In Mexico City, evangelical churches face the problem of a law which requires that all church property be owned by the government. This law was enacted at the time of the Mexican Revolution in the early 1900s and was intended to eliminate the vast property holdings of the Roman Catholic Church. But now the law serves as a serious hindrance to the planting of new evangelical churches. When evangelicals begin to hold services in a private home prior to erecting a building, the landlord often objects and threatens to evict the tenant who allows such services in the house; the landlord fears the property may be taken over by the government. When evangelicals buy property and erect a church building, they must notify government officials and turn over the property to the federal authorities. Even seminary buildings, if properly registered, become federal property in Mexico. Church members pay for the facilities and must maintain the property, but the government holds the title. Even the smallest item of furnishing belongs to the state.

In Muslim countries the erection of a church building often runs into serious difficulty; in strict Muslim nations it may be impossible. We recall what happened to the one Christian church in Kabul, Afghanistan, some years before the Russians invaded the country. This was an international, English-speaking church that with great difficulty obtained permission to erect a building of its own. The building stood there for some time, and then the government bulldozers moved in and demolished it. On the day set for demolition, the Christians cleaned the building and set everything in perfect order, prayed, sang hymns, and thanked God for the time that he had allowed them to use the facility. Then it was destroyed. I have often wondered if the terrible things that have happened to the Afghan government and people since that time are not related somehow to what the Afghan officials did to that church building.

When church buildings are seized to be used for other purposes, they continue to bear silent witness to the Christian faith and the gospel ministry for which they were erected. In China, for instance, where church buildings were seized and used as warehouses and schools for several decades, their original purpose was not forgotten. When the political climate in China changed and permission was granted for Christians to worship openly once again, those same buildings were refurbished and their ministry resumed. They had been closed for a quarter century, but nobody had forgotten that they were church buildings. The buildings had continued to bear witness to the Chinese community.

A final word in favor of church buildings has to do with the feelings of pastors. Most pastors strongly prefer to have their own church building because it gives them a sense of identity, sometimes of pride. This is true in North America and around the world. I have addressed various gatherings of pastors and missionaries on the subject of church property, and I sense that it is an emotional issue with many of them. "Don't take my building away from me," blurted out one young black pastor in Philadelphia, after I had suggested that there might be alternatives to the traditional church building. The same reaction comes from older ministers, who shake their heads at any suggestion that perhaps in the cities we ought to try some other options. They generally regard it as a wild idea that won't work. It is obvious to me that pastors like church buildings, and as long as there is the possibility of erecting and maintaining them, pastors will work hard to have them. This being the case, maybe it is the way of wisdom to keep them. A contented and hard-working pastor is generally the key to an effective and growing church.

The Negative Factors

But we must also consider the negative side of the question. What does it cost to open a new church in New York City, Hong Kong, or Lagos? The costs are tremendous. When mission agencies examine the costs involved in planting a church in major cities, they shudder. Accustomed as most of them are to working in small villages and rural areas, where land is cheap or free, where building materials can be obtained locally, and volunteer labor can be enlisted to erect the structures, they are reluctant to consider urban areas, where land is expensive, building codes extensive, materials must be purchased, and labor costs are high. Mission budgets simply won't allow church planting in such costly places.

Another negative factor has to do with change in the city, change in the ethnic composition of neighborhoods, in property values, in human wants and needs. Western cities have an abundance of church buildings that one generation of Christians built, used, and then abandoned as members moved to other parts of the city or out to the suburbs. Expensive properties lost their value as the social and economic level of the neighborhoods changed.

Dwindling congregations are often left with beautiful buildings that they cannot fill on Sunday or efficiently use and maintain the rest of the week. Splendid old pipe organs are too expensive to repair and fall silent. Plexiglas has to be installed to protect the stained-glass windows from being broken. Many such buildings have been sold to new congregations whose members represent the ethnic groups that now live in the neighborhood.

It's not bad for church buildings to change hands between congregations if the property continues to be used for Christian purposes, and the new church ministers effectively to the people of the neighborhood. But often the old structures are sold to commercial interests instead of being turned over to congregations that might use them to serve the city and its people. For example, the in thing on the East Coast of the United States is to turn churches with classic architecture into apartment buildings and restaurants. I saw one recently which still retained the brass plates identifying the members in whose hallowed memories the stained-glass windows had been donated. In some cases, pipe organs which once contributed to congregational worship now entertain restaurant patrons. Something seems profane about the whole thing.

Given the enormous costs of building and maintaining church property, what should be the response of Christian congregations and mission agencies that want to grow and multiply, witness and serve in the city? If we continue to rely on traditional church structures, how are we ever going to raise enough money to plant all the churches that are needed, and how are we going to minister to the poor when we invest so much in brick and mortar? That is Donald McGavran's main point, and we have to face the question squarely. Are there alternatives that will meet the needs of God's people for worship, fellowship, and ministry, and at the same time avoid the negative factors we have enumerated?

Guidelines for Church Builders

As we wade through this murky issue, various principles and guidelines will prove worthy of consideration.

1. We should always put people before property. Theoretically, all of us would agree with that. But often we don't carry it out in actual ministry, especially when it comes to church buildings. In most instances, a major part of our resources, time, and attention is poured into church property. Yet in the New Testament we find no instruction that Christians should seek to erect special buildings for church use. In Jerusalem believers used the temple as long as they could, but when persecution arose they scattered, and from that point on they used homes, rented quarters, or the outdoors. We find no record of church buildings for more than two hundred years, which was the very time when the gospel enjoyed its greatest expansion and churches multiplied all across the Roman world. Early Christians directed their energy to ministering to people and spreading the gospel rather than serving property.

2. We should put the needs of pastors and Christian workers before property acquisition. The New Testament makes it plain that God's people owe their leaders basic sustenance. Kingdom workers should not have to go around begging for support, nor be forced into "tentmaking" because the building program receives the church's primary attention. But in many Southern World situations and in the inner cities of North America and parts of Europe, young congregations which cannot afford both to pay their pastor and to erect a building opt time after time for the building and let the pastor's family fend largely for themselves.

I have seen cases where pastors' families were suffering severely because the congregations they served were pouring their resources into the building programs rather than supporting their spiritual leaders. There is no biblical justification for such behavior; in fact, the Bible points in the opposite direction. In 1 Corinthians 9 the Bible teaches that religious workers have the right to material support; nowhere does it suggest that a building program should receive more support than do gospel workers.

3. If, after careful consideration of the factors involved, the congregation decides to purchase property and erect a building, attention should be paid to two things—location and design. Poor choices in either will damage the church's ministry for years to come.

For example, if an out-of-the-way location is chosen, perhaps on a side street where property is cheaper but hard to find, the ministry of the church is going to be affected adversely. Yet so often we find churches located in such places. Hidden churches struggle against the constant burden of their own poorly chosen location. In contrast, wise planners such as those of the Christian and Missionary Alliance in South America have found that choosing favorable locations, highly visible and easily accessible from all parts of the city, has been a boon to church growth. It costs more in the beginning to buy property in a good location, but it pays off in the long run.

Equally important is the layout of the church facility itself. The architectural design says a great deal about a congregation's concept of ministry, its sense of stewardship, and its intentions in the neighborhood and the city. Building design should not be left to the whims of the architect, but should express the congregation's philosophy of ministry.

The style of a church building affects the way the church functions. The size and shape of the building can facilitate ministry or hamper it. If the building is only an auditorium, the church will be telling the community that it is merely a place where people come together, sit on pews, face the front, sing, pray, hear preaching, and then go home. Such buildings can be a great blessing, but they also limit ministries which another type of building could facilitate.

Any congregation that decides to erect a building or remodel an existing structure should study the needs of the people they want to reach and the kind of ministries that might be used to reach them. They should then design a building that will best facilitate the ministries they have in mind. Buildings should be ministry-appropriate.

4. If the property is sold at some later date, the overriding concern ought not to be recouping the investment by selling to the highest bidder, but continuation of Christian ministry to the city and its people. We recognize that there are instances where a neighborhood

changes in such a way that nobody lives there any longer. Such cases are rare, yet they do happen occasionally. But wherever people remain to be reached, evangelized, and ministered to, churches have an obligation to use to that end the properties God has given them.

I have seen sad things happen in North American cities when churches sell their property without concern for its continued use for gospel purposes. It is not wrong in itself for a congregation of a particular racial or ethnic group to relocate its center of worship to a place closer to its members' homes. But an attitude of gross materialism is shown by congregations whose main interest is getting top dollar for their old property. Churches leaving the city need to be thinking about the people they are leaving behind and what kind of church could take over their building to minister more effectively to the needs of the neighborhood.

For the gospel to catch hold in the city, every neighborhood needs churches whose worship and ministry are appropriate to the language, culture, and needs of the people in the area. Inappropriate ministries help nobody, so the transfer of buildings from one congregation to another can sometimes be a blessing. But the governing principle should not be profit, but ministry to city people.

5. Mission subsidy and outside assistance do less damage to a young congregation when such funds are used to acquire church property. An unhealthy dependence results when financial subsidy is used to support pastors and programs. Buildings are more neutral somehow, and funding used for their purchase seems less likely to produce dependence.

This relates to what I wrote earlier about the dilemma facing many Southern World churches when they cannot afford to support a pastor and erect a church building at the same time. Often it is the pastor who pays the price, because congregations tend to choose in favor of the building. It has been my experience that the use of mission money to subsidize pastors is generally harmful to church development and eventually undercuts the pastor's effectiveness. This is because the delicate, sensitive relationship between pastor and congregation hinges on mutual trust and dependency. When foreign subsidy is introduced in any form that lessens the pastor's reliance on the congregation, serious damage is done to the pastor-church relationship. But when foreign money buys brick and mortar, or perhaps a city lot on which to erect a building, no long-term dependence is likely to develop; indeed, if a solid congregation is formed, this is frequently a wise use of mission money.

6. Building acquisition should never be made a fixed—that is, assumed and unquestioned—item in the overall mission strategy. I say this because we simply do not have any New Testament basis for insisting that a building is essential to an effective urban strategy.

Arguing from the New Testament, the most we can say is that a building is an option, a pragmatic issue each group of Christians should decide in its own time and place.

In some places today it is impossible to build a special church building because the government won't allow it or because the leaders of the dominant non-Christian religion will prevent it from happening. We read earlier (p. 209) that more than 150 church buildings were destroyed by Muslims in northern Nigeria in 1987. Suddenly congregation after congregation had to decide whether to rebuild or not. At the time this book is being prepared, some of them are still debating whether it is wiser to rebuild or to find alternative meeting places that might be both useful and less vulnerable. The same question is being faced in some parts of the Philippines, where dozens of church buildings have been closed by insurgents.

7. The Holy Spirit can be relied upon to give urban congregations the creativity to find solutions to the building problem. When traditional church buildings were closed by the Chinese government, Christians found alternative ways to worship God and spread the faith. When the first services were held in the reopened buildings, the officials were stunned to hear the worshipers, young and old, singing Christian hymns from memory. Where had they learned the words and the tunes? In the house churches, at underground worship services, and in other places the officials had never heard about.

On the Eastern seaboard of the United States, some downtown churches have sold the air space above their edifices to developers who keep the old church buildings intact while erecting high-rise office buildings around and above them. From the sale of their air space, the congregations have gained an enormous source of revenue for their ministries, while the original buildings remain in their control. From Singapore to Nairobi, churches are finding creative answers to the questions of where and how to gather for worship and witness. This leads me to conclude that a traditional church building is not always a necessity. The question of whether to erect such a structure must be analyzed carefully from every angle.

I suggest that every church and mission agency should continually be experimenting with new strategies which do not depend on buildings. If we keep ourselves locked into one pattern, we may be missing something important. Rented facilities work amazingly well in some urban contexts. Cell groups and house churches account for much of the growth in many of the world's largest congregations. Some of the best-attended weekly services in Manila are not held in church buildings but in schoolyards, hotel banquet rooms, and public auditoriums. These and other examples from around the world indicate that if we don't restrict ourselves to one particular mode of operation, there is no limit to the possibilities.

8. To date, we have found no more effective way to promote growth, local leadership, and group identity than home cells and house churches. Big, united services are helpful, but home cells are the cutting edge of church growth and discipleship. Different configurations can be used to tie the cells together and rally believers periodically in larger gatherings. But in big cities nothing surpasses the small group for effective penetration of every apartment building, language group, social class, and neighborhood.

9. The principle of good stewardship must be applied to building acquisition and design. If we are going to reach the masses in the cities and plant all the churches that are needed, we must do some things we haven't done before and think of some designs we haven't previously considered.

Let's strike out for simplicity of design. We have all heard the familiar argument about how much was spent building Solomon's temple in the Old Testament, and that only the best should be considered good enough for God's house. But let's not forget that all the adornments of Solomon's temple are fulfilled in Jesus Christ. The temple symbolized Christ, and now he has come. We should not try to duplicate or imitate his beauty through something else. The embellishments which Christians commonly put into church buildings, the glory we put into brick and mortar, are hard to justify in the light of the need of missions, the physical plight of the urban masses, the relative poverty of many Christians, and the sacrifices made by many pastors and other kingdom workers. I venture to say that most of the wealth we pour into church buildings is not to glorify God at all, but is nothing more than self-aggrandizement under the guise of religious zeal. I think the angels weep at many a building dedication, and so does the Lord. That is Kagawa's point (see p. 235), and I think he is entirely correct.

In planning a church structure, we should consider the atmosphere of the building and what it ought to convey. If we think scripturally of what the church is all about, the metaphor that comes to mind is the body of Christ and the family of God. That being so, what kind of a design produces the most familylike atmosphere? Rarely is body life, family life, clearly expressed in church architecture. What is so family-like about a Gothic structure with a tall ceiling and ramparts? Where is that suggested in the Bible?

If design is to be instrumental in promoting body life for the people of God, what should a church building look like? What should be the mood and atmosphere, the feel of the building? I suggest that the proper feel is that of a living room, the place where the family gathers. In contrast, I would characterize most of our church buildings as having the architecture of grandeur. I suspect that this all started at a time when church design was intended to convey the grandeur of the episcopacy, of the empire, of hierarchy. It was not the church at its best, but at one of its weaker moments, that came to dominate church architectural design. I think, however, that the domestic atmosphere is more in line with the New Testament symbolism of the church as the body of Christ and the family of God, and this should be built into church design. We need a meeting place with a lower ceiling, a chair configuration which allows people to see one another's faces and not just the backs of heads, a place where interaction is promoted. Such features enhance the fellowship of God's family when they meet for worship and edification.

Consider the question in the light of the difference between a warship and a cruise ship. Cruise ships are beautiful. We have all admired the advertisements of vacation trips aboard these glistening white vessels. Cruise ships have lovely lounges, deck chairs, swimming pools, and staterooms with comfortable beds and furnishings. They are costly to build and maintain. They are beautiful boats, but who would want to fight a battle in one? They are built for pleasure, comfort, and relaxation. But a warship, on the other hand, isn't pretty at all. There is no chrome, no fancy wood, no swimming pool. The sleeping quarters aren't plush, and the designs are strictly utilitarian. But they are good in a battle, because it is for battle they were conceived.

Church buildings can be like pleasure yachts or battleships. What's the church in this world for? What's urban mission all about? Are we here to cruise along comfortably, or are we here to fight the Lord's battle in the city? Our answer will be revealed by the kind of buildings we choose.

Discussion Questions

1. Do you know of a congregation that intentionally gathers for worship in rented facilities? How is the arrangement working out?
2. Evaluate the argument that if church property is going to be sold, it makes sense to try to get the highest possible price, regardless of who the buyer may be or what that party intends to do with the property.
3. What has been your experience in home cells and small groups? Can your spiritual needs be satisfied in the long run without the large gathering and the special building?
4. How do you propose Christian missions tackle the problem of high prices, enormous populations, limited resources, and the need to multiply city churches? Design a strategy.

20

Pastoring in the City
Roger S. Greenway

Some pastors discover that ministering in the city provides them with stimulation and satisfaction; once they have tasted it, they are never fully satisfied ministering anywhere else. Others, however, find pastoring in the city frustrating and disagreeable. Their advice is to avoid city churches if at all possible.

A few years ago, a young city pastor addressed a letter to the editor of a leading evangelical magazine. The letter read as follows:

> Too often it seems that seminary graduates are limited to three options if they want to fulfill their call to a pastoral ministry: (1) youth ministry in a large church (multi-staff), (2) Christian education work in a medium-sized congregation (two or more staff members), or (3) a single-staff pastorate in a small church. Available small churches seem to be the "undesirable" ones—those located in isolated, hard-to-reach places or located in a declining urban area.
>
> Responding to a call to be a pastor-teacher, I came to a declining urban church—what appeared to be the best of my three options. After two years I think I have done everything well, but I feel awful about my lack of love for the congregation and the community. This is a job to me—and a frustrating one at that. The neighborhood has a high crime rate; I fear for my family's safety as well as resent the broken church windows. The congregation is elderly, poorly educated, and set in their ways. In addition, the financial remuneration is extremely oppressive for a young family.
>
> I feel guilty about complaining, but I also know I'm being realistic about my attitudes. I believe God has given me a great deal of ability to be used in the ministry. But already I want to bail out. There seem to be a lot of young ministers like me, working toward their next parish while resenting the present one. Is this sense of failure, frustration, and lack of love normal? Is it necessary? What are some non-simplistic suggestions

for those of us who want to have an enjoyable as well as effective ministry? Can/should ministry be enjoyable?

The editor challenged readers to offer suggestions to the young pastor, but I don't recall seeing any in print. Belatedly, I offer mine, which may help other pastors who find themselves in similar circumstances. I'm also thinking of seminarians, some of whom are considering the possibility of a city ministry. Are frustration and disappointment inevitable in such ministries, or are there ways to make urban churches effective centers of evangelism and service to the community, and a great joy to their leaders?

Let me say first of all that a pastor in this kind of situation needs help, needs it fast, and needs it from someone close enough at hand to observe the situation and assess the problems fairly and adequately. Concerns such as the physical safety of the pastor's family and the adequacy of his salary need to be evaluated objectively. Someone with wisdom, from his own denomination or the neighboring Christian community, ought to be called in to help make a balanced assessment. This can be a great service to the church as well as to the pastor.

Once an objective assessment has been made and some of the concerns have been dealt with responsibly, the next major item is the attitude of the pastor toward the congregation and the community. One thing is certain: in order to minister to people effectively, one has to love them. Christian ministry springs from obedience to Christ's call and a genuine concern for people and their needs. No love, no ministry. But from the letter it is obvious that the young pastor's love-level was dangerously low, and it's safe to surmise that the congregation knew it.

The pastor was afraid that his ministry was failing, his talents wasted, and his years of education largely in vain. He placed the blame on the urban location, which he regarded as "undesirable" and forced upon him because he had no other option. How sad that in his time of frustration he received no support from other people in urban ministry! In every city there are vibrant, effective ministries led by people who have learned how to minister in the city and enjoy it. When problems get too big and numerous, rather than running from them, it is far better to look around and ask for counsel. There is a lesson here for all urban workers: build and maintain support groups that can be turned to when problems arise.

Declining churches are scattered throughout the older cities of Canada, the United States, and Europe. Many of them are pastored by men who would probably describe their ministries in terms similar to those of the young pastor I quoted. Therefore, one of the challenges facing those of us who are concerned for cities is to reach such pastors with the news that there is hope. *Urban ministry doesn't have to be a bed of nails.* Where pastors develop a sense of mission to the city, and congregations take hold of the vision of what a city church can be, urban pastorates become the most exciting and rewarding places anyone can imagine.

The apostle Paul once found himself in a city that disgusted him in many ways. Corinth was big, wicked, and abusive, and Paul was ready to quit and go elsewhere. But the Lord spoke to him in a vision at night, saying: "Do not be afraid; keep on speaking, do not be silent. For I am with you, and no one is going to attack and harm you, because I have many people in this city" (Acts 18:9–10). Paul responded by staying, teaching the gospel, and establishing the church. And those words to Paul also contain a mandate for urban pastors today who are tempted to give up and seek easier places to serve the Lord.

How to Succeed in the City

What kind of men and women are needed in the city, and what does it take to succeed in urban ministry? People often ask me that question, which I will attempt to answer in a nutshell.

1. Those who want to serve in the city must learn to *love* the city and its people. This warrants repeating. There must be a commitment to Christ, a willingness to work hard for his church, and an overall servant attitude. But at the heart of one's ministry there must be love, love for God and love for fellow humans. First Corinthians 13 is a Bible passage that urban workers need to reflect on often. Such love will help overcome unwarranted fear of the city and will release the gifts and energies needed to serve fruitfully.

2. The Christian worker must get to *know* the city. Persons who were born and raised in the city may have a head start. But no one should be overly confident—many city people's knowledge and experience are confined to their own neighborhood, area of work, and school. Be continually inquisitive about the city, its variety of people, and the complex social mechanisms by which the city works. Travel around the city, especially by public transportation. Learn the city's sounds and smells and feel its awesome strength. Respect the city for what it offers culturally, but see through the tinsel and lights to the spiritual core of the city with its alienation from God.

3. The Christian worker must learn to *appreciate the body of Christ* that exists in the city. It is composed of people from many different

ethnic groups, cultures, and social classes. It speaks a variety of languages. Some parts of the body meet in splendid church buildings, with
stained-glass windows, robed choirs, and mighty pipe organs, while
other parts meet in storefronts, crowded living rooms, or shabby facilities. Denominationally, the urban body of Christ covers a wide spectrum, each element with its own strengths and weaknesses. The successful urban worker learns to love them all and praise God for the
variety of ways the Spirit is building Christ's body. And before introduc-
ing a new church or ministry, he or she will ask whether it might be
more effective to serve and strengthen existing ministries of the body
in the city.

4. Successful workers *hurt* for the city. They hurt where the people
hurt. General William Booth, founder of the Salvation Army, used to
tell potential recruits: "If you can't cry over the city, we can't use you."
He was entirely correct, for the sin and pain and suffering of the city are
so intense that only the kind of person who can weep as Jesus wept
over Jerusalem is going to accomplish any salvific good.

5. Good urban workers possess a deep and genuine *passion for evangelism,* for telling people the Good News about Jesus Christ. Along
with all the social, emotional, and material needs heaped high in the
city, there is one need that cuts through all layers of society and
touches every home and individual. It is the need to know God's love
in Christ and experience God's great salvation. In the city there is
always the danger that social needs, because they are so big and many,
will divert attention from the central need, which is Christ. Some
formerly great churches lost their usefulness because they forgot the
gospel while tending exclusively to social needs. Telling the story of
Jesus lies at the heart of the church's ministry in the city as well as
everywhere else.

6. To be effective and successful in urban ministry, the worker must
build genuine *credibility.* This can be achieved only through involvement with people individually and communally.

I often ask city pastors how the community surrounding their church
buildings looks upon the church and its ministry. Some churches, unfortunately, have a bad reputation in their own neighborhoods. Neighbors
may feel unwanted because their race is different from that of the church
members. Or the neighbors may see that the church spends all its time
and resources on the internal needs and activities of the congregation,
disregarding the external needs in the community. Or it may be that
interchurch rivalry has damaged relationships; each branch of the body
is jealous of the others and overly protective of its own interests.

Credibility comes only by way of involvement with outsiders. To be
effective in the city, it is essential to spend a great deal of time and

effort ministering to people outside the church's regular membership. In big and small ways the love we mentioned earlier has to be demonstrated. Alone, no one can ever do everything that needs to be done, nor should anyone try. For that reason pastoral and missionary teams are very helpful in urban ministry, because they harness the resources of more than one person to provide a wider and more holistic witness in the community.

Building credibility in the community is the surest road to bridging ethnic and cross-cultural differences to truly become a neighborhood church. The toughest assignment any pastor can have is to lead a traditional white congregation toward effective ministry in a neighborhood that has changed radically, both culturally and economically. That church's main problem is building credibility in a neighborhood where the perceptions, from both sides, are heavy with ignorance and hostility. In such instances the pastor's main job is leading traditionally oriented members to accept changes that insure the church's future, while building credibility through services to the community.

What does it take to be effective in urban ministry? All of the above and, most importantly, the blessing and power of God. One of the most valued things I've learned in years of ministry is that God uses in amazing ways men and women who don't necessarily possess the highest academic degrees, attractive physical appearance, or a mountain of natural abilities. But they all have this indispensable qualification— they are fully committed to God and his service.

An Agenda for Urban Ministry

Someone once asked me what I thought an appropriate agenda for urban ministry might be. Tell me, he said, what your priorities would be if you were pastoring in the city. I took his question to a meeting of pastors and mission specialists and asked them for their answers. Here is what they gave me, each item representing a participant's top priority for an urban-ministry agenda.

Equip God's people in the city to make ethical decisions about community issues.

Communicate the gospel to the poor.

Help city churches develop holistic ministries.

Find ways to change the rural mentality of city churches so that they effectively minister to city people.

Build churches noted for their caring in the uncaring city.

Promote countercultural ideology in the churches, and help Christians put countercultural principles into practice.

Work toward reconciliation, vertically between people and God and horizontally between races.

Help Christians understand the gospel so that they won't be so frightened of change and the issues associated with urban life.

Sensitize Christians to city issues and to urban applications of love.

Dream biblical dreams for the city instead of just American dreams about wealth and success.

Raise the conscience level of rural, suburban, and small-town Christians concerning city issues.

Proclaim to the church and the community: This city belongs to God!

Challenge ourselves and others to recognize the city's idolatries.

Hold before Christians Mother Teresa's compassionate appeal to give dignity in death to the poorest of the poor, but go beyond it to give them dignity in life.

Insist that Christians work out systematically the changes in city life which the gospel demands and implies.

This is a great list of suggestions for an urban pastorate. Who could argue against the importance of any one of them? Imagine the marvelous changes which would occur in cities if these suggestions were implemented in churches and communities throughout the world!

But is the list complete? Aren't there important things missing? Doesn't it reveal some naive assumptions about cities, the number and character of city churches, the unreached segments of the urban populations, the need for church planting and diligent pastoring?

There is a constant danger that we will build our agendas for ministry on the basis of our own limited understanding of the city and its needs. We think we understand the city, or at least some part of it, and we generalize about the rest. Even veteran city workers may make this mistake, and people with only a smattering of urban experience are in greater jeopardy. Urban ministry has suffered a great deal as a result of limited perspectives on cities and city people.

Our agenda for urban ministry must be governed first of all by the Word of God and its teachings. Good strategy is based on sound mission theology. True, the evaluation of human needs is extremely important. Urban workers must examine slum conditions, understand the nature and causes of suffering, and know the steps that can improve situations. But physical conditions alone do not determine the agenda. The agenda must start with God's Word and its profound assessment of the human condition and the divine solution.

The central item in a biblical agenda is the proclamation of the gospel to saints and sinners in every part of the city. God's Word is needed by all levels of society, from the slums to society hill. It must be proclaimed in a manner that is culturally and linguistically appropriate to the hearers. It is through the teaching of the Word of God that believers are equipped for kingdom living. That is a basic premise which applies everywhere, in all cultures and among all people groups.

The signs of God's kingdom take form and shape as its citizens multiply in number, apply their faith to everyday matters, live by kingdom principles in city neighborhoods, and carry Christian values into the marketplaces, the classrooms, and all the systems by which cities operate. Only then can we expect to see better cities.

I like what was said about Mother Teresa and her deep compassion for the urban poor. What she does in Calcutta and other cities to give dignity in death to society's outcasts bears the aura of Christ about it. Also important is the suggestion that we must go beyond the Calcutta approach and give dignity in life. The quality of life experienced by God's image-bearers is an eminently Christian concern. For that reason we support community development programs which unite compassion and stewardship with professional expertise to make a better life for the poor. The Bible compels us, however, to go well beyond Mother Teresa in our agenda for urban ministry. We want more for the rich and poor of the city than life and death with dignity. We want them to live, die, and spend eternity with Christ.

Furthermore, we want those who repent and believe gathered into churches where they will be pastored, taught, discipled, and equipped for useful service. This requires that cities be dotted with Christian churches—in the slums, in the high-rise apartments, and in the exclusive neighborhoods. Each of these churches will need one or more faithful pastors whose agenda for ministry will be as big as the city and as profound as the whole counsel of God.

Urban-Suburban Coalitions

This is a good place to discuss the challenging concept (as far as Western countries are concerned) of urban-suburban coalitions between congregations. Pastors, whether ministering in the city or in the suburbs, may find that their efforts in developing coalitions between ethnically and culturally diverse segments of Christ's body add valuable new dimensions to congregational life. They may trigger the kind of renewal that many churches are seeking.

Admittedly, close cooperation between city and suburban congregations is rare. Yet many who have tried it have found it richly rewarding. The universality of the church has become real in new and vital ways, and the confession of "one Lord, one faith, one baptism" has taken on new meaning.

There are a few of us who, for personal or professional reasons, move back and forth between city and suburban churches. I often preach in one in the morning and in the other at night. Different languages are sometimes involved. I've learned to cross cultures, adapt my vocabulary, make different applications, and bridge what are really two worlds. I've also learned to recognize the strengths and weaknesses in both worlds. City and suburban churches could experience major renewals if they would get together and learn from one another.

What can suburban Christians learn from city church members? The answers may be surprising! Here is a list of eight, drawn up a few years ago by my inner-city students at CUTS (Center for Urban Theological Studies) in Philadelphia:

1. Worship of God without enslavement to the clock.
2. Willingness to express one's faith and feelings verbally, openly, without embarrassment.
3. Acceptance of heterogeneity of race, social class, and clothing in the assembly.
4. Diaconal service that is local and immediate. Needs are close enough that members see them, feel the hurt, and are challenged to become personally involved.
5. Reverence in the sanctuary and in things pertaining to God. (Many city Christians are appalled by the chitter-chatter that goes on in Protestant suburban church auditoriums before services begin, and by the seeming superficiality of traditional hymns and the way they're sung.)
6. Variety in expressions of piety, prayer, and emotional response to God and his Word.
7. Faith lived out in practical ways, less muddled by theological debate.
8. Willingness to take risks (physical danger and hardship) in order to worship and serve God.

I find these answers profound! They cut to the heart of many of the basic weaknesses in the middle-class suburban expression of evangelical Christianity. Rightly handled, they lay an agenda for suburban church renewal.

Similarly, city Christians—black, white, Hispanic, Oriental—need the love, help, and balancing influence of suburban believers. When I asked a black sister what she wanted most from suburban Christians, she replied: "I'd just like to know they pray for us and care about us." She put her finger on the key issue. Urban-suburban coalitions must begin with communication, concern, relationship, and prayer. Once these are established, partnership in mission will develop naturally.

There are models to help us. A small Presbyterian church in New Jersey has drawn up an inventory of all the skills and talents in the congregation and made them available on Saturdays to an inner-city congregation in Philadelphia. The suburban Christians assist in home repairs and take on inner-city youths as apprentices. They focus on the neighborhood immediately around the city church, combining hard work, friendship, instruction, and evangelism.

In Washington D.C., One Ministries has an Adopt-a-Block program. It is a creative model of a relational ministry linking urban churches and families with their counterparts in the suburbs. If the suburban Washington Cathedral and the urban Third Street Assembly of God can form a partnership for mutual service and mission, why can't it happen all across the metropolitan world? It can, wherever love is plentiful and Christians interact with one another.

In Philadelphia, CUTS serves as a bridge. Bill Krispin, the director, says that CUTS is a place where inner-city church leaders and middle-class suburban pastors and seminarians meet for a common purpose. The cultural gap is closed by the CUTS staff, who are trusted by both sides. "They all come in here with the same suspicions anyone else has, but as they get to know one another the walls come tumbling down," says Krispin. "We need people who will stand in the gap and bring people together. They're 'doorkeepers,' who will meet Christians from the suburbs at the doors of the city, and invite them to come in and share gifts and ministry."

I venture the following suggestions for implementing the concept of building urban-suburban coalitions:

1. Pastors on both sides of city lines should begin praying for one another, privately and in worship services. Sharing information and prayer requests will naturally follow. The burdens borne by some city churches and mission organizations in ministering to the poor and the homeless certainly should provoke prayer in all churches.

2. Using whatever personal or denominational connections may exist, city and suburban churches should begin meeting together regularly, with no fixed agenda except to build relationships and enjoy

fellowship. A suburban church can invite an inner-city congregation to share an outing, a picnic, or a retreat. The less formal it is, the better.

3. Pulpit exchanges can be arranged. Invite a pastor to take the choir along, and show the warmest hospitality possible. It's always frightening for pastors from either side of city lines to preach to a culturally different audience, but through the experience lessons are learned and relationships established.

4. Urban churches can invite suburban Christians for weekend retreats in the city. Few things can be more beneficial than a weekend in the inner city for people who have never experienced city life. Why should retreats invariably be held in the countryside? A couple of nights with a black or Hispanic family, meetings in an inner-city location, and Sunday services with a city congregation are rich experiences for suburban or small-town people.

5. Suburban churches can offer help to inner-city churches in whatever way is needed, remembering that in the city local Christians are in control and the role of suburbanites is service. No crusading "save the city" attitude is needed or desired. Those who come to serve and submit to local leadership will find their gifts and labor appreciated.

6. Suburban churches should consider how they might spend less on nonessentials and channel the funds saved to churches and mission agencies struggling to carry on God's work in the city. It is tragic that some of the best urban work is hampered by lack of funds. May God give us more middle- and upper-class Christians who say: "Everything we possess has been given by God; and we are just stewards, not owners." People of that sort can live where they please, and God will make them and their earning skills a blessing and the salt of salvation in many lives.

Urban and suburban churches cannot afford to ignore one another any longer. E. V. Hill, a black pastor and evangelical leader in Los Angeles, has said that if suburban evangelicals continue to turn their backs on the inner city, the core of our civilization will rot. The edges of the rotting core will grow wider and wider until they engulf suburbia as well.

The Role of the Urban Pulpit

Preaching

Sometimes the impression is given that city pastors generally need not pay much attention to preaching and the careful preparation of sermons. Urban ministry, the impression goes, is for activists, and not for students of the Scriptures, because most of a city pastor's time is spent dealing directly with people's problems, and city congregations don't expect a great sermon on Sunday.

That is a seriously mistaken impression, though it is held not infrequently by pastors and seminarians as well as laypeople. In my experience of urban ministry, I have seen city churches caught in the morass of all sorts of problems, with unmet needs and disappointing ministries. I've asked myself many times, what can be done to help these churches and their burdened, frustrated pastors? I would argue that many of the problems can be traced to the pulpits, and that is where the solutions must begin. The pulpit of a city church can be one of the most exciting places in which to minister. But associated with urban pulpits there are dangers that must be recognized and addressed. The ideas that follow reflect my personal observations and experience with city churches. They are basic to my philosophy of urban preaching, pastoral leadership, and congregational ministry.

Most importantly, preaching in the city must be biblical and comprehensive in scope. The great questions of life must be addressed from the viewpoint of divine revelation. When city people come to church, they must hear the word of the Lord from his Word. The messages preached must boldly address the complexities of urban life and reflect the wide variety of interests and experiences in the average city congregation. When comparing a small-town newspaper with a big-city paper, one is struck by the differences, not only in the size of the paper, but in the breadth of the news coverage and editorial comment. City people are bombarded by a host of ideas, issues, problems, and events, and this breadth of interest must be matched in the sermons they hear on Sunday.

One of the things I enjoy doing in my classes on urban ministry is to search the Scriptures for biblical themes especially appropriate to urban pulpits. I call it "translating theology onto the streets." Isaiah 58, for example, focuses on true knowledge and service of God; Jeremiah 29:7 is a great lesson about the *shalom* of the city and the unity of all urbanites in the pursuit of peace and justice. The themes of mercy, justice, and compassion for the poor spring from the prophets and numerous other Scriptures. The importance of planting and multiplying city churches is written all across Acts and the Epistles. Hope for city dwellers radiates from Revelation 18, where Babylon is seen to fall, and from chapter 21, where the Holy City descends and God in Christ dwells with redeemed humanity.

The range of themes and instruction from Scripture is limitless. Nothing in the city is too big, too evil, or too bewildering for the perceptive messenger of God's Word. Consequently, the Christian pulpit is a very liberating place for the city. Leadership in righteousness, compassion, unity, moral values, family life, and the whole host of issues cities know so well, springs from the Word well spoken and Spirit-directed.

Appropriate Weekly Ministries

Central as preaching is, it must not substitute for responsible programing. Preaching must be directly related to the church's ministries during the week, ministries which represent the church's corporate response to the needs of both members and nonmembers. Without the combination of a strong pulpit and appropriate weekly ministries, preaching will either induce guilt or create illusions about Christian involvement that are without substance. Both preacher and congregation need a viable programmatic framework in which to respond in obedience to the message proclaimed from the Word.

I was reminded of this one Sunday as I made my way to a downtown Philadelphia church and had to step over a man sprawled out on a vent in the sidewalk. The man was asleep or unconscious; he probably had been there all night. He was white and middle-aged, and something in his face made me think that not long before he had been an entirely different person. Perhaps he was one of the new poor who drifted into the city after losing their jobs in the steel mills of western Pennsylvania. What effect did his tragic circumstances have on my preaching and the life of that congregation, many of whom had walked past the same man or one of the other street people who frequent the neighborhood? Can preachers mount urban pulpits and avoid speaking to the issues such people represent?

Submission to the Lord and his Word leads to action, programing, and individual and corporate response to needs and their causes. Consequently, pulpit and program must march in lockstep together. Notes from the pulpit must echo through all the midweek ministries of the church.

Direction and Correction

The pulpit must give direction and stimulation to the total ministry program of the church and also provide correction when the program goes astray. Through sound biblical instruction on the broad themes confronting city dwellers, preaching gives theological depth and meaning to the church's weekly ministries. It also challenges programs that are in danger of losing biblical perspective and content. When the church's program is exposed regularly to the scrutiny of the Word, members can feel secure about what the church is doing. The church can dare to be bold and innovative as long as it submits everything it does to the authority of the Scriptures.

City churches must not allow their programs to overshadow the preaching and teaching of the Word. This mistake has occurred over and over again, with disastrous results. The temptation to allow the church's programs gradually to take precedence over everything else is understandable because the needs are great and the demand for new ministries never ends. Pastors easily become overinvolved in countless worthwhile programs, each of which takes some of their time and energy. When this happens, the pulpit ministry invariably suffers. Pastors and congregations together must heed the instruction of Acts 6 and consistently delegate midweek ministries to gifted members. If the pulpit is weakened, all the other ministries eventually suffer, and the chief source of motivation and direction for urban ministry is muffled.

The Pastor and the Prisoner

While serving as a missionary-pastor in Ceylon (Sri Lanka), I watched as a skilled and committed pastor of a neighboring church brought renewal and evangelistic outreach to a city congregation that had nearly died. His approach consisted of the basics: sound teaching and preaching, frequent visits to urge the members to renewed commitments to the Lord and the church, and an example communicating a great love for evangelism. As a result of his ministry, lay members of the congregation became involved in various programs of outreach and learned to use their places of employment for witnessing. Among them was a matron in a Colombo prison where the nation's worst offenders were held. This obscure woman was used mightily of God to reach the heart of Mrs. W., Ceylon's minister of health.

Mrs. W. was a person of wealth, education, and great devotion to Buddhism. Her late husband had written *Revolt in the Temple,* a book which viciously attacked Christianity and proposed a new Buddhist state for Ceylon. He called for a revival of Buddhism and for ridding the country of Christianity.

After her husband's death, Mrs. W. was elected to government office and later appointed to the post of minister of health, the first woman to serve in such a high capacity. While in that position, she traveled widely throughout the world and promoted the interests of the Buddhist faith wherever she could. For example, one day she thought she saw a cross design in the ornate wrought-iron gates of the Colombo

General Hospital. Immediately she ordered that the gates be removed and replaced by something that contained no Christian symbols.

But disaster struck Mrs. W.'s political career. In 1959 a Buddhist monk assassinated the prime minister, and indirect evidence seemed to implicate Mrs. W. in the plot. Suddenly she found herself in prison, removed completely from the comforts, wealth, and status she had once enjoyed. All alone in her cell, she felt that her career was ended and her life in ruins. But though she did not know it, God was pressing her to Christ.

Among those assigned to Mrs. W. was the matron mentioned earlier, who had been encouraged by her pastor to distribute Bibles to the prisoners. At an hour when Mrs. W. was in total despair, the matron offered her a New Testament and said, "This book has the answer to your predicament." Mrs. W. took the book and, to her own surprise, started reading it. She read and read. For two days and a night she hardly put the book down. Over and over she prayed, "O God, if there is a God, reveal to me the way of light!"

The next time the matron came to her cell, Mrs. W. asked if it would be possible for the matron's pastor to visit her. Within an hour the matron phoned her pastor, asking him to come. Getting in to see a political prisoner was not easy, but the pastor patiently endured the inspections and delays until finally he was taken to a small conference room to meet Mrs. W. The jailer said firmly, "Just five minutes, and I'll be listening to every word!" But in fact, he gave them fifty-five minutes. For it turned out that he too was a Christian, and all the while he sat there listening, he was praying that the pastor would get through to Mrs. W. with the gospel.

For many weeks the pastor visited Mrs. W. every Wednesday and explained to her the basic teachings of the Scriptures. At last the day came when she was released. In the middle of the family celebration in her home, Mrs. W. knelt in prayer to thank God for her twofold deliverance, and then and there she made her first offering to the Lord. Soon afterwards, to the consternation of almost all who had known her, she was baptized. She told everyone that she had met God in the prison and had learned what communion with Christ means. "It's better," she said, "to be inside a prison with God than to be outside without him." Colombo newspapers picked up her story, and on the day of her baptism the church was packed.

The attention then and afterward fell on the former Buddhist who had become an ardent Christian. But behind the scene was a pastor who had led his church members to use their jobs as contact points for the gospel, to place Scriptures in the hands of hurting, seeking people, and to be effective witnesses wherever they were. It is not surprising that the pastor's ministry brought renewal to the congregation and led many to trust Christ. Imagine what could happen if churches in a thousand cities were pastored by people like that!

Discussion Questions

1. Do you know any pastors who really love ministering in the city? What's different about them? Why do they find the city so attractive and exciting?
2. Discuss the value of urban-suburban coalitions between congregations. What arguments pro and con will probably be raised whenever the idea of a coalition is raised in (a) a city congregation? (b) a suburban congregation?
3. Suggest several biblical themes that would probably be more urgent for a city congregation than for a rural or small-town congregation to hear.
4. What advice would you give the young pastor whose letter is found at the beginning of this chapter?

Bibliography

General

Mission Perspective

Adeney, Miriam. *God's Foreign Policy*. Grand Rapids: Eerdmans, 1984.

Aleman, Blanca, and Harley C. Schreck. " 'Community' in the City." *Urban Mission* 6.2 (Nov. 1988): 19–26.

Allen, Frank W. "Toward a Biblical Urban Mission." *Urban Mission* 3.3 (Jan. 1986): 6–13.

Allen, Jimmy R. "Urban Evangelism." In *Toward Creative Urban Strategy*, comp. George A. Torney, pp. 105–21. Waco, Tex.: Word, 1970.

Armstrong, James. *From the Underside: Evangelism from a Third World Vantage Point*. Maryknoll, N.Y.: Orbis, 1981.

Badgero, Ray. "Teaching Tips and Tools: Documentation and Statistics." *Evangelical Missions Quarterly* 21.3 (July 1985): 302–3.

Baird, William. *The Corinthian Church: A Biblical Approach to Urban Culture*. New York: Abingdon, 1964.

Bakke, Raymond J. "The Challenge of World Urbanization to Mission Thinking and Strategy: Perspectives on Demographic Realities." *Urban Mission* 4.1 (Sept. 1986): 6–17.

———. "Strategy for Urban Mission." *TSF Bulletin* 8.4 (Mar.–Apr. 1985): 20–21.

———. *The Urban Christian*. Downers Grove, Ill.: Inter-Varsity, 1987.

———. "Urban Evangelization: A Lausanne Strategy Since 1980." *International Bulletin of Missionary Research* 8.4 (Oct. 1984): 149–54.

Baroni, Geno C., and Ronald D. Pasquariello. "What Can Parishes Do for Our Cities?" *Church and Society* 69.1 (Sept.–Oct. 1978): 5–10.

Barrett, David B. "Annual Statistical Table on Global Mission: 1987." *International Bulletin of Missionary Research* 11.1 (Jan. 1987): 24–25.

————. "Five Statistical Eras of Global Mission: A Thesis and Discussion." *Evangelical Missions Quarterly* 12.1 (Jan. 1984): 21–37.

————. "Silver and Gold Have I None: Church of the Poor or Church of the Rich?" *International Bulletin of Missionary Research* 7.4 (Oct. 1983): 146–51.

————. *World-Class Cities and World Evangelization.* Birmingham, Ala.: New Hope, 1986.

————, ed. *World Christian Encyclopedia: A Comparative Study of Churches and Religions in the Modern World, A.D. 1900 to 2000.* New York: Oxford University Press, 1982.

Bavinck, J. H. *The Church Between Temple and Mosque: A Study of the Relationship Between the Christian Faith and Other Religions.* Grand Rapids: Eerdmans, 1982.

Belew, M. Wendell. *Missions in the Mosaic.* Atlanta: Home Mission Board, Southern Baptist Convention, 1974.

Benjamin, Don C. *Deuteronomy and City Life: A Form Criticism of Texts with the Word City ('îr) in Deuteronomy 4:41–26:19.* Washington: University Press of America, 1983.

Bennett, George. *Effective Urban Church Ministry.* Nashville: Broadman, 1983.

Benton, John W. "Can Prostitutes Be Helped?" *Urban Mission* 3.2 (Nov. 1985): 37–40.

Blaiklock, E. M. *Cities of the New Testament.* Westwood, N.J.: Revell, 1965.

Boer, Jan Harm. *Missions: Heralds of Capitalism or Christ?* Ibadan: Day Star, 1984.

Bosch, David. *Witness to the World: The Christian Mission in Theological Perspective.* Atlanta: John Knox, 1980.

Bouman, Stephen P. "Your Face, Your Cloak, Your Coat, Your Shoes: Parish-Based Community Organization." *Urban Mission* 3.4 (Mar. 1986): 5–18.

Bruce, F. F. *Paul and Jesus.* Grand Rapids: Baker, 1974.

Busia, K. A. *Urban Churches in Britain: A Question of Relevance.* London: Lutterworth, 1966.

Callahan, Daniel, ed. *The Secular City Debate.* New York: Macmillan, 1966.

Carlson, Ronald W. "Films About the City: A Selected Bibliography of Films for Sensitizing Christians to Urban Life and Its Problems." *Urban Mission* 4.1 (Sept. 1986): 24–34.

Cho, Paul Yonggi. *More than Numbers.* Waco, Tex.: Word, 1984.

————. "Reaching Cities with Home Cells." *Urban Mission* 1.3 (Jan. 1984): 4–14.

Claerbaut, David. *Urban Ministry.* Grand Rapids: Zondervan, 1983.

Cohen, Abner, ed. *Urban Ethnicity.* London: Tavistock, 1974.

Conn, Harvie M. "Any Faith Dies in the City." *Missiology* 13.4 (Oct. 1985): 6–19.

———. "Christ and the City." *Urban Mission* 1.2 (Nov. 1983): 25–31.

———. "The City: The New Frontier." *Evangelical Missions Quarterly* 20.4 (Oct. 1984): 395–98.

———. *A Clarified Vision for Urban Mission: Dispelling the Urban Stereotypes.* Grand Rapids: Zondervan, 1987.

———. *Eternal Word and Changing Worlds: Theology, Anthropology and Mission in Trialogue.* Grand Rapids: Zondervan, 1984.

———. *Evangelism: Doing Justice and Preaching Grace.* Grand Rapids: Zondervan, 1982.

———. "In the City, I'm a Number, Not a Person: The Depersonalization Misunderstanding." *Urban Mission* 2.5 (May 1985): 6–19.

———. "The Kingdom of God, Its Advance and the City." *Urban Mission* 1.5 (May 1984): 16–25.

———. "Looking to the Future: Evangelical Missions from North America in the Years Ahead." *Urban Mission* 5.3 (Jan. 1988): 18–31.

———. "Lukan Perspectives and the Cities." *Missiology* 13.4 (Oct. 1985): 409–25.

———. "The Rural/Urban Myth and World." *Reformed Review* 37.3 (Spring 1984): 125–36.

———, ed. *Reaching the Unreached: The Old-New Challenge.* Phillipsburg, N.J.: Presbyterian and Reformed, 1984.

Cook, Harold R. *Strategy of Missions: An Evangelical View.* Chicago: Moody, 1963.

Cook, William. "Evangelical Reflections on the Church of the Poor." *Missiology* 11.1 (Jan. 1983): 47–53.

———. "Evangelizing the World-Class Cities." *Together* 2 (Jan.–Mar. 1984): 30–34.

Copeland, E. Luther. "Can the City Be Saved: Toward a Biblical Urbanology." *Perspectives on Religious Studies* 4 (Spring 1987): 14–22.

Corwin, Charles. "Cultural Diversity as a Dynamic for Growth." *Evangelical Missions Quarterly* 17.1 (Jan. 1981): 15–22.

Costas, Orlando E. *The Church and Its Mission: A Shattering Critique from the Third World.* Wheaton, Ill.: Tyndale, 1974.

Courtney, Thomas J. "Mission to the Urban Poor." *Urban Mission* 1.2 (Nov. 1983): 17–24.

Cox, Harvey. *Religion in the Secular City: Toward a Post-Modern Theology.* New York: Simon and Schuster, 1984.

Crichton, Iain. "Empowering for Effective Urban Ministry: The Center for Urban Theological Studies, Philadelphia." *Urban Mission* 5.2 (Nov. 1987): 33–42.

Cully, Kendig Brubaker, and F. Nile Harper, eds. *Will the Church Lose the City?* New York: World, 1969.

Danwing, Enrique. "God and Large Cities." *Urban Mission* 6.2 (Nov. 1988): 27–32.

Davidson, James D. "Lafayette Urban Ministry." *Review of Religious Research* 18.3 (Spring 1977): 302.

Davidson, James D.; Ronald Elly; Thomas Hull; and Donald Nead. "Increasing the Church's Involvement in Social Concerns: A Model for Urban Ministries." *Review of Religious Research* 20.3 (Summer 1979): 291–314.

Dayton, Donald. "The Urban Church Today: A Report on an Evangelical Congress." *Reformed Journal* 28.8 (Aug. 1978): 9–11.

Dayton, Edward R., and David A. Fraser. *Planning Strategies for World Evangelization.* Grand Rapids: Eerdmans, 1980.

Dayton, Edward R., and Samuel Wilson, eds. *The Refugees Among Us: Unreached Peoples.* Monrovia, Calif.: MARC, 1983.

———. *Unreached Peoples '82: Focus on Urban Peoples.* Elgin, Ill.: David C. Cook, 1982.

———. *Unreached Peoples '84: The Future of World Evangelization.* Monrovia, Calif.: MARC with World Vision International, 1984.

Dekker, T. J. "Unreached Peoples Data: Out of the Computer and into the Fields." *Evangelical Missions Quarterly* 19.3 (July 1983): 232–35.

DeVise, P. R., and E. C. Berry. "Tale of Two Cities." *Renewal* 9.2 (Feb. 1969): 8–13.

Dodson, D. W. "The Dynamic City." *Christianity and Crisis* 29.15 (Sept. 1969): 228–32.

Dougherty, James. *The Fivesquare City: The City in the Religious Imagination.* Notre Dame, Ind.: University of Notre Dame Press, 1980.

Drummond, Henry. *A City Without a Church and Other Addresses.* London: Hodder and Stoughton, 1988.

DuBose, Francis M. "Cities Aren't All Alike: The Common and Contrasting Urban Context of the Christian Global Mission." *Urban Mission* 1.3 (Jan. 1984): 15–23.

———. *How Churches Grow in an Urban World.* Nashville: Broadman, 1978.

Dyrness, Grace R. "Urbanization in the Two-Thirds World." *Urban Mission* 4.4 (Mar. 1987): 6–11.

Eames, Edwin, and Judith Granich Goode. *Urban Poverty in a Cross-Cultural Context.* New York: Free, 1973.

Eckblad, Tom. "Tips for Urban Church Planters." *Urban Mission* 1.3 (Jan. 1984): 24–29.

Ellens, Harold. "Church and Metropolis." *Missiology* 3.2 (Apr. 1975): 169–75.

Ellison, Craig W. "Addressing Felt Needs of Urban Dwellers." *Urban Mission* 4.4 (Mar. 1987): 26–41.

———. "Attitudes and Urban Transition." *Urban Mission* 2.3 (Jan. 1985): 14–26.

———. "Growing Urban Churches Biblically." *Urban Mission* 6.2 (Nov. 1988): 7–18.

———. "Psychology, Christianity and Urban Need." *Journal of Psychology and Theology* 6.4 (Fall 1978): 283–90.

———. "Stress and Urban Ministry." *Urban Mission* 1.2 (Nov. 1983): 5–16.

———, ed. *The Urban Mission.* Grand Rapids: Eerdmans, 1974.

Ellul, Jacques. *The Meaning of the City.* Translated by Dennis Pardee. Grand Rapids: Eerdmans, 1970.

Eppinga, J. D. *A Pastor Speaks to the Soul of the City.* Grand Rapids: Eerdmans, 1954.

Everett, Harvey A. *The Apartment Community: The Church's New Frontier.* Valley Forge, Pa.: Church Strategy Program, American Baptist Home Mission Societies, 1964.

Fackre, Gabriel. *Second Fronts in Metropolitan Mission.* Grand Rapids: Eerdmans, 1968.

Filbeck, David. *Social Context and Proclamation: A Socio-Cognitive Study in Proclaiming the Gospel Cross-Culturally.* Pasadena, Calif.: William Carey Library, 1985.

Fitcher, Joseph H. *Social Relations in the Urban Parish.* Chicago: University of Chicago Press, 1954.

Forrester, Jay W. *Urban Dynamics.* Cambridge, Mass.: MIT Press, 1969.

Frenchak, David J., and Clinton E. Stockwell. *Signs of the Kingdom in the Secular City.* Chicago: Covenant, 1984.

Frenchak, David J., and Sharrel Keyes, eds. *Metro-Ministry: Ways and Means for the Urban Church.* Elgin, Ill.: David C. Cook, 1979.

Frick, Frank S. *The City in Ancient Israel.* Decatur, Ga.: Scholars, 1977.

Fulton, Brent. "Seminary of the Field: A Model for Mission Among the Skyscrapers." *Urban Mission* 4.4 (Mar. 1987): 52–54.

Gant, Edwin P. "Evangelism Explosion: A Tool God Is Using in Many Cities." *Urban Mission* 3.2 (Nov. 1985): 32–36.

Gerber, Virgil. "A New Tool for Winning the City." *Church Growth Bulletin* 12.6 (July 1976): 542–44.

Gheddo, Piero. *Why Is the Third World Poor?* Translated by Kathryn Sullivan. Maryknoll, N.Y.: Orbis, 1973.

Gibbs, Eddie. *I Believe in Church Growth.* Grand Rapids: Eerdmans, 1981.

Gilliland, Dean S. *Pauline Theology and Mission Practice.* Grand Rapids: Baker, 1983.

Glasser, Arthur F., and Eric S. Fife. *Missions in Crisis: Rethinking Missionary Strategy.* Chicago: Inter-Varsity, 1961.

Glasser, Arthur F.; Paul G. Hiebert; C. Peter Wagner; and Ralph B. Winter, eds. *Crucial Dimensions in World Evangelization.* Pasadena, Calif.: William Carey Library, 1976.

Goddard, Burton L., ed. *Encyclopedia of Modern Christian Missions: The Agencies.* Camden, N.J.: Thomas Nelson, 1967.

Goslin, Thomas S., II. *The Church Without Walls.* Pasadena, Calif.: Hope, 1984.

Gration, John. "The Homogeneous Unit Principle: Another Perspective." *Evangelical Missions Quarterly* 17.4 (Oct. 1981): 197–202.

Greenway, Roger S. "An Agenda for the City." *Urban Mission* 3.5 (May 1986): 3–5.

———. *Apostles to the City.* Grand Rapids: Baker, 1978.

———. "The 'Big Mango' and Christian Mission." *Urban Mission* 6.2 (Nov. 1988): 3–6.

———. *Calling Our Cities to Christ.* Nutley, N.J.: Presbyterian and Reformed, 1974.

———. "Children in the City." *Urban Mission* 3.2 (Nov. 1985): 3–6.

———. "A Church Planting Method That Works in Urban Areas." *Evangelical Missions Quarterly* 6.3 (Spring 1970): 152–58.

———. "Cities, Seminaries and Christian Colleges." *Urban Mission* 3.1 (Sept. 1985): 3–6.

———. "Don't Be an Urban Missionary Unless. . . ." *Evangelical Missions Quarterly* 19.2 (Apr. 1983): 86–94.

———. "Don't Let the Parish Perish!" *Urban Mission* 3.4 (Mar. 1986): 3–4.

———. "Gentrification and the Parable of the Bats." *Urban Mission* 1.5 (May 1984): 2–4.

———. "God's Hour in the City." *Urban Mission* 4.5 (May 1987): 3–4.

———. "The Importance of Missionary Research." *Urban Mission* 4.3 (Jan. 1987): 3–5.

———. "Let These Women Go! Prostitution and the Church." *Urban Mission* 1.4 (Mar. 1984): 17–25.

———. "Mission to an Urban World." *Church Growth Bulletin* 12.1 (Sept. 1975): 475–78.

———. "Reaching Apartment Dwellers." *Urban Mission* 1.4 (Mar. 1984): 2–3.

———. "Reaching the Unreached in the Cities." *Urban Mission* 2.5 (May 1985): 3–5.

———. "Role of the Urban Pulpit." *Urban Mission* 4.1 (Sept. 1986): 3–5.

———. "The Shift to Ethnic Mission." *Urban Mission* 1.2 (Nov. 1983): 3–4.

———. "The 'Team' Approach to Urban Church Planting." *Urban Mission* 4.4 (Mar. 1987): 3–5.

———. "Urban Evangelism." In *Let the Earth Hear His Voice,* ed. J. D. Douglas, pp. 109–19. Minneapolis: World Wide, 1975.

———. "Urbanization and Missions." In *Crucial Issues in Missions Tomorrow,* ed. Donald A. McGavran, pp. 227–44. Chicago: Moody, 1972.

———. "Urbanization and Missions." In *Crucial Dimensions in World Evangelization,* ed. Arthur F. Glasser, Paul G. Hiebert, C. Peter Wagner, and Ralph D. Winter, pp. 215–32. Pasadena, Calif.: William Carey Library, 1976.

———. "Urban Spirituality." *Urban Mission* 2.2 (Nov. 1984): 3–4.

———. "The Urban Vision." *Urban Mission* 5.4 (Mar. 1988): 3–4.

———. "Who Lives in This City?" *Urban Mission* 3.5 (May 1986): 57–58.

———, ed. *Discipling the City: Theological Reflections on Urban Mission.* Grand Rapids: Baker, 1979.

———, ed. *Guidelines for Urban Church Planting.* Grand Rapids: Baker, 1976.

———, ed. *The Pastor-Evangelist: Preacher, Model, and Mobilizer for Church Growth.* Phillipsburg, N.J.: Presbyterian and Reformed, 1987.

Greenwood, Elma. *How Churches Fight Poverty: 60 Successful Local Projects.* New York: Friendship, 1967.

Grigg, Viv. "The Poor Wise Man of Calcutta." *Urban Mission* 5.2 (Nov. 1987): 43–44.

———. "Sorry! The Frontier Moved." *Urban Mission* 4.4 (Mar. 1987): 12–25.

Grimes, Barbara F., ed. *Ethnologue.* Huntington Beach, Calif.: Summer Institute of Linguistics, 1974.

———, ed. *Ethnologue: Languages of the World.* 10th ed. Dallas: Summer Institute of Linguistics, 1984.

Hadaway, C. Kirk. "Learning from Urban Church Research." *Urban Mission* 2.3 (Jan. 1985): 33–44.

Hadaway, C. Kirk, and Larry L. Rose, eds. *An Urban World: Churches Face the Future.* Nashville: Broadman, 1984.

Haines, John F. "Reaching Muslims in French Cities." *Urban Mission* 2.1 (Sept. 1984): 20–33.

Hall, Douglas. "The Church and Its Community." *Urban Mission* 4.2 (Nov. 1986): 36–44.

Harrison, Margaret E. "Too Much Separatism?" *Urban Mission* 5.4 (Mar. 1988): 40–41.

Hesselgrave, David J. *Communicating Christ Cross-Culturally.* Grand Rapids: Zondervan, 1978.

———. *Counseling Cross-Culturally.* Grand Rapids: Baker, 1984.

————. *Planting Churches Cross-Culturally: A Guide for Home and Foreign Missions.* Grand Rapids: Baker, 1980.

Hiebert, Paul G. "Barrett and Beyond." *Evangelical Missions Quarterly* 12.1 (Jan. 1984): 63–68.

————. "Window Shopping the Gospel." *Urban Mission* 4.5 (May 1987): 5–12.

Hinton, Keith. *Growing Churches Singapore Style: Ministry in an Urban Style.* Singapore: OMF, 1985.

Hollinger, Dennis, and Joseph Modica. "The Feminization of Poverty: Challenge for the Church." *Urban Mission* 5.5 (May 1988): 14–22.

Hopler, Thom. *A World of Difference: Following Christ Beyond Your Cultural Walls.* Downers Grove, Ill.: Inter-Varsity, 1981.

Howes, Robert Gerard. *Steeples in Metropolis.* Dayton: Pflaum, 1969.

Hull, Roger, Jr. "Urban Ecumenical Program: Missionary Thrust or Bust?" *Evangelical Missions Quarterly* 5.1 (Fall 1968): 26–35.

Innes, William C. *Social Concerns in Calvin's Geneva.* Allison Park, Pa.: Pickwick, 1983.

Janssen, Lawrence H. *These Cities Glorious.* New York: Friendship, 1963.

Jennings, George. "Mission Among Metropolitan Muslim." *Urban Mission* 5.2 (Nov. 1987): 12–18.

Johnston, Arthur. "Essentials for Urban Ministry." *Alliance Witness* 120.5 (Feb. 27, 1985): 9–10.

Joslin, Roy. *Urban Harvest.* Hertfordshire, England: Evangelical, 1982.

Kane, J. Herbert. *A Global View of Christian Missions from Pentecost to the Present.* Rev. ed. Grand Rapids: Baker, 1975.

Keyes, Lawrence E. *The Last Age of Missions: A Study of Third World Missionary Societies.* Pasadena, Calif.: William Carey Library, 1983.

Kidd, Beth. "Inner-City Missionary Nurse." *Urban Mission* 2.4 (Mar. 1985): 12–21.

Kloetzli, Walter. *The Church and the Urban Challenge.* Philadelphia: Muhlenberg, 1961.

————. *Urban Church Planning: The Church Discovers Its Community.* Philadelphia: Muhlenberg, 1958.

————, ed. *Challenge and Response in the City: A Theological Consultation on the Urban Church.* Rock Island, Ill.: Augustana, 1962.

Koning, Gerry. "Kid Power—An Urban Children's Program." *Urban Mission* 3.1 (Sept. 1985): 40–43.

Kyle, John. *Urban Mission.* Downers Grove, Ill.: Inter-Varsity, 1988.

Lappierre, Dominique. *City of Joy.* London: Arrow, 1986.

Lausanne Occasional Paper no. 9. *Christian Witness to Large Cities.* Wheaton, Ill.: Lausanne Committee for World Evangelization, 1980.

Lausanne Occasional Paper no. 22. *Thailand Report: Christian Witness to the Urban Poor*. Wheaton, Ill.: Lausanne Committee for World Evangelization, 1980.

Lee, Robert. *The Church and the Exploding Metropolis*. Richmond: John Knox, 1965.

——, ed. *Cities and Churches: Readings on the Urban Church*. Philadelphia: Westminster, 1962.

Leiffer, Murray H. *The Effective City Church*. Nashville: Abingdon, 1961.

Lightbody, C. Stuart. "New Strategies for a New Era: The Story of a Denominational Mission Turning Urban." *Urban Mission* 3.3 (Jan. 1986): 30–34.

Lim, David S. "The City in the Bible." *Evangelical Review of Theology* 12.2 (Apr. 1988): 138–56.

Lingenfelter, Judith. "Public Transportation and Urban Witness." *Urban Mission* 5.4 (Mar. 1988): 5–10.

Linthicum, Robert C. "Networking: Hope for the Church in the City." *Urban Mission* 4.3 (Jan. 1987): 32–51.

——. "The Urban World and World Vision." *Urban Mission* 5.1 (Sept. 1987): 5–12.

——, and J. Timothy Kauffman. "Urban Reality Today: Thoughts on Worldwide Urban Ministry." *Urban Mission* 5.5 (May 1988): 6–13.

Loomis, Samuel. *Modern Cities and Their Religious Problems*. New York: Baker and Taylor, 1887.

McGavran, Donald A. *The Clash Between Christianity and Cultures*. Washington: Canon, 1974.

——. *Effective Evangelism: A Theological Mandate*. Phillipsburg, N.J.: Presbyterian and Reformed, 1988.

——. "Effective Evangelism in Modern Cities." *Urban Mission* 2.4 (Mar. 1985): 40–43.

——. *Momentous Decisions in Missions Today*. Grand Rapids: Baker, 1984.

——. "New Urban Faces of the Church." *Urban Mission* 1.1 (Sept. 1983): 3–11.

——, ed. *Crucial Issues in Missions Tomorrow*. Chicago: Moody, 1972.

McKaughan, Paul. "Through a Glass Darkly—Reading the Future Signs." *Pulse* 22.5 (Mar. 13, 1987): 5–8.

McKenna, David, ed. *The Urban Crisis. A Symposium on the Racial Problem in the Inner City*. Grand Rapids: Zondervan, 1969.

McNeil, Jesse J. *Mission and Metropolis*. Grand Rapids: Eerdmans, 1965.

McWilliam, John. "Mass Evangelism: Reaching Your City in the Eighties." *Urban Mission* 3.1 (Sept. 1985): 7–14.

Magnuson, Norris. *Salvation in the Slums: Evangelical Social Work, 1865–1920*. Metuchen, N.J.: Scarecrow, 1977.

Meeks, Wayne A. *The First Urban Christians: The Social World of the Apostle Paul.* New Haven: Yale University Press, 1983.

Miller, Kenneth D. *Man and God in the City.* New York: Friendship, 1954.

———, and Ethel P. Miller. *The People Are the City: 150 Years of Social and Religious Concern in New York City.* New York: Macmillan, 1962.

Mitchell, Rudy. "Evangelism in the City." *Urban Mission* 1.3 (Jan. 1984): 30–35.

———, and Eldin Villafane. "The Center for Urban Ministerial Education: A Case Study in Urban Theological Education by Extension." *Urban Mission* 2.2 (Nov. 1984): 31–39.

Mohl, Raymond A., and James F. Richardson. *The Urban Experience.* Belmont, Calif.: Wadsworth, 1973.

Monsma, Timothy. "Homogeneous Networks: A Label That Promotes Good Urban Strategy." *Urban Mission* 5.3 (Jan. 1988): 11–17.

———. "Urban Explosion and Missions Strategy." *Evangelical Missions Quarterly* 17.1 (Jan. 1981): 5–12.

Moore, Paul. *The Church Reclaims the City.* New York: Seabury, 1964.

Moore, Richard E., and Duane L. Day. *Urban Church Breakthrough.* New York: Harper and Row, 1966.

Motte, Mary, and Joseph R. Lang, eds. *Mission in Dialogue: The Sedos Research Seminar on the Future of Mission.* Maryknoll, N.Y.: Orbis, 1982.

Murphy, Edward. "Guidelines for Urban Church Planting." In *Crucial Dimensions in World Evangelization,* ed. Arthur F. Glasser, Paul G. Hiebert, C. Peter Wagner, and Ralph D. Winter, pp. 233–53. Pasadena, Calif.: William Carey Library, 1976.

———. "Guidelines for Urban Church Planting." In *Crucial Issues in Missions Tomorrow,* ed. Donald A. McGavran, pp. 245–65. Chicago: Moody, 1972.

Musselman, G. Paul. *The Church on the Urban Frontier.* New York: Seabury, 1960.

Neighbour, Ralph, Jr., and Cal Thomas. *Target Group Evangelism.* Nashville: Broadman, 1975.

Neill, Stephen; Gerald H. Anderson; and John Goodwin, eds. *Concise Dictionary of the Christian World Mission.* Nashville: Abingdon, 1971.

Newbigin, Lesslie. *Sign of the Kingdom.* Grand Rapids: Eerdmans, 1981.

Nida, Eugene. *Church Growth and Christian Mission.* New York: Harper and Row, 1965.

Nieves, Alvaro L. "Urban Minorities and Christian Higher Education." *Urban Mission* 3.2 (Nov. 1985): 20–28.

Niklaus, Robert. "Cities: Staggering Statistics." *Evangelical Missions Quarterly* 17.4 (Oct. 1981): 246–47.

————. "World: First Religious Census." *Evangelical Missions Quarterly* 18.4 (Oct. 1982): 256–57.

————. "World: Massive Growth." *Evangelical Missions Quarterly* 21.3 (July 1985): 315–16.

————. "World: Megacity Strategies." *Evangelical Missions Quarterly* 21.2 (Apr. 1985): 173–74.

Norton, Perry L. *Church and Metropolis: A City Planner's Viewpoint of the Slow-Changing Church in the Fast-Changing Metropolis.* New York: Seabury, 1964.

Noyce, Gaylord B. *Survival and Mission for the City Church.* Philadelphia: Westminster, 1975.

Oren, Martin Luther. "Aging in the City." *Urban Mission* 3.5 (May 1986): 36–48.

Ortiz, Manuel. "A Church in Missiological Tension." *Urban Mission* 2.1 (Sept. 1984): 12–19.

Ostrom, Karl A., and Donald W. Shriver, Jr. *Is There Hope for the City?* Philadelphia: Westminster, 1977.

Palau, Luis. "The Future of Mass Evangelism." In *Evangelism: The Next Ten Years,* ed. Sherwood Wirt, pp. 154–65. Waco, Tex.: Word, 1978.

Pasquariello, Ronald D.; Donald W. Shriver, Jr.; and Alan Geyer. *Redeeming the City: Theology, Politics and Urban Policy.* New York: Pilgrim, 1982.

Pate, Larry. "Get Ready for Partnerships with Emerging Missions." *Evangelical Missions Quarterly* 22.4 (Oct. 1986): 382–88.

Perkins, John. *With Justice for All.* Ventura, Calif.: Regal, 1982.

Peters, George W. *Saturation Evangelism.* Grand Rapids: Zondervan, 1970.

Phillips, Keith. *They Dare to Love the Ghetto.* Los Angeles: World Impact, 1979.

Pretiz, Paul E. "Church Planters Needed." *Urban Mission* 5.3 (Jan. 1988): 6–10.

————. "What We Mean by Urban Evangelism." *Urban Mission* 4.5 (May 1987): 38–39.

Racine, Carl. "Don't Neglect Third World Suburbia!" *Missiology* 9.2 (Apr. 1981): 171–80.

Ramsay, William. *The Cities of St. Paul: Their Influence on His Life and Thought.* Grand Rapids: Baker, 1979.

Reapsome, Jim. "Editions Analysis: Cities Must Have Our Best Efforts." *Evangelical Missions Quarterly* 19.2 (Apr. 1983): 98–99.

————. "People Groups: Beyond the Push to Reach Them Lie Some Contrary Opinions." *Evangelical Missions Quarterly* 20.1 (Jan. 1984): 6–19.

Recker, Robert. "The Redemptive Focus of the Kingdom of God." *Calvin Theological Journal* 14.2 (Nov. 1979): 154–86.

Ro, Bong Rin. "Urban Missions: A Historical Perspective." *Evangelical Review of Theology* 12.2 (Apr. 1988): 157–73.

Roberts, Vella Kotarathil. "The Urban Mission of the Church from an Urban Anthropological Perspective." D.Miss. diss., Fuller Theological Seminary, 1981.

Rose, Larry, and C. Kirk Hadaway. *An Urban World: Churches Face the Future.* Nashville: Broadman, 1984.

———, eds. *The Urban Challenge.* Nashville: Broadman, 1982.

Rowen, Samuel. "Is Continued Urban Growth Inevitable?" *Evangelical Missions Quarterly* 21.4 (Oct. 1985): 418–20.

Rubingh, Eugene. "The City in the Mission of God." *Urban Mission* 5.2 (Nov. 1987): 5–11.

Sanchez, Daniel. "How to Reach U.S. Ethnic Groups." *Evangelical Missions Quarterly* 13.2 (Apr. 1977): 95–103.

Sawatsky, Ben A. "A Church Planting Strategy for World Class Cities." *Urban Mission* 3.2 (Nov. 1985): 7–19.

Schaeffer, Francis A. *Death in the City.* Downers Grove, Ill.: Inter-Varsity, 1969.

Schlissel, Steve M. "City Singles." *Urban Mission* 3.1 (Sept. 1985): 26–31.

Schmidt, Henry J. "The Urban Ethos: Building Churches in a Pagan Environment." *Mission Focus* 8.2 (June 1980): 25–33.

Schreck, Harley, and David Barrett, eds. *Unreached Peoples: Clarifying the Task.* Monrovia, Calif.: MARC, 1987.

Schuller, David S. *Christianity Encounters the New Urban Society.* St. Louis: Concordia, 1966.

Scott, Waldron. *Bring Forth Justice: A Contemporary Perspective on Mission.* Grand Rapids: Eerdmans, 1980.

———. "Man at His Best and Worst: A Biblical View of Urban Life." *World Christian*, Jan.–Feb. 1988, pp. 27–29.

Sensenig, Joy V. "Why and How to Start a Ministry Among Students." *Urban Mission* 13.1 (Jan. 1977): 27–33.

Sheppard, David. *Built as a City: God and the Urban World Today.* London: Hodder and Stoughton, 1974.

Shriver, Donald W., Jr., and Karl A. Ostrom. *Is There Hope for the City?* Philadelphia: Westminster, 1977.

Siebert, Rudolf J. "Urbanization as a World Trend." *Evangelical Missions Quarterly* 13.4 (Oct. 1985): 429–43.

Sowel, Robert M. "Personal Evangelism in the Inner City." *Urban Mission* 5.2 (Nov. 1987): 19–24.

Steinhouer, Paul. "Unbabbling Pentecost: A Case for Multi-Ethnic Church Planting." *Urban Mission* 4.5 (May 1987): 32–35.

Stockwell, Clinton E. *Urban Research Project: A Handbook for Urban Ministry.* Chicago: Baptist General Conference, Midwest District, 1985.

Stott, John R. W., and Robert Coote. *Down to Earth: Studies in Christianity and Culture.* Grand Rapids: Eerdmans, 1980.

Stravers, David E. "Print Power: An Incarnational Approach to Literature Evangelism in Cities." *Urban Mission* 5.5 (May 1988): 23–37.

Teresa, Mother. *My Life for the Poor.* Edited by Jose Gonzalez-Balado and Janel N. Playfoot. San Francisco: Harper and Row, 1985.

Tidball, Derek. *The Social Context of the New Testament: A Sociological Analysis.* Grand Rapids: Zondervan, 1984.

Tillapaugh, Frank. *The Church Unleashed: Getting God's People Out Where the Needs Are.* Ventura, Calif.: Regal, 1982.

Tonelson, Alan. "What Happened to the Population Explosion?" *Evangelical Missions Quarterly* 15.2 (Apr. 1979): 107–10.

Tonna, Benjamin. *A Gospel for the Cities: A Socio-Theology of Urban Ministry.* Maryknoll, N.Y.: Orbis, 1982.

Torney, George A., comp. *Toward A Creative Urban Strategy.* Waco, Tex.: Word, 1970.

Ujvarosy, Helen, ed. *Signs of the Kingdom in the Secular City: Resources for the Urban Church.* Chicago: Covenant, 1984.

Ulschak, Francis. *Urban Ministry: A Study of Goals.* Chicago: SCUPE, 1977.

Van Houten, Mark. *God's Inner-City Address: Crossing the Boundaries.* Grand Rapids: Zondervan, 1988.

Verkuyl, Johannes. *Contemporary Missiology: An Introduction.* Translated by Dale Cooper. Grand Rapids: Eerdmans, 1978.

Verstraelen, Frans J. "Calculations and Surprise in the *World Christian Encyclopedia.*" *Evangelical Missions Quarterly* 12.1 (Jan. 1984): 55–62.

Vreeman, Jerry. "Mass Media and the Local Church." *Urban Mission* 1.4 (Mar. 1984): 10–16.

Wagner, C. Peter. *Frontiers in Mission Strategy.* Chicago: Moody, 1971.

Wakatama, Pius. *Independence for the Third World Church: An African's Perspective on Missionary Work.* Downers Grove, Ill.: Inter-Varsity, 1976.

Warren, Max. "Church Growth Day After Tomorrow." *Church Growth Bulletin* 1.5 (May 1965): 1–3.

Waymire, Bob, and C. Peter Wagner. *The Church Growth Survey Handbook.* 2d rev. ed. Santa Clara, Calif.: Global Church Growth Bulletin, 1980.

————. "New Global Data Map Promises Results." *Evangelical Missions Quarterly* 19.3 (July 1983): 236–41.

Weber, George W. *The Congregation in Mission: Emerging Structures for the Church in an Urban Society.* New York: Abingdon, 1964.

Westgate, James E. "Emerging Church Planting Strategies for World Class Cities." *Urban Mission* 4.2 (Nov. 1986): 6–13.

Willems, Lisa. "Jungle to City: Enduring yet Endangered, Tribal People Look for Hope in the Urban World." *World Christian Magazine*, Jan.–Feb. 1984, p. 16.

Wilson, Bryan. *Religion in Sociological Perspective.* New York: Oxford University Press, 1982.

Wilson, Samuel. "Hope for the City: A Focus for Mission." *Urban Mission* 3.4 (Mar. 1986): 25–33.

————. "Why Love the City?" *World Christian*, Jan.–Feb. 1988, pp. 16–19, 23–26.

Winter, Gibson. *The Suburban Captivity of the Churches.* New York: Macmillan, 1962.

Wirth, Louis. "Urbanism as a Way of Life." *American Journal of Sociology* 44.1 (July 1938): 1–24.

Wolterstorff, Nicholas. *Until Justice and Peace Embrace.* Grand Rapids: Eerdmans, 1983.

Wright, William B. *Cities of Paul: Beacons of the Past Rekindled for the Present.* Boston: Houghton Mifflin, 1905.

Yamamori, Tetsunao. "How to Reach Urban Ethnics." *Urban Mission* 1.4 (Mar. 1984): 29–35.

Younger, George D. *The Church and Urban Power Structure.* Philadelphia: Westminster, 1963.

Yuen, Bessie Kawaguchi. "Urban Poor-ology: A Theology of Ministry to the World's Urban Poor." *Urban Mission* 5.1 (Sept. 1987): 13–19.

Ziegenhals, Walter E. *Urban Churches in Transition: Reflections on Selected Problems and Approaches to Churches and Communities in Racial Transition Based on the Chicago Experience.* New York: Pilgrim, 1978.

Social-Science Perspective

Abrahamson, Mark. *Urban Sociology.* Englewood Cliffs, N.J.: Prentice-Hall, 1976.

Abu-Lughod, Janet, and Richard Hay, Jr., eds. *Third World Urbanization.* Chicago: Maaroufa, 1977.

————. "Urban-Rural Differences as a Function of the Demographic Transition." In *An Urban World*, ed. Charles Tilly. Boston: Little, Brown, 1964.

Adams, Robert M. "The Origin of Cities." *Scientific American* 203.3 (Sept. 1960): 153–68.

Arensberg, Conrad M., and Solon T. Kimball. *Culture and Community.* New York: Harcourt, Brace and World, 1965.

Ayres, Robert L. *Banking on the Poor: The World Bank and World Poverty.* Cambridge, Mass.: MIT Press, 1984.

Baldwin, Leland D. *The American Quest for the City of God.* Macon, Ga.: Mercer University Press, 1981.

Bardo, John W., and John J. Hartman. *Urban Sociology.* Wichita, Kans.: Wichita State University Press, 1982.

Basham, Richard. *Urban Anthropology.* Palo Alto, Calif.: Mayfield, 1978.

Bender, Thomas. *Toward an Urban Vision: Ideas and Institutions in Nineteenth-Century America.* Baltimore: Johns Hopkins University Press, 1978.

Benjamin, Don C. *Deuteronomy and City Life: A Form Criticism of Texts with the Word City ('ir) in Deuteronomy 4:41–26:19.* Lanham, Md.: University Press of America, 1983.

Bennett, G. Willis. "The Changing Face of the Contemporary City." *Urban Mission* 2.2 (Nov. 1984): 15–25.

Berger, Alan S. *The City: Urban Communities and Their Problems.* Dubuque, Iowa: William C. Brown, 1978.

Berry, Brian J. L. *The Human Consequences of Urbanization: Divergent Paths in the Urban Experience of the Twentieth Century.* New York: St. Martin's, 1973.

———. *Urbanization and Counter-Urbanization.* Beverly Hills, Calif.: Sage, 1976.

Bierman, Arthur K. *The Philosophy of Urban Existence: A Prolegomenon.* Athens, Ohio: Ohio University Press, 1973.

Blackwell, James E., and Philip S. Hart. *Cities, Suburbs and Blacks: A Study of Concerns, Distrust and Alienation.* Bayside, N.Y.: General Hall, 1982.

Bott, Elizabeth. *Family and Social Network: Roles, Norms and External Relationships in Ordering Urban Families.* London: Tavistock, 1957.

Breese, Gerald. *Urbanization in Newly Developing Countries.* Englewood Cliffs, N.J.: Prentice-Hall, 1966.

Carlson, Ronald W. "Films About the City: A Selected Bibliography of Films for Sensitizing Christians to Urban Life and Its Problems." *Urban Mission* 4.1 (Sept. 1986): 24–34.

Chisholm, Michael. *Modern World Development: A Geographical Perspective.* Totowa, N.J.: Barnes and Noble, 1982.

Chudacoff, Howard P. *The Evolution of American Urban Society.* Englewood Cliffs, N.J.: Prentice-Hall, 1975.

Clarke, Susan E., and Jeffrey L. Obler, eds. *Urban Ethnic Conflict: A Comparative Perspective.* Chapel Hill: University of North Carolina Institute for Research in Social Science, 1976.

Cox, Harvey. *The Secular City: Secularization and Urbanization in Theological Perspective.* New York: Macmillan, 1965.

Dantzig, George B., and Thomas L. Saatz. *Compact City: Plan for a Liveable Urban Environment.* San Francisco: Freeman, 1973.

Davis, Kingsley. "The Origin and Growth of Urbanization in the World." *American Journal of Sociology* 60.5 (Mar. 1955): 429–37.

———. "The Urbanization of the Human Population." *Scientific American* 213.3 (Sept. 1965): 41–53.

———. *World Urbanization, 1950–70.* London: Greenwood, 1977.

Dogan, Mattei, and John D. Kasarda, eds. *The Metropolis Era.* Vol. 1, *A World of Giant Cities.* Newbury Park, Calif.: Sage, 1988.

———. *The Metropolis Era.* Vol. 2, *Mega-Cities.* Newbury Park, Calif.: Sage, 1988.

duToit, Brian M., and Helen I. Safa, eds. "Migration and Urbanization." In *International Congress of Anthropological and Ethnological Sciences.* 9th ed. The Hague: Mouton, 1975.

Dwyer, D. J. *The City in the Third World.* London: Macmillan, 1974.

Eames, Edwin, and Judith G. Goode. *Anthropology of the City.* Englewood Cliffs, N.J.: Prentice-Hall, 1977.

Eddy, Elizabeth M., ed. *Urban Anthropology: Research Perspectives and Strategies.* Athens, Ga.: University of Georgia Press, 1968.

Eells, Richard, and Clarence Walton, eds. *Man in the City of the Future: A Symposium of Urban Philosophies.* London: Collier-Macmillan, 1968.

Eisenstadt, S. N., and A. Shachar. *Society, Culture, and Urbanization.* Newbury Park, Calif.: Sage, 1987.

Ellul, Jacques. *The Meaning of the City.* Translated by Dennis Pardee. Grand Rapids: Eerdmans, 1970.

Fava, Sylvia Fleis, ed. *Urbanism in World Perspective: A Reader.* New York: Crowell, 1968.

Fischer, Claude. *To Dwell Among Friends: Personal Networks in Town and City.* Chicago: University of Chicago Press, 1982.

Forrester, Jay W. *Urban Dynamics.* Cambridge, Mass.: MIT Press, 1969.

Foster, G. M., and R. B. Kemper, eds. *Anthropologists in Cities.* Boston: Little, Brown, 1974.

Fox, R. G. *Urban Anthropology: Cities in Their Cultural Settings.* Englewood Cliffs, N.J.: Prentice-Hall, 1976.

Fried, Morton, ed. *Readings in Anthropology.* New York: Crowell, 1959.

Friedl, John, and Noel H. Chrisman, eds. *City Ways: A Selective Reader in Urban Anthropology.* New York: Crowell, 1975.

Gans, Herbert. *The Urban Villagers.* New York: Free, 1962.

Gappert, Gary, and Richard V. Knight. *Cities and the Twenty-First Century.* Beverly Hills, Calif.: Sage, 1982.

Geertz, Clifford, ed. *Old Societies and New States.* New York: New, 1965.

Gibbs, Jack P., ed. *Urban Research Methods.* Princeton, N.J.: Van Nostrand, 1961.

Gist, Noel, and Sylvia F. Fava. *Urban Society.* New York: Crowell, 1964.

Glazer, Nathan, and Daniel Moynihan. *Beyond the Melting Pot: The Negroes, Puerto Ricans, Jews, Italians and Irish of New York City.* 2d ed. Cambridge, Mass.: MIT Press, 1970.

Gmelch, George, and Walter Zenner, eds. *Urban Life: Readings in Urban Anthropology.* New York: St. Martin's, 1980.

Gulick, J. *Urbanization and Family Change.* Atlantic Highlands, N.J.: Humanities, 1968.

Gutkind, P. *Urban Anthropology: Perspective on Third World Urbanization and Urbanism.* New York: Harper and Row, 1974.

Hallman, Howard W. *Neighborhoods: Their Place in Urban Life.* Beverly Hills, Calif.: Sage, 1984.

Hannerz, Ulf. *Exploring the City: Inquiries Toward an Urban Anthropology.* New York: Columbia University Press, 1980.

Hanson, R. C., and O. G. Simmons. "The Role Path: A Concept and Procedure for Studying Migration to Urban Communities." *Human Organization* 27.2 (Summer 1968): 152–58.

Hauser, Philip M. "The Folk-Urban Ideal Types." In *The Study of Urbanization,* ed. P. Hauser and L. F. Schnore, pp. 491–517. New York: John Wiley and Sons, 1965.

Helmer, John, and Neil A. Eddington, eds. *Urbanman: The Psychology of Urban Survival.* New York: Free, 1973.

Herbert, David. *Urban Geography: A Social Perspective.* New York: Praeger, 1972.

Hiebert, Paul G. *Cultural Anthropology.* 2d ed. Grand Rapids: Baker, 1983.

Hoselitz, B. "The Role of Cities in the Economic Growth of Underdeveloped Countries." *Journal of Political Economy* 61.3 (June 1953): 195–208.

Hunter, David E., and Phillip Whitten, eds. *Encyclopedia of Anthropology.* New York: Harper, 1976.

Keating, W. D. "Urban Displacement Research: Local, National, and International." *Urban Affairs Quarterly* 21.1 (Sept. 1985): 132–36.

Kerens, Patrick. *Sinful Social Structures.* New York: Paulist, 1974.

Kish, Leslie. *Survey Sampling.* New York: John Wiley and Sons, 1965.

Leacock, Eleanor, ed. *The Culture of Poverty: A Critique.* New York: Simon and Schuster, 1971.

Leinwand, Gerald. *The City as a Community.* New York: Washington Square, 1970.

Lewis, Oscar. "The Culture of Poverty." *Scientific American* 215.4 (Oct. 1966): 19–25.

———. "The Possessions of the Poor." *Scientific American* 221.4 (Oct. 1969): 114–24.

Lineberry, Robert L., and Louis H. Masotti. *Urban Problems and Public Policy.* Washington, D.C.: Heath, 1975.

Lloyd, Peter. *Slums of Hope? Shanty Towns of the Third World.* New York: Penguin, 1979.

McGee, T. G. "Peasants in the Cities: A Paradox, A Paradox, A Most Ingenious Paradox." *Human Organization* 32.2 (Summer 1973): 135–42.

———. *Urbanization Process in the Third World.* London: Bell, 1971.

McNeill, William H., and Ruth S. Adams, eds. *Human Migration: Patterns and Policies.* Bloomington, Ind.: Indiana University Press, 1979.

Mangin, William. "Squatter Settlements." *Scientific American* 217.4 (Oct. 1967): 21–29.

———, ed. *Peasants in Cities: Readings in the Anthropology of Urbanization.* Boston: Houghton Mifflin, 1970.

Masotti, Louis H., and Jeffrey K. Haden, eds. *The Urbanization of the Suburbs.* Beverly Hills, Calif.: Sage, 1973.

Mayur, R. "Supercities: The Growing Crisis." *Futurist* 19.4 (Aug. 1985): 27–30.

Mead, Margaret, ed. *Cultural Patterns and Technical Change.* New York: New American Library, 1961.

Miner, Horace. "The Folk-Urban Continuum." *American Sociological Review* 17.5 (Oct. 1952): 529–37.

Mitchell, J. Clyde. *Social Networks in Urban Situations.* Manchester, England: University of Manchester Press, 1969.

Moynihan, Daniel Patrick, ed. *Toward a National Urban Policy.* New York: Basic, 1970.

Mumford, Lewis. *The City in History: Its Origins, Its Transformations, and Its Prospects.* New York: Harcourt, Brace and World, 1961.

————. *The Urban Prospect.* New York: Harcourt, Brace and World, 1968.

Nelson, Bryce. "Feeling of Ethnic Pride on the Rise." *Los Angeles Times,* April 30, 1978, pp. 16–18.

Nelson, Joan. *Access to Power: Politics and the Urban Poor in Developing Nations.* Princeton, N.J.: Princeton University Press, 1979.

————. "The Pioneers." *Latin America Press* 16.34 (Sept. 20, 1984): 3.

Oren, Martin L. "Aging in the City." *Urban Mission* 3.5 (May 1986): 36–48.

Orleans, Peter, and Miriam Orleans. *Urban Life: Diversity and Inequality.* Dubuque, Iowa: William C. Brown, 1976.

Palen, J. John. *The Urban World.* 2d ed. New York: McGraw-Hill, 1981.

Piddington, Ralph, ed. *Kinship and Geographical Mobility.* Leiden: E. J. Brill, 1965.

Press, Irwin, and M. Estellie Smith, eds. *Urban Place and Process.* New York: Macmillan, 1980.

Racine, Carl. "Don't Neglect Third World Suburbia!" *Missiology* 9.2 (Apr. 1981): 171–80.

Redfield, Robert. "The Folk Society." *American Journal of Sociology* 52.4 (Jan. 1947): 293–308.

————. *The Little Community: Viewpoints for the Study of a Human Whole.* Chicago: University of Chicago Press, 1955.

————. *Peasant Society and Culture: An Anthropological Approach to Civilization.* Chicago: University of Chicago Press, 1956.

————. *The Primitive World and Its Transformation.* Ithaca, N.Y.: Cornell University Press, 1959.

Redfield, Robert, and Milton B. Singer. "The Cultural Role of Cities." *Economic Development and Cultural Change* 3.1 (Oct. 1954): 53–73.

Sennett, Richard, ed. *Classic Essays on the Culture of Cities.* New York: Appleton-Century-Crofts, 1969.

Scthuranam, S. V. *The Urban Informal Sector in Developing Countries: Employment, Poverty and Environment.* Geneva, Switzerland: International Labor Office, 1981.

Sheppard, David. *Bias to the Poor.* London: Hodder and Stoughton, 1983.

Sjoberg, G. *The Preindustrial City, Past and Present.* New York: Free, 1960.

Southall, Aidan, ed. *Urban Anthropology: Cross-Cultural Studies of Urbanization.* London: Oxford University Press, 1973.

Spindler, Louise S., ed. *Culture Change and Modernization.* New York: Holt, Rinehart and Winston, 1977.

Spradley, James P. *Participant Observation.* New York: Holt, Rinehart and Winston, 1980.

Steinberg, Stephen. *The Ethnic Myth: Race, Ethnicity, and Class in America.* New York: Atheneum, 1981.

Torney, George A., comp. *Toward Creative Urban Strategy.* Waco, Tex.: Word, 1970.

Tringham, Ruth, ed. *Urban Settlements: The Process of Urbanization in Archaeological Settlements.* Andover, Mass.: Warner Modular, 1973.

Ucko, Peter J.; Ruth Tringham; and G. W. Dimbleby. *Man, Settlement and Urbanism.* Cambridge, Mass.: Schenkman, 1972.

United Nations Department of International Economic and Social Affairs. *The World Population Situation in 1983.* Population Studies no. 85. New York: United Nations, 1984.

Wagner, C. Peter. "Culturally Homogeneous Churches and American Pluralism: Some Religious and Ethical Implications." Ph.D. diss., University of Southern California, 1977.

Warren, Donald I. *Helping Networks: How People Cope with Problems in the Urban Community.* South Bend, Ind.: University of Notre Dame Press, 1981.

Weaver, Thomas, and Douglas White, eds. *The Anthropology of Urban Environments.* Boulder, Colo.: Society for Applied Anthropology, 1972.

Weber, Max. *The City.* Translated by S. L. Henderson. Edited by T. Parsons. New York: Free, 1958.

Weitz, Raanan, ed. *Urbanization and the Developing Countries.* New York: Praeger, 1973.

White, Douglas, and Thomas Weaver, eds. *The Anthropology of Urban Environments.* Boulder, Colo.: Society for Applied Anthropology, 1972.

Whorf, Benjamin Lee. *Language, Thought, and Reality.* Cambridge, Mass.: MIT Press, 1956.

Winter, Gibson. *The New Creation as Metropolis.* New York: Macmillan, 1963.

Wirth, Louis. "Urbanism as a Way of Life." *American Journal of Sociology* 44.1 (July 1938): 1–24.

Africa

Mission Perspective

Alexander, Frank. "Mission in Malawi." Missiological Abstract. Pasadena, Calif.: Fuller Theological Seminary, 1969.

Anderrson, Afraim. *Churches at the Grass Roots: A Study in Congo–Brazzaville.* London: Lutterworth, 1968.

Braun, Willys K. *Advance of the Church in Africa.* Hong Kong: New Life Litho, 1980.

Casaleggio, Enrico. *The Land Will Yield Its Fruit.* Translated by J. Orffer. Mkar, Nigeria: SUM/CRC, 1963.

Christian Council of Nigeria. *Christian Responsibility in an Independent Nigeria.* Ibadan: Christian Council of Nigeria, 1960.

Crampton, Edmund Patrick Thurman. *Christianity in Northern Nigeria.* Zaria: Gaskiya, 1975.

Falk, Peter. *The Growth of the Church in Africa.* Grand Rapids: Zondervan, 1979.

Fleming, Kenneth C. "The Gospel to the Urban Zulu: Three Cultures in Conflict." *Evangelical Missions Quarterly* 22.1 (Jan. 1986): 24–31.

Fritz, Paul J. "Summer Urban Church-Planting Internships for Seminary Students: Nigeria." *Urban Mission* 5.5 (May 1988): 38–42.

Gilliland, Dean S. "How 'Christian' Are African Independent Churches?" *Missiology* 14.3 (July 1986): 259–72.

Glasser, Arthur, and Eric Fife. *Missions in Crisis: Rethinking Missionary Strategy.* Downers Grove, Ill.: Inter-Varsity, 1961.

Goba, Bonganjalo. "Role of the Urban Church: A Black South African Perspective." *Evangelical Review of Theology* 8.1 (Apr. 1984): 90–99.

Grimley, John B., and Gordon E. Robinson. *Church Growth in Central and Southern Nigeria.* Grand Rapids: Eerdmans, 1966.

Hastings, Adrian. *African Christianity.* New York: Seabury, 1976.

Hogan, J. Philip. "The Assemblies of God in Nairobi, Kenya." In *Guidelines for Urban Church Planting,* ed. Roger S. Greenway, pp. 37–43. Grand Rapids: Baker, 1976.

Hopler, Thom. "A Bibliography and Review of Literature Leading to an Understanding of Church Growth in Nakuru, Kenya." Missiological Abstract. Pasadena, Calif.: Fuller Theological Seminary, 1975.

———. "Guidelines for Urban Church Planting." *Missiology* 6.2 (Apr. 1978): 247.

Hostetter, Richard. "Voluntary Associations and Urban African Churches." *Missiology* 4.4 (Oct. 1976): 427–30.

Jacobs, Sylvia M., ed. *Black Americans and the Missionary Movement in Africa.* Westport, Conn.: Greenwood, 1982.

Monsma, Timothy M. "African Cities: Choosing New Urban Fields." *Urban Mission* 3.5 (May 1986): 49–50.

———. "African Urban Missiology: A Synthesis of Nigerian Case Studies and Biblical Principles." Doctoral dissertation. Pasadena, Calif.: Fuller Theological Seminary, 1977.

———. "Reaching Africa's Growing Cities." In *Guidelines for Urban Church Planting,* ed. Roger S. Greenway, pp. 63–70. Grand Rapids: Baker, 1976.

———. "The Tiv Soldiers of Nigeria." *Urban Mission* 1.1 (Sept. 1983): 29–31.

————. *An Urban Strategy for Africa.* Pasadena, Calif.: William Carey Library, 1979.

Mwantila, Simalike. "Urban Missions in Tanzania, East Africa." *Urban Mission* 2.4 (Mar. 1985): 44–47.

Nikkel, Steve. "Holistic Ministry in Freetown, Sierra Leone." *Urban Mission* 5.4 (Mar. 1988): 35–39.

Oosthuisen, G. C. *Pentecostal Penetration into the Indian Community in Metropolitan Durban, South Africa.* Durban: Human Sciences Research Council, Pretoria, 1975.

Paden, John N. *Religion and Political Culture in Kano.* Berkeley: University of California Press, 1973.

Parrinder, Geoffrey. *Religion in an African City.* London: Oxford University Press, 1953.

Polding, M. Fred. "Kinshasa, Zaire: An African Strategy for Urban Church Growth." *Urban Mission* 3.4 (Mar. 1986): 36–38.

Riddle, Norman G. "Church Growth and the Communication of the Gospel in Kinshasa." Master's thesis, Fuller Theological Seminary, 1971.

Schreiber, Dale. "The Urban Muslims of Ivory Coast." *Urban Mission* 3.3 (Jan. 1986): 39–44.

Shorter, Aylward. "Social Change, Political Ideology and Urbanization." In *African Culture and the Christian Church*, pp. 14–43. Maryknoll, N.Y.: Orbis, 1974.

Shreck, Harley C. "African Urban People Groups." *Urban Mission* 4.4 (Mar. 1987): 42–51.

Stevens, R. S. O. *The Church in Urban Nigeria.* London: Church Missionary Society, 1963.

Swank, Gerald O. *Frontier Peoples of Central Nigeria, and A Strategy for Outreach.* Pasadena, Calif.: William Carey Library, 1977.

Taber, Charles R., ed. *The Church in Africa 1977: Papers Presented at a Symposium at Milligan College, March 31–April 3.* Pasadena, Calif.: William Carey Library, 1978.

Tate, Francis V. "Patterns of Church Growth in Nairobi." Master's thesis. Pasadena, Calif.: Fuller Theological Seminary, 1970.

Tucker, Ruth. "African Women's Movement Finds Massive Response." *Evangelical Missions Quarterly* 22.3 (July 1986): 282–90.

Udo, Reuben K. "Migration and Urbanization in Nigeria." In *Population Growth and Socioeconomic Change in West Africa*, ed. J. C. Caldwell, pp. 298–307. New York: Columbia University Press, 1975.

Van Rheenen, Gailyn. *Church Planting in Uganda: A Comparative Study.* Pasadena, Calif.: William Carey Library, 1976.

Watts, Hilstan L. "Some Structural Problems of Urban Religion: A Case Study from the City of Durban." *Social Compass* 19.1 (1972): 63–81.

Wold, Joseph Conrad. *God's Impatience in Liberia.* Grand Rapids: Eerdmans, 1968.

Social-Science Perspective

Adollo, John J. *Nigeria Year Book.* Lagos: Times, 1972.

Ajaegbu, Hyacinth I. *African Urbanization: A Bibliography.* London: International African Institute, 1972.

———. *Urban and Rural Development in Nigeria.* London: Heinemann, 1976.

Aldous, Joan. "Urbanization, the Extended Family, and Kinship Ties in West Africa." In *Urbanism in World Perspective: A Reader,* ed. S. F. Fava, pp. 297–305. New York: Crowell, 1968.

Barbour, K. M., and R. M. Prothero, eds. *Essays on African Population.* London: Routledge and Kegan Paul, 1961.

Barrett, David B. *Schism and Renewal in Africa. An Analysis of Six Thousand Contemporary Religious Movements.* Nairobi: Oxford University Press, 1968.

Bascom, William R. "The Urban African and His World." In *Urbanism in World Perspective: A Reader,* ed. S. F. Fava, pp. 81–93. New York: Crowell, 1968.

———. "Urbanism as a Traditional African Pattern." *Urbanization and Migration in West Africa Sociological Review* 7 (1959): 30ff.

Beaver, R. Pierce. *Christianity and African Education.* Grand Rapids: Eerdmans, 1966.

Benue-Plateau State (Ministry of Internal Affairs and Information). "Toward a Just Egalitarian Society." *Monthly Newsletter,* Feb. 1974, p. 1.

Bohannan, Laura, and Paul Bohannan. *African Outline: A General Introduction.* New York: Doubleday, 1964.

Bryant, K. J. *A Guide to Kaduna.* Zaria: Norla, 1958.

Burns, Alan. *History of Nigeria.* London: Allen and Unwin, 1969.

Caldwell, John C. *African Rural-Urban Migration: The Movement to Ghana's Towns.* London: Hurst, 1969.

———, ed. *Population Growth and Socioeconomic Change in West Africa.* New York: Columbia University Press, 1975.

Cohen, Abner. *Custom and Politics in Urban Africa: A Study of Hausa Migrants in Yoruba Towns.* Berkeley: University of California Press, 1969.

De Ridder, J. C. *The Personality of the Urban African in South Africa: A Thematic Apperception Test Study.* London: Routledge and Kegan Paul, 1961.

Dike, A. A. "Environmental Problems in Third World Cities: A Nigerian Example." *Current Anthropology* 26.4 (Aug.–Oct. 1985): 501–5.

Dogan, Mattei, and John D. Kasarda. *The Metropolis Era.* Vol. 1, *A World of Giant Cities.* Newbury Park, Calif.: Sage, 1988.

———. *The Metropolis Era.* Vol. 2, *Mega-Cities.* Newbury Park, Calif.: Sage, 1988.

duToit, Brian M. "Cultural Continuity and African Urbanization." In *Urban Anthropology: Research Perspectives and Strategies,* ed. Elizabeth M. Eddy. Athens, Ga.: University of Georgia Press, 1968.

Edinburgh University Department of Anthropology. *African Urbanization: A Reading List of Selected Books, Articles and Reports.* London: International African Institute, 1965.

Eisenstadt, S. N., and A. Shachar. *Society, Culture, and Urbanization.* Newbury Park, Calif.: Sage, 1987.

Epstein, A. L. *Africa South of the Sahara.* London: Europa, 1985.

———. *Politics in an Urban African Community.* Manchester: Manchester, 1958.

———. "Urbanization and Social Change in Africa." *Current Anthropology* 8.4 (Oct. 1967): 275–95.

Fava, Sylvia F., ed. *Urbanism in World Perspective: A Reader.* New York: Crowell, 1968.

Feldman, S., and W. E. Moore, eds. *Labour Commitment and Social Change in Developing Areas.* New York: Social Research Council, 1960.

Gamble, D. P. "The Temne Family in a Modern Town (Lunsar) in Sierra Leone." *Africa* 33.3 (July 1963): 209–26.

Geertz, Clifford, ed. *Old Societies and New States.* New York: Free, 1965.

Goldthorpe, J. E. "Educated Africans: Some Conceptual and Terminological Problems." In *Social Change in Modern Africa,* ed. A. Southall. London: Oxford University Press, 1969.

Green, Harry A. *Urban Conditions in Nigeria: A Preliminary Bibliography.* Zaria: Ahmadu Bello University, 1972.

Green, Leslie, and Vincent Milone. *Urbanization in Nigeria: A Planning Commentary.* New York: Ford Foundation, 1971.

Gugler, Joseph. *Urban Growth in Sub-Saharan Africa.* Kampala: Makerere University, 1970.

Gugler, Joseph, and William Flanagan. *Urbanization and Social Change in West Africa.* Cambridge: Cambridge University Press, 1978.

———. "Urbanization in East Africa." In *Urban Challenge in East Africa,* ed. John Hutton. Nairobi: East African, 1972.

Gutkind, Peter C. W. "African Urbanism, Mobility and the Social Network."

In *Kinship and Geographical Mobility*, ed. R. Piddington, pp. 48–60. Leiden: E. J. Brill, 1965.

————. *Urban Anthropology*. Assen: Van Gorcin, 1974.

Hance, William A. *Population, Migration and Urbanization in Africa*. New York: Columbia University Press, 1970.

Hanna, William J., and Judith L. Hanna. *Urban Dynamics in Black Africa*. Chicago: Aldine-Atherton, 1971.

Hogben, S. J. *An Introduction to the History of the Islamic States of Northern Nigeria*. Ibadan: Oxford University Press, 1967.

Hunter, David E., and Phillip Whitten, eds. *Encyclopedia of Anthropology*. New York: Harper, 1976.

Kraft-Askari, Eva. *Yoruba Towns and Cities: An Enquiry into the Nature of Urban Social Phenomena*. Oxford: Clarendon, 1969.

Kuper, Hilda. *An African Aristocracy: Rank Among the Swazi of Bechuanaland*. London: Oxford University Press, 1947.

————, ed. *Urbanization and Migration in West Africa*. Westport, Conn.: Greenwood, 1977.

Leslie, J. A. K. *A Social Survey of Dar-es-Salaam*. London: Oxford University Press, 1963.

Levine, Robert A.; Nancy H. Klein; and Constance R. Owen. "Father-Child Relationships and Changing Life-Styles in Ibadan, Nigeria." In *The City in Modern Africa*, ed. Horace Miner, pp. 215–55. London: Praeger, 1967.

Little, Kenneth. *Some Aspects of African Urbanization South of the Sahara*. Reading, Mass.: Addison-Wesley, 1971.

————. *Urbanization as a Social Process: An Essay on Movement and Change in Contemporary Africa*. London: Routledge and Kegan Paul, 1974.

————. *West African Urbanization: A Study of Voluntary Associations in Social Change*. London: Cambridge University Press, 1970.

Lloyd, Peter C. *Power and Independence: Urban Africans' Perception of Social Inequality*. London: Routledge and Kegan Paul, 1974.

————, A. L. Mabogunje, and B. Awe, eds. *The City of Ibadan: A Symposium on Its Structure and Development*. Ibadan: Cambridge University Press, 1967.

Lock, Max. *Kaduna 1917, 1967, 2017*. London: Faber and Faber, 1967.

Maasdorp, Garvis, and A. S. B. Humphreys. *From Shantytown to Township*. Cape Town: Juta, 1975.

Mabogunje, Akin L. *Urbanization in Nigeria*. London: Oxford University Press, 1968.

————. "Urban Land Policy and Population Growth in Nigeria." In *Population*

Growth and Development in Africa, ed. S. A. Ominde and C. N. Ejiogu. London: Heinemann, 1972.

McCall, D. F. "Dynamics of Urbanization in Africa." *Annals of the American Academy of Politics and Social Science* 298 (Mar. 1955): 151–60.

Marris, Peter. *Family and Social Change in an African City: A Study of Rehousing in Lagos.* London: Routledge and Kegan Paul, 1966.

————. "Motives and Methods: Reflections on a Study in Lagos." In *The City in Modern Africa,* ed. Horace Miner, pp. 39–54. New York: Praeger, 1967.

Mayer, Philip. *Townsmen or Tribesmen: Conservatism and the Process of Urbanization in a South African City.* New York: Oxford University Press, 1971.

Mead, Margaret. "The Tiv of Nigeria." In *Cultural Patterns and Technical Change,* pp. 114–44. New York: New American Library, 1961.

Meillassoux, Claude. *Urbanization of an African Community: Voluntary Associations in Bamako.* AES monograph 45. Seattle: University of Washington Press, 1968.

Miner, Horace, ed. *The City in Modern Africa.* New York: Praeger, 1967.

Ministry of Information and Home Affairs, Government of Eastern Nigeria. *Enugu.* Enugu: Government of Eastern Nigeria, 1965.

Mitchel, N. C. "Yoruba Towns." In *Essays on African Population,* ed. K. M. Barbour and R. M. Prothero, pp. 279–301. London: Routledge and Kegan Paul, 1961.

Mitchell, J. Clyde. "Distance, Transportation, and Urban Involvement in Zambia." In *Social Change in Modern Africa,* ed. A. Southall. London: Oxford University Press, 1969.

————. *The Kalela Dance: Aspects of Social Relationship Among Urban Africans in Northern Rhodesia.* Manchester: Manchester University Press, 1959.

————. *Social Networks in Urban Situations: Analyses of Personal Relationships in Central African Towns.* Manchester: Manchester University Press, 1969.

————. "Theoretical Orientations in African Urban Studies." In *The Social Anthropology of Complex Societies,* ed. Michael Banton. London: Tavistock, 1966.

————. *Tribalism and the Plural Society.* Salisbury: University College of Rhodesia, 1966.

Mortimore, M. J., ed. *Zaria and Its Region: A Nigerian Savanna City and Its Environs.* Zaria: Ahmadu Bello University, 1970.

Nelson, Robert, and Howard Wolpe, eds. *Nigeria: Modernization and the Politics of Communalism.* East Lansing: Michigan State University Press, 1971.

Obudho, R. A., and Salah El-Shakhs, eds. *Development of Urban Systems in Africa.* New York: Praeger, 1979.

O'Connor, Anthony M. "The Distribution of Towns in Sub-Saharan Africa." In *Urban Growth in Sub-Saharan Africa*, ed. J. Gugler. Kampala: Makerere University, 1970.

———. *Urbanization in Tropical Africa: An Annotated Bibliography*. Boston: G. K. Hall, 1981.

Ominde, S. H., and C. N. Ejiogu, eds. *Population Growth and Economic Development in Africa*. London: Heinemann, 1972.

Parrinder, Geoffrey. *Religion in an African City*. London: Oxford University Press, 1953.

Pastoral Institute, Bodija. "Development in Towns: Report of a Seminar Sponsored by the Community Development Group." Bodija, Western Nigeria, 1970.

Peil, Margaret. *Cities and Suburbs: Urban Life in West Africa*. New York: Holmes and Meier, 1981.

———, and David Lucas. *Survey and Research Methods for West Africa*. Lagos: University of Lagos, 1972.

Plotnicov, Leonard. *Strangers to the City: Urban Man in Jos, Nigeria*. Pittsburgh: University of Pittsburgh Press, 1967.

Sandbrook, Richard. *The Politics of Basic Needs: Urban Aspects of Assaulting Poverty in Africa*. Toronto: University of Toronto Press, 1982.

Schawb, William B. "Comparative Field Techniques in Urban Research in Africa." In *Marginal Natives: Anthropologists at Work*, ed. M. Freilich. New York: Harper and Row, 1970.

Schwerdtfeger, Friedrich W. "Urban Settlement Patterns in Northern Nigeria (Hausaland)." In *Man, Settlement and Urbanism*, ed. P. J. Ucko, R. Tringham, and G. W. Dimbleby. Cambridge, Mass.: Schenkman, 1972.

Shack, W. A. "Urban Ethnicity and the Cultural Process of Urbanization in Ethiopia." In *Cross-Cultural Studies of Urbanization*, ed. Aidan Southall. New York: Oxford University Press, 1973.

Shorter, Aylward. *East African Societies*. London: Routledge and Kegan Paul, 1974.

Simms, Ruth P. *Urbanization in West Africa: A Review of Current Literature*. Evanston, Ill.: Northwestern University Press, 1965.

Skapa, Barbara A. *A Select Preliminary Bibliography on Urbanism in Eastern Africa*. Syracuse, N.Y.: Syracuse University, Maxwell Graduate School of Citizenship and Public Affairs, 1967.

Smythe, Hugh H. L., and Mabel M. Smythe. *The New Nigerian Elite*. Stanford, Calif.: Stanford University Press, 1960.

Southall, Aidan, ed. *Social Change in Modern Africa*. London: Oxford University Press, 1969.

Thompson, R. W. "Rural-Urban Differences in Individual Modernization in Buganda." *Urban Anthropology* 3.3 (Spring 1984): 64–78.

Wachtel, Andy A. D. "Toward a Model of Urbanism in an African City: The Dual Focus Career of Formal Sector Workers in Nakuru, Kenya." Master's thesis, Northwestern University, 1978.

Wolpe, Howard. *Urban Politics in Nigeria: A Study of Port Harcourt.* Berkeley: University of California Press, 1974.

Asia

Mission Perspective

Allen, Frank W. "Kamuning, Philippines—An Urban Church-Planting Model." *Urban Mission* 6.2 (Nov. 1988): 56–60.

Arthur, Joseph. "The Sleeping Giant: A Strategy for a Student Program of Evangelism and Church Planting in the Philippines." Ph.D. diss., Fuller Theological Seminary, 1974.

Barthold, Stan, and Mary Barthold. "Japan Apartment House Evangelism: The Kuzuha Bible Church." *Urban Mission* 2.1 (Sept. 1984): 44–46.

Benet, F. "The Ideology of Islamic Urbanization." In *Urbanism and Urbanization,* ed. Nels Anderson, pp. 1–6. Leiden: E. J. Brill, 1964.

Bolton, Robert J. *Treasure Island: Church Growth Among Taiwan's Urban Minnan Chinese.* Pasadena, Calif.: William Carey Library, 1976.

Bowie, Vaughan. "Scaffolding: Urban Mission in Australia." *Urban Mission* 2.5 (May 1985): 46–51.

Castillo, Metosalem Q. *The Church in Thy House.* Manila: Alliance, 1982.

Childs, Lloyd. "Teams Multiplying Churches in Malaysia/Singapore." *Urban Mission* 2.5 (May 1985): 33–39.

Cho, Cheong Shik. "The Church's Strategy for Evangelism and Program for Follow Up." D.Min. diss., Fuller Theological Seminary, 1985.

Cho, Paul Yonggi. *More than Numbers.* Waco, Tex.: Word, 1984.

———. "Reaching Cities with Home Cells." *Urban Mission* 1.3 (Jan. 1984): 4–14.

———. *Successful Home Cell Groups.* Plainfield, N.J.: Logos, 1981.

Conklin, James E. "Worldview Evangelism: A Study of the Karen Baptist Church in Thailand." D.Miss. diss., Fuller Theological Seminary, 1984.

de Silva, Ranjit. "Discipling in Three Sri Lankan Cities." *Urban Mission* 2.4 (Mar. 1985): 33–39.

———. "Discipling the Cities in Sri Lanka: A Challenge to the Church Today." M. A. thesis, Fuller Theological Seminary, 1979.

English, Paul Ward. *City and Village in Iran: Settlement and Economy in the Kirman Basin.* Madison: University of Wisconsin Press, 1966.

Finnell, David. *Evangelism in Singapore: A Research Analysis Among Baptists*. Singapore: Singapore Baptist Bookstore, 1986.

Fryman, Jeleta. "Alexandria: Signs of Hope." *World Christian Magazine*, Nov.–Dec. 1984, pp. 17ff.

Fugmann, Gernot. "Church Growth and Urbanization in New Guinea: A Preliminary Study in an Area of Young Christianity." Master's thesis, Fuller Theological Seminary, 1969.

Greenway, Roger S. "Kagawa of Japan: Evangelist cum Reformer." *Urban Mission* 3.5 (May 1986): 20–35.

Griffiths, Michael. *Changing Asia*. Downers Grove, Ill.: Inter-Varsity, 1977.

Grigg, Viv. *Companion to the Poor*. Sutherland, Australia: Albatross, 1984.

Haines, John F. "Reaching Muslims in French Cities." *Urban Mission* 2.1 (Sept. 1984): 20–33.

Hayward, Victor, ed. *The Church as Christian Community: Three Studies of North Indian Churches*. London: Lutterworth, 1966.

Hedlund, Roger, ed. *Church in the Third World*. Bombay: Gospel Literature Service, 1977.

———. "Urbanization and Evangelization in South Asia." *Urban Mission* 4.3 (Jan. 1987): 16–31.

Hinton, Keith. *Growing Churches Singapore Style: Ministry in an Urban Context*. Singapore: Overseas Missionary Fellowship, 1985.

Houghton, Graham, and Ezra Sargunam. "Church Planting Among the Urban Poor." *Asia Pulse* 15.2 (May 1982): 2–6.

John, A. J. "Women and the Evangelization of Indian Cities." *Urban Mission* 3.1 (Sept. 1985): 15–25.

Kim, Ick Won. "A Study of the Korean Church Growth in Context of the Korean National Characteristics." D.Min. diss., Fuller Theological Seminary, 1983.

Lausanne Occasional Paper no. 9. *Christian Witness to Large Cities*. Wheaton, Ill.: Lausanne Committee for World Evangelization, 1980.

Lee, Jae Bum. "Full Gospel Central Church, Seoul, Korea: A Church Growth Analysis." Master's thesis, Fuller Theological Seminary, 1982.

Lee, Robert. *Stranger in the Land. A Study of the Church in Japan*. New York: Friendship, 1967.

Lodwick, Kathleen L., ed. *The Chinese Recorder Index: A Guide to Christian Missions in Asia*. 2 vols. Wilmington, Del.: Scholarly Resources, 1986.

Madany, Bassam M. "Forgotten Christians of the Middle East." *Urban Mission* 1.4 (Mar. 1984): 4–9.

Mak, Arthur F. "The Case of a Threatened Church: A Study of the Hong Kong Christian Confession in View of the 1997 Communist Takeover." *Urban Mission* 5.3 (Jan. 1988): 32–39.

Matheny, Tim. *Reaching the Arabs: A Felt Need Approach.* Pasadena, Calif.: William Carey Library, 1981.

Mumper, Sharon E. "Taiwan's Urban Population—Time for a Harvest." *Urban Mission* 4.1 (Sept. 1986): 35–38.

Neff, Dale R. "Manila '85." *Urban Mission* 2.2 (Nov. 1984): 26–30.

Nelson, Amirtharaj. *A New Day in Madras: A Study of Protestant Churches in Madras.* Pasadena, Calif.: William Carey Library, 1975.

Niklaus, Robert. "Hong Kong: Familiarity Factor." *Evangelical Missions Quarterly* 20.4 (Oct. 1984): 410–14.

————. "Korea: The Prayer Way." *Evangelical Missions Quarterly* 20.4 (Oct. 1984): 408–10.

O'Connor, Richard A. *Urbanism and Religion: Urban Thai Buddhist Temples.* Ann Arbor: University of Michigan Press, 1982.

Pernia, Ernesto D. *Urbanization, Population Growth, and Economic Development in the Philippines.* London: Greenwood, 1977.

Pickett, J. Waskom. *Christian Mass Movements in India: A Study with Recommendations.* Lucknow, India: Lucknow, 1933.

Poethig, Richard P. "Theological Education and the Urban Situation in Asia." *South East Asia Journal of Theology* 13.2 (1972): 61–67.

Ramseyer, Robert L. "Church Planting in Hiroshima, Japan." *Urban Mission* 1.3 (Jan. 1984): 43–47.

Ro, Bong Rin. *Urban Ministry in Asia.* Taichung, Taiwan: Asia Theological Association, 1989.

Rosner, Victor. "Schools for Calcutta's Pavement Children." *Urban Mission* 2.3 (Jan. 1985): 44–46.

Rowland, Trent. "Streets of Gold: Turkey's Villagers Seek Riches in the City." *World Christian Magazine*, July–Aug. 1986, pp. 16ff.

Shelley, Mark. "Toward an Urban Strategy for Mindanao, Philippines." *Urban Mission* 4.5 (May 1987): 21–31.

Tsai, Kuo-shan. "How to Reach the Industrial Workers in Taiwan." *Chinese Around the World* 4.5 (June 1985).

Tuggy, A. L., and R. Toliver. *Seeing the Church in the Philippines.* Manila: OMF, 1972.

Van Houten, Richard L. "Mission Options in Hong Kong: Hong Kong's Status." *Urban Mission* 2.1 (Sept. 1984): 5–11.

Wong, James. *Singapore: The Church in the Midst of Social Change.* Singapore: Church Growth Study Centre, 1973.

Yamamori, Tetsunao. "Christians Prepare for China Takeover." *World Christian Magazine*, July–Aug. 1985, p. 12.

————. *Church Growth in Japan: A Study in the Development of Eight Denominations, 1859–1939.* Pasadena, Calif.: William Carey Library, 1975.

Zechariah, Chelliah. "Growth Patterns in the Assemblies of God Congregations in Tamil Nadu, India." *Urban Mission* 2.2 (Nov. 1984): 40–43.

Social-Science Perspective

Agassi, Joseph, and I. C. Jarvie, eds. *Hong Kong. A Society in Transition— Contributions to the Study of Hong Kong Society.* London: Routledge and Kegan Paul, 1969.

Berkowitz, Morris I.; Frederick P. Brandans; and John H. Reed. "Folk Religion in an Urban Setting: A Study of Hakka Villagers in Transition." *Ching Feng* 12 (Mar.–Apr. 1969): 1–167.

Blake, G. H., and R. I. Lawless, eds. *The Changing Middle Eastern City.* New York: Barnes and Noble, 1980.

Bogue, D. J., and K. C. Zachariah. "Urbanization and Migration in India." In *India's Urban Future,* ed. Roy Turner. Berkeley: University of California Press, 1962.

Bose, N. K. "Calcutta: A Premature Metropolis." *Scientific American* 213.3 (Sept. 1965): 90–102.

Bruner, Edward M. "Urbanization and Ethnic Identity in North Sumatra." *American Anthropologist* 63.3 (June 1961): 508–21.

Buck, David. *Urban Change in China: Politics and Development in Tsinan, Shantung, 1890–1949.* Madison: University of Wisconsin Press, 1978.

Bulsara, Jal F. *Problems of Rapid Urbanisation in India.* Bombay: Popular Prakashan, 1964.

Cheng, Tong-yung. "Hong Kong: A Classical Growth Model: A Survey of Hong Kong Industrialization, 1948–1968." *Weltwirtschaftliches Archive* 104.1 (1970): 138–58.

Chou, K'ai-jen. *The Hong Kong Economy: A Miracle of Growth.* Hong Kong: Academic, 1966.

Costello, V. V. *Urbanization in the Middle East.* Cambridge: Cambridge University Press, 1977.

Crissman, L. W. "Town and Country: Central Place Theory and Chinese Marketing, with Particular Reference to Southwestern Changhua Hsien, Taiwan." Ph.D. diss., Cornell University, 1973.

Davis, Kingsley. "Urbanization in India: Past and Future." In *India's Urban Future,* ed. Roy Turner. Berkeley: University of California Press, 1962.

DeSouza, Alfred, ed. *The Indian City.* New Delhi: Manohar, 1978.

Dore, R. P. *City Life in Japan: A Study of a Tokyo Ward.* Berkeley: University of California Press, 1963.

Dowling, J. N. "A Rural Indian Community in an Urban Setting." *Human Organization* 27.3 (Fall 1968): 236–40.

Drakakis-Smith, D. W. "Traditional and Modern Aspects of Urban Systems in the Third World: A Case Study in Hong Kong." *Pacific Viewpoint*, May 1971, pp. 21–40.

Dwyer, D. J., ed. *Asian Urbanization. A Hong Kong Casebook.* Hong Kong: Hong Kong University Press, 1972.

———, ed. *The Changing Face of Hong Kong.* Hong Kong: Royal Asiatic Society, Hong Kong Branch, 1971.

———, ed. *The City as a Centre of Change in Asia.* Hong Kong: Hong Kong University Press, 1972.

Elvin, Mark, and G. William Skinner, eds. *The Chinese City Between Two Worlds.* Stanford: Stanford University Press, 1974.

Endacott, G. B. *Government and People in Hong Kong, 1841–1962: A Constitutional History.* Hong Kong: Hong Kong University Press, 1962.

———, and A. Hinton. *Fragrant Harbor: A Short History of Hong Kong.* Hong Kong: Oxford University Press, 1962.

Firth, J. R. "The Work of the Hong Kong Housing Authority." *Journal of the Royal Society of Architects* 113 (Feb. 1965): 175–95.

Freed, S. A., and R. S. Freed. "Shanti Aagar: The Effects of Urbanization in a Village in North India." Vol. 53, pt. 1, *Anthropological Papers of the American Museum of Natural History,* 1976.

Ghurye, G. S. *Anatomy of a Rururban Community.* Bombay: Popular Prakashan, 1963.

Hari, Purwanto. "The Problems of Chinese Assimilation and Integration in Indonesia." *Philippine Sociological Review,* Jan.–Oct. 1976, pp. 51–55.

Hedlund, Roger E. "Urbanization and Evangelization in South Asia." *Urban Mission* 4.3 (Jan. 1987): 16–31.

Hinton, Keith. *Growing Churches Singapore Style: Ministry in an Urban Context.* Singapore: Overseas Missionary Fellowship, 1985.

Hoadley, John S. "The Government and Politics of Hong Kong: A Descriptive Study with Special Reference to the Analytical Framework of Gabriel Almond." Ph.D. diss., University of California at Santa Barbara, 1968.

Hopkins, Keith, ed. *Hong Kong: The Industrial Colony.* Hong Kong: Oxford University Press, 1971.

Hsueh, S. S. *Government and Administration of Hong Kong.* Hong Kong: University Bookstore, 1962.

Hughes, Richard. *Hong Kong: Borrowed Place—Borrowed Time.* London: Andre Deutsch, 1968.

Hugo-Brunt, Michael. "Hong Kong Housing." In *Taming Megalopolis,* ed. H. W. Eldredge, pp. 477–93. Garden City, N.Y.: Doubleday, 1967.

Hurlimann, Martin. *Hong Kong.* New York: Viking, 1962.

Ingrams, Harold. "Hong Kong and Its Place in the Far East." *Journal of the Royal Central Asian Society* 40.3–4 (1953): 255–65.

Johnson, Graham Edward. "Natives, Immigrants and Associations: A Study of Voluntary Associations and Leadership in an Expanding Town in Hong Kong's New Territories." Ph.D. diss., Cornell University, 1970.

Jones, P. H. M. *Golden Guide to Hong Kong–Macao.* Hong Kong: Far Eastern Economic Review, 1969.

Karpat, Kemal H. *The Gecekondu: Rural Migration and Urbanization.* Cambridge: Cambridge University Press, 1976.

Khoo, Siew-Ean; Peter C. Smith; and James J. Fawcett. "The Migration of Women to Cities: The Asian Situation in Comparative Perspective." *International Migration Review* 18.4 (Winter 1984): 1247–63.

Lapidus, Ira, ed. *Middle Eastern Cities: A Symposium on Ancient, Islamic and Contemporary Middle Eastern Urbanism.* Berkeley: University of California Press, 1969.

———. "Muslim Urban Society in Mamluk, Syria." In *The Islamic City: A Colloquium,* ed. A. H. Hourani and S. M. Stern. Oxford: Bruno Cassirer, 1970.

Lappierre, Dominique. *City of Joy.* London: Arrow, 1986.

Lee, Kit-chung. "Religious Practices and Buildings in Western District: A Study of Their Role in an Urban Environment." Master's thesis, University of Hong Kong, 1970.

Lee, On-jook. *Urban-to-Rural Migration in Korea.* Seoul: Seoul National University Press, 1980.

Levine, Hal B., and Marlene Wolfzahn Levine. *Urbanization in Papua, New Guinea: A Study of Ambivalent Townsmen.* Cambridge: Cambridge University Press, 1979.

Lewis, John W., ed. *The City in Communist China.* Stanford: Stanford University Press, 1971.

McGee, T. G. *Southeast Asian City: A Social Geography of the Primate Cities of Southeast Asia.* New York: Praeger, 1967.

Matsushita, Masatoshi. "Tokyo in 2000 A.D." In *Man in the City of the Future,* ed. Richard Eells and Clarence Walton, pp. 59–72. New York: Macmillan, 1968.

Meier, Richard L. "The Performance of Cities: An Assessment of Hong Kong and Its Future." Working paper no. 136. Berkeley: University of California, Berkeley, Institute of Urban and Regional Development, Nov. 1970.

———. *Urban Futures Observed in the Asian Third World.* New York: Pergamon, 1980.

Mulay, Sumati. *Towards Modernization: A Study of Peasantry in Rural Delhi.* Philadelphia: International Publications Service, 1973.

Murphey, Rhoads. *The Fading of the Maoist Vision: City and Country in China's Development.* New York: Methuen, 1980.

Norbeck, Edward. *Country to City: The Urbanization of a Japanese Hamlet.* Salt Lake City: University of Utah, 1978.

Pillsi, K. S. "Hong Kong Kaifongs." *Far Eastern Economic Review* 42.4 (Oct. 24, 1963): 205–7.

Rao, V. K. R. V., and P. B. Desai. *Greater Delhi: A Study in Urbanization, 1940–57.* New York: Asia, 1965.

Rew, Alan. *Social Images and Process in Urban New Guinea: A Study of Port Moresby.* St. Paul: West, 1974.

Rowe, William L. "Caste, Kinship, and Association in Urban India." In *Urban Anthropology: Cross-Cultural Studies in Urbanization,* ed. A. Southall. New York: Oxford University Press, 1973.

Royal Asiatic Society of Great Britain and Ireland, Hong Kong Branch. *Some Traditional Chinese Ideas and Conceptions in Hong Kong Social Life Today.* Hong Kong: Royal Asiatic Society, 1967.

Rozman, Gilbert. *Urban Networks in Ching, China and Tokugawa, Japan.* Princeton, N.J.: Princeton University Press, 1973.

Salisbury, Richard F., and Mary E. Salisbury. "The Rural Oriented Strategy of Urban Adaptation: Some Migrants in Port Moresby." *Anthropology of Urban Environments* 11. Boulder, Colo.: Society of Applied Anthropology, 1972.

Sarikwal, R. C. *Sociology of a Growing Town: Ghaziabad, India.* Delhi: M. R. Prints, 1978.

Schmitt, Robert C. "Implications of Density in Hong Kong." *Journal of the American Institute of Planners* 29.3 (Aug. 1963): 210–17.

Scofield, John. "Hong Kong Has Many Faces." *National Geographic* 121.1 (Jan. 1962): 1–41.

Sethuraman, S. V. *Jakarta: Urban Development and Employment.* Geneva, Switzerland: International Labor Office, 1976.

Seymour, Susan, ed. *The Transformation of a Sacred Town: Bhubaneswar, India.* Boulder, Colo.: Westview, 1980.

Shibata, T. "Tokyo: Bright Present, Foreboding Future." *Japan Quarterly* 32.4 (Oct.–Dec. 1985): 350–55.

Skinner, G. William, ed. *The City in Late Imperial China.* Stanford: Stanford University Press, 1977.

Smith, Robert J. "Town and City in Pre-Modern Japan." In *Urban Anthropology,* ed. A. Southall. New York: Oxford University Press, 1973.

Sovani, N. *Urbanization and Urban Studies.* New York: Asia, 1966.

Taeuber, Irene B. "Hong Kong: Migrants and Metropolis." *Population Index* 29.1 (Jan. 1963): 3–25.

Topley, Marjorie, ed. *Anthropology and Sociology in Hong Kong.* Hong Kong: Centre of Asian Studies, University of Hong Kong, 1969.

Trager, L. "Family Strategies and the Migration of Women: Migrants to Dagupan City, Philippines." *International Migration Review* 18.4 (Winter 1984): 1264–77.

Tse, N. Q. "Industrialization and Social Adjustment in Hong Kong." *Sociology and Social Research* 52.3 (Apr. 1968): 237–51.

Vatuk, Sylvia. *Kinship and Urbanization: White Collar Migrants in Northern India.* Berkeley: University of California Press, 1973.

Wheatley, P. *Pivot of the Four Quarters: A Preliminary Inquiry into the Origins and Character of the Ancient Chinese City.* Hawthorne, N.J.: Aldine, 1971.

Wong, Fai-Ming. "Modern Ideology, Industrialisation, and the Middle Class Family in Hong Kong." Ph.D. diss., University of California at Santa Barbara, 1969.

Woo, Irene. "City Without a Soul." *Far Eastern Economic Review* 60.26 (June 23–29, 1968): 669–70.

Wright, B. R. "Social Aspects of Change in the Chinese Family Pattern in Hong Kong." *Journal of Social Psychology* 63 (June 1964): 31–39.

Yazaki, Takeo. *Social Change and the City in Japan.* Briarcliff Manor, N.Y.: Japan Publications, 1968.

Yeung, Y. M., and C. P. Yo, eds. *Changing Southeast Asian Cities: Readings on Urbanization.* New York: Oxford University Press, 1977.

Latin America

Missionary Perspective

Avila, Mariano. "Ministering in Nezahualcoyotl." *Urban Mission* 6.2 (Nov. 1988): 33–42.

Bergsma, Paul J. "Holistic Urban Ministry in Tegucigalpa, Honduras." *Urban Mission* 1.3 (Jan. 1984): 40–42.

Cook, William. "Interview with Chilean Pentecostals." *International Review of Missions* 72.288 (Oct. 1983): 591–95.

Costas, Orlando E. *The Church and Its Mission: A Shattering Critique from the Third World.* Wheaton, Ill.: Tyndale, 1974.

———. "Church Growth as a Multidimensional Phenomenon: Some Lessons from Chile." *International Bulletin of Missionary Research* 5.1 (Jan. 1981): 2–8.

Courtney, Thomas J. "Mission to the Urban Poor." *Urban Mission* 1.2 (Nov. 1983): 17–24.

Cruickshank, Mary. *The Sun Rises: The Story of the Birth, Growth, and*

Present-Day Life of the Peruvian Evangelical Church. London: Evangelical Union of South America, 1979.

Dye, Richard. "Church Growth in Acapulco: Planting a Whole Presbytery." *Urban Mission* 3.3 (Jan. 1986): 34–39.

Gates, C. W. *Industrialization. Brazil's Catalyst for Church Growth: A Study of the Rio Area.* Pasadena, Calif.: William Carey Library, 1972.

Gibbs, Eddie. *Urban Church Growth: Clues from South America and Britain.* Bramcote, Notts: Grove, 1978.

Greenway, Roger S. "Cities of Latin America: Do the Millions Know Christ?" *Urban Mission* 2.3 (Jan. 1985): 3–5.

———. "The 'Luz Del Mundo' Movement in Mexico." *Missiology* 1.2 (Apr. 1973): 113–24.

———. *An Urban Strategy for Latin America.* Grand Rapids: Baker, 1973.

Hamao, F. "Visit to Japanese Settlements in Latin America." *Japanese Missionary Bulletin* 27.8 (1973): 480–84.

Isidro, Lucas. *The Browning of America: The Hispanic Revolution in the American Church.* Chicago: Fides/Claretian, 1981.

Kessler, J. B. A. *A Study of the Older Protestant Missions and Churches in Peru and Chile.* Goes, Netherlands: Oosterbaan and LeCointre, 1967.

Klassen, Jacob. "Quito, Ecuador: Transferable Principles of Urban Outreach." *Urban Mission* 3.1 (Sept. 1985): 32–40.

Kratzig, Guillermo. "Tent Evangelism in Argentine Cities." *Urban Mission* 3.5 (May 1986): 51–56.

———. *Urbanization: Analysis of the Obstacles to Evangelistic Action in Large Urban Centers.* Buenos Aires: Junto Bautista de Publicaciones, 1975.

Lalive D'Epinay, Christian. *Haven of the Masses: A Study of the Pentecostal Movement in Chile.* London: Lutterworth, 1969.

Lightbody, C. Stuart. "History in the Making in Lima." *Latin America Evangelist* 66.3 (July–Sept. 1986): 4–8.

———. "New Christian Agency in Peru Helps Small Businessmen." *Pulse* 19.22 (Nov. 21, 1984): 3–4.

———. "New Strategies for a New Era. The Story of a Denominational Mission Turning Urban." *Urban Mission* 3.3 (Jan. 1986): 30–34.

Long, Loran. "Preparing for Holistic Church Planting Among Mexico's Urban Poor." Master's thesis. Pasadena, Calif.: Fuller Theological Seminary, 1982.

McGavran, Donald A.; John Huegel; and Jack Taylor. *Church Growth in Mexico.* Grand Rapids: Eerdmans, 1963.

Maust, John. *Cities of Change: Urban Growth and God's People in Ten Latin American Cities.* Coral Gables, Fla.: Latin America Mission, 1984.

Mitchell, James Erskine. *The Emergence of a Mexican Church: The Associate*

Reformed Presbyterian Church of Mexico. Pasadena, Calif.: William Carey Library, 1970.

Niklaus, Robert. "Colombia: Flashpoint of Growth." *Evangelical Missions Quarterly* 21.2 (Apr. 1985): 174–76.

———. "Latin America: Counter Evangelism." *Evangelical Missions Quarterly* 19.3 (July 1983): 259–60.

Nyberg, Lennart. "An Exploration and Evaluation of a New Field in Brazil for Scandinavians in Mission." Master's thesis. Pasadena, Calif.: Fuller Theological Seminary, 1977.

Paredes-Alfaro, Ruben Elias. "The Protestant Movement in Ecuador and Peru: A Comparative Socio-Anthropological Study of the Establishment and Diffusion of Protestantism in Two Central Highland Regions." Ph.D. diss., University of California, 1983.

Platt, Daryl L. "New Hope for Santo Domingo: A Preliminary Church Growth Survey of the Protestant and Evangelical Churches in the Dominican Republic, W. I." Master's thesis. Pasadena, Calif.: Fuller Theological Seminary, 1975.

Pretiz, Paul E. "Medellin, Colombia: Research Can Be Motivational." *Urban Mission* 4.3 (Jan. 1987): 52–54.

Racine, Carl. "Don't Neglect Third World Suburbia!" *Missiology* 9.2 (Apr. 1981): 71–80.

Read, William R., and Frank A. Ineson. *Brazil 1980: The Protestant Handbook.* Monrovia, Calif.: MARC, 1973.

Rycroft, W. Stanley, and Myrtle M. Clemmer. *A Study of Urbanization in Latin America.* New York: United Presbyterian Church, USA, 1962.

Schreck, Harley C. "Mexico City: A Church-Based Model of Community Service." *Urban Mission* 6.2 (Nov. 1988): 43–55.

Scott, Kenneth D. "Latin America: Peruvian New Religious Movements." *Missiology* 13.1 (Jan. 1985): 44–59.

Sebastian, Paul R. "Peru: A Regional Missionary Congress in the Missions." *World Missions* 31.2 (1980): 44–49.

Silvoso, Eduardo. "In Rosario It Was Different: Crusade Converts Are in the Churches." *Evangelical Missions Quarterly* 14.2 (Apr. 1978): 83–87.

———. "Renewal from Within: The Bruno Model from South America." *Urban Mission* 2.5 (May 1985): 40–45.

Smith, Fred H. "Growth Through Evangelism." *Urban Mission* 1.1 (Sept. 1983): 19–28.

Sobrino, Jon. *The True Church and the Poor.* Translated by Matthew J. O'Connell. Maryknoll, N.Y.: Orbis, 1984.

Tyson, Brady. "The Mission of the Church in Contemporary Brazil: The Case of a Church in a Land of Poverty and Repression." *Missiology* 3.3 (July 1975): 287–306.

Volstad, David K. "The Christian and Missionary Alliance in Lima, Peru." In *Guidelines for Urban Church Planting,* ed. Roger S. Greenway, pp. 45–55. Grand Rapids: Baker, 1976.

Walsh, William B. *Yanqui, Come Back! The Story of Hope in Peru.* New York: E. P. Dutton, 1966.

Social-Science Perspective

Beals, R. L. "Social Stratification in Latin America." *American Journal of Sociology* 58.4 (Jan. 1953): 327–39.

Beyer, Glenn, ed. *The Urban Explosion in Latin America: A Continent in Process of Modernization.* Ithaca, N.Y.: Cornell University Press, 1967.

Bonilla, Frank. "The Urban Worker." In *Continuity and Change in Latin America,* ed. J. J. Johnson, pp. 186–205. Stanford, Calif.: Stanford University Press, 1964.

Butterworth, Douglas, and John K. Chance. *Latin American Urbanization.* Cambridge: Cambridge University Press, 1981.

Calderon Alvarado, Luis. *Problems of Urbanization in Latin America.* Freiburg, Switzerland: Oficina Internacional de Investigaciones Sociales de FERES, 1963. Written in Spanish.

Cornelius, Wayne A., and F. Trueblood, eds. *Latin America Urban Research,* vol. 4. Beverly Hills, Calif.: Sage, 1974.

Cornelius, Wayne A., and Robert V. Kemper, eds. *Metropolitan Latin America: The Challenge and the Response.* Beverly Hills, Calif.: Sage, 1978.

Epstein, D. G. "The Genesis and Function of Squatter Settlements in Brasilia." In *The Anthropology of Urban Environments* 11. Edited by T. Weaver and D. White. Boulder, Colo.: Society for Applied Anthropology, 1972.

Forman, Shepard. *The Brazilian Peasantry.* New York: Columbia University Press, 1975.

Garvin, Paul L., and Madeline Mathiot. "The Urbanization of the Guaraní Language." In *An Urban World,* ed. Charles Tilly, pp. 152–60. Boston: Little, Brown, 1974.

Gilbert, Alan, and Jorge E. Hardoy, eds. *Urbanization in Contemporary Latin America.* Chichester: John Wiley and Sons, 1982.

Greenway, Roger S. *An Urban Strategy for Latin America.* Grand Rapids: Baker, 1973.

Hardoy, Jorge E., ed. *Urbanization in Latin America: Approaches and Issues.* Garden City, N.Y.: Doubleday, 1975.

Harris, Marvin. *Town and Country in Brazil.* New York: Columbia University Press, 1956.

Harris, Walter D., Jr. *The Growth of Latin American Cities.* Athens: Ohio University Press, 1971.

Hauser, Philip M., ed. *Urbanization in Latin America.* New York: Columbia University Press, 1961.

Heath, D. B., and R. N. Adams, eds. *Contemporary Cultures and Societies of Latin America.* New York: Random, 1965.

Kemper, Robert V. "The Anthropological Study of Migration to Latin American Cities." *Kroeber Anthropological Society Papers* 42 (1970): 1–25.

Klassen, Jacob P. "Quito, Ecuador—Transferable Principles of Urban Outreach." *Urban Mission* 3.1 (Sept. 1985): 32–40.

Leeds, A. "Brazil and the Myth of Urban Rurality: Urban Expense and Want in Squatments in Rio de Janeiro and Lima." In *City and Country in the Third World,* ed. A. J. Field. Cambridge, Mass.: Schenkman, 1969.

Lewis, Oscar. *The Children of Sanchez: An Autobiography of a Mexican Family.* New York: Vintage, 1966.

———. *Five Families: Mexican Case Studies in the Culture of Poverty.* New York: Basic, 1959.

———. "Some Perspectives on Urbanization with Special Reference to Mexico City." In *Urban Anthropology: Cross-Cultural Studies of Urbanization,* ed. A. Southall. New York: Oxford University Press, 1973.

———. *La Vida: A Puerto Rican Family in the Culture of Poverty.* New York: Random, 1965.

Light, Ivan. *Cities in World Perspective.* New York: Macmillan, 1983.

McDowell, Bart. "Mexico City: An Alarming Giant." *National Geographic Magazine* 166.2 (Aug. 1984): 139–72.

Mangin, William. "Sociological, Cultural, and Political Characteristics of Some Urban Migrants in Peru." In *Urban Anthropology: Cross-Cultural Studies of Urbanization,* ed. A. Southall. New York: Oxford University Press, 1973.

Millon, R. *Urbanization at Teotihuacan.* Austin: University of Texas Press, 1965.

Nutini, Hugo G. *The Latin American City: A Cultural/Historical Approach in the Anthropology of Urban Environments,* ed. Thomas Weaver and Douglas White. Boulder, Colo.: Society for Applied Anthropology, 1972.

Parsons, J. R. "Prehistoric Settlement Patterns in the Texcoco Region, Mexico." Museum of Anthropology, University of Michigan, 1972.

Pearse, Andrew. "Some Characteristics of Urbanization in the City of Rio de

Janeiro." In *Urbanization in Latin America*, ed. Philip Hauser. New York: UNESCO, 1961.

Peattie, Lisa. *The View from the Barrio*. Ann Arbor: University of Michigan Press, 1968.

Portes, Alejandro, and Harley L. Browning, eds. *Current Perspectives in Latin American Urban Research*. Austin, Tex.: Institute of Latin American Studies, University of Texas, 1976.

———, and John Walton. *Urban Latin America: The Political Condition from Above and Below*. Austin: University of Texas Press, 1976.

Rabinovitz, Francine F., and Felicity M. Trueblood, eds. *Latin American Urban Research*, vol. 1. Beverly Hills, Calif.: Sage, 1971.

Redfield, Robert. *The Folk Culture of Yucatan*. Chicago: University of Chicago Press, 1955.

Reina, Ruben. *Parana: Social Boundaries in an Argentine City*. Austin: University of Texas Press, 1973.

Ressler, J. Q. "Indian and Spanish Water-Control on New Spain's Northwest Frontier." *Journal of the West* 7.1 (Jan. 1968): 10–17.

Roberts, Bryan R. *Organizing Strangers: Poor Families in Guatemala City*. Austin: University of Texas Press, 1973.

Safa, Helen. *The Urban Poor of Puerto Rico: A Study in Development and Inequality*. New York: Holt, Rinehart and Winston, 1974.

———, and B. M. duToit, eds. *Migration and Ethnicity: Implications for Urban Policy and Development*. The Hague: Mouton, 1975.

Sanders, W. T. *Cultural Ecology of the Teotihuacan Valley, Mexico*. University Park: Penn State University Press, 1965.

Scott, Ian. *Urban and Spatial Development in Mexico*. Baltimore: Johns Hopkins University Press, 1982.

Smith, Lynn T. "Urbanization in Latin America." In *Urbanism and Urbanization*, ed. Nels Anderson, pp. 127–42. Leiden: E. J. Brill, 1964.

Uzzell, J. D. "Bound for Places I'm Not Known To: Adaptation of Migrants and Residents in Four Irregular Settlements in Lima, Peru." Ph.D. diss., University of Texas, 1972.

———. "The Interaction of Population and Locality in the Development of Squatter Settlements in Lima." In *Latin American Urban Research*, vol. 4, ed. W. Cornelius and F. Trueblood. Beverly Hills, Calif.: Sage, 1974.

———. "A Strategic Analysis of Social Structure in Lima, Peru, Using the Concept of Plays." *Urban Anthropology* 3.1 (Spring 1974): 34–46.

Vaughan, Denton R. *Urbanization in the Twentieth Century in Latin America: A Working Bibliography*. Austin: University of Texas Press, 1970.

Wadell, J. O., and O. M. Watson, eds. *The American Indian in Urban Society*. Boston: Little, Brown, 1971.

Whiteford, Andrew H. *Two Cities of Latin America: A Comparative Description of Social Class.* Garden City, N.Y.: Doubleday, 1964.

Willems, Emilio. *Followers of the New Faith: Culture Change and the Rise of Protestantism in Brazil and Chile.* Nashville: Vanderbilt University Press, 1967.

Wirth, John D., and Robert L. Jones, eds. *Manchester and Sao Paulo: Problems of Rapid Urban Growth.* Stanford, Calif.: Stanford University Press, 1978.

Wonderly, William L. "Urbanization: The Challenge of Latin America in Transition." *Practical Anthropology* 7.5 (Sept.–Oct. 1960): 205–9.

United States, Canada, Europe, Australia, and New Zealand

Missionary Perspective

Abell, A. I. *The Urban Impact on American Protestantism 1865–1900.* Cambridge: Harvard University Press, 1943.

Allen, Jimmy R. "Urban Evangelism." In *Toward Creative Urban Strategy,* comp. George A. Torney, pp. 105–21. Waco, Tex.: Word, 1970.

Angell, James W. *Put Your Arms Around the City.* Old Tappan, N.J.: Revell, 1970.

Arn, Win, and Charles Arn. *The Master's Plan for Making Disciples: How Every Christian Can Be an Effective Witness Through an Enabling Church.* Pasadena, Calif.: Church Growth, 1982.

Baird, William. *The Corinthian Church. A Biblical Approach to Urban Culture.* New York: Abingdon, 1964.

Banfield, Edward C. *The Unheavenly City Revisited.* Boston: Little, Brown, 1974.

Baroni, Geno C., and Ronald D. Pasquariello. "What Can Parishes Do for Our Cities?" *Church and Society* 69.1 (Sept.–Oct. 1978): 5–10.

Barrett, David B. *World-Class Cities and World Evangelization.* Birmingham, Ala.: New Hope, 1986.

Belew, M. Wendell. *Churches and How They Grow.* Nashville: Broadman, 1971.

———. *Missions in the Mosaic.* Atlanta: Home Mission Board, Southern Baptist Convention, 1974.

Benjamin, Don C. *Deuteronomy and City Life: A Form Criticism of Texts with the Word City ('îr) in Deuteronomy 4:41–26:19.* Lanham, Md.: University Press of America, 1983.

Bennett, George. *Effective Urban Church Ministry.* Nashville: Broadman, 1983.

Bowie, Vaughan. "Scaffolding: Urban Mission in Australia." *Urban Mission* 2.5 (May 1985): 46–51.

Bull, Geoffrey T. *The City and the Sign.* Grand Rapids: Baker, 1972.

Callahan, Daniel, ed. *The Secular City Debate.* New York: Macmillan, 1966.

Callahan, Kennon L. *Twelve Keys to an Effective Church: Strategic Planning for Mission.* New York: Harper and Row, 1983.

Chaney, Charles L. *Church Planting at the End of the Twentieth Century.* Wheaton, Ill.: Tyndale, 1982.

Cho, Paul Yonggi. "Reaching Cities with Home Cells." *Urban Mission* 1.3 (Jan. 1984): 4–14.

Claerbaut, David. *Urban Ministry.* Grand Rapids: Zondervan, 1983.

Coleman, Robert E. *The Master Plan of Evangelism.* Old Tappan, N.J.: Revell, 1964.

Conn, Harvie M. *Evangelism: Doing Justice and Preaching Grace.* Grand Rapids: Zondervan, 1982.

————. "In the City, I'm a Number, Not a Person: The Depersonalization Misunderstanding." *Urban Mission* 2.5 (May 1985): 6–19.

Coote, Robert, ed. *The Gospel and Urbanization.* Ventnor, N.J.: Overseas Ministries Study Center, 1984.

Copeland, E. Luther. "Can the City Be Saved: Toward a Biblical Urbanology." *Perspectives on Religious Studies* 4.1 (Spring 1977): 14–22.

Cork, Dolores Freeman. *Farming the Inner City for Christ: The Gladys Farmer Story.* Nashville: Broadman, 1980.

Costas, Orlando. "Evangelism and the Gospel of Salvation." *International Review of Missions* 63.249 (Jan. 1974): 24–37.

Courtney, Thomas J. "Mission to the Urban Poor." *Urban Mission* 1.2 (Nov. 1983): 17–24.

Cox, Harvey. "Mission in a World of Cities." *International Review of Missions* 55.219 (July 1966): 273–81.

————. *The Secular City: Secularization and Urbanization in Theological Perspective.* New York: Macmillan, 1965.

Craddock, Fred B. *Overhearing the Gospel: Preaching and Teaching the Faith to Persons Who Have Already Heard.* Nashville: Abingdon, 1978.

Cross, Robert D. *The Church and the City: 1865–1910.* Indianapolis: Bobbs-Merrill, 1967.

Cully, Kendig B., and F. Nile Harper, eds. *Will the Church Lose the City?* New York: World, 1969.

Davidson, James D.; Ronald Elly; Thomas Hull; and Donald Nead. "Increasing the Church's Involvement in Social Concerns: A Model for Urban Ministries." *Review of Religious Research* 20.3 (Summer 1979): 291–314.

Dayton, Donald. "The Urban Church Today: A Report on an Evangelical Congress." *Reformed Journal* 28.8 (Aug. 1978): 9–11.

Dayton, Edward R., and Samuel Wilson, eds. *Unreached Peoples '82: Focus on Urban Peoples.* Elgin, Ill.: David C. Cook, 1982.

DeRidder, Richard R., and Roger S. Greenway. *Let the Whole World Know: Resources for Preaching on Missions.* Grand Rapids: Baker, 1988.

Driggers, B. Carlyle. *Models of Metropolitan Ministry.* Nashville: Broadman, 1979.

Du Bose, Francis M. *How Churches Grow in an Urban World.* Nashville: Broadman, 1978.

Dudley, Carl S. *Where Have All Our People Gone? New Choices for Old Churches.* New York: Pilgrim, 1979.

Ellison, Craig W., ed. "Attitudes and Urban Transition." *Urban Mission* 2.3 (Jan. 1985): 14–26.

———. "Psychology, Christianity and Urban Need." *Journal of Psychology and Theology* 6.4 (Fall 1978): 283–90.

———. "Stress and Urban Ministry." *Urban Mission* 1.2 (Nov. 1983): 5–16.

———. *The Urban Mission.* Grand Rapids: Eerdmans, 1974.

Ellul, Jacques. *The Meaning of the City.* Grand Rapids: Eerdmans, 1975.

Engel, James F. *Contemporary Christian Communications: Its Theory and Practice.* New York: Thomas Nelson, 1979.

———. *How Can I Get Them to Listen?* Grand Rapids: Zondervan, 1977.

———, and H. Wilbert Norton. *What's Gone Wrong with the Harvest? A Communication Strategy for the Church and World Evangelization.* Grand Rapids: Zondervan, 1975.

Enroth, M. Ronald; Edward E. Ericson, Jr.; and C. Peter Breckinridge. *The Jesus People: Old-Time Religion in the Age of Aquarius.* Grand Rapids: Eerdmans, 1972.

Eppinga, J. D. *A Pastor Speaks to the Soul of the City.* Grand Rapids: Eerdmans, 1954.

Everett, Harvey A. *The Apartment Community: The Church's New Frontier.* Valley Forge, Pa.: Church Strategy Program, American Baptist Home Mission Societies, 1964.

Fackre, Gabriel. *Second Fronts in Metropolitan Mission.* Grand Rapids: Eerdmans, 1968.

———. *Word in Deed: Theological Themes in Evangelism.* Grand Rapids: Eerdmans, 1975.

Falwell, Jerry. *Capturing a Town for Christ.* Old Tappan, N.J.: Revell, 1973.

———, and Elmer Towns. *Church Aflame.* Nashville: Impact, 1971.

Frenchak, David, and Sharrel Keyes, eds. *Metro-Ministry: Ways and Means for the Urban Church*. Elgin, Ill.: David C. Cook, 1979.

Frenchak, David, and Clinton E. Stockwell. *The Signs of the Kingdom in the Secular City*. Chicago: Covenant, 1984.

Fung, Raymond. "The Forgotten Side of Evangelism." *The Other Side* 15.10 (Oct. 1979): 16–25.

Gant, Edwin P. "Evangelism Explosion: A Tool God Is Using in Many Cities." *Urban Mission* 3.2 (Nov. 1985): 32–36.

Gerber, Virgil. "A New Tool for Winning the City." *Church Growth Bulletin* 12.6 (July 1976): 542–44.

Gladwin, John. *God's People in God's World: Biblical Motives for Social Involvement*. Downers Grove, Ill.: Inter-Varsity, 1979.

Globe, E. Philip. *Everything You Need to Grow a Messianic Synagogue*. Pasadena, Calif.: William Carey Library, 1974.

Graf, Arthur E. *The Church in the Community: An Effective Evangelism Program for the Christian Congregation*. Grand Rapids: Eerdmans, 1965.

Graham, W. Fred. "Declining Church Membership: Can Anything Be Done?" *Reformed Journal* 30.1 (Jan. 1980): 7–13.

Greenway, Roger S. "An Agenda for the City." *Urban Mission* 3.5 (May 1986): 3–5.

———. *Apostles to the City: Biblical Strategies for Urban Missions*. Grand Rapids: Baker, 1978.

———. *Calling Our Cities to Christ*. Nutley, N.J.: Presbyterian and Reformed, 1973.

———. "Children in the City." *Urban Mission* 3.2 (Nov. 1985): 3–6.

———. "Cities, Seminaries and Christian Colleges." *Urban Mission* 3.1 (Sept. 1985): 3–6.

———. "Don't Let the Parish Perish!" *Urban Mission* 3.4 (Mar. 1986): 3–4.

———. "Gentrification and the Parable of the Bats." *Urban Mission* 1.5 (Sept. 1983): 2–4.

———. "The Homeless on Our Streets: How Can the Church Minister to Them?" *Urban Mission* 2.1 (Sept. 1984): 34–43.

———. "Let These Women Go! Prostitution and the Church." *Urban Mission* 1.4 (Mar. 1984): 17–25.

———. "Reaching the Unreached in the Cities." *Urban Mission* 2.5 (May 1985): 3–5.

———. "Role of Urban Pulpits." *Urban Mission* 4.1 (Sept. 1986): 3–5.

———. "The Shift to Ethnic Mission." *Urban Mission* 1.2 (Nov. 1983): 3–4.

———. "Urban Evangelism." In *Let the Earth Hear His Voice*, ed. J. D. Douglas. Minneapolis: World Wide, 1975.

————. "Urban Ministry—No Bed of Nails." *Urban Mission* 3.3 (Jan. 1986): 3–5.

————. "Urban-Suburban Coalitions for Mission and Renewal." *Urban Mission* 2.4 (Mar. 1985): 3–5.

————. "Who Lives in This City?" *Urban Mission* 3.5 (May 1986): 57–58.

————, ed. *Discipling the City: Theological Reflections on Urban Mission.* Grand Rapids: Baker, 1979.

————, ed. *Guidelines for Urban Church Planting.* Grand Rapids: Baker, 1976.

Greenwood, Elma. *How Churches Fight Poverty.* New York: Friendship, 1967.

Griffioen, Donald J. *Open Windows and Open Doors: Open to Renewal and Growth.* Grand Rapids: Christian Reformed Board of Evangelism of Greater Grand Rapids, 1984.

Hadaway, C. Kirk. "Learning from Urban Church Research." *Urban Mission* 2.3 (Jan. 1985): 33–44.

Haines, John F. "Reaching Muslims in French Cities." *Urban Mission* 2.1 (Sept. 1984): 20–33.

Hale, J. Russell. *Who Are the Unchurched? An Exploratory Study.* Washington, D.C.: Glenmary Research Center, 1977.

Hall, Douglas. "Emmanuel Gospel Center, Boston: Contextualized Urban Ministry." *Urban Mission* 1.2 (Nov. 1983): 31–36.

Halvorson, Loren E. *Exodus into the World.* Minneapolis: Augsburg, 1966.

Harper, Michael. *Let My People Grow: Ministry and Leadership in the Church.* Plainfield, N.J.: Logos International, 1977.

Harrod, Howard L. "Formation of Ministers of an Urban Society." *Encounter* 29.4 (Fall 1968): 348–54.

Haughey, John C., ed. *The Faith That Does Justice: Examining the Christian Sources for Social Change.* New York: Paulist, 1977.

Hefley, James, and Marti Hefley. *The Church That Takes On Trouble.* Elgin, Ill.: David C. Cook, 1976.

Hesselgrave, David J. *Communicating Christ Cross-Culturally.* Grand Rapids: Zondervan, 1978.

Holthaus, Lee. "Changing Lives Since 1891: The Union Rescue Mission of Los Angeles." *Urban Mission* 2.2 (Nov. 1984): 5–14.

Howes, Robert Gerard. *Steeples in Metropolis.* Dayton: Pflaum, 1969.

Hunter, George G. *The Contagious Congregation: Frontiers in Evangelism and Church Growth.* Nashville: Abingdon, 1979.

Hurn, Raymond W. *Black Evangelism.* Kansas City, Mo.: Nazarene, 1974.

Jennings, Alvin. *How Christianity Grows in the City.* Fort Worth: Star Bible, 1985.

————. *Three Rs of Urban Church Growth.* Fort Worth: Star Bible, 1981.

Johnson, Ben. *An Evangelism Primer: Practical Principles for Congregations.* Atlanta: John Knox, 1983.

Johnson, Douglas, and George Cornell. *Punctured Preconceptions: What North American Christians Think About the Church.* New York: Friendship, 1972.

Jones, Major J. *Black Awareness: A Theology of Hope.* Nashville: Abingdon, 1971.

Joslin, Roy. *Urban Harvest.* Hertfordshire, England: Evangelical, 1982.

Kelley, Dean M. *Why Conservative Churches Are Growing: A Study in Sociology of Religion.* New York: Harper and Row, 1972.

Kidd, Beth. "Inner-City Missionary Nurse." *Urban Mission* 2.4 (Mar. 1985): 12–21.

Kloetzli, Walter, ed. *Challenge and Response in the City: A Theological Consultation on the Urban Church.* Rock Island, Ill.: Augustana, 1962.

———. *The Church and the Urban Challenge.* Minneapolis: Muhlenberg, 1961.

———. *Urban Church Planting: The Church Discovers Its Community.* Minneapolis: Muhlenberg, 1958.

Kromminga, Carl G. *The Communication of the Gospel Through Neighboring: A Study of the Basis and Practice of Lay Witnessing Through Neighborly Relationships.* Franeker, Netherlands: T. Wever, 1964.

Lausanne Occasional Paper no. 1. *The Pasadena Consultation on the Homogeneous Unit Principle.* Wheaton, Ill.: Lausanne Committee for World Evangelization, 1978.

Lausanne Occasional Paper no. 7. *Christian Witness to the Jewish People.* Wheaton, Ill.: Lausanne Committee for World Evangelization, 1980.

Lausanne Occasional Paper no. 8. *Christian Witness to Secularized People.* Wheaton, Ill.: Lausanne Committee for World Evangelization, 1980.

Lausanne Occasional Paper no. 9. *Christian Witness to Large Cities.* Wheaton, Ill.: Lausanne Committee for World Evangelization, 1980.

Lausanne Occasional Paper no. 10. *Christian Witness to Nominal Christians Among Roman Catholics.* Wheaton, Ill.: Lausanne Committee for World Evangelization, 1980.

Lausanne Occasional Paper no. 12. *Christian Witness to Marxists.* Wheaton, Ill.: Lausanne Committee for World Evangelization, 1980.

Lausanne Occasional Paper no. 19. *Christian Witness to Nominal Christians Among the Orthodox.* Wheaton, Ill.: Lausanne Committee for World Evangelization, 1980.

Lausanne Occasional Paper no. 22. *Christian Witness to the Urban Poor.* Wheaton, Ill.: Lausanne Committee for World Evangelization, 1980.

Lee, Robert. *The Church and the Exploding Metropolis.* Richmond: John Knox, 1965.

————. *Cities and Churches: Readings on the Urban Church.* Philadelphia: Westminster, 1962.

Leiffer, Murray H. *The Effective City Church.* Nashville: Abingdon, 1955.

Lindberg, Milton B. *Witnessing to Jews: A Handbook of Practical Aids.* Chicago: American Messianic Fellowship, 1954.

Lyon, David. *Christians and Sociology.* Downers Grove, Ill.: Inter-Varsity, 1975.

McConnel, C. Douglas. *Urban Ministries Training: Evaluating for Effectiveness.* Altadena, Calif.: Barnabas Resources, 1985.

McGavran, Donald A. *Momentous Decisions in Missions Today.* Grand Rapids: Baker, 1984.

————. "New Urban Faces of the Church." *Urban Mission* 1.1 (Sept. 1983): 3–10.

————, and Winfield C. Arn. *Ten Steps for Church Growth.* New York: Harper and Row, 1977.

McGray, Walter Arthur. *Toward a Wholistic Liberation of Black People.* Chicago: National Black Christian Students Conference, 1977.

McKenna, David, ed. *The Urban Crisis.* Grand Rapids: Zondervan, 1969.

McNeil, Jesse J. *Mission and Metropolis.* Grand Rapids: Eerdmans, 1965.

Magnuson, Norris. *Salvation in the Slums: Evangelical Social Work, 1865–1920.* Metuchen, N.J.: Scarecrow, 1977.

Marsden, George M. *Fundamentalism and American Culture: The Shaping of Twentieth-Century Evangelicalism, 1870–1925.* New York: Oxford University Press, 1980.

Maust, John. *Cities of Change: Urban Growth and God's People in Ten Latin American Cities.* Coral Gables, Fla.: Latin America Mission, 1984.

Miller, Kenneth Dexter. *Man and God in the City.* New York: Friendship, 1954.

Miller, Vern. "Evangelizing the Central City: Problems and Possibilities." In *Missions, Evangelism, and Church Growth,* ed. C. Norman Kraus, pp. 123–39. Scottdale, Pa.: Herald, 1980.

Mitchell, Rudy. "Evangelism in the City." *Urban Mission* 1.3 (Jan. 1984): 30–35.

————, and Eldin Villafane. "The Center for Urban Ministerial Education: A Case Study in Urban Theological Education by Extension." *Urban Mission* 2.2 (Nov. 1984): 31–39.

Moberg, David O. *The Great Reversal: Evangelism Versus Social Concern.* Philadelphia: Lippincott, 1972.

Moore, Paul. *The Church Reclaims the City.* New York: Seabury, 1964.

Moore, Richard E., and Duane L. Day. *Urban Church Breakthrough.* New York: Harper and Row, 1966.

Musselman, G. Paul. *The Church on the Urban Frontier.* New York: Seabury, 1960.

Nichols, Bruce, ed. *In Word and Deed: Evangelistic and Social Responsibility.* Grand Rapids: Eerdmans, 1985.

Nieves, Alvaro L. "Minority Issues in the Justice System." *Urban Mission* 5.4 (Mar. 1988): 27–34.

———. "Urban Minorities and Christian Higher Education." *Urban Mission* 3.2 (Nov. 1985): 20–28.

Norton, Perry L. *Church and Metropolis.* New York: Seabury, 1964.

Noyce, Gaylord B. *Survival and Mission for the City Church.* Philadelphia: Westminster, 1975.

Oren, Martin L. "Aging in the City." *Urban Mission* 3.5 (May 1986): 36–48.

Orr, J. Edwin. *Campus Aflame: Dynamic of Student Religious Revolution.* Glendale, Calif.: Regal, 1971.

Ortiz, Manuel. "The Rise of Spiritism in North America." *Urban Mission* 5.4 (Mar. 1988): 11–17.

Owens, Virginia S. *The Total Image: or, Selling Jesus in the Modern Age.* Grand Rapids: Eerdmans, 1980.

Palmer, Donald C. *Explosion of People Evangelism.* Chicago: Moody, 1974.

Pasquariello, Ronald D.; Donald W. Shriver, Jr.; and Alan Geyer. *Redeeming the City: Theology, Politics and Urban Policy.* New York: Pilgrim, 1982.

Perkins, John. *With Justice for All.* Ventura, Calif.: Regal, 1982.

Phillips, Keith W. *Everybody's Afraid in the Ghetto.* Ventura, Calif.: Regal, 1975.

Racine, Carl. "Don't Neglect Third World Suburbia." *Missiology* 9.2 (Apr. 1981): 171–80.

Roberts, J. Deotis. *Roots of a Black Future: Family and Church.* Philadelphia: Westminster, 1980.

Rose, Larry L., and C. Kirk Hadaway. *An Urban World: Churches Face the Future.* Nashville: Broadman, 1984.

———, eds. *The Urban Challenge.* Nashville: Broadman, 1982.

Rubingh, Eugene. *Strategies for Evangelization in Cities.* Grand Rapids: Christian Reformed Church, 1986.

Sample, Tex. *Blue Collar Ministry: Facing Economic and Social Realities of Working People.* Valley Forge, Pa.: Judson, 1984.

Sanderson, Ross W. *The Church Serves the Changing City.* New York: Harper, 1955.

Sawatsky, Ben A. "A Church Planting Strategy for World Class Cities." *Urban Mission* 3.2 (Nov. 1985): 7–19.

Schaeffer, Francis A. *Death in the City.* Downers Grove, Ill.: Inter-Varsity, 1969.

Schaller, Lyle. *Assimilating New Members.* Nashville: Abingdon, 1978.

———. *The Change Agent.* Nashville: Abingdon, 1972.

———. *Hey, That's Our Church.* Nashville: Abingdon, 1975.

———. *Planning for Protestantism in Urban America.* Nashville: Abingdon, 1965.

Schlissel, Steve M. "City Singles." *Urban Mission* 3.1 (Sept. 1985): 26–31.

Schuller, David S. *The New Urban Society.* St. Louis: Concordia, 1966.

Sheppard, David. *Built as a City: God and the Urban World Today.* London: Hodder and Stoughton, 1974.

Shriver, Donald W., Jr., and Karl A. Ostrom. *Is There Hope for the City?* Philadelphia: Westminster, 1977.

Sider, Ronald J., ed. *Evangelicals and Development: Toward a Theology of Social Change.* Philadelphia: Westminster, 1981.

Smit, William. *Christian Perspectives in Sociology.* Grand Rapids: Calvin College Sociology Department, 1978.

Smith, Sandy. "Chester's Troubled Youth: An In-Depth Study of Young People in an Old American City." *Urban Mission* 5.1 (Sept. 1987): 20–29.

Smith, Timothy L. *Revivalism and Social Reform in Mid-Nineteenth-Century America.* Nashville: Abingdon, 1957.

Snyder, Howard A. *The Problem of Wineskins: Church Structure in a Technological Age.* Downers Grove, Ill.: Inter-Varsity, 1975.

——— *The Radical Wesley and Patterns for Church Renewal.* Downers Grove, Ill.: Inter-Varsity, 1980.

Stackhouse, Max L. *Ethics and the Urban Ethos: An Essay in Social Theory and Theological Reconstruction.* Boston: Beacon, 1972.

Stark, Rodney, and William Sims Bainbridge. "Networks of Faith: Interpersonal Bonds and Recruitment to Cults and Sects." *American Journal of Sociology* 85.6 (May 1980): 1376–95.

Stockwell, Clinton. *Urban Research Project.* Arlington Heights, Ill.: Harvest, 1985.

Stott, Jack L. *Shalom: The Search for a Peaceable City.* Nashville: Abingdon, 1973.

Stott, John R. W., and Robert Coote. *Down to Earth: Studies in Christianity and Culture.* Grand Rapids: Eerdmans, 1980.

Tillapaugh, Frank R. *Unleashing the Church: Getting People Out of the Fortress and into Ministry.* Ventura, Calif.: Regal, 1982.

Tonna, Benjamin. *A Gospel for the Cities: A Socio-Theology of Urban Ministry.* Maryknoll, N.Y.: Orbis, 1982.

Torney, George A., comp. *Toward a Creative Urban Strategy.* Waco, Tex.: Word, 1970.

Ujvarosy, Helen, ed. *Signs of the Kingdom in the Secular City: Resources for the Urban Church.* Chicago: Covenant, 1984.

Ulschak, Francis. *Urban Ministry: A Study of Goals.* Chicago: SCUPE, 1977.

Van Houten, Mark E. *God's Inner-City Address: Crossing the Boundaries.* Grand Rapids: Zondervan, 1988.

Vaughan, John N. *The World's Twenty Largest Churches: Church Growth Principles in Action.* Grand Rapids: Baker, 1984.

Wagner, C. Peter. "From 'Melting Pot' to 'Stew Pot': American Social Pluralism and the Church." *Theology, News and Notes* 26.3 (Oct. 1979): 4–8.

―――. *Frontiers in Missionary Strategy.* Chicago: Moody, 1971.

―――. *Our Kind of People: The Ethical Dimensions of Church Growth in America.* Atlanta: John Knox, 1979.

―――. *Strategies for Church Growth: Tools for Effective Mission and Evangelism.* Ventura, Calif.: Regal, 1987.

―――. *Your Church Can Be Healthy.* Nashville: Abingdon, 1979.

―――. *Your Church Can Grow.* Ventura, Calif.: Regal, 1976.

Webber, George W. *The Congregation in Mission: Emerging Structures for the Church in an Urban Society.* Nashville: Abingdon, 1964.

―――. *God's Colony in Man's World: Christian Love in Action.* New York: Abingdon, 1960.

―――. *Today's Church: A Community of Exiles and Pilgrims.* Nashville: Abingdon, 1979.

Weitz, Raanan, ed. *Urbanization and the Developing Countries.* New York: Praeger, 1973.

White, Ronald C., Jr., and C. Howard Hopkins, eds. *The Social Gospel: Religion and Reform in Changing America.* Philadelphia: Temple University Press, 1976.

Wilson, Robert L. *Questions City Churches Must Answer.* New York: Methodist Church, 1962.

Wimberly, Edward P. *Pastoral Care in the Black Church.* Nashville: Abingdon, 1979.

Winter, Gibson. *The New Creation as Metropolis.* New York: Macmillan, 1963.

―――. *The Suburban Captivity of the Churches: An Analysis of Protestant Responsibility in the Expanding Metropolis.* New York: Macmillan, 1962.

Wood, Stephanie. "The Red Lights of Chicago: A Case Study in Urban Ministry." *World Christian* 7.1 (Jan.–Feb. 1988): 20–21.

Younger, George D. *The Church and Urban Power Structure.* Philadelphia: Westminster, 1963.

Ziegenhals, Walter E. *Urban Churches in Transition: Reflections on Selected Problems and Approaches to Churches and Communities in Racial Transition Based on the Chicago Experience.* New York: Pilgrim, 1978.

Social-Science Perspective

Adams, Robert M. "The Origin of Cities." *Scientific American* 203.3 (Sept. 1960): 153–68.

Bailey, Robert, Jr. *Radicals in Urban Politics: The Alinsky Approach.* Chicago: University of Chicago Press, 1974.

Bentley, H. William. *The Meaning of History for Black Americans.* Chicago: National Black Evangelical Association, 1979.

Bentley, Ruth Lewis. "Response to Psychology as Urban Ministry Presentation." *Journal of Psychology and Theology* 6.4 (Fall 1978): 305–8.

Bergel, Egon E. *Social Stratification.* New York: McGraw-Hill, 1962.

———. *Urban Sociology.* New York: McGraw-Hill, 1955.

Berger, Alan S. *The City: Urban Communities and Their Problems.* Dubuque, Iowa: William C. Brown, 1978.

Blackwell, James E. *The Black Community: Diversity and Unity.* New York: Harper and Row, 1975.

Bobick, Michael W. "New York's New Neighbors: Reaching Chinese Immigrants in the 1980's." *Urban Mission* 2.5 (May 1985): 20–32.

Boorstin, Daniel. *The Republic of Technology: Reflections on Our Future Community.* New York: Harper and Row, 1978.

Bowden, Charles, and Lew Kreinberg. *Street Signs Chicago: Neighborhood and Other Illusions of Big-City Life.* Chicago: Chicago Review, 1981.

Callow, Alexander B., Jr., ed. *American Urban History: An Interpretive Reader with Commentaries.* 3d ed. New York: Oxford University Press, 1982.

Caro, Robert A. *The Power Broker: Robert Moses and the Fall of New York.* New York: Knopf, 1974.

Clarke, Susan E., and Jeffrey L. Obler, eds. *Urban Ethnic Conflict: A Comparative Perspective.* Chapel Hill: University of North Carolina Press, 1976.

Collins, Thomas, ed. *Cities in a Larger Context.* Athens, Ga.: University of Georgia Press, 1980.

Cox, Kevin R. *Location and Public Problems: A Political Geography of the Contemporary World.* Chicago: Maaroufa, 1979.

Dantzig, George B., and Thomas L. Saat. *Compact City: A Plan for a Liveable Urban Environment.* San Francisco: Freeman, 1973.

Davidson, James D. "Lafayette Urban Ministry." *Review of Religious Research* 18.3 (Spring 1977): 302.

Davies, Ross L. *The Nature of Cities.* Oxford: Pergamon, 1973.

Davis, Kingsley. *Cities: Their Origin, Growth and Human Impact.* San Francisco: Freeman, 1973.

De Vise, P. R., and E. C. Berry. "A Tale of Two Cities." *Renewal* 9.2 (Feb. 1969): 8–13.

Eames, Edwin, and Judith G. Goode. *Urban Poverty in a Cross-Cultural Context.* New York: Free, 1973.

Feagin, Joe R., et al. *The Urban Scene: Myths and Realities.* New York: Random, 1973.

Feldman, Philip, and Jim Orford. *Psychological Problems: The Social Context.* Chichester, N.Y.: John Wiley and Sons, 1980.

Fischer, Claude. *To Dwell Among Friends: Personal Networks in Town and City.* Chicago: University of Chicago Press, 1982.

Forrester, Jay W. *Urban Dynamics.* Cambridge, Mass.: MIT Press, 1969.

Gappert, Gary, and Richard V. Knight. *Cities of the Twentieth Century.* Beverly Hills, Calif.: Sage, 1982.

Gibbs, Eddie. *Urban Church Growth: Clues from South America and Britain.* Bramcote: Grove, 1977.

Gibbs, Jack P., ed. *Urban Research Methods.* Princeton, N.J.: Van Nostrand, 1961.

Gilbert, Alan, and Joseph Gugler. *Cities, Poverty and Development.* London: Oxford University Press, 1982.

Glazer, Nathan, and Daniel Moynihan. *Beyond the Melting Pot.* 2d ed. Cambridge, Mass.: MIT Press, 1970.

Gottmann, Jean. *Megalopolis: The Urbanized Northeastern Seaboard of the United States.* New York: Twentieth Century Fund, 1961.

Goudzwaard, Bob. *Capitalism and Progress: A Diagnosis of Western Society.* Toronto: Wedge, 1979.

Greeley, Andrew. *Ethnicity in the United States: A Preliminary Reconnaissance.* New York: John Wiley, 1974.

Gulick, J. *Urbanization and Family Change.* Atlantic Highlands, N.J.: Humanities, 1968.

Hannerz, Ulf. *Exploring the City: Inquiries Toward an Urban Anthropology.* New York: Columbia University Press, 1980.

Helmer, John, and Neil A. Eddington, eds. *Urbanman: The Psychology of Urban Survival.* New York: Macmillan, 1973.

Herbert, David. *Urban Geography: A Social Perspective.* New York: Praeger, 1972.

Hessel, Dieter. *Social Ministry.* Philadelphia: Westminster, 1982.

Hine, Virginia H. "The Basic Paradigm of a Future Socio-Cultural System." *World Issues* 2.2 (Apr.–May 1977): 19–22.

Hogan, L. Lloyd, ed. *The Review of Black Political Economy*. Atlanta: National Economic Association, 1980.

Holli, Melvin G., and Peter d'A. Jones, eds. *Ethnic Chicago*. Grand Rapids: Eerdmans, 1981.

Ianni, Francis A. J. "New Mafia: Black, Hispanic and Italian Styles." *Society* 11.3 (Mar.–Apr. 1974): 26–39.

Jacobs, Jane. *The Death and Life of the Great American Cities*. New York: Random, 1961.

———. *The Economy of Cities*. New York: Random, 1969.

Janssen, Lawrence. *These Cities Glorious*. New York: Friendship, 1963.

Knoke, David, and David L. Rogers. "A Blockmodel Analysis of Interorganizational Networks." *Sociology and Social Research* 64.1 (Oct. 1979): 28–52.

Leacock, Eleanor B., ed. *The Culture of Poverty: A Critique*. New York: Simon and Schuster, 1971.

Leinwand, Gerald. *The City as a Community*. New York: Washington Square, 1970.

Lewis, Oscar. *La Vida: A Puerto Rican Family in the Culture of Poverty*. New York: Random, 1965.

Lineberry, Robert L., and Louis H. Masotti. *Urban Problems and Public Policy*. Washington, D.C.: Heath, 1975.

Lowry, Ritchie P. *Who's Running This Town! Community Leadership and Social Change*. New York: Harper and Row, 1968.

McGee, T. G. "Peasants in the Cities: A Paradox, A Paradox, A Most Ingenious Paradox." *Human Organization* 32.2 (Summer 1973): 135–42.

McLuhan, Marshall. *Understanding Media: The Extensions of Man*. New York: McGraw-Hill, 1964.

Mangin, William, ed. *Peasants in Cities: Readings in the Anthropology of Urbanization*. Boston: Houghton Mifflin, 1970.

Mann, Phillip. *Community Psychology: Concepts and Applications*. New York: Free, 1978.

Miller, Zane L. *The Urbanization of America: A Brief History*. New York: Harcourt Brace Jovanovich, 1973.

Mohl, Raymond A., ed. *The Making of Urban America*. Wilmington, Del.: Scholarly Resources, 1988.

Mohl, Raymond A., and James F. Richardson. *The Urban Experience*. Belmont, Calif.: Wadsworth, 1973.

Mowry, George E., and Blaine L. Brownell. *The Urban Nation: 1920–1980*. New York: Hill and Wang, 1981.

Moynihan, Daniel Patrick, ed. *Toward a National Urban Policy*. New York: Basic, 1970.

Naisbitt, John. *Megatrends: Ten New Directions Transforming Our Lives.* New York: Warner, 1982.

Niemeyer, Oscar. "A City for the Year 2000." *UNESCO Courier* 38.3 (Mar. 1985): 18–19.

Novak, Michael. *The Spirit of Democratic Capitalism.* New York: Simon and Schuster, 1982.

Orleans, Peter, and Miriam Orleans. *Urban Life: Diversity and Equality.* Dubuque, Iowa: William C. Brown, 1976.

Orwell, George. *1984.* New York: Harcourt Brace Jovanovich, 1961.

Palen, J. John. *The Urban World.* New York: McGraw-Hill, 1975.

Perry, David C., and Alfred J. Watkins. *The Rise of the Sunbelt Cities.* Beverly Hills, Calif.: Sage, 1977.

Price, Frances V. "Only Connect? Issues in Charting Social Networks." *Sociological Review* 29.2 (May 1981): 283–312.

Redfield, Robert, and Milton Singer. *The Cultural Role of Cities.* Chicago: University of Chicago Press, 1954.

Scherer, Jacqueline. *Contemporary Community: Sociological Illusion or Reality?* London: Tavistock, 1972.

Schiller, John. *The American Poor.* Minneapolis: Augsburg, 1982.

Sennett, Richard, ed. *Classic Essays on the Culture of Cities.* New York: Appleton-Century-Crofts, 1969.

Sjoberg, G. *The Preindustrial City, Past and Present.* Glencoe, Ill.: Free, 1960.

Snow, David A.; Louis A. Zurcher, Jr.; and Sheldon Ekland-Olson. "Social Networks and Social Movements: A Microstructural Approach to Differential Recruitment." *American Sociological Review* 45.5 (Oct. 1980): 787–801.

Spradley, James P., and David W. McCurdy. *The Cultural Experience: Ethnography in Complex Society.* Chicago: Science Research Associates, 1972.

Toffler, Alvin. *Future Shock.* New York: Random, 1970.

Valentine, Bettylou. *Hustling and Other Hard Work: Life Styles in the Ghetto.* New York: Free, 1978.

Waddell, Jack O., and Michael O. Watson. *The American Indian in Urban Society.* Boston: Little, Brown, 1971.

Warren, Rachelle B., and Donald I. Warren. *Neighborhood Organizers Handbook.* South Bend, Ind.: University of Notre Dame Press, 1977.

Winter, J. Alan, ed. *The Poor: A Culture of Poverty or a Poverty of Culture?* Grand Rapids: Eerdmans, 1971.

Index